"Beyond Our Wildest Dreams"

RECONSIDERATIONS IN
SOUTHERN AFRICAN HISTORY

Richard Elphick and Jeffrey Butler, Editors

"*Beyond Our Wildest Dreams*"

The United Democratic Front and the Transformation of South Africa

Ineke van Kessel

University Press of Virginia

Charlottesville and London

Publication of this work was assisted by a grant from the African Studies Centre, Leiden, the Netherlands.

The University Press of Virginia
© 2000 by the Rector and Visitors of the University of Virginia
All rights reserved
Printed in the United States of America
First published in 2000

The paper used in this publication meets the minimum requirements of the American National Standard for Information Sciences—Permanence of Paper for Printed Library Materials, ANSI Z39.48-1984.

Library of Congress Cataloging-in-Publication Data

van Kessel, Ineke.
    Beyond our wildest dreams : the United Democratic Front and the transformation of South Africa / Ineke van Kessel.
        p. cm. — (Reconsiderations in southern African history)
    Includes bibliographical references and index.
        ISBN 0-8139-1861-8 (cloth : alk. paper). — ISBN 0-8139-1868-5 (paper : alk. paper)
        1. United Democratic Front (South Africa) 2. South Africa—History—Autonomy and independence movements. 3. South Africa—Politics and government—1948– I. Title. II. Series.
    DT1945.K47 1999
    968.06'3—dc21   99-39892
                                                               CIP

Contents

List of Illustrations   *vii*
Acknowledgments   *ix*
Abbreviations   *xiii*
Chronology   *xvii*

Introduction   *1*

Part One
 Redrawing the Boundaries: Changing the Terms of Exclusion
   and Incorporation

 ONE
 The UDF and South Africa in the 1980s: The Events   *15*

 TWO
 Making Sense of Events: Interpreting the 1980s   *48*

Part Two
 The Struggles behind the Struggle: Three Case Studies

 THREE
 "From Confusion to Lusaka": The UDF in Sekhukhuneland   *75*

 FOUR
 "Yah, God Is on Our Side": The Krugersdorp Residents Organisation
   and Township Revolt   *150*

F I V E
Grassroots: From Community Paper to Activist Playground　*224*

Conclusion　*288*

Note on Methodology and Sources　*309*
Notes　*315*
Bibliography　*343*
Index　*359*

Illustrations

Maps

1. The Northern Transvaal   76
2. The West Rand   151
3. Cape Town and surroundings   225

Tables

1. Standard 10 examination results in Lebowa, 1980–1986   90
2. 1994 election results in Sekhukhuneland, Krugersdorp, and
       the Western Cape   306

Illustrations

1. UDF launch in Mitchell's Plain, 20 August 1983   19
2. Mass funeral, Lingelihle, Cradock, Eastern Cape, July 1985   31
3. Mass Democratic Movement demonstration in Durban,
       September 1989   32
4. Funeral of Peter Nchabeleng, Apel, 3 May 1986   130
5. UDF poster of Peter Nchabeleng   131
6. Poster announcing a civic meeting in Kagiso, 1985   177
7. Sister Mary Bernard Ncube after her release from detention,
       October 1987   216
8. Comic strip in *Grassroots*   242
9. Frank Chikane addresses the *Grassroots* Annual General Meeting   251

Acknowledgments

MANY PEOPLE HAVE in various ways contributed to this book. The Algemeen Nederlands Persbureau (ANP—the Dutch news agency) provided an environment that stimulated my interest in sub-Sahara Africa. My first visit to South Africa, and my first encounter with the subject of this book—the United Democratic Front—was in 1984, when covering the South African elections as a journalist for ANP.

This book is an adaptation of my doctoral thesis, submitted to the University of Leiden in 1995. Reconciling my ambition to write a book on contemporary South Africa with the obligation to meet the requirements of a Ph.D. thesis was not as self-evident as it had seemed at the outset. Professor H. L. Wesseling of Leiden University provided the space to pursue both objectives. Rob Buijtenhuijs and Stephen Ellis of the African Studies Centre in Leiden and Robert Ross, coordinator of African Studies at the University of Leiden, read and commented on the drafts of all chapters. I am grateful to the African Studies Centre for enabling me to undertake this research project and for financial assistance with the publication of the book. Annette van Andel en Ria van Santen provided moral support during the defence of the thesis in November 1995.

Jeremy Seekings of the University of Cape Town, author of numerous publications on the UDF, generously exchanged ideas, comments, and papers. Peter Delius of the History Department of the University of the Witwatersrand and Tony Harding, an educationalist with working experience in Sekhukhuneland, gave useful advice for my work in Sekhukhuneland. Tom Lodge of the University of the Witwatersrand allowed me to read the draft manuscript of his chapter in *All, Here, and Now* and thus gave me the timely opportunity to reorient my own research toward local case studies. Eric Louw of the University of Natal sent a generous supply of his publications on the South African media. George Moiloa provided background information on Kagiso as well as a copy of the oral history project on the Krugersdorp Residents Organisation, which he had undertaken with fellow students at Khanya College in Johannesburg. Ann Cunningham and Michelle Pickover of the Historical and Literary Papers Library of the University of the Witwatersrand in Johannesburg guided me through their extensive collection. Razia Saleh of the South African History Archives helped me find my way through the avalanche of documents that kept pouring into SAHA's offices and later checked a number of references. Erik van den Bergh and Hans Hartman of the Werkgroep Kairos in Utrecht provided useful advice in the initial stage of this research and supplied a regular flow of press clippings and other items throughout the period of research and writing. Anton Dekker and Kier Schuringa of the Netherlands Institute for Southern Africa in Amsterdam and the staff of the African Studies Centre library in Leiden also were most helpful. Thanks are also due to Sydney Ramushu, who provided me with a written version of his poem "From Confusion to Lusaka" and consented to its publication here, and to Lawrence Ntlokoa, who gave permission to use sections of his diary.

Dr. C. F. Beyers Naudé lent support during the difficult first phase of this project. The South African ambassador in the Netherlands, Albert Nothnagel, persevered in obtaining a visa for my fieldwork after an initial visa request was turned down in Pretoria. Willem Veerman of the African Studies Centre demonstrated an admirable patience in the instruction of computer illiterates and produced the graphics. Nel van Betlehem designed the maps. The Inter-church Organisation for Development Cooperation (ICCO) in Zeist and the *Grassroots* staff in Cape Town generously allowed me access to their files. Parts of chapter 3 have been previously published in my article "'From Confusion to Lusaka': The Youth Revolt in Sekhukhuneland," which appeared in the *Journal of Southern African Studies* 19, no. 4 (December 1993), pp. 593–614, and are reprinted here by permission of Carfax Publishing Ltd. (P.O. Box 25, Abingdon, Oxfordshire OX14 3UE, United Kingdom).

Ena Jansen, Pat Sidley, Carina LeGrange, and Liesbeth Botha made me feel at home in Johannesburg. I am particularly grateful to Ena for her unfailing hospitality and to Pat, who was always there in moments that called for crisis management. Gertrude Nchabeleng and her sons and daughters provided another home in Sekhukhuneland. Maurice Nchabeleng was a much appre-ciated companion in the Northern Transvaal and occasionally also in Johan-nesburg. Guidance to Sekhukhuneland was also provided by Philip Mnisi, who met an untimely death in 1992. Laurine Platzky, Eric Miller, and Joshua James Platzky Miller brought a South African dimension to our house in Leid-schendam while I wrote my thesis. My husband, Johan van Workum, shared the ups and downs that marked the production of thesis cum book.

Many people have facilitated this research and greatly enhanced my pleas-ure in this project by rendering hospitality and companionship. The house of Joyce Mabudafhasi was a hospitable base in Mankweng. Josette Cole and Vir-ginia Zweigenthal generously provided accommodation and companionship in Cape Town, Nadeem Hendricks and his family introduced me to the intri-cacies of left-wing politics in Cape Town, while Anari van der Merwe allowed me the use of her house on the foot of Table Mountain. Carol and John Vin-sen, whom I first met during my journalistic explorations in 1984, provided a hospitable port of call in Durban.

Last but not least, I wish to express my appreciation for all the people who were willing to share their experiences and ideas with an inquisitive stranger, who were so concerned about my safety and well-being, and who introduced me to the multifarious realities of this fascinating but bewildering society. My never-ending questions were patiently endured even by those interviewees who doubted the relevance of historical research, as was eloquently expressed by one young man in Cape Town, to whom I had explained my research project: "The UDF?? Eh, that is *history,* man."

Abbreviations

AGM	Annual General Meeting
ANC	African National Congress
anti-PC	Anti–President's Council Committee
anti-SAIC	Anti–South African Indian Council Committee
ASCA	African Spiritual Churches Association
AWB	Afrikaner Weerstandsbeweging (Afrikaner Resistance Movement)
AZANYU	Azanian Youth Organisation
AZAPO	Azanian People's Organisation
AZASM	Azanian Students Movement
AZASO	Azanian Students' Organisation
BC	Black Consciousness
BCM	Black Consciousness Movement
BPC	Black People's Convention
CACE	Centre for Adult and Continuing Education
CAHAC	Cape Areas Housing Action Committee
CAL	Cape Action League
CAST	Civic Associations of the Southern Transvaal
CAYCO	Cape Youth Congress
CBC	Consumer Boycott Committee
CONTRADOSA	Congress of Traditional Doctors
CONTRALESA	Congress of Traditional Leaders of South Africa
COSAS	Congress of South African Students
COSATU	Congress of South African Trade Unions
CUPC	Churches' Urban Planning Commission
CUSA	Council of Unions of South Africa
DBAC	Disorderly Bills Action Committee
DC	Disciplinary Committee
FBWU	Food and Beverage Workers Union
FCCA	Federation of Cape Civic Associations
FCWU	Food and Canning Workers' Union
FEDSAW	Federation of South African Women
FEDTRAW	Federation of Transvaal Women
FOSATU	Federation of South African Trade Unions
FRELIMO	Frente de Libertaçao de Moçambique

GAWU	General and Allied Workers Union
GWU	General Workers' Union
HDA	Hostel Dwellers' Association
ICCO	Interchurch Organisation for Development Cooperation
IYCC	Interdenominational Youth Christian Club
JORAC	Joint Rent Action Committee
KAFCOC	Kagiso Interim Co-ordinating Committee
KAYCO	Kagiso Youth Congress
KCA	Kagiso Civic Association
KCBC	Krugersdorp Consumer Boycott Committee
KCO	Kagiso Civic Organisation
KICC	Kagiso Interim Co-ordinating Committee
KRO	Krugersdorp [Kagiso] Residents Organisation
MAYCO	Mankweng Youth Congress
MAYO	Mamelodi Youth Congress
MDM	Mass Democratic Movement
MK	Umkhonto we Sizwe
MUYCO	Munsieville Youth Congress
NACTU	National Confederation of Trade Unions
NEC	National Executive Committee
NECC	National Education Crisis Committee
NEUM	Non-European Unity Movement
NEUSA	National Educational Union of South Africa
NEYCO	Nebo Youth Congress
NGK	Nederduits Gereformeerde Kerk (Dutch Reformed Church)
NGSK	Nederduits Gereformeerde Sendingkerk) (Dutch Reformed Mission Church)
NIC	Natal Indian Congress
NOTPECO	Northern Transvaal People's Congress
NP	National Party
NUM	New Unity Movement
NUMSA	National Union of Metalworkers
NUSAS	National Union of South African Students
PAC	Pan Africanist Congress
PEBCO	Port Elizabeth Black Civic Organisation
PHT	Popular History Trust
PWV	Pretoria-Witwatersrand-Vereeniging
REC	Regional Executive Committee
RENAMO	Resistência Nacional Moçambicana

RMC	Release Mandela Campaign
SAAWU	South African Allied Workers Union
SAB	South African Breweries
SACC	South African Council of Churches
SACP	South African Communist Party
SACTU	South African Congress of Trade Unions
SACTWU	South African Clothing and Textile Workers' Union
SADF	South African Defence Force
SAHA	South African History Archives
SAIC	South African Indian Council
SAIRR	South African Institute of Race Relations
SANSCO	South African National Students' Congress
SAP	South African Police
SAPA	South African Press Association
SASO	South African Students' Organisation
SASPU	South African Students' Press Union
SATHC	South African Traditional Healers Council
SAYCO	South African Youth Congress
SCA	Soweto Civic Association
SEYO	Sekhukhune Youth Organisation
SPCC	Sekhukhune Parents' Crisis Committee
SRC	Student Representative Council
SWAPO	South West Africa People's Organisation
TIC	Transvaal Indian Congress
TUATA	Transvaal United African Teachers Association
UBJ	Union of Black Journalists
UDF	United Democratic Front
UNISA	University of South Africa
UNITA	Uniâo Nacional para a Independência Total de Angola
UWC	University of the Western Cape
UWO	United Women's Organisation
UWUSA	United Workers' Union of South Africa
VCA	Vaal Civic Association
WACC	World Association for Christian Communication
WASA	Writers' Association of South Africa
WCCA	Western Cape Civic Association
WF	Women's Front
YCW	Young Christian Workers
ZANU	Zimbabwe African National Union
ZAPU	Zimbabwe African People's Union
ZCC	Zion Christian Church

A Chronology of Rebellion

1983 to August 1984

The first one and half years in the life of the UDF were largely reactive. The Front was formed in a reaction to government reforms. High-profile campaigns against the tricameral parliament dominated. This focus on the tricameral elections meant that colored and Indian organizations within the UDF were in the forefront of activity.

September 1984 to July 1985

Beginning with the uprising in the townships of the Vaal Triangle, this period was marked by a groundswell from below. The focus shifted from the tricameral parliament to the African townships, where initially localized protests around schools and rents gradually evolved into a challenge of the authority of the local and central state. In many cases, this escalation was provoked by the violent intervention of the security forces. While the state perceived the UDF as the agitating force behind the civic protests, the impact of the UDF on the townships was mostly indirect. Most action was spontaneous rather than orchestrated.

July 1985 to June 1986

By proclaiming a partial State of Emergency, the government attempted to act against the threat of "ungovernability." In reaction to heavy-handed repression, new forms of organization and opposition emerged, such as street committees and consumer boycotts. The period of "people's power" is characterized by a peak in violence and messianic expectations of impending liberation.

June 1986 to 1988

The second State of Emergency was marked by intensified rebellion and repression, with townships coming under virtual military rule. After some months of euphoria when liberation seemed imminent, the opposition became fragmented and demoralized. By early 1987, black resistance appeared

to be at an end, with the UDF in danger of losing authority over their constituencies, most notably in the case of youth.

1989 to 1991

January 1989 was marked by a revival of a spirit of resistance, beginning with
a hunger strike by political detainees that acquired increasing momentum. The
mass release of detainees helped to restore confidence. The UDF regrouped
with the new umbrella federation of trade unions, COSATU, to form a broad
alliance, the Mass Democratic Movement. The MDM proved successful in
reconstructing a popular protest movement. After the unbanning of the
African National Congress and the return of the ANC leadership from prison
and exile, the UDF lapsed into inactivity, uncertain about its role. The Front
was finally disbanded in 1991.

"Beyond Our Wildest Dreams"

Introduction

To create a new country, you have to go beyond the
boundaries of the mind.

Transnet advertisement

In a booklet with basic facts on South Africa presented to Dutch
tourists in the mid-1980s, the prospective visitor is offered a brief introduction
to the African population. Squeezed in between entries on steam locomotives
and wine routes, the tourist guidebook provides the following information on
the "Life of the Natives": "The life of the natives is not so easily accessible, as
it is located in remote areas of the country. One can get a glimpse of this native
life in the form of tribal dances, which are held regularly in some parts of
Natal, at the Goldmine Museum in Johannesburg and in certain holiday
resorts. In some rural areas the local black population can be seen in characteristic costumes."[1] In the early 1990s, a more solid-looking guidebook
informed the traveler about government policy vis-à-vis the African population: "When the Union of South Africa was founded in 1910 the total population included 10 black ethnic groups who by the late 1960s respectively
ranged in numbers from a few hundred thousand to four million. Each had—
and still has—a territorial base reasonably well-defined by history over more
than a century, as well as a cultural identity, including language, and a distinctive socio-political system. The central question confronting South African
governments since 1910 has been the manner in which these 10 black ethnic
groups should be democratically fused into the political system."[2]

Both contentions, of course, are equally absurd. Far from being an exotic
backdrop in a country otherwise characterized by modern amenities and nostalgic trains, South African blacks in the 1980s acted on the center stage of
society. From the moment of landing at the airport, the visitor would have
been aware that these supposedly "third-world peoples" were indispensable
for the functioning of what has been wrongly labeled a "first-world economy."
Whatever newspaper the visitor bought on the streets of Johannesburg, Cape
Town, or Durban, the front page would inevitably relate information about
new outbursts of black anger, coupled with dire warnings from white authorities. And far from being concerned with the democratic participation of

blacks, South African governments during most of this century were obsessed
with the question of how to exclude blacks from the political system.

This, however, is the significant point when comparing the official hand-
outs of 1985 and 1992: state publications had shifted from the language of
exclusion to a discourse of incorporation. To be fair, the tourist guide lagged
somewhat behind government policy. State attempts at redrawing the map of
apartheid society had begun in the late 1970s and continued throughout the
1980s. But during the 1980s, the "natives" made sure that this time the blue-
print of a new society would not be drawn without them. Even in 1992, the
state's information service had not come to terms with the events that had led
to the much hailed new partnership. The historical survey in the 1992 guidebook conveniently skips the 1984–86 revolt, the most turbulent period in
South African history since the Anglo-Boer War.

In the past decade, South Africa's political and socioeconomic landscape
has been profoundly reshaped. The new cycle of revolt was triggered by the
state's reform policy, which in turn was a response to the changing nature of
the South African economy. A key actor during the crucial years of reform and
rebellion in the 1980s was the United Democratic Front (UDF), an umbrella
for a great variety of organizations that shared a total rejection of apartheid
and a willingness to take to the streets in a public demonstration. The UDF
played a vital role in bringing the banned African National Congress (ANC)
back on the center stage of South African politics, thus paving the way for its
unbanning and for the subsequent stage of negotiating and power sharing.

It is always tempting to read history backwards, taking the outcome as
point of departure and assuming that preceding developments were the stepping stones in the process that led, more or less inevitably, to the now known
results. Moreover, if the actual outcome correlates largely with the desired
results, the actors in the process are naturally tempted to claim their due cred-
its. With the wisdom of hindsight, the UDF can be depicted as a transitional
front, having prepared the ground for the leaders of the "authentic" liberation
movement to come home from exile and from prison and to take over power.
Once the ANC had taken its rightful position, the UDF ceded its political
role. After some deliberations, the Front decided in 1991 to disband. But the
founding fathers of the UDF initially had much more modest ambitions: they
were cementing an ad hoc alliance to combat the new constitutional dispensation that the government had promulgated in 1982. As Azhar Cachalia, one
of the UDF's core activists, later explained: "Look, when we founded the
UDF, we had never in our wildest dreams expected that events would take
off in the way they did. What happened was beyond everybody's expectations."[3] This assertion was echoed in interviews with many other leading personalities in the UDF.

The UDF years have been a crucial episode in the transformation of South African society. Many of the old boundaries of the apartheid state have been wiped out, at least from the statute books if not always in real life. The process of partial incorporation began in 1979 with trade union reforms, intended to draw the black labor force into the industrial bargaining system, in the hope of creating a stabilized labor aristocracy whose political aspirations could be bought off with the promise of modest prosperity. With the center of gravity shifting from mining and agriculture to manufacturing, the economy expressed a growing demand for skilled, semiskilled, clerical, and managerial staff. In the words of Anglo-American director Harry Oppenheimer, the South African economy was moving from a "labour-intensive, low-wage, low-productivity economic system—typical of industrial development in its earliest stage—to the capital-intensive, high-wage, high-productivity system which characterises the advanced industrialised countries."[4]

Fulfilling these demands implied the acceptance of a permanent black urban population and raising educational levels for blacks. The educational system was restructured in order to better attune the curriculum to the increasingly differentiated needs of the economy. Recommendations to work toward equal quality of education for all racial groups under one single education ministry were rejected. However, racial restrictions on admission to private schools and to universities were allowed to lapse.[5]

Having dropped the illusion that African workers could be considered life-long migrants who would exercise their political rights in "their" homelands, the state had to come to terms with the fact that millions of Africans were regarded now as permanent residents of "white" South Africa. To this end, the state differentiated between "urban blacks" and "rural blacks." State policy in this respect was largely based on the recommendations of the Riekert Commission on Manpower (1979). Riekert abandoned one of the central fictions of apartheid, namely that there would eventually be no black citizens of "white" South Africa because all blacks would exercise their political rights in the Bantustans. Urban blacks were henceforth to be treated as permanent residents, not as temporary sojourners in "white" South Africa. But more security for urban blacks was to be achieved at the expense of rural Africans, notably in the homelands. Riekert favored a strict system of influx control from the rural areas to the urban centers, with labor bureaus ensuring that labor would be released from the homelands only in response to demand in the white areas. While the boundaries around the Bantustans were tightened, a solution was devised for the political incorporation of the "urban insiders." The 1982 Black Local Authorities Act granted limited powers of local government to elected town councils in the urban townships. It was hoped that increased opportunities for local political competition and patronage would draw attention and energy away from the battle for state power. President P. W. Botha envisaged an archipelago of semi-autonomous black city-states, scattered around the white industrial centers: if Luxemburg could be an independent state, then why not Soweto? The combined set of bills that were drawn up to implement Riekert's recommendations became known as the Koornhof Bills, after Minister of Co-operation and Development Piet Koornhof.[6]

Having thus disposed of rural blacks and having accommodated urban blacks, the government devised policies aimed at the co-optation of two other population groups, situated in an intermediary position in the racial stratification: coloreds and Indians. The exclusively white parliament was transformed into a tricameral parliament, with separate chambers and cabinets for whites, coloreds, and Indians. The 1983 constitution had sufficient built-in guarantees to ensure that final control remained firmly in white hands. The African majority remained excluded from political power at a national level. This unilateral restructuring of the political landscape provided the impetus for the formation of the United Democratic Front, under the slogan "Apartheid divides, UDF unites."

In contrast to the exclusivist nationalism of the Afrikaners, the UDF advocated the inclusive nationalism of the Freedom Charter: South Africa belongs to all who live in it, black and white. In contrast to the long-term policy goal of replacing the racial stratification of the apartheid state with the social stratification of a modern market economy, the UDF proposed its own utopia of an egalitarian society, governed by a participatory democracy, strongly rooted in grassroots structures. However, in the process of contesting this unilaterally imposed change in the terms of exclusion and incorporation, the UDF was drawing its own boundaries, though these were certainly less rigid than those of the apartheid state. The UDF's Programme of Action announced the intention "to establish the United Democratic Front as the only representative front representing all sections of our people."[7]

The UDF leadership frequently spoke on behalf of "our people" or "the people." Although the UDF could safely claim to be the most representative movement in South African history, it was clear that not all inhabitants of South Africa were deemed to belong to "the people." While the apartheid state drew geographic borderlines around Bantustans and racially defined Group Areas, the UDF demarcated its constituency along more symbolic lines. "Who are the people?" asked one of the speakers at a UDF conference. "We have stated in the past that the people consist of all those classes, parts of classes, organisations, groups and individuals who form part of or support the struggle against apartheid. The people, therefore, do not consist of one class or race. Indeed, they consist of persons from all racial groups who have an interest in a struggle to destroy apartheid. . . . On the other hand, the forces of apartheid are all those classes, sections of classes, organisations, groups and individuals who form part of or support the machinery of apartheid. This category includes Blacks as well as whites."[8]

Here, "the people" are all those actively opposed to apartheid. But often "the people" were more narrowly defined, with political loyalties as the decisive criterion. In another widely held interpretation of "the people," the term refers exclusively to ANC adherents. Steve Tshwete, president of the UDF's Border region and simultaneously a cadre in the ANC underground, recalled the discussions on Robben Island, where he was imprisoned for fifteen years for activities in Umkhonto we Sizwe (MK), the ANC's armed wing: "You know, the word 'people,' it pervades the whole Charter: 'The people shall govern' and 'land to the people.' We had to engage in intensive politicisation, because 'people,' as far as we were concerned, are all those classes, those social groups, irrespective of race, colour, or creed, who rallied around the banner of the ANC for a non-racial, united, democratic South Africa."[9]

Similarly, at a meeting of student activists from UDF- and ANC-aligned organizations in a rural village in the Northern Transvaal, the term "the people" referred exclusively to people and organizations in the ANC camp. The "Zimzims," students belonging to rival organizations aligned to the Pan Africanist Congress (PAC), were not seen as belonging to "the people." They were just "persons."[10] The terms "the people" and another UDF favorite, "the community," were frequently employed to demarcate the borderlines in a dichotomy between "us and them," between good and evil.

Race, Class, and Evil

The conflict in South Africa has been depicted as a clash between two nationalisms, the exclusivist nationalism of the Afrikaners versus the inclusive nationalism of the Freedom Charter, which represents the mainstream ideology in African resistance. Alternatively, the focus is not on Afrikaner ideology but more generally on white prejudice and privilege. In much of the more recent academic literature, the factor of race is seen as subordinate to another factor: class interest. For this revisionist school, the central fact in South African history is not archaic Afrikaner ideology or white prejudice but "the super-exploitation of black labour by a racially structured capitalism."[11] The rigid either/or character of this "race-class debate," requiring a hierarchical ranking of the categories of race and class, has been criticized by participants on both sides of the debate.[12] In recent years, the focus has shifted toward the dual structure of racial oppression and class exploitation, allowing for a more nuanced discussion. The race-class debate and its implications in terms of opposition politics are explored in somewhat more detail in the section on the historiography of the conflict in South Africa.

A consequence of these theoretical paradigms is a rather one-dimensional portrayal of the main protagonists. They tend to be reduced to either greedy capitalists versus downtrodden proletarians or white supremacists versus black freedom fighters. The more balanced approach, which recognizes the validity of concepts of race and ethnicity as well as the insights provided by a class analysis, has the virtue of restoring at least two dimensions to the protagonists. But in order to do justice to South Africans of all colors and classes, more dimensions are needed. Fortunately, just like people elsewhere, real-life people in South Africa are not one- or two-dimensional actors; they are multidimensional human beings.

The struggle in South Africa was not only about redefining the political and the social order. It was also about competing concepts of the desired moral order. In his speech at the 1983 conference where the idea of a United Front was discussed, Allan Boesak condemned the constitutional proposals not only as politically untenable but also as "morally wrong and unacceptable." He exhorted his audience to join forces, as "co-workers with God," against an evil government.[13] At a UDF meeting in Kroonvale, the colored township of Graaff Reinet, a resolution was passed stating that the people were against apartheid because it was immoral and sinful.[14] When a delegation of church leaders went to meet government ministers to discuss an upsurge of violence in the Vaal Triangle, they claimed to act on divine instructions. Bishop Desmond Tutu said the church leaders came as Christians with no political axe to grind. "We went on the mandate of the Gospel."[15]

The stakes in the contest included material resources, political rights, and human values, but the competition was equally about access to and control over spiritual resources. Both sides claimed to be fighting the forces of evil and darkness, and both sides laid claim to having "God on our side." The conflict over South Africa has indeed been characterized as "first and foremost . . . a type of spiritual warfare."[16] The God of the National Party and the South African Police was locked in battle with the God of the oppressed. The highly controversial 1983 constitution declares that "The people of the Republic of South Africa acknowledge the sovereignty and guidance of Almighty God."[17] This is the God of the Afrikaner people, the God who "gathered our forebears together from many lands and gave them this their own, who has guided them from generation to generation, who has wondrously delivered them from the dangers that beset them."[18] This is also the God of the Christian National education imposed by the National Party on South African schools. In his autobiography, Frank Chikane, vice-president of the UDF Transvaal and later secretary general of the South African Council of Churches (SACC), gives a vivid description of this competition for divine backing. In South African textbooks, God is on the side of the settlers who dispossess the indigenous people. The whites came and took the land and the freedom of the blacks in exchange for the Bible. On whose side was God, if the whites claimed to have been helped by God to subdue the blacks? "Did they defeat our forefathers because God was on their side?"[19]

Calvinist doctrine was also used to provide supernatural legitimacy for the police force. A manual used at the police colleges explained that "the State has received its authority from God, and has, in his turn, given authority to the police."[20] Both the South African Police (SAP) and the South African Defence Force (SADF) frequently invoked religious backing for their mission. "When the men in uniform defy the Marxist danger with arms, they are assisted by the Chaplain with the weapon of the Gospel."[21]

On the other side of the front line, the combatants were equally on a divinely ordained mission. An article entitled "Christianity and Revolution: A Battle Fought on Many Fronts," published in the ANC magazine *Sechaba,* explained how national liberation and spiritual salvation went hand in hand in "taking up the cross to follow Jesus, who voluntarily chose the dangerous path of confronting violence himself to open the way for a new society."[22] Calvinist doctrine was invoked by Allan Boesak when he wrote an open letter to the minister of justice, pointing out that the Bible teaches that "where justice is lacking . . . the government's authority is no longer derived from God, but it is in conflict with God. In such a case, resistance against such a government is justified and becomes a duty."[23] The Kairos document, published in 1985 by leading South African adherents of liberation theology, provided legitimacy on biblical grounds for resistance against tyranny. The Kairos document asserts that "God sides with the Oppressed" and recommends reshaping church rituals "to promote the liberating mission of God in our present crisis. The evil forces we speak of in baptism, for example, must be named. We know what these evil forces are in South Africa today."[24]

The contest about spiritual resources, of course, was not limited to the discourse of Christianity. Various Christian denominations branded apartheid as heresy. Hindu organizations asserted that "Hinduism believes that all people are equal."[25] Numerous Moslem leaders proclaimed similar verdicts, declaring participation in the government's new dispensation *haraam,* unlawful by religious law. The Dutch Reformed Church did not watch in idleness while the enemy appropriated God. Following a proposal of Dominee Stoffel Colyn, chaplain general of the South African Police, the general synod resolved that Islam was a false religion and that "the gospel of Jesus Christ [is] the only answer to the onslaught of Islam."[26]

On the ideological as well as on the actual battlefield, control over supernatural resources was hotly contested. Describing the battles in Natal between Inkatha warriors and UDF-aligned youth, one of the "comrades" on the UDF side explained how both sides prepared themselves for the fight. "They take muti. They have wizards to weaken us. We take muti. We sing: 'kill the wizards'. . . . It is difficult to find strong muti if you are a comrade."[27] Speaking at a cultural conference, Thabo Mbeki (then the ANC director of information) exhorted his audience to remember what the Zulu king Dingaan had said when he faced the enemy: "Bulala abathakathi—Kill the Sorcerers."[28] In these battles between "us and them," the other side was portrayed as the forces of evil, as the Antichrist, as witches and sorcerers, who had to be removed from society.

The autobiography of Ronnie Kasrils, the head of military intelligence for the ANC armed wing Umkhonto we Sizwe (MK), provides an interesting glimpse of discussions among MK recruits. Having watched a volleyball competition between two MK teams in which one side invoked *muti* powers (African medicine with supposedly magic qualities), he proceeded to discuss the subject in the classroom. He told his students about an incident during Zimbabwe's liberation war, where the ANC had fought alongside Zimbabwean guerrillas against Ian Smith's white minority regime. A group of guerrillas had sought sanctuary in the hills near a village, where they were advised that a famous *sangoma* (a traditional healer) would be visiting the village. The guerrillas were divided on what to do: go and meet the sangoma in order to show respect for traditional custom and to benefit from the spiritual powers of the sangoma; or let security considerations prevail and avoid contact. This last argument was underpinned with the assertion that there was no power in muti anyway. The outcome was that some of the guerrillas indeed went to meet the sangoma, who performed a ritual to make them invisible to their enemies and subsequently betrayed them to the Rhodesian army. The lesson, as Kasrils spelled out for his students, was that magic could not bring safety. "There was no muti that could make you invincible. Victory depended not on muti, but on skill, preparation, and the fact that we were waging a just war."[29] If the issue, as Kasrils explained to the director of the training center in the German Democratic Republic, centered on a debate between the protagonists of dialectal materialism and of idealism, then Kasrils after all placed himself in the camp of the idealists, along with the adherents of the sangoma. A moral legitimation, the conviction of fighting a just war, would guarantee ultimate victory.

In order to build a new society, a new moral order, the forces of evil had to be driven out. Not only white authorities, capitalist bosses, black town councillors and policemen, and Bantustan leaders were excluded from the definition of "the people." Those who controlled the forces of evil magic, witches and sorcerers, were equally excluded. Purging the forces of evil from the body of society could take various forms: ostracizing black policemen, boycotting the shops of town councillors, and burning government property, *impimpis* (suspected informers), and, indeed, witches. Allan Boesak proposed to exorcize the forces of evil with prayer. "If the rulers will not hear the cries of the people, if they will not change, if they continue to prevent justice, let us pray them out of existence. . . . We do not believe in the power of violence, but we do believe in the power of prayer."[30] Some, however, chose violent methods of exorcism. Persons suspected of having acted as informers were publicly eliminated with the notorious "necklace"—they were burned to death with a gasoline-doused car tire around the neck. Other cleansing rituals were less dramatic. During the peak of the period of "people's power" in 1985–86, the few feverish months when liberation seemed around the corner, frequent references were made to various cleanup activities. One of the duties of the street committees in Alexandra township was "to look to the cleanliness, to clean the yard of dirt and crime."[31] People's courts, aspiring to eliminate crime and to restore harmony within the family or between neighbors, were instrumental in mostly short-lived attempts at building both a political and a moral community in the townships. People's parks—open spaces cleared of rubbish and crudely decorated with flowers and symbols of liberation—were the signals of a new order, until the police moved in to root out what to them appeared as the symbols of evil.

Macro and Micro Perspectives

At stake in the battles of the 1980s was the contest about changing the borderlines in the racial and social stratification of South Africa. In this contest, participants developed their own visions of a future society, of a new political and social order as well as a new moral order. In the birth process of a new society, symbolic borderlines were drawn and redrawn by rituals of exclusion and incorporation.

This book is an attempt to contribute to our understanding of a dramatic period in South African history by looking at these processes at a local level. I have chosen to focus on the UDF as a social movement from below, taking three local organizations as my vantage point. Part 2, the main body of this book (chapters 3–5), consists of three case studies, which look in detail at locally based attempts at shaping a new society. I have selected three different settings and three different phenomena: a youth movement in Sekhukhuneland, a rural part of Lebowa, one of the former Bantustans in the Northern Transvaal; a civic association (a residents organization) in Kagiso, a township adjacent to

Krugersdorp, west of Johannesburg; and a community newspaper in the Cape Peninsula. All three have in common that they were aligned to the UDF. The Northern Transvaal, Sekhukhuneland in particular, was known as a stronghold of rural youth congresses. Sekhukhuneland was the scene of rural resistance in the 1950s and was reputed to be an ANC bastion. The choice of Sekhukhuneland as a case study provided the opportunity both to investigate a rural youth movement and to explore the continuities and discontinuities over the past decades. Apart from the Krugersdorp Residents Organisation (KRO) being a well-organized civic group, it had the additional advantage of being well documented because of a court case that it initiated against the minister of law and order. The choice of the third case study was perhaps less obvious than the selection of a rural and an urban case study. Since one of the characteristic features of the UDF was the massive use of various forms of media, I chose the newspaper *Grassroots,* which was one of the earliest community papers and thus served as a model for similar ventures in other parts of South Africa. The *Grassroots* target areas in the Cape Peninsula also provided the opportunity to glimpse the difficulties involved in trying to operate across racial boundaries between coloreds and Africans. An additional advantage was the availability of abundant documentation, since *Grassroots*'s main source of funding was a nongovernmental organization (NGO) based in the Netherlands.

The history of the UDF as a political organization and its role in national political life has already been the subject of several books. The present book therefore includes only a brief chronological outline of major events and trends in the 1980s, followed by a historiographical section, discussing various interpretations of the struggles in the 1980s: What did it all mean? What were the causes of the revolt? How was the white power bastion tackled? Who was fighting whom, with whom, and why? The politics of alliances can be discussed in terms of race and class, as is commonly done in both academic and activist literature. Although that obviously is a relevant perspective, alliances can also be discussed from other angles, such as generation or gender or the urban-rural divide. The historiographical section returns to the questions raised in this introduction: Who are "the people" on whose behalf the battles were waged? What were the terms of inclusion or exclusion? These themes are then pursued in the three case studies. In the conclusion I attempt to link these perspectives from the micro level to the macro story: How do local struggles fit into the overall pattern? Most of the literature deals either with the overall story of resistance and repression in the 1980s or with local case studies. The relationship between local struggles and national movements is virtually a missing link. As I pursued my case studies, the academic paradigms proved at times inadequate. The case studies are situated at a local level, while the paradigms in the academic literature are derived from the study of South African society at a national level. Which dimensions are missing in the literature, when viewed from this micro perspective?

In addition to the overall struggle against apartheid and for a more just socioeconomic order, other agendas as well were pursued on the micro level. Situations of near anarchy or power vacuum allow for a shift in power relations, often best visible at a local level. A common feature of many wars of liberation (for example, in Eritrea or Mozambique) was the—mostly temporary—rise in status of previously fairly powerless groups such as women, youth, or the poor. The anti-apartheid struggle was not a classical war of liberation, but the phase of popular mobilization in the mid-1980s shared some of these features. The young men and boys, who were the most visible actors in the battles of the 1980s, were no doubt motivated by anger against the oppressive and humiliating condition of apartheid. But they were also contesting patterns of authority within African society, they were in search of adventure and excitement, and they formed competing bands in the battle for control over territory, resources, and girlfriends. For women, the opportunities inherent in the "times of ungovernability" were more ambivalent. Some types of activities—for example, in the field of media—opened avenues for women's empowerment; elsewhere, women were increasingly marginalized as the macho culture of street fighters began to dominate "struggle culture" in the townships. These "struggles behind the struggle" are a central theme of the three case studies.

Another dimension, missing from most of the literature but emerging strongly from the case studies, is the importance of religion and local belief systems as a source of inspiration and legitimation. The actors in the 1980s were motivated by a mixture of African nationalism, the ideal of a nonracial society, and the vision of an egalitarian order. Many—probably most—were not acting within a purely secular framework. They engaged in a battle against the apartheid state and its accomplices, but they were also fighting a spiritual battle against the forces of darkness, cleansing society of evil in the search for a harmonious moral order.

Part One

Redrawing the Boundaries: Changing the Terms
of Exclusion and Incorporation

CHAPTER ONE

The UDF and South Africa in the 1980s: The Events

We remember only too well the township situation during the period described as a "period of people's power." Community councillors left their jobs, and a huge vacuum was formed. We did not know what to do with the authority, the power, that had already come into the hands of the people. Perhaps history is on our side in that liberation did not come then. It has given us another chance . . . to reflect and develop our position to stronger heights.

Murphy Morobe

Getting off the Ground: 1983–1984

THE CONVENTIONAL STORY of the United Democratic Front traces the origins of the Front to a call made by Allan Boesak at a congress held by the Anti–South African Indian Council Committee (anti-SAIC) on 22 and 23 January 1983 in Johannesburg. The anti-SAIC had been established in 1981 with the limited goal of opposing the elections for the South African Indian Council (SAIC), an advisory body that the government had devised as a platform for Indian politics. After a successful boycott campaign by this ad hoc alliance of Indian organizations, the turnout in the 1981 poll stood at a dismal 10 percent. This campaign marked the revival of Charterist politics inside South Africa: the boycott was supported by a coalition of 110 organizations that adopted the Charter for Change, a document strongly reminiscent of the Freedom Charter, the basic policy document of the Congress Alliance.[1]

The meeting in Johannesburg was convened in early 1983 to consolidate the "victory and the gains" of the boycott campaign with the establishment of a more permanent political organization.[2] The Indian delegates decided to revive the Transvaal Indian Congress (TIC), which had existed in the 1950s as part of the Congress Alliance, binding the ANC in a partnership with organizations of progressive Indians, coloreds, and whites. More importantly, at least in retrospect, it responded to a call by a colored church minister, Dr. Allan Boesak, president of the World Alliance of Reformed Churches, to form a broad front of organizations all over the country to respond to the constitutional proposals and the Koornhof Bills. In the same month, exiled ANC president Oliver Tambo had called for the formation of "strong mass democratic organisation" inside South Africa, mentioning the examples of trade unions, youth, students, women, and civics, or civic associations. Declaring 1983 "The Year of United Action," Tambo urged his listeners "to organise all democratic forces into one front for national liberation."[3]

When Allan Boesak accepted the invitation to be a guest speaker at the anti-SAIC congress, he was not aware of Tambo's call.[4] In his speech, he advocated "the politics of refusal, . . . the only dignified response that blacks can give in this situation. In order to succeed we need a united front. . . . There is no reason why churches, civic associations, trade unions, student organizations, and sports bodies should not unite on this issue, pool our resources, inform the people of the fraud that is about to be perpetrated in its name, and on the day of the election expose these plans for what they are."[5] Allan Boesak is a talented orator, whose fiery rhetoric held mass audiences spellbound, whether in church halls or at UDF rallies. For this reason, perhaps, Boesak's speech is remembered as marking the birth of the UDF, but he was by no means the only one who exhorted anti-apartheid groupings to join forces. Already in 1981–82, the idea of a United Front was much debated in black political circles.

Only with hindsight did the anti-SAIC congress gain its momentous significance. The UDF was initially conceived as an ad hoc alliance, with the limited goal of fighting the constitutional proposals and the Koornhof Bills. Although the UDF declaration is clearly inspired by ANC heritage, the UDF decided against adopting the Freedom Charter. Two reasons were given: advocating the Freedom Charter would most likely invite state repression and would limit the opportunities of the Front to broaden out to include a wide political spectrum, reaching out beyond the known Charterist organizations. The core organizations were clearly Charterist oriented, but the Front aspired to unite "all our people, wherever they may be in the cities and the countryside, the factories and mines, schools, colleges, and universities, houses and sport fields, churches, mosques and temples, to fight for our freedom."[6] Only in August 1987, after many of its constituent organizations and the largest trade union federation had decided to adopt the Freedom Charter, did the UDF follow suit.

The Front's Charterist credentials were equally obvious in the choice of its three presidents: Albertina Sisulu, the wife of the imprisoned ANC leader Walter Sisulu, from the Transvaal, and two other ANC veterans from the 1950s, Archie Gumede, a lawyer from Natal, and Oscar Mpetha, a trade unionist from the Western Cape. The geographical spread is indicative of the lack of national cohesion at the time. Regional chauvinism was still so strong that the regions could not have agreed on one national president.

The extent of direct ANC involvement in the launch of the UDF remains ambiguous. For years, the ANC had been trying to move back into mainstream black politics inside South Africa. One early venture, which hoped to exploit new space opened by the creation of self-governing Bantustans, was the formation of Inkatha in 1975, initially actively supported by the ANC.[7] A popular front rather than a new political organization had obvious advantages. A new political organization could be tempted to supplant the liberation movement, as the example of Inkatha had demonstrated. The UDF's working principles state that the Front "does not and will not purport to be a substitute movement to accredited people's liberation movements."[8] All UDF activists whom I interviewed were adamant that the initiative came from inside, while acknowledging that known ANC adherents inside South Africa played an active part in the formation of the UDF and that consultations had taken place with the ANC in exile.

Between May and July 1983, regional United Democratic Front committees were set up in the Transvaal, Natal, and the Western Cape, while provisional structures were formed in the Eastern Cape and the Orange Free State. The national launch took place on 20 August in Mitchell's Plain, a colored area near Cape Town. The conference, which officially marked the formation of the UDF, was attended by about a thousand delegates, representing some 575 community organizations, trade unions, sporting bodies, and women's and youth organizations. As more organizations joined in the course of the year, UDF spokespeople usually measured the strength of the Front in a convenient shorthand: 600 organizations representing two million people. On closer inspection, it is impossible to estimate the constituency of these organizations. Of the 575 organizations represented at the launch, 235 were branches of the Western Cape Inter Church Youth, a recently founded organization of which not much was heard in subsequent years. For media consumption, however, the original formula was eminently digestible. The UDF would stick in popular memory as a front representing some 600 organizations and two million people.

The conference adopted a declaration stating that the UDF's aim was the creation of a united democratic South Africa, free of Bantustans and Group Areas and based on the will of the people. Apart from electing the three presidents, the delegates also approved a pantheon of "patrons" to illustrate that the UDF could build on wide-ranging support. The patrons included famous ANC names and many religious leaders, a combination that served to demonstrate both political and moral legitimacy. In addition to the official conference, over twelve thousand people attended a mass rally that gave a standing ovation to the defiant reading of messages of greetings from Nelson Mandela and other ANC leaders in prison.

The Revival of Charterist Politics

The launch of the UDF was the best organized display of support for the ANC in almost a quarter century. After the banning of the ANC in 1960, Black Consciousness (BC) had emerged as the dominant force in black opposition. Black Consciousness was a movement rather than an organization. Having originated on black university campuses, it was a movement of psychological self-liberation that mainly attracted intellectuals, such as students, teachers, ministers of religion, and journalists. BC widened the definition of *black* to include not only Africans but also the other oppressed population groups: coloreds and Indians. The comeback of Charterist organizations, which would dominate black politics during the 1980s, occurred from 1980 to 1981. Unlike the African National Congress, the Indian Congresses had never been banned. But the Transvaal branch had withered away, and the Natal Indian Congress (NIC) had shrunk to a narrow core of intellectuals and professionals. In the late 1970s, the NIC was revived by an infusion of young student activists who set out to build a mass base for the organization by focusing on local concerns such as housing, rents, and transportation. In the same period, civic organizations were being formed in other parts of the country.

When the Black People's Convention (BPC) was banned in October 1977, the Azanian People's Organisation (AZAPO) was launched in 1978 as its successor organization. The BPC had focused on race, aspiring to give a positive content to black identity in the belief that psychological self-liberation was a necessary prerequisite for political liberation. AZAPO moved away from the exclusive focus on race toward a class analysis. In theory, that would have opened the way for cooperation with the white left. But AZAPO held that, in South African conditions, race and class coincided.

In the discussions on the formation of a broad front, problems arose in respect to nonracial organizations that included a white membership, such as the South African Council of Churches (SACC) and the recently formed Federation of South African Trade Unions (FOSATU). The Black Consciousness position was that white people had a role to play in advancing the process of change in the white community. AZAPO did not want white people in "organisations of the oppressed"; nor did it want to participate in joint programs with organizations that had white members. Ideologically, the Black Consciousness Movement (BCM) and AZAPO were more closely related to the Africanist position of the Pan Africanist Congress (PAC) than to the multiracial or nonracial principles of the ANC.

1. UDF launch in Mitchell's Plain, 20 August 1983. Joe Marks, vice-president of the UDF Western Cape, brings the Amandla salute, flanked by Popo Molefe and Trevor Manuel. Photograph courtesy of Paul Weinberg.

Divisions within BC organizations between orthodox adherents of BC and people who increasingly leaned toward the ANC led to an exodus of activists such as AZAPO president Curtis Nkondo and Popo Molefe, chair of AZAPO's Soweto branch, who found a new political home in the UDF. Nkondo clearly demarcated the lines between BC and Charterism, leaving no room for compromise. Raising the issue of the Freedom Charter, Nkondo now asserted that "anybody who deviates from the demands of the 'Charter' is a traitor, and a fraud, or a downright quisling."[9]

Moves toward regional coordination were underway in various areas of the country. Apart from the churches, the only organizations that could truly claim a nationwide following were the emerging independent trade unions and the student organizations, which—like apartheid education—were structured along racial lines. The National Union of South African Students (NUSAS) organized on the campuses of white liberal, English-language universities, the Azanian Students Organisation (AZASO) organized black students at postsecondary institutions, and the Congress of South African Students (COSAS) provided a political home for black high school students. All three joined the UDF, but COSAS was to play the most crucial role, notably in the formation of a wide range of youth organizations. Student organizations proved important as recruiting and training grounds for activists. More than most UDF affiliates, student organizations had access to a range of resources and facilities, ranging from printing equipment and photocopiers to meeting halls. They not only had the means to collect and disseminate information, but they were also in a position to work as nearly full-time activists. Lastly, although school grounds and university campuses became major battlefields during the 1980s, during at least the first half of the decade they were preserves of relative freedom.

COSAS, formed in 1979, initially aimed to draw students into community issues and wider anti-apartheid struggles. A reappraisal of strategy around 1983 led to COSAS focusing on school and student matters and consequently limiting its membership to high school students. The exodus of experienced, older leaders led to temporary disruption but also to a wider range of youth organizations. The excluded former students were instrumental in the formation of Charterist youth congresses, which took off in mid-1983.[10] Although the Soweto uprising of 1976 had been an isolated student revolt, since 1979 student activists actively sought to link up with community and worker protests. School boycotts, rent and bus boycotts, the anti-SAIC campaign, the Release Mandela Campaign, the anti–Republic Day campaign of 1981, and the campaign against the imposed "independence" of the Ciskei all contributed to a sense of optimism about the renewed phenomenon of mass mobilization.

The need to link up student organizations, trade unions, and women's groups, and to link local issues to national politics, was widely discussed in student circles. Protest politics was shifting from uncompromising noncollaborationism to a more pragmatic result-oriented approach. The advantage of the new focus on bread-and-butter issues was that ordinary people could be involved in building local organizations and that activists were restrained from marching too far ahead of the mainstream. The drawback was the danger of concentrating on winning limited gains, becoming reformist in the process. As student leader Auret van Heerden pointed out in an influential address in 1982: "we need organisations making demands which cannot be met within the framework of an oppressive and exploitative society."[11]

How Broad a Front?

The participants at the anti-SAIC congress believed that the Front could be broad enough to accommodate Black Consciousness groupings. But although the UDF provided a new political home for many individuals with a history in BC organizations, the major organizations in the BC tradition remained outside the Front. The question whether Inkatha would be eligible to join the UDF was initially left open for future deliberation.[12] Like the UDF and AZAPO, Inkatha leader Gatsha Buthelezi had reacted sharply to the new constitution. He even invited the ANC and the PAC to join him in what he called a marriage of convenience. But by the end of 1983, a bitter enmity had grown between the UDF and Inkatha. Planned talks were scuttled by clashes at the University of Zululand, which left five students dead. In January 1984, the UDF National Executive Committee (NEC) decided that there would be no meeting with Inkatha.

The criteria for inclusion and exclusion were spelled out in a memorandum by the newly formed UDF secretariat in early August 1983.[13] The emphasis again was on the broad character: "There is a place for everyone." But the need for a "consistent approach" necessitated some guidelines. A requirement for affiliation was the unqualified acceptance of the whole UDF declaration. The criteria for exclusion were more detailed. Organizations working within the framework of the homelands were not eligible for membership, as this was contrary to the UDF's stated belief in a unitary South Africa. Organizations operating within the state machinery at the central, provincial, or local level were equally unacceptable.

A rapprochement with AZAPO was pursued for some time. But from 1984, relations deteriorated to the point of violent clashes, although it later transpired that some of the clashes, notably in the Eastern Cape, had been instigated by agents provocateurs employed by the security services. In spite of its adherence to a class analysis, AZAPO stood committed "to the fact that the struggle will continue to be manifested in terms of colour, of black and white."[14] Two issues—the role of progressive whites and the compatibility of nonracial democratic principles with the existence of racially based organizations such as the Indian Congresses—became the major points of division between the UDF and AZAPO.[15]

AZAPO's attempts at building a broader platform resulted in the launch of the National Forum on 11 and 12 June, where about two hundred organizations adopted a "Manifesto of the Azanian People." It declared that the people's struggle was directed against "the system of racial capitalism which holds the people of Azania in bondage for the benefit of the small minority of white capitalists and their allies, the white workers and the reactionary sections of the black middle class." The black working class was identified as the "driving force of the struggle."[16]

In the Western Cape, known for its ideological factionalism, the inclusion of organizations such as the white student organization NUSAS ("The sons and daughters of the ruling class") and colored and Indian traders was the issue that caused a split in the shaky local coalition of anti-apartheid groupings. Trotskyites and other ultraleft elements criticized the proposed UDF as a popular alliance that would inevitably end up in a betrayal of the working class. Notwithstanding the rhetoric about the leading role of the working class, AZAPO, the Cape Trotskyites, and other independent socialist groups were dominated by middle-class intellectuals. What was the position of the major organizations of the black working class, the independent trade unions? They were not nearly as hostile as the ideological puritans, but for the next few years the most influential grouping of unions preferred to go it alone.

The most important independent trade unions were grouped in two federations: the Federation of South African Trade Unions (FOSATU), founded in 1979, and the Council of Unions of South Africa (CUSA), founded in 1980. The CUSA unions tended toward BC positions, emphasizing the need for black leadership. The FOSATU leadership took both a nonracial and a militant pro-worker position, advocating the need for worker leadership. Although recognizing the leading role of the ANC as the major liberation movement on the international scene, the FOSATU leadership strove toward building an independent workers party internally. The ANC had a legitimate role to play in the struggle against the apartheid regime, but it was "essential that workers must strive to build their own powerful and effective organisation even whilst they are part of a wider popular struggle."[17] General Secretary Joe Foster warned against the danger of workers being swamped by the powerful tradition of populist politics and against the confusion caused by the introduction into the political debate of "an empty and misleading political category called the community."[18] The United Front formula, so ran Foster's argument, poses the danger of focusing on protest politics and the risk of worker leadership being wasted by adventurist actions.

The UDF obviously was such a front. FOSATU decided against affiliation, although it was prepared to enter into ad hoc alliances, as in the boycott campaign against the tricameral parliament. CUSA affiliated with both the UDF and the National Forum but ceased active participation in 1985, giving priority to the unity talks with FOSATU on the merger of both federations. Another source of trade union support was the so-called community unions. Unlike FOSATU unions, the community unions were general unions, not organized along the lines of the industry. They held the view that workplace issues were inseparable from community interests. General unions like the South African Allied Workers Union (SAAWU) and the General and Allied Workers Union (GAWU) did affiliate with the UDF. A single all-embracing federation of unions proved an elusive ideal, but in November 1985 FOSATU unions and the major CUSA unions merged into a new federation, the Congress of South African Trade Unions (COSATU). COSATU became an overtly Charterist trade union federation, far more inclined to work with the UDF than its predecessors. Non-Charterist unions formed into two smaller federations. During the 1980s, union membership tripled from 808,000 in 1980 to 2.46 million in 1990.[19]

The UDF and the unions shared platforms in the campaigns against the Koornhof Bills and the elections for the tricameral parliament. They advocated a boycott of the municipal elections under the Black Local Authorities Act, held during the last months of 1983. Only 21 percent of the potential electorate voted in this series of elections for the new councils. But the real test of the UDF's strength was the campaign against the 1984 tricameral elections. From this tour de force the UDF emerged as the major force in extra-parliamentary opposition, but it first had to overcome serious internal controversy.

Before the year 1983 was over, the UDF had almost fallen apart on an issue that has proved divisive in the history of black politics: to participate or not to participate. The government had submitted its constitutional proposals to a referendum for the white electorate, which approved the constitution with a comfortable majority of 65 percent. Next, the constitution bill would be the subject of referenda among the prospective Indian and colored voters. To discuss its position, the UDF in December called a National General Conference in Port Elizabeth. Three options were considered: to boycott the referendum, to participate in the referendum and campaign for a "no" vote, or to allow each region freedom of choice. The debate became particularly vicious as it unfolded partially along racial lines, with Indian delegates making eloquent pleas in favor of participation. It was argued that the UDF would make a show of strength by delivering a massive "no." African delegates from the Transvaal felt betrayed: calling for a racial referendum would amount to a negation of the nonracial principles of the UDF. In the end, it was decided to leave the decision to the UDF National Executive Committee.[20]

The discussions revealed not only a difference in preparation among delegations but also vastly differing levels of education and ideological sophistication. The Indian Congresses argued their case invoking Gandhi, Lenin, and Gramsci. And had the example of the trade unions not demonstrated that one could operate within the system without becoming a collaborator? Opponents of participation also used some ideological ammunition. They retorted that Lenin favored participation because political consciousness among the masses had been low, while in South Africa people were more politicized. If they were as yet insufficiently politicized, then one should go out and politicize the masses. The UDF ought to follow Mao's recipe: guerrillas of Umkhonto we Sizwe (MK) should be able to find support bases among the people; they should be like fish in water. This again brought a racial dimension in focus: some of the Indian and colored delegates privately made it clear that they preferred to wage battle from the benches of parliament, not from the trenches of the struggle. The armed struggle was better left to Africans. Illustrative of lingering tensions and prejudice is a "struggle joke" that circulated some years later. Within the struggle, it was said, there is a certain division of labor: the whites will do the thinking, the Indians will take care of the money, the Africans will do the fighting and the dying, and when it is all over, the coloreds will celebrate.

At its meeting in late January in Pretoria, the NEC decided to call for a nonracial referendum while simultaneously allowing flexibility for affiliates "to oppose the constitution on the basis determined by local conditions."[21] The UDF was finally saved by the government, which—equally uncertain of the outcome—decided against holding a referendum among Indians and coloreds. The failure to formulate a common position raised the question of the nature of the UDF as a front: Did affiliation mean that affiliated organizations were bound to UDF decisions?

The Organization of the UDF

The Front had three levels of leadership: national, regional, and local. The National Executive Committee consisted of three presidents, a secretary, a publicity secretary, a treasurer, and representatives from the regions. Initially only the secretary (Popo Molefe) and the publicity secretary (Terror Lekota) were paid, full-time officials. Mohammed Valli Moosa was added in October 1983 as assistant secretary. Later the list of officials on the UDF's payroll grew to about eighty. The NEC met periodically to make administrative decisions and plan national campaigns. The supreme policymaking forum was the National General Council, which was required to meet every two years but in fact met only twice, in 1985 and 1991. Convening large conferences became impossible under the State of Emergency. To speed up the process of decision making, in 1985 it was decided to set up a National Working Committee, which in practice became the highest policymaking body. The Working Committee consisted of the entire NEC plus two members from each region. Decision-making powers rested largely with the regions, which grew in number from six in 1983 to ten in later years. Regional executive committees (RECs) were elected at regional council meetings, where all local organizations carried equal voting powers, irrespective of strength. The Western Cape was an exception to this rule, allowing two votes for organizations with a "mass base." Decision making involved a complex process of mandates.[22] To a large extent, local UDF affiliates maintained their autonomy, but as the UDF developed into a more cohesive political movement, more organizational discipline was urged.

After the paralyzing participation debate, there remained the more practical job of building the UDF. The challenge here was to reach beyond the limited circle of activists, to involve ordinary people, to "politicize the masses." In the Million Signature Campaign, held during the first half of 1984, South Africans from all walks of life were invited to make their mark against apartheid by signing a statement. The intention of the campaign was twofold: to mobilize large numbers of people in the UDF and to build cores of activists with organizing and mobilizing skills. The campaign proved successful in colored and Indian areas, but for the African townships, where people lived under harsher repression, it was at the same time too bold and too tame. For those with vivid memories of repression, it seemed risky to sign a document that might fall into the wrong hands. Those eager to fight the system dismissed this petition-type activity as "a waste of time and reformist."[23] Elaborate handbooks were produced, exhorting the volunteers to be models of good behavior. First of all, the UDF needed to become respectable among apolitical people. "Dress neatly, be polite, do not argue, do not impress people with big words."[24] Although less than one third of the target number was reached, the campaign proved useful as a training ground for activists who could then move on to the central issue in UDF campaigns in 1984: the election boycott.

Culminating in a series of nationwide protest meetings in the middle of August 1984, the boycott campaign against the tricameral elections was a resounding success. In the elections for the (colored) House of Representatives the voter turnout was 30.9 percent of registered voters and 19 percent of potential voters (the total number of people qualified to vote). A week later, the boycott of the (Indian) House of Delegates fared even better, with only 20.2 percent of registered voters and 16.2 percent of potential voters going to the polls.

As part of the protests, widespread school boycotts were held in colored and African schools, and on a much smaller scale in some Indian and white schools. African schools had experienced sporadic boycotts since the beginning of the year. With some local variations, grievances followed a similar pattern. Upholding an age limit criterion of twenty years for re-admission to high schools, schools at the beginning of the year had excluded over three hundred students because they were over twenty. In numerous cases, students felt that the age limit was being used to victimize older, more experienced, and more outspoken student leaders. Other key issues were an end to corporal punishment and sexual harassment, free textbooks and stationery, the demand for elected student representative councils, and complaints about poor teacher qualifications. Student protests began with school-specific issues and only gradually moved on to the phase of more overt political protest, initially targeting "Bantu Education" and the Department of Education and Training but subsequently challenging local and central state power.[25] On the grounds of a school in Atteridgeville near Pretoria, a fifteen-year-old schoolgirl was run over by a police vehicle. The death of Emma Sathekga became a symbolic marker: she was the first "unrest victim" in the statistics on casualties of political violence, which would exceed five thousand before the decade was over. Next to election boycotts and school protests, a third source of "unrest" was developing: local community-based protests against rising bus fares and rent increases.

A Groundswell of Anger: September 1984–July 1985

The first major eruption of civil unrest occurred on 3 September 1984 in the townships of the Vaal Triangle, a heavily industrialized and economically depressed region south of Johannesburg. After the announcement of a rent increase, the recently formed Vaal Civic Association held protest meetings where it was decided that residents would pay what they considered an "affordable" rent (i.e., 30 Rand a month). There was no suggestion of a rent boycott.[26] The call for a two-day stay-away from work was massively heeded.

The events sparking the Vaal uprising took place in Sharpeville, a name that already stood as a day of remembrance on the resistance calendar. In the early morning of 3 September, groups gathered in the streets to march to the administration office where the rents were paid. On their way, stones were thrown at the house of deputy mayor Kuzwayo Jacob Dlamini. The beleaguered Dlamini opened fire and injured at least one person. The incensed crowd responded with firebombs. Dlamini fled his burning house, fell down, and lay unconscious. He was dragged to his already burning car and set afire. When police arrived, Dlamini was dead.[27] Before the day was over, riots had spread throughout the Vaal Triangle. The events of 3 September were to become a familiar pattern over the next few years. Hostility to councillors constituted the pivot around which township politics were radicalized and the transition to confrontation occurred.[28]

This outburst of popular anger coincided with the installation of the tricameral parliament in Cape Town, but the residents of Sebokeng, Evaton, and Sharpeville who took to the streets were mostly unaware of the coincidence. Widespread rioting coursed through this dense cluster of bleak townships. In Sharpeville, the deputy major and a councillor were killed, while homes of council officials were gutted; the chair of the Lekoa Council was killed by an angry crowd; in Sebokeng a councillor was stoned to death. Shopping centers, gas stations, a bus depot, administration buildings, beer halls, and schools were destroyed. Large contingents of police and the army moved in to quell the rebellion, leaving twenty-six people dead and more than three hundred injured. This swoop through the Vaal marked the first use of army troops on a large scale in the African townships. At least ten councils agreed to suspend rent and service increases. The Vaal uprising was to play a central role in the Delmas treason trial, named after a rural Transvaal town where most of the proceedings of this longest treason trial since the 1950s took place. Leading members of the UDF, along with activists from the Vaal Civic Association (VCA), were charged with treason and conspiring with the ANC. The state held that the UDF and indirectly the ANC had inspired the Vaal uprising. In fact, the UDF leadership had been overtaken by events and was largely unable to provide direction.

These disparate strands of protest were pulled together in a major stay-away from school and work in the Pretoria-Witwatersrand-Vereeniging(PWV) area on 5 and 6 November.[29] One significant aspect of this stay-away was the participation of the major trade union federations FOSATU and CUSA, which for the first time took an active part in an overtly political protest action. Student activists from COSAS were instrumental in the distribution of hundreds of thousands of pamphlets in the townships, calling on residents to observe the stay-away. This joint effort of unions and student organizations provided the basis for optimistic speculations about the newly emerging student-worker alliance. About half a million workers stayed away from work, which amounted to about 60 percent of the black workforce in the PWV.

By the end of 1984 it was becoming clear that South Africa had entered a phase of unrest that would be more serious than the disturbances of 1976. Alarming footage appeared on television screens in European and American living rooms, showing white policemen whipping and shooting black school-children. Western governments came under increasing pressure from broad anti-apartheid coalitions to move beyond rhetorical condemnation to more effective pressure. During 1985, Pretoria continued its piecemeal reform initiatives, but measures such as the repeal of the acts prohibiting mixed marriages and interracial sex were insufficient to restore confidence abroad that Pretoria was indeed moving in the right direction. The failure by President P. W. Botha to live up to expectations that he would announce significant reforms in his 15 August "Rubicon" speech in Durban led to increased dissatisfaction with the government internationally and in business and opposition circles in South Africa. The refusal by Chase Manhattan Bank to roll over the loans of the South African state was an indication of faltering confidence on the part of the international business community. Under increasing congressional pressure, in September 1985 the Reagan administration imposed limited sanctions against South Africa. Similar pressures were building up in Europe, but it took the European Community until September 1986 to follow suit. At the beginning of October 1986, the American Congress overrode a presidential veto and imposed further sanctions.

The UDF made effective use of mounting international indignation. Whatever the effectiveness of the sanctions, international support and solidarity had psychological and material significance. Such support offered some measure of protection against repression, although this was largely limited to persons with international fame. It shored up the conviction that South Africans were fighting for a just cause; and it provided resources. Most of the UDF's finances came from abroad. UDF spokespeople displayed considerable skills in handling the media, both at home and abroad. While becoming versed in public relations, in addressing overseas audiences, and in capturing media attention with high-profile activities such as a long sit-in by UDF activists in the British consulate in Durban, the UDF was struggling to find a new role with the rank and file.

Finding a New Role for the Front

After the tricameral elections, a sense of malaise set in as the immediate raison d'être of the Front had now disappeared. From an ad hoc alliance, the UDF was transforming itself into a more permanent movement, concerned with a broad range of issues. It would take the UDF about half a year to pull itself together. The organizational structure of the UDF lacked a backup system. Detention of key leaders paralyzed the Front. In various discussion papers the UDF's performance was evaluated and its future role discussed. Among the shortcomings were a lack of participation by workers, a weak presence in the African areas, failure to draw in the major trade unions, a cumbersome process of decision making, and weak organization in rural areas.[30]

Searching for a new role and a more appropriate organizational formula, the UDF again had to confront the issue of the nature of the Front: What exactly was the relationship between the Front and its affiliates? Complaints that the UDF drained the affiliates by absorbing the most capable activists and by diverting attention from the organizations' own concerns, whether township rents or liberation theology, were widespread.

In defining its new role, the UDF needed to strike a balance between a narrow focus on national politics and the risk of dissipating its energies in all directions by taking on more tasks than it could hope to handle. The problematic aspects of the Front's strategic formula, which aimed to link local concerns to the national liberation struggle, can be seen most clearly in its relationship with civic organizations.

The rediscovery of the mobilizing potential of bread-and-butter issues was one of the innovations of social movements in South Africa in the 1980s. Civic associations, dealing with everyday concerns such as rents, electricity, water, and public transportation, had the potential to mobilize large numbers of not very politically minded township residents. But political activists were needed to bring out the political content of these basic struggles and to make certain that these struggles were coordinated into an assault on the state, both at the local and national levels.

A paper prepared for a 1984 workshop establishes a clear link between struggles engaging the local state, the central state, and capitalism. The high cost of living is blamed on market mechanisms: housing, electricity, and water are so expensive because they are produced and sold for profit. "Our struggle at local level is both a fight against the Black Local Authorities and huge profits made by Employers at the expense of residents. It is a fight against Apartheid and Capitalism at local level."[31]

Like the UDF itself, civics were presented in the image of progress and modernity. The UDF was not inclined to reach out to conservative or traditionalist sectors of society, such as the African independent churches or traditional healers. Similarly, civics made little effort to link up with apolitical groupings in township life such as *stokvels* (mutual benefit societies) and burial societies. Popular participation in civic organizations fluctuated strongly. By early 1985, the UDF attempted to develop a more coherent strategy toward civics. While the Front had only a tenuous grip on township activity, the state saw the UDF as the agitating force behind civic protests. According to the charge sheet in the Delmas trial, the UDF had used civics "to condition and incite the masses regarding emotional issues in the black communities . . . which are identified as so-called 'day-to-day issues.'"[32] However, the UDF was largely uninvolved in the growing township crisis during 1984. The UDF did not take up the issue of rents and only briefly was involved with the education issue. The focus was on opposition to the tricameral parliament.

While the South African state feared the revolutionary potential of civics, the ANC worried about their reformist character. In 1985, ANC voices in policy statements and polemics were critical of local-level negotiations that were occurring between civic organizations and state bodies.[33] But without local deals, civics could not deliver the goods. Popular support for community organizations was precisely predicated on their capacity to stop a rent increase or to negotiate an improved bus service. The pendulum between reform and revolution, between the perspective of a negotiated settlement or an insurrectionary seizure of power, would keep swinging back and forth for the rest of the decade.

The recognition that the UDF's campaigns and structures were generally reactive and insensitive to grassroots issues and militancy led to a strategic shift at the UDF's April 1985 National General Council, held under the slogan "from protest to challenge, from mobilisation to organisation."[34] State harassment hampered organizational efforts, but part of the blame lay with the UDF itself. It had not managed to effectively harness local forms of resistance.[35] The UDF's remoteness from the African townships can in part be explained by the composition of its national leadership. Formed with the primary goal of combating the tricameral elections, the UDF National Executive Committee was dominated by Indians and coloreds. The twenty-five members of the first NEC included twelve Africans, five coloreds, and eight Indians.[36] The UDF emerged from its 1985 conference with a newly elected leadership that had closer links with the African townships.

Forcing Black Local Authorities out of office confronted the UDF with a new challenge. The Front or its affiliates now had to set up alternative structures. Civics were being thrust into a new role, for which they were hardly equipped: they had to be transformed from watchdog bodies into embryonic forms of local government.

The UDF had proved that it could fill stadiums. Could it also take on the state in a direct challenge? That would require a coherent strategy and unity within the UDF's own ranks, overcoming regional divisions and factionalism. Black resistance had escalated to a state of rebellion during the first half of 1985. Massive school boycotts continued in the Eastern Cape, and rent boycotts spread through the Vaal Triangle. Violence intensified when the security forces moved into the townships with a massive show of strength. People associated with "the system" found themselves increasingly under attack. Acts of insurgency escalated, and conflict within the black community reached new levels of intensity with clashes between the UDF and Inkatha in Natal and between the UDF and AZAPO in the Eastern Cape.[37]

On 21 March 1985, the twenty-fifth anniversary of the massacre in Sharpeville, police in the Eastern Cape opened fire on a crowd in Langa, killing nineteen people. Intense rioting erupted in Langa and the other Uitenhage township, KwaNobuhle, leaving ten people dead. On 2 July, the bodies of three civic leaders from Cradock, a small town in the Eastern Cape, were found. Matthew Goniwe, Fort Calata, and Michael Mkhonto had mysteriously disappeared a couple of days before. Schoolmaster Goniwe had acquired national fame as the driving force behind youth and civic organizations in rural parts of the Eastern Cape, where he was the UDF's rural organizer. Cradock was reputed to have a strong civic based on street committees, thus welding a strong political community in a previously sleepy rural town. The murder sparked widespread violent protest. The funeral of the assassinated Cradock activists drew a crowd of forty thousand, with a massive display of flags of the ANC and the South African Communist Party (SACP).[38]

2. Mass funeral, Lingelihle, Cradock, Eastern Cape, July 1985.
Photograph courtesy of Gille de Vlieg.

On 21 July 1985, the government declared a partial State of Emergency that covered the Witwatersrand, the Eastern Cape, and was later extended to include the Western Cape. Police and army were given extensive powers to search and arrest, to restrict access, to impose curfews, and to counter school boycotts. The media were subjected to severe restrictions. Between July 1985 and March 1986 nearly eight thousand people were detained under emergency regulations. Thousands more were detained under various laws, including the notorious Internal Security Act, which allowed for detention without trial. UDF activists and trade unionists were the major targets of these sweeping

3. High visibility was one of the characteristics of the new social movements in the 1980s. Here the Mass Democratic Movement takes to the streets in Durban, 22 September 1989. Photograph courtesy of Rafs Mayet.

detention powers. In August 1985, COSAS became the first UDF affiliate to be declared an unlawful organization. COSAS, the largest UDF affiliate, was also particularly hard hit by detentions, for the security forces believed that student leaders were among the main instigators of unrest.

Two major treason trials ensured that a sizable part of the UDF leadership was taken out of circulation. In the Pietermaritzburg Treason Trial, eight UDF executive members, including Albertina Sisulu, Cassim Salojee, Ismail Mohamed, and Frank Chikane, stood trial together with trade unionists on charges of conspiring with a "revolutionary alliance" that included the ANC and the SACP. Although no acts of violence were charged, the state intended to prove that they had employed "means which envisaged violence."[39] In December 1985, the state withdrew charges against twelve of the accused, and in June 1986, charges were dropped against the remainder. Meanwhile, however, another treason trial had robbed the UDF of some its most capable and dynamic leadership. In April 1986, Terror Lekota, Popo Molefe, and Moss Chikane were detained by the security police. These three UDF leaders were joined in court by nineteen other members of the UDF and of the Vaal Civic Association. Central to the indictment was the allegation that the UDF formed part of a conspiracy with the ANC to overthrow the state by violence. The trial, which drew intense national and international attention, dragged on until November 1988. Lekota was sentenced to twelve years and Molefe and Chikane to ten years, with lighter sentences for two other accused. The five Delmas treason trial defendants were freed in December 1989 after the Appellate Division of the Supreme Court overturned their convictions and sentences.

Ungovernability and the First State of Emergency: July 1985–June 1986

The first State of Emergency did not crush the rebellion but, rather, inspired new tactics and new forms of political organization. Consumer boycotts were introduced as a new political weapon. As mass gatherings were outlawed, street committees proliferated, after the model of local organization that Matthew Goniwe had tested in Cradock. In mid-July a two-month consumer boycott against white-owned shops was launched in Port Elizabeth and Uitenhage to demand the withdrawal of the police and the army from the townships and to force attention on a series of local grievances. From the Eastern Cape, the boycott movement had spread by August to the Western Cape and the Transvaal. The new weapon was initially greeted with euphoria. Shopkeepers, experiencing a sharp drop in turnover, were brought to the negotiating table. The Port Elizabeth Chamber of Commerce began working with the Port Elizabeth Black Civic Organisation (PEBCO).

But it soon became apparent that these victories were of a limited scope. Local and regional negotiations failed because of the lack of commitment of the central government. Moreover, conditions in other parts of the country were less conducive to boycotts than those in the Eastern Cape. Boycott monitors had an easier job in the compact townships of the Eastern Cape than in the sprawling settlements of the Western Cape or the huge conglomerates of the Witwatersrand. In addition, the Eastern Cape townships were politically and economically more homogeneous. Successful boycott campaigns that were upheld by broad-based township organizations relying on participatory structures of decision making served to reinforce the political and moral authority of the emerging "organs of people's power." Conversely, coercion, intimidation, and abuse by undisciplined youth would often weaken support for the boycott. Bad organization, as in Soweto, also produced disastrous results. Without consultations and monitoring of black shopkeepers, profiteering was likely as township shops exploited their monopoly position to impose stiff price increases. If white shops were to be boycotted, it was essential for township stores to be well stocked. But delivery vans became favorite targets for youth roaming the streets in search of offenders. If the civic was unable to set up a tightly controlled operation, consumer boycotts could alienate residents rather than galvanize mass support. If delivery trucks were stoned and plundered and buses set alight, the drivers were naturally not inclined to sympathize with the boycotters. And the drivers were usually black workers, living in townships. The Transvaal bus company PUTCO, which served the township routes in the Johannesburg area, reported 4 drivers killed and 232 injured between October 1984 and April 1986.[40] Boycott campaigns could set youth against adults, residents against migrants, and UDF adherents against supporters of other political tendencies. The boycotts not only tested the staying power of white business and white authorities; they also tested the authority of the UDF and the ANC.

At the end of 1985, students in many black schools were writing their exams under armed guard. With school boycotts becoming a chronic rather than intermittent means of protest, the Soweto Parents' Crisis Committee was formed in September 1985 with the aim of getting students to return to school. It approached the ANC to lend support to a "back to school" campaign. Now the ANC found itself in a dilemma. If masses of black youth failed to heed the ANC's call, it would be a terrible blow to the ANC's prestige. Eventually, in December 1985, the ANC gave its blessing to the parents' initiative, which later widened into a nationwide campaign under the banner of the National Education Crisis Committee (NECC). Transforming the student slogan "no education before liberation" into "People's Education for People's Power," the NECC called on students to return to school, while supporting their demands for a rescheduling of exams, reinstatement of all teachers who had been dismissed because of the school crisis, repair of damaged school buildings, withdrawal of the army from the townships, lifting of the State of Emergency, unbanning of COSAS, and allowing student representative councils (SRCs) in the high schools.[41] The parents' initiative had some success in getting children back to school, but this partial success was undermined by cabinet ministers' reneging on deals and by the detention of NECC leaders. In other cases, police action prompted students to resume the boycott, as is described in chapter 4 on Kagiso.

Boycotts gave ordinary people a sense of power, but actors and observers alike could become intoxicated with a false sense of power that underestimated the tenacity of the adversary. Many activists believed that a phase of "dual power" had arrived, as in the days preceding the storming of the Winter Palace in St. Petersburg. But the pattern of resistance was uneven, and coordination was lacking. It was not the UDF itself but local affiliates and people loosely associated with the UDF that wielded power. Although the South African state experienced a crisis of authority and legitimacy as never before, it was not on the verge of collapse, as was suggested by slogans such as "liberation is around the corner."

Boycotts were hailed as essentially peaceful Gandhian tactics of passive resistance, but the enforcement of boycotts could frequently entail the use of physical force and harsh punishments. The UDF did not formally support actions of this kind, but it was reluctant to condemn excesses and to enforce discipline within its own ranks. Fear of alienating militant followers and doubts about its capacity to exercise some control combined to make the UDF reticent in condemning certain methods of struggle, such as the use of the "necklace" to liquidate suspected informers. Officially, the UDF stuck to non-violent methods, but in numerous speeches and funeral orations, local leaders called on the people to hit back.

The first instance of necklacing occurred in March 1985 in the Eastern Cape, township of KwaNobuhle. The victim was Tamsanqa Kinikini, the only councillor who had not resigned. He had wielded a reign of terror with a vigilante group. This highly symbolic method of purging evil forces from the community spread rapidly throughout South Africa. A year later, the necklace was used as a method of execution in remote parts of the Northern Transvaal Bantustans.

The most outspoken opposition to necklacing came from church leaders such as Bishop Tutu and Allan Boesak. They expressed the same concern as horrified parents, who feared that the necklace would brutalize the executors as much as their victims. From 1985 on, church leaders came under pressure to condone certain forms of violence. Frank Chikane conceded that the question of violence was not important to the people in the townships and that people had no other option but to defend themselves.[42]

The role of the ANC was equally ambivalent. The ANC's call to make the townships ungovernable served as a legitimation for all sorts of violent behavior, from necklacing town councillors to hijacking the cars of the "bourgeoisie." This is not to say that violence erupted in response to ANC calls. When the ANC exhorted its followers to make the townships ungovernable, that process was already in full swing. Neither the UDF nor the ANC were able to harness township revolt into a coordinated offensive. Nor was the liberation movement able to stop practices such as necklacing, which were certainly harmful to the ANC's international image, to its standing among South African whites, and most likely also to its reputation among a majority of blacks. The renouncing of necklace executions by ANC president Tambo in 1986 had no visible effect inside South Africa.

More durable perhaps than the fledgling structures of people's power was the workers' power that was now manifested in a new giant federation of trade unions, the Congress of South African Trade Unions (COSATU). On 1 December 1985, over ten thousand people attended the launch of COSATU in Durban, uniting thirty-three trade unions. In contrast to the focus of the Federation of South African Trade Unions (FOSATU) on the shop floor,

COSATU held that unions ought to be involved in community struggles and the wider political arena, if only to secure that worker interests would be paramount in the liberation struggle. The UDF's union affiliates had to leave the Front in order to join the new federation, but this loss was easily compensated by a much better working relationship between the UDF and the major trade union movement.

COSATU played a particularly active role in the unfolding conflict in Natal, where the UDF was plagued by several weaknesses, including a lack of African leadership. Up to mid-1985, Natal had been fairly quiet, but in the second half of the decade the Natal Midlands and the Durban townships became major flash points. The core of the UDF was formed by the Natal Indian Congress (NIC) and by youth and student organizations in the townships. The UDF in Natal was a loose alliance of small and large organizations with different agendas, lacking political and organizational coherence. Civics were virtually absent in the townships located within KwaZulu and in the area around Pietermaritzburg. In the Durban townships, civics had developed during rent and transportation struggles in the early 1980s. These civic activists were an important source of African leadership in the early days of the UDF, but their organization collapsed when it overextended its limited capacities, leaving a vacuum of African leadership. The dominant position of the NIC proved a mixed blessing. The Indian Congress made a significant contribution in terms of talented activists and resources, but Indian organizers were not familiar with the dynamics of township life. Some aspects of the furore caused by a supposedly Indian-led cabal are examined in chapter 2. Here it suffices to state that NIC dominance and the lack of senior African leadership exacerbated the crisis in Natal. Regional COSATU leadership was drawn in to fill the vacuum, but with only modest success. Amidst clear signs of collusion between Inkatha and the police, detentions and the assassination of union members hampered COSATU's effectiveness in trying to mediate the crisis. Union leadership could exert little control over school students and unemployed youth. Particularly in rural areas, the generational gap was pronounced, with the older generation resentful of impatient youth who tried to undermine the authority of the chieftaincy and to force revolution on a basically conservative rural population.[43] The UDF leadership almost abdicated responsibility for the conduct of its youthful constituency. Speaking about the violence in the Pietermaritzburg area, Archie Gumede, the most prominent UDF leader in Natal, claimed that "the UDF itself does not have the machinery to supervise the activities of its affiliates. . . . I am not able to control 10 year-olds . . . the only people we believe can make a meaningful agreement are these men, the ones in jail—Mandela, Sisulu."[44]

"Now, There Can Be No Turning Back"

In March 1986, the State of Emergency was lifted. During seven months of emergency rule, about 600 unrest-related deaths were recorded, bringing the total number of fatalities over the eighteen months of unrest to 1,237. With rebellion spreading into remote corners of South Africa, boycotts flaring up, mounting international solidarity campaigns, and increasing signs of nervousness in the South African business community, the UDF felt confident that soon "the people" would be empowered to shape their destiny. "The strength and sacrifice of our people, their will to be free, cannot be crushed," stated the UDF's secretarial report in February 1986: "Now, there can be no turning back." Listing the victories, the report recalled that of thirty-four town and village councils set up in 1983 under the Black Local Authorities Act, only five were still in operation after two years of resistance; 240 councillors had resigned, most of them in the Eastern Cape.[45] But the report also spelled out that a heavy price was being paid in terms of detentions, deaths, and disappearances.

This period is the high-water mark of people's power, of the belief that representatives of the people, or even "the people themselves" were marching ahead to take control over certain "liberated areas." These areas were defined in geographical terms, as with townships that became no-go areas. But the term could equally apply to spheres of life where "the people" were taking over, as in schools, community media, or organs of popular justice. People's courts signified perhaps the most fundamental challenge of state authority, for they exposed the lack of legitimacy of the criminal justice system of the apartheid state. In some townships people's courts were widely appreciated for their role in curbing crime, disciplining unruly youth, and solving domestic conflicts. These courts enforced "a new morality, a people's morality that conformed to the political ideals of their liberatory projects," thus prefiguring a new moral order.[46] But elsewhere these popular courts were resented for harsh and arbitrary punishments. Particularly if run by youth, the courts lacked legitimacy in the eyes of older residents.

In response to the uprising in the townships, the ANC military strategy switched from "armed propaganda" to the stage of "people's war." Debated at the ANC's consultative conference in Kabwe, Zambia, in June 1985, the concept of *people's war* meant the expansion of the social base of guerrilla operations inside South Africa. Emotional sentiment had to be converted into disciplined support, spontaneous outbursts of rebellion needed to get a sense of direction, military activities had to be linked to action on the political terrain.[47] Following the Kabwe conference, the activity of the ANC armed wing

Umkhonto we Sizwe (MK) increased significantly, but the toll in terms of guerrillas killed or captured was heavy. In reality, MK never posed a substantial military threat to its formidable opponent. But although its military effectiveness was limited, Umkhonto's psychological impact was important: MK fighters provided role models for the young street fighters.

Under the combined pressures of repression, impatient youth, and the millenarian belief in the advent of people's power, the UDF was becoming more and more intolerant of those who refused to join forces under its wide umbrella. By early 1986, the UDF had excluded its Africanist rivals from "the people's camp" and was identifying them as enemy forces. The National Working Committee, meeting in May, resolved that AZAPO, AZANYU (Azanian Youth Organisation), the Azanian Youth Congress, and AZASM (Azanian Students Movement) had "wittingly or unwittingly become agents of Pretoria." The UDF called on members of these organizations "to publicly disassociate themselves from these reactionary activities and join the forces of progress."[48] The UDF's attempts to impose hegemonic control were largely limited to black South Africa. The Front was more accommodating toward whites who had rejected apartheid but who were as yet uncertain about their organizational alignment.

The Rise and Fall of People's Power: June 1986–1988

This episode marks the transition from euphoria to despair. The second State of Emergency, imposed nationwide on 12 June 1986 and lifted only in 1990, amounted to virtual military rule. Some of the UDF leadership were by now prepared for a semi-underground existence, but most of the rank and file were taken by surprise when police and army moved into the townships in the early morning of 12 June. In the first six months of the emergency, nearly twenty-five thousand people were arrested and isolated from contact with families and lawyers. Although many were released within weeks, thousands remained imprisoned, with the prospect of indefinite detention without trial. The waves of detentions swept through all layers of the Front: by August 1986 fifty national and regional UDF leaders had been arrested.[49] About eight thousand detainees were under the age of eighteen; some were even under ten. Stories of torture, abuse, and intimidation horrified public opinion, not only in South Africa but also in the wider world. The exposure of South Africa's "war against children" led to increased international pressure on Pretoria.[50] Inside South Africa, most of these expositions were banned. Press censorship was tightened, with further restrictions introduced in December 1986. Newspapers were reduced to printing the bland "unrest reports" from the state's Bureau of Information, soon nicknamed the Ministry of Truth.

Paradoxically, as repression mounted, a remarkable series of "meet the ANC" encounters gained momentum. Delegations of white South African businessmen, clergy, journalists, students, and academics traveled to meetings in African and European capitals and returned home favorably impressed, spreading the word that these diabolical terrorists were, after all, fellow South Africans, burdened perhaps with unlikely socialist visions but not with anti-white sentiments. To the surprise of a delegation of visiting South African businessmen, Oliver Tambo said prayers before lunch.[51] The UDF leadership itself had its first publicly known encounter with the ANC during a visit to Sweden in January 1986.[52]

The first years of the second State of Emergency were characterized by the militarization of township administration. In addition to the army, the regular police force, and a notorious new corps of assistant policemen, nicknamed *kitskonstabels* (instant police) because they were deployed after only three weeks' training, extra-state repression was also on the increase. UDF activists became targets of faceless death squads and vigilantes.[53] Vigilantes often operated at the behest of beleaguered town councillors and African businessmen. Sometimes gangs of heavies were formed by men who had reason to resent the attempts of youthful comrades to impose their rule, as in the case of members of the Zion Christian Church (ZCC) in the Northern Transvaal or the adult men in the Crossroads squatter camp near Cape Town. In KwaNdebele, ministers in the homeland government unleashed vigilantes on residents opposed to "independence."

At times, the vigilantes operated in connivance with the police. Crossroads and its satellite camps, where youth activists were driven out after days of sustained battle, became one of the most notorious examples of such open collusion. Vigilantes proved more effective and more selective than the police. Police confronted protest manifestations with indiscriminate violence, but vigilante terror was more specifically aimed at the leaders of popular organizations.

Unofficial repression combined with a sophisticated network of state repression and surveillance. Policy shifted to the counterinsurgency tactic known as WHAM: Winning Hearts and Minds. WHAM had a two-pronged approach: elimination of all "troublemakers" combined with addressing "genuine" grievances of the township population. Upgrading the townships entailed refuse removal, sewage disposal, improvement of the living environment, recreational facilities, and new housing schemes. Models of people's power like Alexandra, the township in Johannesburg that had become a no-go area, off-limits to the police, and Cradock's township of Lingelihle were targeted for upgrading.

WHAM ideologues ignored that grievances were somehow linked to government policies. Moreover, upgrading the living environment could also backfire, as these improvements raised expectations.[54] If an aspiring middle-class black saw that protests yielded improvements, would not more protests yield more improvements?

Upgrading posed a problem for the UDF because the Front had never developed a strategy of how to deal with concessions. The politics of refusal had resulted in a rejectionist stance: concessions were rejected as "sham reforms," as attempts to make apartheid livable, rather than claimed as victories. When sympathetic service organizations later attempted to plan and implement improvements in the township living environment, they often encountered disinterest or hostility: "reformist" initiatives were rejected because these would blunt the impetus for revolution.

In October 1986, the UDF was declared an affected organization and was thereby prohibited from receiving funds from abroad. According to the UDF's national treasurer, "a lot more than half" of the Front's income came from abroad.[55] But the formula of a front again proved suitable to South African conditions: many of its six to seven hundred affiliates were still able to raise funds on their own, while money could also be channeled through sympathetic churches, human rights organizations, educational institutions, and service organizations. Foreign funding became essential to keep some kind of organization going. According to the treasurer, overseas money came in without strings attached, but there was nevertheless a drawback. When the need to raise internal funds became less urgent, local fund-raising campaigns fizzled out.

In defense of its harsh emergency rule, the government cited lower death tolls. But a declining death rate did not result in a restoration of confidence in South Africa's future. The year 1986 witnessed the highest number of strikes in a decade. For the first time since 1978, more people emigrated from South Africa than immigrated to the country. Disinvestment by overseas companies and the international sanctions campaign gathered momentum.

A Changing Pattern of Violence

The bare statistics obscure the changing pattern of violence. In the first years of revolt, until 1985, most fatalities were caused by actions of the security forces. The second leading cause of death was a category ranked "black on black" violence, a convenient but very imprecise blanket term that could include political feuding between UDF and Inkatha, between UDF and AZAPO, vigilante activity, killings of black town councilors, policemen or suspected informers, or the settling of other scores.

But starting in 1986, the tendency was toward a proliferation of indirect conflicts in which more and more groupings were drawn into internecine violence.[56] This trend would continue and progressively worsen in the first half of the 1990s. However, it does not follow that the state was always absent in "black on black" violence. Vigilantes, which in Natal could include Inkatha groups, sometimes acted at the behest of the security forces. In the Western Cape, the involvement of the security forces in the squatter struggles in Crossroads was blatantly visible even at the time, but elsewhere the role of the state would be revealed only in later years.

Although the UDF was badly hit during the second State of Emergency, the state did not succeed in a normalization of the townships. Rent boycotts continued and provided a key rallying point for township activists. Street committees organized youth brigades to prevent the eviction of rent defaulters or to forcibly evict people who had moved into houses from which rent boycotters had been expelled by the municipal police. Where electricity had been cut off, volunteers moved in to reconnect township houses. Once rent boycotts had taken off, they acquired their own momentum. Even without the political message, a boycott of rents and service charges had obvious advantages for heads of households since it augmented family income. Moreover, since town councils generally insisted on payment of all arrears as a condition for the resumption of services, ending the boycott became virtually impossible. Rent boycotts continued beyond 1990 and even beyond the 1994 elections, posing a problematic legacy for the new government.

Consumer and bus boycotts flared up intermittently, but township residents began to show signs of exhaustion and a loss of patience with the "rule of the comrades," which was frequently characterized by lack of consultation and coercive methods. The comrades had initially gained popularity with their anticrime campaigns and cleanup activities, but at times the dividing line between political and criminal activity became rather blurred. The rise of the *comtsotsis* (a confluence of comrades and *tsotsis,* or township gang members) can be traced to the period of the second emergency. Most likely, many of the abuses were perpetrated by unorganized youth, rather than by members of UDF organizations. But the distinction was not always evident. The omnipresent UDF T-shirts were, of course, also used by nonmembers, and the slogans and symbols of UDF, ANC, and SACP had become part of popular culture in the townships.

The first State of Emergency had left the UDF largely intact and had actually made the leadership more confident that the Front could withstand stormy weather. The few buoyant months between the two States of Emergency boosted confidence as resistance once more could be openly displayed. But the second State of Emergency was far more comprehensive and ferocious. This time the Front was badly hit, and to many it seemed like a mortal blow. The ruling National Party was returned to power with an overwhelming majority

in a whites-only general election in May 1987, and the right-wing Conservative Party replaced the Progressive Federal Party as the official opposition.

The years 1987–88 have gone down in activist memory as marking the depth
of despair. But out of this state of hopelessness grew a new realism. The forced
period of lying low and the abandoning of high-profile politics afforded the
opportunity to reflect on past performance and future strategies. Activists
emerged from detention with a more sober mind, no longer intoxicated with
the belief in imminent liberation but prepared to set out on the inglorious task
of painstakingly rebuilding the organizations.

Prolonged school boycotts and detentions of student leaders meant the loss
of an organizing base, which initially had been provided by the schools and by
the now banned student organization COSAS. With tens of thousands of
youth, both those in school and those who had completed school or prema-
turely dropped out, roaming the streets, it was vital to provide them with a
sense of direction and some organizational discipline.

In order to make its organization less unwieldy, the UDF began restructuring its constituency along sectoral lines. The first steps toward consolida-
tion were taken in 1987, with the formation of an umbrella organization for
youth, the South African Youth Congress (SAYCO). SAYCO was launched at
a clandestine meeting of 150 delegates in March 1987 in Cape Town, after the
venue had been changed repeatedly to shake off the security police. Attempts
to form a UDF Women's Congress faltered, as did attempts to form a national
civic movement. SAYCO, boasting more than half a million members, was
easily the largest UDF affiliate. SAYCO's cadres were gearing themselves for
a protracted battle. They attempted to bridge the generational gap through
close contacts with COSATU and the acknowledgment that student representative councils could not run schools on their own. Schools ought to be
run by "the community," which meant the involvement of parents, students,
and teachers. Now that liberation was no longer around the corner, students
ought to go back to school to prepare themselves for a future in a liberated
South Africa. The "back to school" campaign would also bring more coherence in the student movement. The school was seen as a more suitable basis
for organization than the street.[57]

With the formation of another sectoral organization, the Congress of Traditional Leaders (CONTRALESA), the UDF moved into uncharted waters.
Chiefs in the Bantustans were widely portrayed as the rural equivalent of the
town councilors: collaborators of "puppet structures." The change came in the
wake of the revolt in KwaNdebele, where several members of the Royal House
played a prominent role in the campaign against independence. Royal princes
sought the advice of the UDF. With the support of the ANC, which had seen
the disastrous consequences of FRELIMO's (Frente de Libertaçao de Moçam-

bique) alienation of traditional authorities in Mozambique, the chiefs were advised to organize their own sector within the Democratic Movement, under the banner of CONTRALESA.

The eclipse of the Front seemed sealed when, in February 1988, it was effectively banned. Along with seventeen other organizations, the UDF received a restriction order outlawing all forms of organized activity. By 1988, P. W. Botha had withdrawn into the laager, and his envoys were telling the world to "do its damnedest." Also restricted were the NECC and AZAPO. Unrest continued at a lower pitch, without dying down completely. While national and regional structures survived, the links with local organizations became tenuous and participation in grassroots structures dropped sharply. Youth organizations could adapt to a semi-underground existence, but civics by their very nature could hardly function under severe repression. One year after the imposition of the second State of Emergency, nearly all civics had collapsed.

The Revival of Popular Protest: 1989–1990

A new spirit of defiance was manifested by the same people who were locked up in order to silence dissent. By January 1989, a hunger strike begun by defiant women in the Northern Transvaal had been joined by political detainees in prisons and detention centers all over the country. By April 1989, their protest had succeeded in persuading the minister of law and order to release nine hundred detainees, including a sizable number of the UDF leadership. The hunger strikers were probably greatly helped by a stroke of luck. The gradual palace coup by which F. W. de Klerk took over from P. W. Botha opened the way toward a liberalization of the political climate. The emergency restrictions remained in place but were less strictly implemented. After the elections for the white parliament in September 1989, De Klerk was sworn in as state president. With unexpected vigor, he set the country on a breathtaking course of genuine change. A first sign of things to come was the release of the ANC leaders who had been sentenced with Nelson Mandela in the 1964 Rivonia trial. Rallies to welcome Walter Sisulu and the other veterans when released from the prison on Robben Island gave an impetus to regional UDF leaders to pick up the pieces and rebuild their organizations.

The first signs of the resurgence of popular protest movements had already emerged in the early months of 1989, this time without public launches, press conferences, and lists of affiliated organizations. The Mass Democratic Movement (MDM) had no constitution, no policy guidelines, no elected leadership, no members, and no address. The MDM asserted itself on the streets with such vigor that it ousted the political wrangling for the white elections from the front pages. The core of the MDM consisted of the UDF, COSATU, and a number of prominent clergy. COSATU had abandoned its reluctance to enter into a more or less formal alliance with the UDF. The trade union federation could now be confident that it was the strongest partner in the alliance. COSATU had been hit as well by the successive States of Emergency, but its organization had remained intact. COSATU "locals" (horizontal, township-based networks of shop stewards from various COSATU unions) were instrumental in rebuilding the civic structures.

The MDM, in fact, was a flexible alliance, drawing in new partners as the occasion required. It revived popular protest with a series of "defiance campaigns" against segregation, reminiscent of the ANC in the 1950s. In August, thousands of black patients demanded treatment in white hospitals. "Open the beaches" was a popular and low-risk campaign as the holiday season came near, allowing for protest picnics on the beaches of Durban and Cape Town, under the slogan "The People Shall Swim." Repression had not all of a sudden come to an end, but overall the state—no doubt emboldened by the demise of communism—allowed opposition forces space to regroup.

MDM strategy was not limited to scoring largely symbolic victories but was gearing itself toward negotiations. In the context of a changing international environment and the series of peace talks on Namibia, Angola, and Mozambique, a negotiated solution was becoming a realistic prospect. Leadership and followers of the liberation movement were grappling to come to terms with causes and effects of the fall of the Berlin Wall, but they were not paralyzed by the resulting ideological confusion. The ANC in effect unbanned itself before the government followed suit in February 1990. ANC T-shirts and publications and Mandela pictures appeared on the streets, with police—for the most part—standing by as impassive onlookers. By formulating a set of constitutional principles, the ANC gave its allies inside South Africa a new sense of direction.

The Harare Declaration, published in August 1989, stated that South Africa would be a unitary state under one central legislature and that the constitution would include a Bill of Rights. With this move, the ANC gained a strategic advantage. The constitutional principles were subsequently adopted by the Organisation of African Unity and favorably received in circles of the United Nations. With the end of the Cold War, both the ANC and Pretoria came under increasing pressure from their allies to work toward a negotiated settlement. Because the Harare Declaration was moderate in tone and content, it also served to some extent to allay white fears. An essential part of MDM strategy was the broadening of the movement for change. With talks coming near, it became vital to lure as many groupings as possible away from the "enemy camp" toward the "people's camp." Hegemonic control over the broad opposition took on a new urgency. Speaking on the possibility of a negotiated settlement, the UDF's acting publicity secretary Murphy Morobe stated: "After all is said and done there can only be two parties at the negotiating table the leaders of the present minority government, the NP, and those of the democratic majority led by the ANC."[58] Contacts were intensified with big business, white liberals, black entrepreneurs, Bantustan leaders, chiefs, and even disgruntled members of the despised police and prison service.

Broadening out was to culminate in a huge "Conference for a Democratic Future" meant to cement a united position vis-à-vis the government. As before, the issue of alliance politics was sure to generate ideological heat. Several COSATU unions expressed fears that middle-class groupings and "bourgeois leadership" could hijack the struggle for their own benefit. The Conference for a Democratic Future finally took place in December 1989, convened by the MDM and the Black Consciousness Movement and attended by 4,462 delegates representing 2,138 organizations. Much of its momentum, however, was lost in disputes about the criteria for inclusion and exclusion. The invitation to homeland leaders and parties was particularly controversial. Among the absentees were Inkatha and organizations aligned to the Pan Africanist Congress (PAC). The conference resolved to adopt the Harare Declaration and to call for a nonracial constituent assembly representing all the people of South Africa, which would draw up a new constitution.

This year of transition from semi-legality toward full legalization of the ANC, SACP, and PAC was characterized by a new mood of pragmatism. UDF leaders sat down with the ANC leadership to make an assessment of the balance of forces. While acknowledging the military strength of the government, they exploited its lack of legitimacy and the widening rifts within the "ruling camp." A series of local negotiations prepared the way for talks about the central issue of state power.

Disbanding or Transforming the UDF? 1990–1991

With the unbanning of the ANC and the release of Nelson Mandela in February 1990, the UDF was once again forced to redefine its role. The mood was one of expectation, mixed with distrust of the government's real intentions and suspicion that the ANC leadership might be tempted to compromise the revolution. Only years later was it revealed that Nelson Mandela had for some years already been engaged in private meetings with government officials.[59] In spite of the general veneration for Mandela, in the polarized atmosphere of 1990 such a series of meetings would easily have been interpreted as an attempt by "the old man" to conclude a secret deal behind the back of "the people."

Although the unbanning of the ANC had been anticipated for some time, the actual announcement caught the UDF leadership by surprise. It had not given much thought to the future role of the Front. For several reasons, a simple merger of the UDF with the ANC was not in the cards. As long as the transition process toward majority rule was not irreversible, it would be imprudent to disband the UDF. Moreover, the ANC—a liberation movement in the process of becoming a political party—would be based on individual membership, while the UDF constituents were organizations of which not all members would be joining the ANC. Two sectors of the UDF, however, were absorbed into the ANC: women's organizations and SAYCO both disbanded and formed the reconstituted ANC Women's League and the ANC Youth League. Because of an increasing awareness of the importance of a vibrant and autonomous civil society, it was ruled out that civics or student organizations should be simply subsumed in the ANC.

Within the UDF, three options were discussed: to disband, to transform itself into a coordinating structure for the organizations of civil society, or to wait and decide later.[60] The argument for disbanding the UDF was that the Front had served its purpose, and now the unbanned liberation movement could resume its legitimate place. The UDF's continued existence would only cause duplication and confusion. The second option was to transform the UDF into a coordinating structure for civics, student organizations, religious bodies, and those youth and women's organizations that decided against merging with the ANC's Youth League or Women's League. This position was favored both by activists, who argued that an umbrella structure was needed to exercise hegemonic control, and by the proponents of "civil society," who stressed the need to promote an independent social movement to keep an eye on the present as well as on a future government. The discussion on the future role of civics also vacillated between these two poles of Charterist hegemony versus an autonomous civil society. One position was that civic structures should fold since the ANC would now address the needs of the people. But the dominant position held that civics ought to be rebuilt as independent watchdog bodies to ensure democracy and accountability on a local level, representing all residents, regardless of political affiliation.[61] The third option was to postpone making a decision since the UDF presently had a role to play in areas where the ANC was weak. If the Front became irrelevant, it could disband at a later stage. This last option prevailed during 1990, but in 1991 the UDF decided to disband.

Frictions between ANC and UDF and between ANC and COSATU occurred occasionally as the top-down commandist style of the ANC leadership clashed with the culture of grassroots participation that had characterized black opposition inside South Africa. Complaints about lack of consultation were heard frequently when the ANC leadership flew into Bantustans to woo discredited homeland politicians without consulting the regional UDF leadership, or when leaders appointed regional ANC organizers without consulting UDF structures. When ANC national organizer Steve Tshwete went to open a Chamber of Commerce in the Venda homeland in the Northern Transvaal, a joint rally with Venda's military ruler Brigadier Gabriel Ramushwana was boycotted by the local youth congress.

By early 1991, the dissolution of the UDF had become a foregone conclusion. Its most capable activists were absorbed into the ANC. For those missing out on coveted positions in the ANC, the civic movement provided an alternative platform. Paradoxically, the unbanning of the ANC had a demobilizing effect: many people believed that they could now rely on the ANC to solve their problems. It was decided that the UDF would officially disband on 20 August 1991, exactly eight years after its launch in Mitchell's Plain. Whatever movements or forums would emerge after the UDF's dissolution was left undecided. A dissenting voice came from Allan Boesak, who objected to dissolving the UDF. He believed that colored people in the Western Cape were left without a political home now that ANC exiles and former prisoners "with little feeling for local dynamics" had taken over the region. Coloreds saw the ANC as an African-dominated movement. Boesak believed that the ANC should have made better use of the UDF to bring coloreds on board. He felt the UDF should have been dissolved gradually as the need for it disappeared, not abruptly.[62] This position, however, was linked to the specific conditions of the Western Cape and was not shared in other regions. Allan Boesak, the star speaker at the birth of the Front, was not invited for the UDF's final conference.

In spite of its numerous shortcomings, the United Democratic Front played a vital role during the crucial years of the 1980s. The Front provided a sense of direction, some ideological cohesion, and a sense of legitimacy by virtue of its identification with the African National Congress. It gave its broad following access to resources, to media and publicity, and to know-how, ranging from legal advice to workshops for printing T-shirts. Through informal networks, which could include non-UDF people, ideas and people circulated throughout South Africa. It paved the way for the return of the ANC as the dominant force in black politics. It boosted the confidence of many thousands of ordinary people to believe that they were capable of changing their living conditions and that organization was the key to change. One of the UDF's vital contributions was the forging of a broad South African national identity. Regional and ethnic chauvinism, so prominent at the beginning of the decade, had dwindled into insignificance—or so it seemed in the exuberant mood in the first months of 1990. Soon the fault lines—some old and some new—would cause cracks in the "new South Africa."

CHAPTER TWO

Making Sense of Events:
Interpreting the 1980s

Aside from civic leaders and activists, there were four groups who learned lessons from the 1986 uprising. . . . First were the academics, whose fashionably cynical analyses we must scrutinize very carefully.

Mzwanele Mayekiso

AN INTERESTING DIMENSION of the historiography of the South African liberation struggle is the interaction between actors and authors. It is rare for the recorders of history to have an immediate impact on the makers of history and, vice versa, for the actors to have an input in the portrayal of their struggles. Dissatisfied over the portrayal of civic struggles in Alexandra in the media and in the academic literature, civic activist Mzwanele Mayekiso wrote his own account of the battle for the township, engaging in a vivid debate with his academic critics.[1] This survey of literature is therefore not limited to academic debates but includes the perspectives of contemporary actors and observers. In practice, the categories of academics, journalists, other professional observers, and activists were to some extent overlapping. In the unfolding of the South African drama, there were few dispassionate observers.

Turning to various interpretations of the South African story in the 1980s, we first look at the causes: Why did it all happen? And in what type of society did it happen? In the literature on the nature of the South African conflict some fundamental questions are asked: Was apartheid policy motivated primarily by economic or by ideological factors? Are we to regard race or ethnicity as in itself an explanation of apartheid, or should it be seen as subordinate to another factor, class interest? How unique was (and is) South Africa?[2] This debate on the primacy of race or class was of some practical relevance for the actors in the 1980s. If the apartheid state was defined as the main enemy, then the opponent could be engaged by a broad front of anti-apartheid forces. If capital was seen as the prime mover, it followed that there were obvious limitations to alliance politics.

Next we turn to the mode of events: How did it happen? Then we summarize some divergent views on the constituency of the UDF, its leadership, and its rank and file: Who made it happen? Under this heading, a discussion follows on the politics of alliances. Finally, we examine the contents of the struggles of the 1980s: What was it all about?[3]

The discussion of these themes is meant to provide a unifying perspective for the three case studies, which are otherwise highly differentiated. The questions raised in this chapter are mostly concerned with the UDF on a national level. In the case studies, we descend from the macro to the micro level, pursuing the same themes in the local context of Sekhukhuneland, Kagiso, and the Western Cape.

Why Did It Happen? Causes and Conditions

Causes and conditions sometimes tend to get conflated. Authors commonly list conditions conducive to rebellion, such as an economic crisis with soaring unemployment or the oppressive condition of apartheid itself. The mere presence of these conditions, however, is insufficient to induce support for a liberation movement or to cause a revolt by a process of self-ignition. What caused large numbers of South Africans to rise up in protest during the 1980s? Although much of the literature focuses on material conditions conducive to rebellion, both the ANC and the South African state were inclined to attach more weight to human agency than to structural conditions as the cause of revolution.

Both the state and the liberation movement had a vested interest in projecting an image of a planned and organized offensive: the revolt occurred because strategists had been plotting to strike at the heart of the state. From about 1975, staff at the Ministry of Defense were referring to a "total onslaught" against the South African state. The ANC was seen as either the conscious or the inadvertent agent of international communism. The total onslaught was to be countered by a "total strategy," involving not just military and policing operations but also counteroffensives on the political, diplomatic, religious, psychological, cultural, economic, and social fronts.

The "total onslaught" thesis was perfectly suitable to ANC strategists. If the state wanted to see the ANC's hidden hand behind each and every riot, bomb blast, or pamphlet, the ANC was willing to oblige. The image of omnipresence was obviously in the interest of an exiled liberation movement trying to make a domestic impact with modest military resources. Claiming all acts of resistance as ANC-inspired acts boosted the image of the exiled movement, but it did not always suit the internal UDF leadership, which had to face the consequences. There was no question of remote control from Lusaka, although the movement in exile certainly was influential in a more symbolic sense, while cadres in the ANC underground actively participated in the UDF. As the UDF came to be perceived as the internal wing of the ANC, by numerous adherents and the state alike, it was seen as playing its part in this grand design. If South Africa was in a state of insurrection, this had happened because the ANC and the UDF made it happen.

Most accounts of the 1980s start out with a description of various kinds of crises besetting South Africa, which then serve as the explanatory context for subsequent events. The focus is on the economy, the education crisis, the legitimacy crisis of the state, the urban crisis, and—infrequently—the rural crisis. Subsuming all these crises is the notion of an organic crisis.

The economic crisis, with rising unemployment and declining standards of living as its most notable features, is frequently mentioned as one of the main causes of the rebellion. Real wages suffered their sharpest decline in a decade during 1985. By mid-1985, officially registered unemployment was increasing at the alarming rate of about ten thousand people a month. By mid-1986, it was estimated that 80 percent of blacks between eighteen and twenty-six years of age were unemployed.[4]

The consequences of the recession were unevenly felt. Rather than an overall decline in living standards, a pattern emerges of increasing socioeconomic differentiation in the African townships. Although sections of the black population were affected by increasing marginalization, sizable numbers enjoyed modest prosperity. In terms of economic power, blacks constituted not only the largest part of the workforce but also came to occupy a large chunk of the consumer market.

The economic crisis, characterized by widespread unemployment and growing insecurity, and coinciding with the growth of an urban middle class, compounded the structural flaws in the state's urbanization policies. Salient aspects of the urban crisis are the shortage of housing, the issue of rents, and the role of local government. The housing backlog is related to the migrant labor system. Since early 1970, policymakers had concentrated on creating peri-urban high-density living areas—or dormitory towns—in the homelands, from which commuters could travel to their places of work. This coincided with the drastic curtailment of all new housing in black townships within commuting distance of the homelands. While the state attempted to limit the number of "permanent urban blacks," there was a dramatic upturn in migrant labor. The state could not cope with the pace and scale of black urbanization.

In the context of its reform policy, the government aimed at providing more extensive public housing and public services for a more differentiated labor force. The state's urban policy, however, was fatally flawed. Although it was now accepted that Africans were no longer temporary sojourners in "white" South Africa but permanent urban residents, no viable means of financing township expansion and improvement were made available. Townships were expected to become financially self-supporting. Lack of revenue made local government totally inadequate, accumulating colossal deficits without being able to deliver proper services.[5] The problem was compounded by the lack of popular legitimacy of the township administration. But only in the Vaal did rent struggles lead directly to confrontation. Elsewhere it was student and school protests that provided the link between limited rent struggles and broader confrontation.

The education system was not able to cope with the massive influx of African schoolchildren, nor was the labor market able to absorb graduates and dropouts from the understaffed and overcrowded black high schools. In the 1960s and 1970s, secondary education had been the privilege of a lucky few. But between 1980 and 1984, African secondary school enrollment doubled from 577,000 to over a million, while the student population at universities more than tripled, from 10,564 to 36,604.[6]

The rapid expansion of secondary education was followed by a sharp decline in the pass rate for the final exam, known as matriculation or "matric." In 1978, 76.2 percent of high school students passed their exam. In 1983 this figure was down to 48.2 percent.[7] Students' fear of repeatedly failing their exams contributed to their sense of frustration and at times to their enthusiasm for exam boycotts. Simultaneous with the rapid expansion of African secondary and postsecondary education, the economy began slowing down, leading to spiraling black unemployment. For many teenagers, the experience of secondary education turned into a bottleneck of frustration rather than a window of opportunity.

The generation that produced the student movement of the 1980s had some characteristics likely to contribute to their militancy. Demographically, the age distribution within the black population was changing, producing an overwhelming preponderance of young people. According to the 1980 census, the majority of the African population was under twenty-one. The new generation of students demonstrated a strong generational consciousness and a "distinctively urban youth culture" that was "relatively educated, totally urbanized, sympathetic to statements of black political identity."[8] Militant youth action was certainly not limited to school students: dropouts and unemployed youth also provided troops for street battles.

Student protest began in 1984 around limited educational and school-specific issues. Radicalization only happened in the process. One major difference with earlier student struggles was the role of student organization. Through COSAS (Congress of South African Students), high school students had a nationwide organization that could make calls to action evoking a national response. Its leadership had a clear strategy of using short-term demands on education as a basis for mobilizing students and then using the level of organization thus achieved as a platform for action on national political issues.[9]

Ideological cleavages within the ruling elite contributed to a sense of moral

crisis. When the government shifted from old-style apartheid based on ideological justifications specific to Afrikanerdom toward technocratic rule invoking a free market ideology, it did not manage to manufacture a new legitimacy.
The Afrikaner's own belief in the God-given right of the Afrikaner nation to
rule over disenfranchised blacks was unraveling. It was this crisis of will and
the attempted transformation from ideological apartheid to a technocratic,
market-related system of preserving white privilege that opened up the space
for the opposition to organize and expand, thus in turn exacerbating the political crisis.

Race or Class?

What was the fundamental cause of South Africa's woes? Opinions differed
regarding the nature of the problem: Was it a crisis caused by apartheid, to be
overcome by the political incorporation of blacks and the abolition of irrational restrictions on the mobility of capital and labor? Could South Africa
revert to "normal" by abandoning racial restrictions and simply allowing market forces to operate? Or was this a crisis of the peculiar South African variant of capitalism, racial capitalism? Or even a crisis of world capitalism, which
now manifested itself in one of the outposts of monopoly capitalism (in which
case the recipes pointed respectively to a socialist revolution in South Africa
or a global revolution)? Diagnosis and prescriptions depended, of course, on
one's analysis of the nature of the conflict in South Africa.

   Liberals see capitalism and apartheid as being essentially dysfunctional vis-
à-vis each other. The unfettered expansion of industrial capitalism would in
itself result in the dismantling of apartheid. Industry's increasing demand for
skilled labor and labor mobility (as opposed to the mining and agricultural
sectors, with their demand for a massive, cheap, largely unskilled or semiskilled labor force) increasingly made apartheid a burden to a rational operation of the South African economy. Freeing market forces would gradually
result not only in economic progress for blacks but also, through economic
empowerment, in their political incorporation.

   Revisionists present a diametrically opposed argument: the relationship
between capitalism and apartheid is entirely functional. Characteristic for
South Africa is a racially structured capitalism in which whites have monopolized state power to achieve economic domination. From the mid-1970s, the
revisionist school has been ascendant in the academic debate. This debate ran
out of steam in the mid-1980s. Class analysis was not abandoned, but academics widened their horizon. A new interest in "history from below" sensi-
tized academics to other dimensions of the human experience.

   The race-class debate was not limited to scholarly publications. From the late 1970s, Marxist and neo-Marxist thought became increasingly influential in the syllabi of the "liberal" white universities. Through student publications and student (and ex-student) networks, Marxism-Leninism filtered from the campus into the trade union movement, nonstudent youth organizations, and nuclei of township activists. As shown in the case studies, youth proved a particularly receptive audience.

The debate on the nature of the South African state had some obvious practical implications in terms of strategy and tactics. Should resistance be mobilized along the lines of race or class? Could only the oppressed blacks bring down the bastion of white privilege? Could apartheid be defeated by a broad alliance of all anti-apartheid forces? But if apartheid was just a smoke screen for capitalist exploitation, then the leading role in the struggle ought to be played by the African working class. The issue of alliance politics in turn raises the question of the ultimate objective of the struggle: national liberation or socialist transformation.

The cumulative effect of the various crises, it was argued, amounted to a crisis of a qualitatively different nature: an organic crisis. An organic crisis requires formative intervention: constructing a new balance of forces, new political configurations and philosophies, a profound restructuring of the state and the ideological discourse.[10]

How Did It Happen? Strategy and Tactics

The UDF spent a great deal of energy on mobilizing massive numbers of people. Less attention was paid to the need to sustain the movement by building organizational structures that were less susceptible to the barometer of popular moods. By the time organization building figured more prominently on the agenda, state repression made progress virtually impossible. Popular protest developed its own momentum, moving far ahead of the strategists and far beyond their "wildest dreams." This ground swell of anger from below thrust the UDF into further prominence and greatly enhanced the stature of the ANC, but it does not follow that movements or persons who reaped the benefits of revolt are therefore also its architects. Although the UDF was often not the actual instigator of these protests, it became the vehicle that transformed protest into a challenge to the state. In a very real way, the UDF made sense of events. In giving meaning to a great variety of struggles, the UDF carried multiple meanings, which ranged from a human rights discourse to class struggle. The UDF meant different things to different people. One key to understanding the UDF's success lays in its adroit use of a wide range of media.

Focusing on bread-and-butter issues of immediate relevance to ordinary people proved an effective mobilizing technique. But by themselves, localized protests did not amount to a challenge to the state. School boycotts, rent protests, bus boycotts, strikes, and stay-aways came to be perceived as part of the liberation struggle only because these protests occurred in a context of generalized political mobilization. By linking local issues to national politics and the central question of state power, the UDF infused bread-and-butter struggles with a new meaning. By boycotting rent increases or school classes, people not only demonstrated their anger about inadequate incomes, housing conditions, or lack of textbooks; they were also taking part in the liberation struggle.

The binding element in this variety of struggles was a common allegiance to the ANC. The UDF's high-profile campaign style was in part inspired by the example set by the ANC in the 1950s with its civil disobedience campaigns. After its banning, the ANC had become skeptical about the possibilities for mass political organization. The exile community concentrated its efforts on the armed struggle, with political activity relegated to an auxiliary role. The perspective of the ANC strategists was that of a "future all-out war which will eventually lead to the conquest of power."[11]

As a consequence of this strong focus on military action, the ANC was slow to recognize the new potential for political organization. A strategic review, undertaken in 1978–79 after the Black Consciousness Movement and the reemergence of the black trade union movement had indicated new space for organization, ostensibly shifted the emphasis from the military to the political as detonator for a mass uprising. After a visit to Vietnam, an ANC delegation concluded that the main means for developing a popular revolutionary base inside South Africa should be the building of a broad popular political front on issues of immediate and material relevance to the ANC's potential constituency inside South Africa.[12]

If this reads like a recipe for the United Democratic Front, it does not follow that the UDF was therefore conceived by the ANC. Members of the ANC underground had been actively involved in preparing the foundation for the UDF, but the ANC in exile had not. The discussion of how to strengthen political organization was essentially an internal one. Only after the UDF had demonstrated the potential for popular mass mobilization did the ANC begin to act on the recommendations of the 1979 review.

The UDF explicitly acknowledged the primacy of the ANC. Nearly all UDF activists identified with the ANC: even though they were not acting on ANC instructions, they were doing what they thought the ANC wanted them to do. For the ANC, the UDF provided a much needed internal support base. The survival rate of ANC guerrilla fighters increased gradually in the years after 1983 due to the more favorable political climate and greater number of people willing to help.[13] The years after 1984 witnessed an unprecedented growth of MK inside South Africa and a marked increase in the number of MK attacks.

The popular uprising in South Africa presented not only new opportunities but also new problems: How would the ANC control a popular insurrection? Only after 1986, with Operation Vula, did the ANC attempt to set up a unified command center inside the country staffed by senior officials who were charged with the coordination of both political work and military activity.[14] Operation Vula was set up to provide internal leadership to both overt and covert structures, including the Mass Democratic Movement. The irony of this slow movement was that the ANC and MK began strengthening and coordinating command structures inside South Africa only when the main thrust of the popular uprising was subsiding and the government was regaining control.

The existence of the UDF as an aboveground mass movement changed the terrain of struggle, away from the strong emphasis on military operations and toward a political contest. At the height of the euphoria of people's power, leading activists believed that spontaneous mass action would succeed in making the situation intractable for the government. Reflecting later with a more rational mind on the events of the 1980s, UDF leaders had lost their idyllic ideas about the virtues of spontaneity. Anarchy posed a threat not only to the National Party government but also to the new government-in-waiting. The UDF's reluctance to impose control was not caused by just romantic notions of popular spontaneity. The UDF leadership doubted whether it would be able to enforce discipline; if not, it would have been exposed as impotent.

In the international arena, the UDF could operate more flexibly than the ANC. The liberation movement was tainted by its ties with the communist countries, which served as its main suppliers of weapons and military training as well as its ideological beacons. But the Front was successful in tapping material and moral support from the West, where public opinion was generally sympathetic to the UDF, which was perceived as a nonviolent anti-apartheid alliance. By 1987, the UDF itself had a budget of over 2 million Rand, with over 200 million Rand donated to Charterist organizations aligned with the Front.[15] The majority of these funds came from European donors. The UDF's church leaders and some other public figures proved particularly successful in soliciting funds. Money channeled through the South African Council of Churches and the Kagiso Trust to various service organizations, media, and educational and human rights projects also benefited the Charterist cause.[16] Overseas funding was also essential to sustain the UDF's massive output of media and its publicity campaigns. International solidarity was important for activists inside the country for its material benefits and because it also bolstered the belief that one was fighting for a just cause.

Targeting Audiences: Movements and Media

Both the South African state and its opponents were engaged in a massive propaganda battle, on the home front as well as in the international arena. From its inception the UDF was acutely aware of the importance of media and propaganda. Over the years, the Front produced a massive outpouring of newspapers, pamphlets, periodicals, T-shirts, banners, buttons, posters, songs. It arranged workshops and seminars, engaging the services of sympathetic journalists and academics for training in both a theoretical understanding of the role of the media and in the practical art of producing press statements or newsletters. An interesting phenomenon of the 1980s was the proliferation of alternative newspapers, most of which were not formally aligned to the UDF, but nearly all of which were supportive of the UDF and the ANC.

A conscious decision was made to spend a major portion of UDF resources on media in order to create a public presence for the Front.[17] UDF activists could bank on considerable experience and resources, drawing from the student press, service organizations, the trade union movement, and professional journalists. Some of the most capable activists were assigned posts as publicity secretaries. Leading activists such as Terror Lekota, Murphy Morobe, Mohammed Valli, and Jonathan de Vries had no background in public relations but proved natural talents. They were accessible, articulate, easygoing, and sensitive to the needs of the mass media. In targeting vastly different audiences such as white business, township youth, trade unionists, and international diplomacy, the UDF performed much better than the ANC.

In the anticapitalist rhetoric typical of the struggle jargon and much of the left-wing academic discourse as well, the main newspapers—dubbed "the commercial press"—were routinely depicted as servants of the establishment, faithfully reproducing the "master's voice." Ideological purists would thus be inclined to give up on the commercial media, but the pragmatic instincts of the UDF leadership made sure that enemy terrain was not left to the opponents. In its dealings with the mainstream media, both domestic and international, the UDF was definitely much more successful than the South African government. In spite of all the diatribes about the lackeys of big business, most English language newspapers gave sympathetic coverage to the UDF. This is a fact often ignored or denied in the more crude propaganda during the 1980s, but later it was readily admitted by the UDF's leading publicity officials. "By and large, the UDF had a favorable press," acknowledged Murphy Morobe. "Not only because we possessed these charming personalities, but also because we had some common ground. The UDF saw the press as an ally in the struggle for freedom of expression. The press was also gagged, so we had a common cause."[18]

The UDF Western Cape region was particularly reputed for its strong media presentation. Here the UDF leadership benefited from the advice of some professional journalists. As Western Cape secretary Trevor Manuel recalled: "Two days before the big launch in Cape Town we rehearsed the press conference with journalists and a video crew. When we watched the video, we saw that this could not go on. We laughed for about one hour, and then we set out to put our act together. To begin with, we went out to purchase ties."[19]

This image of respectability proved most useful in media contacts. Far from being hostile, the major newspapers were delighted with this new bunch of respectable and articulate blacks, recalled Jonathan de Vries, publicity secretary of the UDF Western Cape. In retrospect, he identified two elements that made the publicity efforts of the Western Cape region highly successful. First, this region was dominated by a few charismatic leadership figures, such as Trevor Manuel, Cheryl Carolus, and Allan Boesak. The second element was his own input:

> Initially, I did put a lot of effort in my publicity job. I organized press conferences, I put flowers on the table, I bought myself a suit and tie, and at that time I was quite good at my job. I had the gift to come up with the right clichés at the right moment. I could deliver what the media wanted. We also had a good budget for media. . . . I cultivated contacts at the newspapers, I took journalists out to lunch, I made them feel special. I gave them the impression that they were getting special treatment, being the first to get information. The liberal media were anyway against apartheid, and we got quite sympathetic coverage. Liberal media are always in search of respectable darkies to interview, to invite to parties. The commercial press was by and large sympathetic; they played the role we wanted them to play.[20]

The UDF publicity managers had every reason to look back with satisfaction on media performance in the 1980s. The propaganda effort was effective, agreed Mohammed Valli, one of the UDF's strategic brains: "Most of the time, the UDF was barking louder than it could bite."[21] The UDF won the propaganda battle.

It was precisely the high-visibility profile of the UDF and its massive propaganda campaign that were cited as reasons for the 1986 government decision to declare the UDF an affected organization, thus banning the receipt of foreign funding. New restrictions against the media, mainly aimed at the alternative press, were announced in August 1987. Elements of the media, said Stoffel Botha, the minister of home affairs, "are generating support for the revolutionary organisations through idolising and propagating their symbols . . . and their symbols are those of revolution."[22] This was, of course, quite correct. When Botha referred to the media activists of the alternative press as "media terrorists," the insulted party could not agree more. "We glowed with pride. We even printed it on T-shirts and went into the townships spreading the legend: 'I am a media terrorist.'"[23]

Adli Jacobs, who worked for one of *Grassroots*'s offshoots, the rather dogmatic leftist magazine *New Era,* later wrote a critical assessment: "In our attempts to hang apartheid and its perpetrators we became infected by the very methods—and perhaps values—that we found abhorrent." Fighting back from a cornered position, the media activists employed the weapons nearest at hand: stereotyped images and clichéd rhetoric, "charismatic revolutionary leaders, clenched fists, toyi-toying crowds, rabid police, casspirs, barricades and flaming townships with the echoes of 'we the people' and 'Forward to this, forward to that.'" Support for progressive organizations was given without asking questions. In the process, the popular support for these organizations was often overestimated. As Jacobs frankly acknowledged, the ANC and the Mass Democratic Movement were falsely presented as being interchangeable with "the people." "We need to acknowledge that we are not 'the people,' nor is any single political organisation, or all of them put together."[24] But this sober assessment could only be aired in the post–February 1990 period. During the 1980s, the alternative media did not question their position on the side of the people, truth, and history.

Who Made It Happen? The Actors

Commenting on the outbreak of violence in the Vaal Triangle, the *Citizen* newspaper described the actors as an irrational mob on the rampage. "When Blacks riot, they turn on other Blacks, razing their homes, looting shops, robbing, maiming and killing other Blacks."[25] From a different perspective, UDF general secretary Popo Molefe gave credit to the actors in the 1980s for having won their own liberation: "The masses are the makers of history."[26] These different perceptions have nevertheless one element in common: the actors are perceived as an undifferentiated mass of anonymous faces. These broad categories of "the masses," "blacks," "the oppressed," the "underclass," "the people," "workers," and "youth," are typical of the discourse of the 1980s. Who actually were the people who helped to transform the political landscape in the 1980s?

Were the agents of change located within the ruling elite or among the subject population? Reform initiatives by the ruling elite created the space for the extra-institutional opposition to regroup forces and mobilize a protest movement that mounted a fundamental challenge to the apartheid state.

Several authors have focused on the class composition of the UDF in order to gauge its revolutionary potential. Apart from its academic interest, this issue is evidently of vital importance to those who wanted to carry the struggle beyond national liberation to a socialist transformation. In these analyses, some basic questions are raised: How divisible is the black working class? How co-optable is the petty bourgeoisie? Would the class base of today's alliances determine which class would rule a post-apartheid society? From a radical perspective, the pivotal role in the revolt is attributed to the proletariat, which had nothing to lose but its chains. Authors with non-Marxist credentials tend to look elsewhere: to the aspiring middle class, which saw its ambitions frustrated.

Allowing for some regional differentiation, it has been argued that, while the UDF was largely a movement of the poor, a disproportionate share of the original UDF leadership came from a radicalized middle-class intelligentsia who spoke a language removed from working-class experience and culture.[27] Another argument defends the UDF against allegations of "petty bourgeois" leadership and demonstrates that the working class was strongly represented in the regional executives.[28] The UDF leadership in six regions reflected the existence of both a working class and an intellectual/professional leadership.

Saul and Gelb's analysis of the class map of South Africa and the social composition of the liberation movement is typical of numerous publications in which the petty bourgeoisie is cast in the role of potential traitor, ready to betray the revolutionary cause and to abandon their working-class allies in favor of a reformed, nonracial capitalism.[29] With such an evil image, it is small wonder that the UDF and its advocates hastened to reject the dreaded label "petty bourgeois." Other authors, to whom social revolution is a less enticing project, take a more positive view of the role of the petty bourgeoisie. Not the proletariat, but the aspiring middle class is here perceived as the driving force.[30] The revolutionary potential is mostly concentrated among the youth and the intelligentsia.

Anthony Marx asserts that recessions have a radicalizing effect on paupers and on the working class but less of an effect on the black middle class, which is careful not to lose its advantages. He sees the urban poor as the most militant section, citing as examples the 1976–77 unrest and the 1984–87 revolt.[31] This, as shown later in the book, is doubtful. The more vulnerable groups are precisely the ones less inclined to expose themselves to the risks of collective action and confrontational politics. Migrant workers proved a fertile recruiting ground for conservative forces, both in 1976 and in the 1980s. Squatters at times have been led to direct their frustrations against their better-off township neighbors, rather than against the forces of the state. Nor is it clear why the working class is lumped together with the marginalized poor. Workers with permanent jobs also stood to lose a lot in times of recession.

Race and Class: Who Are "the People"?

In ANC ideology, the principle of nonracialism had to be reconciled with two more doctrines: African leadership and working-class leadership. African leadership was not mentioned in the Declaration or the Working Principles of the UDF. However, after some frictions caused by the dominance of Indian and colored activists in the early years of the battle against the tricameral parliament, the 1985 National General Council of the UDF adopted the principle of African leadership in addition to the earlier proclaimed principle of nonracialism.

UDF publications gave different connotations to "the people." In much of the UDF's discourse, "the people" are those on "our side," with political loyalties as the decisive test. But the term is also frequently used with a racial implication: "the people" are "blacks" or "oppressed South Africans." Defending the UDF against accusations of populism, the UDF's theoretical journal *Isizwe* gave the following justification: "It is important to understand how WE use the term 'the people.' We use this term to distinguish between the two major camps in our society—the *enemy camp* and the *people's camp*. The people's camp is made up of the overwhelming majority of South Africans—the black working class, the rural masses, the black petty bourgeoisie (traders), and black middle strata (clerks, teachers, nurses, intellectuals). The people's camp also includes several thousand whites who stand shoulder to shoulder in struggle with the majority."[32] The article then goes on to explain that the UDF aspires to a broad popular alliance, which ought not to be confused with a populist movement. The UDF has identified the working class as the leading class, as the "key to victory for the whole people's camp." Because of its "scientific understanding" of different class interests within this broad alliance, the UDF ought not to be accused of populism, which is "an ideology that obscures class and other differences within the broad ranks of the people."[33]

As with "petty bourgeoisie," "populism" was a notion from which progressive intellectuals sought to distance themselves, reserving these labels for rival movements. Left-wing critics of the UDF and the ANC aimed their critique at their populist rhetoric, which invokes "the will of the people" as a source of legitimacy. They rightly point out that "the people" are far from homogeneous. But it is not helpful to simply substitute "the working class" for "the people." The uncritical use of the notion of a working class obscures the fact that the working class was not homogeneous either. Nor was it always clear what was meant by "the working class." Sometimes it seemed to include only the trade union membership, while on other occasions "black" was used as synonymous with "working class."

Similar to "the people" or "our people," "the community" was another term used by the UDF to appropriate support and to claim an exclusive legitimacy.

In many instances, self-appointed "community leaders" articulated the supposed needs of "the people." Analysts have distinguished between a bottom-up process of slow politicization, resulting in well-organized structures of residents with a community of purpose and action such as in the small towns of Cradock and Port Alfred, and a top-down approach of mass actions imposed by national or regional leaders on local residents without adequate consultation and organizations, as exemplified by some consumer boycotts. The boundaries of communities are symbolic and exist by virtue of people's belief in them. Communities are not static, but dynamic. Certain events, such as an external threat, might engender a community spirit, but this is mostly a passing phenomenon.[34]

Although the UDF was conceived as an inclusive front, it was not a political home for all South Africans opposed to apartheid. As we have seen, some opposition groupings preferred to stay outside the UDF ambit. The main trade unions jealously guarded their autonomy, although a better working relationship developed in the second half of the decade. Liberal whites were mostly reluctant to fully associate themselves with this increasingly radical social movement but found common platforms on anti-apartheid and human rights issues. Big business could not be an ally, for "the UDF believes that there is an international conspiracy among the South African government, certain foreign governments, foreign and local big business to continue the oppression and exploitation of the majority in South Africa in one form or another."[35] Big business was not a potential ally, but it could be lured away from Botha's cul-de-sac policies. The UDF approached business with appeals to denounce government policies and solicited support for its positions. The Front also benefited from some material support from business circles.

Big business was by definition white business. What about black—and mostly small—business? With very few exceptions, such as the Western Cape Traders' Association, organizations of businesspeople did not join the UDF. At the local level, working relationships often developed between community organizations and associations of traders, taverners, and taxi owners. The UDF cannot be said to have had a business component, although it did maintain contacts at various levels. By the late 1980s, the UDF was reaching out to black business associations in order to further broaden its base.

Some sections of South African society were notably absent, both from the UDF structures and from the discussions on organizational strategy. For example, hovering on the margins of the UDF are the African independent churches, domestic workers, farm laborers, migrant workers, and squatters. Although the rapid growth of trade unions brought substantial improvements for migrant workers along with changes in the balance of power in the migrant hostels, the migrants by and large remained marginal to the concerns of civic associations and the UDF. Most community mobilization concerned issues of little interest to migrants, with some exceptions, such as transportation. Migrants felt that their interests were properly represented by trade unions that operated with democratic elections and mandates from the membership, but migrants were often distrustful of community organizations. There was a widespread feeling that many urban residents were profiteering from the disadvantages of the migrants. Residents were seen as relatively privileged and uncaring about issues of pressing concern to the migrants, such as influx control and the contract system, which did not allow them to seek jobs other than at their allocated places of work.

During the outbreak of violence between residents and hostel dwellers in 1990, ethnicity came to the fore as a powerful force. Home-based allegiances often proved stronger than the communality of working-class interests. Ethnic identities provided the link with the rural home base. Community organizations in the 1980s were urban centered, focusing on issues concerning permanent urban residents. Hostel dwellers became more marginalized as organizations hardly attempted, let alone succeeded, to translate rural and migrant experiences into the national political program. This marginalization was reinforced by the popular strategies of stay-aways and rent boycotts. Hostel dwellers felt that they had not been consulted and that their interests were not represented in the civic. Many saw the civic as an organ of the ANC, not as a neutral body accommodating the interests of all people. They disapproved of township lifestyle and culture and particularly of the cheeky comrades who showed such disrespect for elders. Zulu hostel dwellers interviewed in a survey on the East Rand categorically placed the youth at the center of their alienation from the township: the role of youth in enforcing stay-aways and boycotts was seen as particularly obnoxious.[36]

Unlike migrants, squatters see themselves as permanent dwellers in urban areas and in peri-urban areas, where vast dormitory towns existed in the midst of rural settings. Most squatters in the 1980s were not recent arrivals from rural areas but were long-settled inhabitants of the PWV. New waves of rural migrants began arriving in substantial numbers only at the end of the 1980s. Like migrant labor, squatting is not a marginal affair but involves millions of South Africans. Until 1989, squatters were less overtly confrontational toward the state than township residents. Many were illegal dwellers and therefore vulnerable. The visible, confrontational politics of civics and youth organizations had little appeal for squatters. Their extreme vulnerability helps to explain why they did not flock in large numbers toward township-based community organizations. In the course of the 1980s, new associations sprang up for hostel dwellers and squatters that did not seek affiliation with the UDF or existing umbrella bodies for civic organizations. Occasionally, isolated voices drew attention to the millions of South Africans who were left in the cold. COSATU secretary general Jay Naidoo acknowledged a major weakness of the struggle was being urban based, with very few resources to be channeled to rural areas to build organizations there.

By 1990, UDF leaders had become more sensible about all-encompassing notions such as "the people" and "the community." A UDF official then acknowledged the problematic aspects of the increase in mass activity. Violent conflict had erupted between migrant workers on the one side and youth and township dwellers on the other. Various conflicts were raging between residents and taxi owners, between youth and traditional leaders, and between youth and parents. Vigilantes associated with Bantustan governments had unleashed violent campaigns.[37] Significant sections of South African society apparently felt excluded from the UDF's definition of "the people."

Race Is Class: The Cabal

In studying social movements such as the UDF, class obviously is a relevant category. But the obsession with class tended to obscure other fissures in the UDF, such as the strained relationship between coloreds and Africans in the Western Cape and the suspicions between Africans and Indians, which were articulated particularly in Natal in numerous allegations about a power-hungry Indian cabal in the UDF. The doctrine of nonracialism did not permit conflicts to be expressed in racial terms. Allegations about "petty bourgeois elements and interests" became code words for complaints about the dominant position of Indians and coloreds. The stories about the Indian cabal clearly illustrate the conflation of race and class.

Rumors about a cabal in the UDF began spreading around 1985. The gist of the allegations was that a nucleus of highly ambitious Indians had amassed an extraordinary amount of power by establishing control over the purse strings and by hatching policy decisions in secret caucuses. It was pointed out that the treasurers in the UDF National Executive were invariably Indians and that fund-raising on behalf of the UDF was controlled by Indians.[38] The cabal's power base was deemed to be in Natal, but its network allegedly extended to the Transvaal and the Western Cape. The accusations emanated from African nationalists and militant youth within the UDF, but they also came from within the Indian community, notably from some of the old guard political activists who felt sidelined by the young Turks taking the front stage in the 1980s. From the cabal stories, a picture emerges of a small group of determined and highly ambitious Indian activists, who were building their own power base by establishing control over the flow of funding, creating their own network of patronage, infiltrating their agents into other progressive organizations, and setting up front organizations.

Donors were particularly generous in providing funds for the defense in political trials. The cabal had supposedly established control over the assignment of legal cases, with the most attractive cases—in terms of money and prestige—being given to their friends and allies. Accusations and resentment kept building up, culminating at the ANC's first regional conference in Natal in November 1990. All activists supposedly associated with the cabal were purged from the ANC structures in southern Natal. The conference, which should have been a memorable occasion, was an uncomfortable experience for Indian activists, who sensed a clear feeling of resentment among African delegates against "Indian cliquism."[39]

Fact and fiction are not easily distinguished in these cabal stories. Critics held the cabal partly responsible for the disastrous situation that had developed in Natal. The spiraling violence in the province was to some extent blamed on the absence of strong, locally rooted UDF organizations. The UDF leadership in Natal was dominated by Indian professionals who were not familiar with the African areas. Organizational structures in the African townships, even those outside KwaZulu, were weak. Apart from the Natal Indian Congress (NIC), the UDF in Natal consisted basically of youth congresses. Indian organizers stood accused of highly irresponsible behavior, inciting militant township youth whom they were subsequently unable to control. Although African education in the townships was in a state of near collapse, education in the Indian areas continued relatively unhindered. The UDF's Indian leadership, so the charges went, were using the youth as shock troops of the revolution, and they were using not their own children but the children of the Africans. The absence of African leadership in the UDF in Natal was deemed to be both the cause and the effect of the cabal. By virtue of their superior resources, the Indians had been able to take control, effectively preventing an authoritative African leadership to emerge in the UDF in Natal. As several informants summed up the charges against the cabal, "what they cannot control, they want to destroy."

What was the cabal's presumed political agenda? While the critics broadly agreed on the charge sheet against the cabal, the motives attributed to the alleged conspirators varied greatly. Three scenarios can be distinguished: the cabal as a reformist bourgeois plot, as a communist plot, and as an Indian plot. In the first scenario, the cabal's political agenda favored the establishment of a nonracial democracy through negotiations, avoiding a violent seizure of power and preserving the socioeconomic status quo. Within the Indian community, the cabal was sometimes perceived in class terms. It was pointed out that the

NIC executive was dominated by Moslem Indians, who were mainly professionals and businessmen. Hindu Indians, the descendants of indentured laborers brought over in the nineteenth century to work on the sugar plantations, were generally identified as working class.[40]

Proponents of the communist scenario believed that the cabal had the backing of the SACP in London, which had supposedly given the cabalists a blank check to take control of Natal. Attention was also drawn to the considerable overlap between the cabal and the personnel involved in Operation Vula, which was portrayed by some as a red plot in the ANC aimed at sabotaging the negotiation process. One accusation against the cabal was its stance in favor of participation. This could be interpreted as a bourgeois position, moving into reformist politics. But it could equally be explained as a typical communist strategy of entrance into established state institutions with the aim of subverting them, as Lenin had done with the Duma.

In the third scenario, the cabal was perceived as an Indian plot without a particular political line; the cabal was intent on building its own power base, a kind of Broederbond in the UDF. The alleged core members of this power-hungry clique believed the anti-cabal campaign to be inspired by anti-Indianism.[41] To the cabal's detractors, the issue appeared precisely in reverse. The tradition of nonracialism had resulted in taboos: one could not raise the issue of the cabal for fear of being branded anti-Indian.

The cabal stories may not tell us what actually happened, but they do tell us what people believed to be happening. These tales can be used to illustrate several aspects of the UDF. There was an element of generational tension, with the respectable gentlemen of the old guard in the NIC resenting the takeover by young rebels who showed insufficient respect for seniority. On a different level, there were clear signs of antagonism between Natal and the Transvaal. Delegations from Natal, comprising a fair number of Indian intellectuals, used to arrive with prepared papers and cogent arguments, which allowed them to steer the meeting. With these demonstrations of their advanced politicization and superior organization, the Natal UDF leadership caused both admiration and irritation. But the overriding sentiment in the cabal stories is indeed one of tensions between Indians and Africans, between the relatively well-off, educated, sophisticated Indian activists with considerable resources and the African activists. Feeling threatened by Inkatha and the state on the one hand and overshadowed by the Indians on the other, Africans resented their marginalization. In the Charterist tradition of nonracialism, it was taboo to criticize Indians for building their own power base. Because of this taboo on the discourse of race and ethnicity, criticism was expressed in class terms: Indians are bourgeois, Africans are working class.

The Politics of Alliances

Debates on alliance politics tended to be highly ideological, for the proposed
type of alliance depended on one's analysis of the nature of the apartheid state,
the preferred characteristics of post-apartheid society, and the perceived way
of achieving these changes. If one envisaged a two-stage strategy—as formu-
lated by the SACP and adopted by many in the ANC—then each phase called
for a different type of alliance: a broad popular alliance in the struggle for
national liberation, to be followed by a movement under the direction of the
working class (or its vanguard) in order to proceed to a socialist transformation of South African society.

   Within the left, the two-stage strategy was contested: Would joining forces
for the national democratic revolution not preempt the socialist revolution?
If today one would allow the petty bourgeoisie to grab the initiative, the
prospects of a socialist transformation tomorrow would become dim. Conversely, if liberals today allowed themselves to be used as useful idiots in order
to gain legitimacy with the Mass Democratic Movement, they were digging
the grave for the cause of liberalism in South Africa.[42]

   The debate on the nature of front politics, of course, was far from new. But
between the 1950s and the 1980s, the interpretation of the nature of the
apartheid state had changed. In the 1950s, both liberal and Marxist orthodoxy
held that economic expansion and apartheid were essentially in contradiction
with one another. In the 1980s, liberals mostly continued to espouse this position, but Marxists now regarded apartheid and capitalism as complementary
rather than contradictory. In the 1950s as well as the 1980s, the relationship
between trade unions and nationalist movements was a subject of fierce
debate. The debate on the role of the South African Congress of Trade Unions
(SACTU) in the Congress Alliance in the 1950s was carried over into the
1980s: Was SACTU's demise to be blamed on the use of trade unionists as foot
soldiers in ill-considered populist campaigns? Or was SACTU to be credited
with bringing much more of a working-class perspective into an essentially
petty bourgeois nationalist movement?[43]

   Similar arguments resurfaced in the discussions on the relationship between
the UDF and the trade union movement. As discussed previously, the leadership of FOSATU (Federation of South African Trade Unions) held that the
existence of an independent working-class movement was necessary if the
working class as a social force was to have influence within the liberation
movement.[44] The achievement of majority rule without addressing the issue
of economic transformation would leave the exploitative economic structures
intact. With the formation of COSATU, which placed political goals at the top
of its agenda, the debates subsided somewhat.

In pamphlets and speeches, student leaders paid lip service to the "leading role of the working class" while simultaneously claiming for themselves the vanguard role in the liberation struggle. This apparent paradox could be explained away as students proclaimed themselves part of the working class by virtue of being the children of workers. The "student-worker alliance" is a catchword in many UDF publications and sympathetic accounts, with the November 1984 stay-away being celebrated as a particularly successful example of student-worker alliances being forged in concrete action.

The vanguard role of youth was not just self-proclaimed. The ANC had made a conscious decision to use youth as the vanguard of the liberation struggle, encouraging the "young lions" to take up a position in the most forward trenches. The need for student-worker alliances was indeed a recurrent theme in the statements of youth organizations affiliated with the UDF. Time and again it was stressed that this was the lesson learned by the youth from the 1976 revolt by high school students in Soweto: the leading role in the struggle belongs to the workers. While these statements adequately reflect the lessons learned in political education courses, they do not necessarily reflect the prevailing strand in youth consciousness. The mood is perhaps more accurately captured in another recurrent phrase: "The future is in the hands of the youth."[45] Student and youth conferences and publications reflect the dominant official position of the intellectual leadership of youth organizations. Many less sophisticated youth had no patience with theoretical and strategizing sessions: they wanted action. In spite of the lessons of 1976, frictions between township youth and migrants were again a recurrent feature of township protest in the 1980s. The prominent role of youth, challenging not only the apartheid state but parental authority as well, produced a generational backlash. Adult men sometimes resorted to violent means, individually or collectively as vigilantes, to reassert their authority as elders and heads of families.

When resistance and conflict broadened during the 1980s, the street fighter joined the articulate activist. Officially workers were still identified as the pillars of the struggle, but it was the youth on the township streets who were actually liberating the country.[46]

The generational dimension was without doubt a central feature of the revolt in the 1980s. But the undifferentiated concept of *youth* is not much more helpful than sweeping generalizations about *workers* or *blacks* when trying to make sense of the events in the decade. Only with the benefit of hindsight were some attempts made to fill in the rough outlines by asking more specific questions: Who was involved, in which protests or events, and at which times?[47] *Youth* in this context cannot be equated with *young people*—a category that would include the vast majority of South Africans—but is clearly linked to political activism. As a consequence of interrupted schooling and long bouts of unemployment, *youth* could be a long-term career. The median age of African schoolchildren in the higher forms of secondary schools is relatively high. School graduates, engaging in youth activities, could also be considered as youth as long as they had not established a family. The constitution of the Alexandra Youth Congress, for example, stated that membership was open to "all who fall within the accepted definition of youth," without further elaboration. Some activists took this to mean everybody between twelve and thirty-six years of age, whether or not they were students.[48]

Youth was differentiated by race and gender, by class and occupation, by religion and language, by the distinction between students and nonstudents, and between workers and unemployed. Between the formation of COSAS in 1979 and the launch of SAYCO (South African Youth Congress) in 1987, South Africa experienced a massive growth in youth organization. The formal leadership of youth organizations was usually dominated by young workers and university and high school students. Unemployed youth were also involved, but these unemployed were a different category from the unemployed and often unemployable lumpen youth. They were frequently former students who had not yet managed to find a job or politicized workers who had been dismissed. The student leaders were relatively well educated: they were the successes rather than the failures of the school system.

There were regional differences, of course. In the colored areas of the Western Cape, political youth movements were a relatively new phenomenon, if one excludes the highly intellectual fringe of the Unity Movement. Before the formation of the Cape Youth Congress (CAYCO), "youth in coloured areas had two options: street gangs and church groups. CAYCO became a third option."[49] But CAYCO was not successful in organizing working youth or unemployed youth.

As violent confrontation unfolded, a more informal, less educated leadership emerged. Motives for joining could be manifold, ranging from political idealism to group conformity, the search for affirmation, an experience of adventure and excitement, a feeling of intoxication with *toyi-toyi* (a militant dance, expressing defiance and preparedness for battle) and freedom songs, and a sense of identity provided by a culture of militaristic camaraderie.[50] Rising levels of violence encouraged people to behave in unusual ways: normally nonviolent people acted violently.

In discussing the gender composition of youth organizations, Jeremy Seekings contends that the leadership of youth organizations was almost entirely male, but that young women formed a sizable portion of the membership. Women members were generally younger than male members, and most were attending school.[51] Why were women rarely prominent in the youth organizations during the violent confrontations of the mid-1980s? In looking for explanations, Seekings points to the prevailing conservatism with regard to gender roles in township politics and the macho culture that became more pronounced as violent confrontations escalated.

What Was It All About?

Perceptions of the UDF's role changed in the course of the 1980s. From its modest beginnings as an hoc alliance with limited goals, the Front was thrust forward on waves of popular militancy toward an all-out challenge of the apartheid state. In the process, it became less of a front and more of a political organization as it tried to develop more ideological cohesion. In view of the political and ideological diversity within the Front, pinpointing the basic tenets of the UDF's ideology is not an easy task.

Yet, under the UDF's wide anti-apartheid umbrella, three broad objectives can be discerned: the establishment of Charterist hegemony, the building of democratic organizations that ought to be prefigurative for a system of majority rule characterized by popular participation, and a more egalitarian society in socioeconomic terms.

In his court testimony, UDF general secretary Popo Molefe explained that the Front aspired to be "the only representative front representing all sections of our people."[52] The UDF was not unique in having hegemonic aspirations, but it was more successful than such uncompromising rivals as AZAPO (Azanian People's Organisation). The more pragmatic strategy, as pursued by the UDF, was the building of a broad front, which could expand further through tactical ad hoc alliances. This did not imply ideological abstentionism but rather a hegemonic aspiration to impose one's own agenda on this broad front. Alliance politics was seen as a zero-sum game: a gain for one side implied a loss for the other side. Imposing Charterist hegemony was not an end in itself, of course, but a means to conquer state power.

In the ANC's insurrectionary perspective, people's power was largely understood in military terms: the creation of liberated zones to serve as bases for revolutionary warfare. With this strategic concept, local negotiations, such as with neighboring white municipalities, are ruled out. The strategy is not to share power but to take the war into the white areas.[53] The UDF, however, saw the new strategy of people's power as a mechanism of promoting discipline and organization, not just as a confrontational strategy.[54] In the 1985–86 period of dual power, civic leaders attempted to establish some control over radical youth and to provide some protection against the security forces. In this perspective, dual power was not the prelude to a revolutionary seizure of power. On the contrary, dual power created the conditions for the first-ever significant negotiations between whites and blacks on the local level, either with local businesspeople or with local administrators.[55]

But there remained a dilemma. If successful civics could deliver some goods and perform some functions of local government, how far should this go? How great was the danger of co-optation? Would reformist initiatives act as a break on the insurrectionary potential? Whatever the strategic perspective—insurrection or negotiation—it was evident that the heady experience of people's power generated an increasingly radical conception of a liberated society. Even if many victories were short-lived, street committees and boycott campaigns gave ordinary people a sense of power for the first time.

There is an important distinction between the ANC and the UDF discourses on people's power. The UDF's strong focus on popular participation is lacking in the ANC and SACP publications, where people's power is seen as a means to an end: hegemonic control. People's power, stated the ANC's historian Francis Meli, is total power. "In South Africa, there is no question of power sharing. The people of South Africa are fighting for total power, people's power. There is no question of our sharing it with Botha; nor with Gatsha Buthelezi, for Inkatha's many crimes against our people . . . preclude this."[56]

What would the "Democratic People's Republic of South Africa," in which "all our people enjoy security, peace and comfort," look like?[57] In 1987, the UDF outlined some of its democratic ideals in a conference paper.[58] Democracy is spelled out as both a means and an end. The UDF's democratic goal is not simply about replacing white faces in parliament with black faces. The essence of democracy is that people, and in particular the working class, have control over all areas of daily existence, "from national policy to housing, from schooling to working conditions, from transport to the consumption of food." This understanding of democracy is fundamentally different from the various power-sharing constitutional models that were being juggled around. "In other words, we are talking about direct as opposed to indirect political representation, mass participation rather than passive docility and ignorance, a momentum where ordinary people feel that they can do the job themselves, rather than waiting for their local MP to intercede on their behalf." Although dismissive of conventional party politics, the paper acknowledged that a plurality of different viewpoints is important for a democracy.

The vices and virtues of liberal democracy and popular democracy have been a theme of discussion in numerous other liberation movements. The decline of the African state in the 1980s inspired a new round of discussions about the most appropriate form of government in the present state of economic development.[59] However, discussions in the UDF remained largely isolated from the wider African debate. Charterists rarely turned to Africa to find sources of inspiration or to learn the lessons of history. Their frame of reference was largely shaped by Marxism-Leninism, the Russian Revolution of 1917, the models provided by Eastern European communist countries, notably the German Democratic Republic, and a handful of third-world models in which Nicaragua and Cuba figured most prominently.

Was a just and nonexploitative society a socialist society? Anticapitalist rhetoric was pervasive in UDF publications and speeches, but this does not necessarily indicate a choice for orthodox Marxism. Non-Marxists in the UDF, such as Allan Boesak, advocated communalism rather than socialism, using moral arguments rather than Marxist textbooks. Communalism was also an element in the concept of people's education, controlled by "the people themselves." Free-marketeers, however, were virtually absent from UDF ranks, one notable exception being Soweto physician and entrepreneur Nthatho Motlana, chair of the Soweto Civic Association (SCA). Socialist preferences were manifest among trade unionists and students, including white students. But the middle-class nationalists in the UDF were basically fighting to establish their place in the socioeconomic system, not to destroy the system.

Clearly, the UDF could mean different things to different people. These ideological tenets are largely constructed on the basis of UDF publications and academic writings. To what extent was the UDF's ideological discourse and the academic analysis consonant with the beliefs and aspirations of its followers at the grassroots level? What kind of society was envisaged by the youth movement in Sekhukhuneland, civic activists in Kagiso, and media workers in the *Grassroots* office in the Western Cape?

Part Two

The Struggles behind the Struggle:
Three Case Studies

CHAPTER THREE

"From Confusion to Lusaka":
The UDF in Sekhukhuneland

There is a confusion between the parents and the sons
There is a confusion between the tribal authority and the community

Poem composed in Sekhukhuneland, 1986

The UDF's Rural Policy

IN SUPPORT OF THE STATE's allegation that the UDF leadership was the driving force behind a nationwide insurrection, the prosecution in the Delmas treason trial stated that the "organisation, politicisation and mobilisation of the black people in the rural areas is a very important part of the aims and the objects of the UDF."[1] The state's claim fitted well with the image of omnipresence that the UDF liked to portray in its propaganda. In rural areas, so the UDF claimed, "tribal authorities are being replaced by democratically elected village councils."[2] Among the Bantustans in the Northern Transvaal, Lebowa and KwaNdebele were reputed to be UDF strongholds (see map 1).

In a press statement issued in 1986, the UDF Head Office presented a survey of the state of rebellion and repression in the Northern Transvaal. Concerning Sekhukhuneland, a district of Lebowa with a history of resistance, the press release boasted that the "people of Sekhukhuneland under the leadership of SEYO [Sekhukhune Youth Organisation], the Sekhukhune Parents' Crisis Committee and the UDF established entrenched organs of people's power such as street, block and village committees which won the support and the hearts and minds of the people."[3] The sequence of actors is remarkable, with the youth organization SEYO being ranked first among the leaders of "the people of Sekhukhuneland." As this chapter demonstrates, this order of actors was quite appropriate. But the claim that people's power had been entrenched in local organization based on mass participation was wishful thinking. Sekhukhuneland, like many other rural areas, experienced an extraordinary

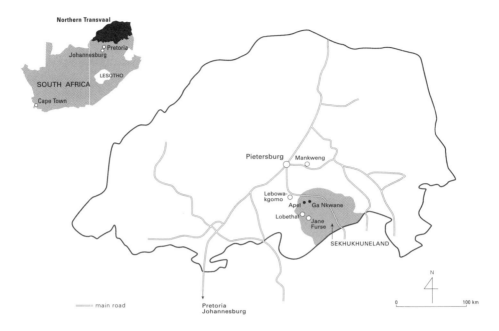

1. The Northern Transvaal. Map by Nel van Bethlehem.

episode of youth mobilization, which for the first time brought great numbers of rural youth in contact with liberation politics. But the relationship between youth and parents was antagonistic. There were hardly any joint efforts to set up "organs of people's power" such as civic associations. The backbone of the UDF in the Northern Transvaal consisted of youth movements, which pursued their own liberation agenda while maintaining fleeting contacts with the formal structures of the Front.

Since its inception, the UDF had been strongly focused on urban areas and national politics. Initially, the primary focus was on the new constitution and on the colored and Indian constituency. In the Northern Transvaal, coloreds and Indians are a negligible quantity. Second came the campaign against the Black Local Authorities in the African townships. In 1984, severe repression against trade unionists and political activists in the Ciskei placed "fighting Bantustans" higher on the political agenda. From 1985 onward, insurrection spread from the townships to remote rural areas. But beyond calls for the abolition of the Bantustans and the return of the land to the people, the UDF did not develop a coherent strategy toward rural issues.

Farm workers, who were virtually inaccessible on the white-owned and strictly controlled farms, remained outside the scope of the UDF. But in other rural communities where the UDF could have made an impact, the Front made no major effort at organization. The UDF did not manage to link up with ongoing local struggles of communities that were organizing resistance against forced removals. Forced removals on a massive scale—of rural black communities from white-designated areas, of farmworkers from white farms, and of squatters from peri-urban areas—were one of the most obnoxious features of apartheid policy. Between 1960 and 1983, an estimated 3.5 million forced removals were implemented. Yet, the matter had low priority on the UDF's national agenda.

Aware of its weak performance in rural areas, the UDF-Transvaal in 1985 appointed Murphy Morobe to the newly created post of rural secretary. Soweto-born Morobe, part of the 1976 Soweto generation that had served time on Robben Island, was not the most likely candidate for rural organizer: he was a city boy who had earned his credentials in student politics and trade union work in Soweto. Shortly after his appointment he was sent on an international tour and subsequently had to take over duties from his detained colleagues. He then served as acting publicity secretary on the UDF National Executive and never really began his work as rural secretary.

From 1985, the UDF's national leadership began strategizing how rural grievances could be converted into formal organization. One obvious way of obtaining access to the Bantustan villages was through migrants, who could be reached in the hostels and compounds and who would carry the message to their home areas, "so that these men can give the seal of approval to the organisation."[4] This strategy of organizing migrant workers in the cities in order to bring organization from their point of employment to their place of residence was outlined in the UDF's 1985 secretarial report. "The migrant workers living in hostels and elsewhere must also be organised. These people provide a vital link with the rural communities. The skills that they learn and the political consciousness they develop can be transferred to the next of kin, friends and acquaintances in these areas. The extent to which we mobilise and organise the migrants will determine the pace of organisation of rural communities."[5] The Northern Transvaal was the only region where the UDF leadership actively promoted networks of migrants in order to reach the rural villages, but even here the strategy of urban-rural linkages was not pursued with much vigor.

Mobilizing the countryside via this urban-rural network was not a novel idea. Contesting the prevailing view in scholarly literature that the ANC and the Communist Party in the 1940s and 1950s were urban based and quite remote from rural concerns and rural constituencies, Peter Delius has drawn attention to the role of migrant workers' organizations in the Northern Trans-vaal, such as the Zoutpansberg Balemi Association in the 1940s and Sebatak-gomo, an organization of BaPedi migrants from Sekhukhuneland, in the 1950s.[6] The ANC organizational strategy aimed at establishing rural branches through chiefs. This approach limited its capacity to mobilize a mass con-stituency, as popular grievances were accumulating against chiefs. In the eyes of many, the office had been corrupted by the control exercised by the Native Affairs Department. This erosion of the legitimacy of the chieftaincy was exac-erbated by the imposition of the Bantu Authorities Act in the 1950s, which aimed at self-rule and ultimately independence for the Bantustans. Chiefs were transformed into salaried officials, totally dependent on the Bantustan admin-istration. State recognition had become more vital for the chieftaincy than popular support.

But while the ANC organizational strategy had reached the end of its potential by the early 1950s, the communist partners in the Congress Alliance provided the primary impetus toward the formation of organizations with a different social base than the chiefly elite: associations of migrant workers.

Sebatakgomo, which had originated as a mutual support organization among BaPedi migrants in the PWV region, played a crucial role in linking rural grievances to national political movements. Through this network, Sekhukhuneland became known as an ANC stronghold. The revolts of the 1950s in Sekhukhuneland and other rural districts were provoked by the intro-duction of Bantu Authorities, stock culling, and environmental rehabilitation schemes. Although these matters were primarily peasant concerns, they were also of vital interest to migrants for whom a rural foothold remained an essen-tial part of their survival strategy. These revolts had been crushed with severe repression, but the ANC nevertheless remained hopeful about the revolu-tionary potential in the Bantustans. In the initial period of armed struggle, stated the ANC document on Strategy and Tactics (1969), "the main physical environment . . . is outside the enemy strongholds in the cities, in the vast stretches of our countryside."[7] Organized sabotage in urban areas was seen as an auxiliary activity. Only much later, in the strategic review undertaken after the Soweto rising, did the urban areas become central to the ANC military strategy. This initial prioritization of rural areas in strategizing the armed struggle was presumably not so much a reflection of the actual support bases of the ANC within South Africa but rather a reflection of revolutionary the-ories and examples from Asia and Latin America. The head of military intelli-gence for Umkhonto we Sizwe (MK), Ronnie Kasrils, was much inspired by Fidel Castro's advance on Havana from his base in the Sierra Maestra, where he recruited a guerrilla force among the peasantry. "I sensed . . . that the key reason for the limitation of our armed struggle was that we had not linked with our rural people, as Fidel had, and did not fully appreciate the role they could play."[8] After the series of rural revolts in the 1950s, the Bantustans remained largely quiescent for the next twenty-five years, while African urban areas exploded periodically in waves of open protest. Only in the insurrectionary climate of the mid-1980s did rural areas once again become the scene of widespread protest and resistance.

It is tempting to draw parallels between the rural struggles of the 1950s and the 1980s. However, behind the appearance of continuity lay significant shifts in the social composition of rural resistance movements as well as in the issues at stake. Delius has explored both the Sekhukhune revolt of the 1950s and the uprising of 1985–86.[9] He points to elements of continuity—notably the role of a broadly ANC-oriented political tradition—but also underlines major discontinuities. In the 1950s, an ANC-linked organization of migrant workers—Sebatakgomo—played a crucial role, in alliance with a number of local chiefs who resisted the encroachment of Bantu Authorities on the chieftaincy. In focusing on the vital importance of urban-based migrant organizations, Delius modifies the classic picture of "peasant revolts." Migrants played some role in the 1980s, but the driving force of the uprising was youth.

This change of actors from migrants and chiefs to youth is the vital difference between the 1950s and the 1980s. The Sekhukhune revolt of 1958 was not a clear-cut example of a peasant revolt, but the migrant workers who played such a crucial role shared many peasant concerns. The insurrection in the mid-1980s in Sekhukhuneland and other parts of Lebowa was definitely not a peasant revolt. This was above all a youth revolt, drawing its inspiration not from struggles for land or from working-class nationalism in the cities but from orthodox Marxist textbooks disseminated through student organizations, from a strong generational youth-consciousness, and from romanticized and sometimes misunderstood notions about the ANC's armed struggle. The leadership of the revolt had no peasant aspirations. The same is true for their following: they had no taste for farming. The main actors were high school students, for whom land issues were only a marginal concern. They were motivated by grievances concerning the conditions in the schools and the use and abuse of chiefly power.

The UDF in Lebowa, as in most of the Northern Transvaal, did not develop into a broad-based social movement. With few exceptions, the bulk of its following was youth, under the leadership of students from secondary and post-secondary schools. After some further observations on the UDF's rural policy and the issue of chieftaincy, this chapter examines the formation of the UDF in the Northern Transvaal, the role of the University of the North, and the spread of rebellion from the urban setting to the villages. We then turn to one of the main centers of rural revolt: Sekhukhuneland.

The UDF and Chieftaincy

Just as the UDF gave scant attention to communities threatened with removal, farmworkers, and migrant workers, the Front also failed to develop a policy toward chieftaincy. Publicity secretary Terror Lekota suggested that chiefs were a dying institution: "As the pressures of the capitalist economy penetrate even those rural areas, more and more people are making a break with the tribal ties of loyalties to the chief—who are being seen to be serving not the community but themselves. What we are going to see is the building of new leaders, not on the basis of old tradition."[10] Chiefs were generally equated with Bantustan structures. Since the UDF stood for a unitary state without ethnically based Bantustans, it followed that not only did the homeland governments have to go, but so did the tribal hierarchies, which had become part and parcel of the Bantustan administrations. The National Working Committee of the UDF resolved in 1986 that "organisation [in the Bantustans] must be intensified and tribal structures should be replaced with democratic organisations."[11]

The 1987 rural report recalled that "the anti-chief campaigns and anti-bantustan campaigns took off" in 1985, depicting chiefs and Bantustans as a tandem.[12] Combating chiefs was identified as a most suitable issue to unite a broad range of people, but the report also considered the expediency of alliances with chiefs, opposition parties in homelands, and elements in homeland civil services. The issue was left unresolved with the noncommittal conclusion that these alliances are inherently problematic. On the one hand, "our inability to control them, or take them further may mean that the victories we win are limited, in yet other circumstances people who are our allies during a specific period may in fact turn against us." On the other hand, "these alliances can also offer us protection and there are situations in which we can change the politics and attitudes of our allies so that they will move closer to us in the long term."

Indeed, migrants, women, and youth all had reason to resent abuse of power and corruption by chiefs. Grievances centered around taxes and tributes, and authoritarian rule. Special tributes were exacted from migrant workers, as a form of thanksgiving to the chief for looking after the migrant's household during his absence. Prior to the abolition of the pass laws in 1986, migrants needed to obtain a permit from the tribal labor bureau in order to qualify for employment and to pay a registration fee. The system also ensured that the chief had considerable control over the movements of his subjects. He could penalize recalcitrant villagers by refusing to have them registered.[13] The abolition of the pass system meant that migrants no longer had to present themselves at the chief's office. Chiefs lost their income from registration fees and also missed the opportunity to collect arrears from their migrant subjects.

Faced with diminishing control, chiefs frequently reacted by imposing new taxes to make up for the lost revenue.

Taxes, being a levy exacted from all members of the tribe, could be raised for special purposes after the chief's council gained approval from the formal gathering of adult men. In practice, these meetings were often called during weekdays, thus excluding the migrants from the consultation process. Upon their return to the village, migrants were presented with the bill upon which the chief and the elder men had decided. The special purposes generally included the building of a school, clinic, or post office, paying for legal advice in cases involving the chief or the tribe, contributing to the chief's marriage goods or to the costs of his funeral, or procuring the services of rainmakers.

In rural areas, the provision of school buildings was the responsibility of the local community. Control over school building funds and over the school committees responsible for running the school became one of the stakes in the controversy between chiefs, principals, parents, and students. Complaints about misappropriation of community funds by the chiefly elite were commonly voiced by youth and adults alike.[14]

Village meetings could be held only with permission from the chief. Chiefs generally opposed attempts to establish a civic association, which they rightly perceived as an alternative power structure. Chiefs had good reason to obstruct the formation of residents' organizations, as these were likely to become platforms for villagers to voice their grievances about taxes and missing funds.

Frequently, the taxes were of more benefit to the chief's private affairs than to the community. Taxes were raised to build a house for the chief, to buy a car, or to pay his repair bill. Some informants came up with even more extreme examples of arbitrary chiefly taxes, such as levies to pay for his traffic fines and diapers for his children.[15] This system of taxation without representation was at the root of many grievances against the chieftaincy. The migrants' organization NOTPECO (Northern Transvaal People's Congress), launched in the 1980s as the successor organization to Sebatakgomo, mobilized its following mainly on this issue, by impressing on the migrants that they were entitled to be part of the decision-making process.

Apart from taxation, free labor was also perceived as a form of exploitation. Free labor, involving work on the chief's homestead and on the tribal land, was exacted mainly from women and schoolchildren. Youth could be called upon to provide free labor in the period before initiation.[16] Chiefs used this prerogative to provide labor for agricultural schemes run by the Lebowa Development Corporation and usually managed by whites. Women were poorly paid for often strenuous work and would then spend their meager wages in the shops owned by the chiefly elite. Abolition of "forced labor" became a common demand of the youth congresses. Faced with these challenges to their authority from different quarters, many chiefs reacted by forming armed vigilante groups to combat rebellious youth. Weapons were provided by the Lebowa government. The tribal authorities were among the pillars of the pacification strategy of the SADF (South African Defence Force) in the Northern Transvaal and particularly in Lebowa.[17]

The imposition of the Bantu Authorities Act in the 1950s had not only changed the relationship between the chief and his subjects but had also upset the balance within the tribal hierarchy. Sekhukhuneland provides a clear example of the consequences of this divide-and-rule strategy. After the promulgation of this act, the government wanted to establish one single tribal authority under the paramount chief for the whole of Sekhukhuneland. The introduction of this new system was linked to a program of agricultural planning that included unpopular measures such as cattle culling and land demarcation. Beginning in 1956, resistance built up against Bantu Authorities and agricultural betterment alike, culminating in open revolt in 1958. The acting paramount chief, Morwamoche Sekhukhune, and a majority of his tribe were opposed to the Bantu Authorities system. The Native Affairs Department undermined the opposition by breaking up the power of the paramountcy. Morwamoche was deported, and the plan to institute one tribal authority was shelved. Subordinate headmen were offered recognition as chiefs if they accepted the establishment of Tribal Authorities. This scheme resulted in a proliferation of chieftaincies. In the early 1950s Sekhukhuneland counted three chieftaincies, but by the mid-1970s more than fifty chiefs had been officially recognized.[18] The doubtful origins of many chieftaincies served to further weaken their legitimacy, since many chiefs were considered to be only headmen who had usurped chiefly power. The disintegration of the paramountcy resulted in more factional conflict as the traditional system of consultation, conflict solving, and interdependence fell into disuse.

On the other hand, this history of resistance on the part of the paramount chief and a number of subordinate chiefs could be drawn upon to demonstrate the role played by traditional rulers in the fight against white domination. This placed chiefs in a different category from township councillors, who lacked any historical legitimacy. Chiefs were, after all, part of Africa's heritage. Although many individual chiefs were seen as corrupt and self-serving, the institution of the chieftaincy could not be dismissed so lightly.

As it moved from one crisis to the next, the UDF never managed to map out a policy on local government in the rural areas. Nor could it draw on a coherent ANC policy, although most ANC pronouncements assumed that chieftaincy either would die of its own accord or would be abolished. Govan Mbeki, writing on the peasant revolts of the 1950s, questioned the role of chiefs in the industrial age: "If the Africans have had chiefs, it was because all human societies have had them at one stage or another. But when a people have developed to a stage which discards chieftainship, when their social development contradicts the need for such an institution, then to force it on them is not liberation but enslavement."[19] Writing a quarter of a century later, another leading ANC intellectual was more straightforward: "Backward tribal and other relationships, such as the role of the chiefs in such situations, will by replaced by democratic institutions founded on the organs of people's power."[20]

Against this background, it is not surprising that the emergence of a Charterist organization of chiefs came as a shock to many UDF and ANC adherents. The formation of the Congress of Traditional Leaders of South Africa (CONTRALESA) in 1987 encountered an ambivalent reception in UDF circles.[21] Could progressive chiefs be organized to further the liberation struggle?

CONTRALESA had its origins in the battle against independence in KwaNdebele and the resistance in the district of Moutse against incorporation into KwaNdebele, the most recently established Bantustan, which was scheduled for "independence" in 1986. Moutse residents feared that the planned excision of their district from Lebowa and its incorporation into KwaNdebele would entail the loss of their South African citizenship. One of the prime movers of the anti-independence camp was Prince Klaas Makhosana Mahlangu, who belongs to the Ndzundza royal family in KwaNdebele. Klaas Mahlangu and other opponents of independence, many of whom had to flee KwaNdebele in fear of their lives, flocked to Johannesburg looking for help. Now a new problem posed itself to the UDF leadership, which by this time was itself in considerable disarray: What was the UDF to do with chiefs who supported a "progressive cause," such as the anti-independence struggle in the Bantustans? Would organizing chiefs serve the purpose of broadening out and further isolating the enemy?

After consultations with UDF leaders, trade unionists, and Peter Mokaba, the president of the South African Youth Congress (SAYCO)—all of whom came from the Northern Transvaal—CONTRALESA was launched in September 1987 in Johannesburg, claiming a membership of thirty-eight chiefs and subchiefs from KwaNdebele and Moutse. According to its constitution, CONTRALESA aimed to unite all traditional leaders in the country, to fight for the eradication of the Bantustan system, to "school the traditional leaders about the aims of the South African liberation struggle and their role in it," to win back "the land of our forefathers and share it among those who work it in order to banish famine and land hunger," and to fight for a unitary, nonracial, and democratic South Africa.[22]

The involvement of SAYCO in the launch of CONTRALESA gave rise to the suspicion that this organization was being formed with the ultimate goal of abolishing the institution of chieftaincy. That suspicion was not unfounded. Some of the activists involved in the formation of CONTRALESA were indeed motivated by the belief that there was no place for chiefs in the class-less society for which they were striving. In the meantime, however, harness-ing chiefs to the progressive cause would prevent them from subverting the struggle. Heeding the lessons from Angola and Mozambique, where "the destabilising factors such as Unita and Renamo found fertile ground in the dis-illusionment of rural people," the founders of CONTRALESA felt it was imperative to "organise and unite all traditional leaders of our country and to refrain from aligning ourselves with any particular oppressive system today or in the future."[23]

Combining "struggle" rhetoric with wooing chiefs proved a difficult feat. CONTRALESA advertised itself as a "progressive grassroots and community-based organisation." This phrase was usually used to denote civics or village committees—the very organizations that chiefs saw as undermining their authority. In line with the practice of UDF organizations and trade unions, CONTRALESA handed out T-shirts to its distinguished members, who would have preferred a tie or a classy briefcase. The relationship between CONTRALESA and the UDF is not quite clear. Press reports at the time of the launch and later present CONTRALESA as a UDF affiliate.[24] However, CONTRALESA's director of projects Samson Ndou stated in an interview in 1990 that CONTRALESA was not affiliated with the UDF or any other polit-ical movement.[25] But Murphy Morobe, who held the rural portfolio in the UDF Transvaal Regional Executive Committee (REC), had always assumed that CONTRALESA was indeed a UDF affiliate.[26] CONTRALESA's draft constitution does not mention UDF affiliation.

While the formation of CONTRALESA as a partner in the Mass Democ-ratic Movement was shocking news to many activists inside South Africa, the ANC was quick to give its blessing. In February 1988, a CONTRALESA dep-utation visited Lusaka to meet an ANC delegation headed by Secretary-General Alfred Nzo. The ANC, UDF, and SAYCO all hailed the "heroic role" that chiefs had played in the past against the forces of colonialism, pointed at the significant role of the chiefs in the early years of the ANC, and welcomed the "chiefs coming back to the people."[27]

This welcome is better explained by changes in overall ANC strategy than by a changing mood in the rural villages. Grievances festered on, but the wide-spread complaints were not translated into a broad popular movement against chiefly rule. While UDF propaganda upheld an image of widespread popular mobilization in the Bantustans, its internal assessments struck a more sober note. The 1987 rural report acknowledged that active organizational involve-ment was largely limited to youth, while organization of the civic associations and women remained extremely weak. The report noted that resistance against the Bantustans was mostly passive, "a spontaneous reflection of the alienation of the rural masses from the homeland structures." What organization there was had been smashed under the second State of Emergency. Rebuilding organization and regrouping around the remaining core groups proved a difficult process. "More serious is the fact that the government's vigilante and kitskonstabel strategy is based on the capacity of the state to recruit rural and unemployed youth. In many areas youth structures have found that people who flocked to them during the height of mass struggle in late 1985 and early 1986 have now joined the security forces in one form or another. This has not only demoralised organisation, but has exposed many activists to severe repression at the hands of the ex-comrades."

The report acknowledged that in many instances the Front had failed to link up with local initiatives of people faced with removals or incorporation into Bantustans and had neglected to address the organization of farmworkers in white rural areas. Excluded from the 1979 trade union reforms, farmworkers remained the most isolated and neglected category of workers. The report noted that rival organizations, such as Inkatha, had been more successful in this sector.[28]

There is substance to the claim in the rural report that, for the first time in decades, mass organizations were attempting to incorporate "the rural masses within the mainstream of the national struggle." But most initiatives had local or regional origins, and incorporating "the masses" did not advance much beyond youth. The national UDF leadership was largely innocent of any central planning or coordination with regard to rural areas.

The Northern Transvaal: The Rural Crisis

The Northern Transvaal is a vast, predominantly rural area with a few middle-sized towns and some industrial and mining centers.[29] The majority of the white population supported political parties and movements to the right of the ruling National Party (NP). This was the heartland of the Conservative Party and the Afrikaner Weerstandsbeweging (AWB). During election times their posters proclaimed an unequivocal message: *"Die land is ons land"* (The land is ours).

In many respects, the Northern Transvaal is the most economically backward region of South Africa. It is by far the most rural region, with a low urbanization rate and the highest rate of male absenteeism as a consequence of migrant labor. Official unemployment figures roughly trebled between 1980 and 1990.[30] Two homelands in the Northern Transvaal, Lebowa and KwaNdebele, became the scene of rural revolts in the mid-1980s. The other

Bantustans in this region—Venda and Gazankulu—do not figure prominently in accounts of rural struggles. In KwaNdebele, widespread resistance
against government plans to impose independence led to an unusual coalition
of the royal house, commuters, and youth.

Lebowa, a much longer established Bantustan, had consistently refused to
accept independence. Like most Bantustans, Lebowa was not one consolidated
territory but thirteen bits and pieces, scattered over the Northern Transvaal.
Most parts of Lebowa were remote from the main centers of employment.
Migrant labor provided the main source of income, with migrants returning
home perhaps on a monthly visit and for a longer period during the Christmas
holidays. Some 30 percent of the potentially economically active population
were employed outside Lebowa.[31] Unemployment in Lebowa in 1986 was officially estimated at 37 percent of the labor force. Salaried employment in Lebowa
could accommodate only approximately 21 percent of the labor force.[32]

Global statistics for the Northern Transvaal obscure the vast difference
between the living conditions of whites and Africans. For example, the population density in Lebowa was twenty-three times higher than in the white-
designated part of the Northern Transvaal. People living in white areas earned
seven to eight times the income of people living in Lebowa. Whites earned on
average more than fifteen times the salary of blacks, who primarily worked in
unskilled or semiskilled work. For black migrants working in the "white"
areas, income was on the average double the mean income earned in the homelands. Agriculture in "white" areas was marked by highly capital-intensive,
mechanized large farms, while homeland agriculture was characterized by
unmechanized subsistence farming on small plots. Stock farming was the most
viable form of agriculture but resulted in overgrazing and erosion. It was estimated that at least one-half (but probably more) of all households living in the
homelands were landless.[33]

The function of Bantustans has changed over the past decades. Their initial
function in the beginning of the twentieth century was the reproduction of
cheap labor power: subsistence agriculture in the African reserves subsidized
the growth of South African mining and industry. The mines could pay wages
below subsistence level because household incomes were supplemented by
homeland agriculture. But the productive capacity of the homelands soon
reached its limits, as a consequence of population pressure, overgrazing, and
the long absence of the strongest inhabitants. By the 1920s, agricultural output per capita was falling. Households came to rely increasingly on income
from migrant labor. Gradually, the roles were reversed: homeland agriculture
was now subsidized by migrant labor. Migrants sent remittances to the countryside to maintain an often tenuous rural foothold. The homelands became
importers of food. By the late 1980s, only 30 percent of the food consumed in
the Bantustans was produced internally.[34]

With the rapid industrialization of the 1940s, white farms experienced a shortage of labor. Farmers were unable to offer wages to compete with manufacturing. The NP, in government since 1948, came to the aid of Afrikaner farmers, one of its main constituencies. The mobility of African labor was drastically curtailed. Labor bureaus in the Bantustans channeled the labor supply between the mines, industry, and commercial agriculture. Without a permit from these labor bureaus, Bantustan residents were not allowed to look for jobs in "white" South Africa. Tightening of the pass laws, which in 1952 were extended to African women, served to contain and control the "surplus Africans" in the homelands. Apart from their role in labor allocation, Bantustans assumed more political functions of control. The 1953 Bantu Authorities Act was a key element in this process, in which control was delegated to a quasi-independent administration of Bantustan officials and chiefs.[35]

Bantustans in general, and the Lebowa administration in particular, were reputed to be havens of corruption and incompetence. Commissions of inquiry came up with damning evidence, but not much was done about the Lebowa government until 1993, when the South African government took responsibility for Lebowa's financial affairs, personnel matters, security, administration, pensions, and the tender board. It was revealed that hundreds of Lebowa government officials had been awarded enormous backdated salary increases, and that the Lebowa government had also appointed more than a thousand teachers whose salaries had not been included in its budget.[36]

In spite of rising unemployment in the industrial and mining centers, the use of migrant workers remained a widespread phenomenon. One of its obvious consequences is the uneven makeup of the population, with disproportionate numbers of women and children. Among the permanent residents of Lebowa, adults are a minority group. In 1980, 56 percent of the de facto population of Lebowa were under 20. Five years later, a staggering 72.3 percent were under 20.[37]

The rural crisis shared some aspects of the crisis in urban areas but also had some definite characteristics of its own. Township priorities such as housing, rents, and service charges were not high on the list of grievances. Most people owned their houses, and services were in any case mostly nonexistent. The structural conditions that help to explain the rural revolts in the Northern Transvaal center around the economic crisis with its high unemployment figures, the crisis in the schools, and the chieftaincy. These conditions feature prominently in accounts of the Sekhukhune rebellion.

Sekhukhuneland has been described as "a country of row upon row of hills and mountains, well-covered with trees and shrubs."[38] These days, Sekhukhuneland is best described as a dust bowl with mountains. The land is heavily eroded, and trees are scarce. As a consequence of high birth rates and forced resettlement, Sekhukhuneland experienced a rapid growth in population. The population virtually doubled between 1970 and 1980, resulting in increased pressure for land and a drastic reduction of the role of cattle in the rural economy. In 1986, the population reached 393,000.[39] The Sekhukhune Chamber of Commerce stated that trade had dropped by 65 percent between 1984 and 1986. Recruiting for the mines had come to a standstill.[40] Sekhukhuneland was one of the poorest districts of Lebowa. Because of drought, environmental degradation, and population density, rural dwellers could no longer rely on subsistence agriculture as a buffer against bad times.

While employment opportunities diminished, education opportunities grew at a spectacular rate. Rising standards of education resulted in rising expectations. High school students expected to get better jobs than their parents, who were mostly working in mines or factories, on white farms, or as domestic workers. But during the economic slump of the 1980s, few new opportunities opened up, while existing employment patterns could not absorb all newcomers. Opportunities for upward social mobility were mostly limited to employment in the teaching and nursing professions, the homeland administration, and the police force.

In line with tendencies nationwide, the 1980s saw a spectacular growth of enrollment in secondary schools in Lebowa. In 1986, almost 79 percent of young adults in the age group between fifteen and nineteen years and older were attending a secondary school.[41] The number of students in secondary schools more than doubled in five years, from 91,965 in 1980 to 199,429 in 1986, an average annual increase of 13.8 percent.[42] The massive influx of students was paralleled by an equally massive increase in the number of teachers, many of whom were young, inexperienced, and not properly qualified.

But the growth of classrooms lagged behind. Twenty-five years before, there had been only one secondary school for the whole of Sekhukhuneland. In 1980, the average number of pupils per classroom was 49.6, while in 1986 a classroom on average contained 62.1 pupils.[43] Classrooms in Sekhukhuneland were sometimes literally overflowing. A high school in GaMankopane had to accommodate 600 students in three classrooms. It was a common sight to see children sitting squeezed on windowsills, outside on a few bricks, or simply on the ground. Schools had a chronic shortage of books and teaching materials. Many teachers made excessive use of corporal punishment.

School careers frequently had to be interrupted as black students needed to work for a while to earn money for school fees, school uniforms, and textbooks. For white high school students, education was free. As a consequence, there was a wide range in age among students in African high schools. In the highest grades, students were frequently in their mid-twenties. Guidelines from the Education Department ensured that the percentage of failures was limited. This policy had two consequences. Since many weak students were promoted to the next standard or grade level, passing or failing a school year seemed completely arbitrary. Nevertheless, students who failed would be blamed by their parents for being lazy. Hence the demand "pass one, pass all" was introduced by protesting students. The second consequence was that students got stuck in standard ten, the final year, where they had to pass matric, the standardized final exams. Thus, matric classes were grossly overcrowded, sometimes having to accommodate a hundred or more students.

Between 1984 and 1986, the number of high school students in Lebowa in standard ten doubled, from 10,900 to 20,300. With the growth of enrollment figures came an ever increasing rate of dropouts and failures. The pass rate fell from 56.6 percent in 1984 to 41.5 percent in 1986, which placed Lebowa well below the national average of a 50 percent pass rate for African schools in 1986 (see table 1). By 1989, only 34 percent of Lebowa matriculants passed their exams.[44] These students often spent not just one or two years in standard ten but three or four years before they either passed matric or dropped out. The threat that students older than twenty-two years would no longer be readmitted added to the general dissatisfaction, although it never materialized. COSAS (Congress of South African Students) was mainly run by older students and former students, giving the government an extra motive to exclude these "troublemakers" by imposing an age limit.

These various components of the rural crisis—poverty, resettlement, overpopulation, drought, unemployment, and the crisis in the schools—all played a role in shaping revolts in Lebowa. But these structural conditions by themselves cannot explain the specific characteristics of the uprisings. The next section explores the role of human agency: Why would these conditions result in a youth revolt? Why would that happen at this particular time? After sketching the broader context of the UDF in the Northern Transvaal, the focus then shifts to the actors in the Sekhukhune revolt.

The UDF in the Northern Transvaal

When the UDF was launched in 1983, the Transvaal region of the UDF covered the whole province. But the heavy dominance of the urban conglomerate of the Witwatersrand led to early complaints of neglect from the rural areas. Rural activists felt that the urban leadership lacked sensitivity to rural issues. A Northern Transvaal Coordinating Committee of the UDF was formed in May 1984 to link up with existing organizations and scattered activists. Its backbone consisted of the student organizations COSAS and AZASO (Azanian Students' Organisation), some township-based youth congresses, and a general trade union, SAAWU (South African Allied Workers Union). An anonymous memorandum written in the same year is sharply

Table 1
Standard 10 examination results in Lebowa, 1980–1986

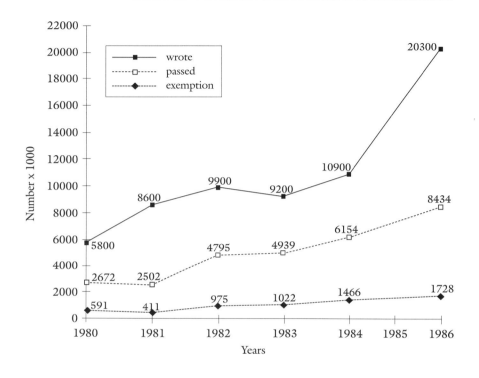

Source: Reprinted from *Lebowa: Introductory Economic and Social Memorandum* (1988), 61;
courtesy Development Bank of Southern Africa and C. J. Meintjes.

critical of the arrogance of the Johannesburg-based activists and the marginalization of the northern areas, which felt "treated as a bantustan . . . with no
right of participation." The people in the Northern Transvaal "are made to welcome the idea that their liberators would one day emerge from Johannesburg,"
and thus people's "confidence in being their own liberators was significantly
dwarfed." The memorandum complained that the UDF-Johannesburg was
using the Northern Transvaal as a labor reserve: the "advanced section of our
activists are usually drawn in the urban centres while the fate of the masses is
left to providence." It was pointed out that rural areas require different strategies from urban areas. In order to unite the rapidly growing number of youth
organizations and the emerging women's organizations, trade unions, and
church struggles into an anti-Bantustan offensive, the Northern Transvaal

would have to become a region in its own right. If a Northern Transvaal region were established and activities and efforts were coordinated with those of the southern region, the memorandum concluded, the activists would be "overstretching the enemy's resources beyond his limits. And nobody, not even the imperialists would save apartheid from its death pangs."[45]

The accompanying Programme of Action, however, did not come up with ideas that were different from those of other UDF regions.[46] The most original idea concerned Sekhukhuneland, where the Northern Transvaal activists planned to revive Sebatakgomo, the migrant workers' organization that played an active role in the revolt in the 1950s. This plan resulted in the formation of the Northern Transvaal People's Congress (NOTPECO), the only organization of migrant workers among UDF affiliates. But NOTPECO would deviate substantially from what its founding fathers had in mind.

The first UDF rally in the Northern Transvaal was held in August 1984 in the Pietersburg township of Seshego. The UDF coordinating committee claimed that, with more than five thousand people attending, it was the biggest political rally ever held in the history of the Northern Transvaal. After some delay, in February 1986 the UDF Northern Transvaal was constituted as a UDF region in its own right. Now that the coordinating committee was transformed into a regional executive committee (REC), it could draw up its own budget and employ its own organizers. By early 1986, the number of affiliates had grown to sixty-three.[47] But servicing the vast rural areas with their poor communications and bad roads was a task far beyond the means of the central core of UDF activists, who clustered around Pietersburg and the University of the North, with its adjoining township of Mankweng. The formation of a separate Northern Transvaal region did not bring the expected flow of resources from Johannesburg, nor did it stop the flow of activists to Johannesburg. Unlike the UDF in the Southern Transvaal or other regions, the UDF Northern Transvaal did not have its own office. For a while it shared some office facilities with SAAWU at the office of the Northern Transvaal Council of Churches in Pietersburg. Later it used the office of a sympathetic lawyer. The UDF Northern Transvaal was trying to cope with meager means, but the regional center in Pietersburg was relatively well off in comparison with facilities in the Bantustans. In the perception of rural activists, resources and manpower centered on Pietersburg and Mankweng and did not filter down to rural areas. Outlying areas voiced complaints against the REC in Pietersburg that were fairly similar to the grievances expressed in the memorandum with regard to the leadership in Johannesburg. The center-periphery problem was replicated on a smaller scale.

The UDF leadership in the Northern Transvaal spanned several generations. It included ANC veterans from the 1950s with a working-class background and intellectuals whose political schooling had begun in the 1970s in the student organizations oriented to Black Consciousness (BC). Chair of the UDF Northern Transvaal region was Peter Nchabeleng, an ANC activist from the 1950s who had served eight years on Robben Island for involvement in Umkhonto we Sizwe (MK). He had been branch secretary of the ANC-aligned trade union SACTU (South African Congress of Trade Unions) in Pretoria as well as a member of the executive of the ANC's Pretoria branch and of the Sebatakgomo migrants' organization. On his release in 1970, Nchabeleng was banished to Apel, the village of his birth in Sekhukhuneland. Meanwhile, some of the core activists from Sebatakgomo, led by Flag Boshielo and John Nkadimeng, had resumed organizing underground Umkhonto structures in the Transvaal. Boshielo, who had gone to Johannesburg as a migrant from Sekhukhuneland to work as a garden boy, later became a commissar of MK in exile. He was killed in an ambush in 1970, on his way home to organize the underground.[48] Nkadimeng, who had been served with a banning order, worked in Soweto at building the ANC underground. Around 1975, Peter Nchabeleng and his co-accused, Nelson Diale, linked up with this network. Before the underground network was properly organized, a group of MK fighters, led by Mosima ("Tokyo") Sexwale, crossed from Swaziland into the Transvaal, spurred on by the 1976 Soweto rising. They made contact with the old Sebatakgomo network in Sekhukhuneland and organized political instruction and military training for new recruits, including Nchabeleng's son Elleck. After a clash with police, where Sexwale wounded two constables with a hand grenade, the whole Transvaal network was rounded up. Sexwale and some others were sentenced to long prison terms, but Peter Nchabeleng, Diale, and Joe Gqabi were acquitted and served with internal banning orders. Gqabi was later assassinated while serving as ANC representative in Zimbabwe. Elleck Nchabeleng was sentenced to six years, most of which were spent on Robben Island. John Nkadimeng had managed to slip out of the country.[49]

In 1984, Peter Nchabeleng was among the first members of the UDF coordinating committee of the Northern Transvaal. While serving in the UDF organization, he remained involved in the ANC underground, where he was in charge of the ANC network in the whole of the Northern Transvaal, one of the few areas where the ANC had some measure of success in the integration of political and military structures.[50] With the formation of the UDF Northern Transvaal, Nchabeleng was elected regional chair. Barely two months later, Peter Nchabeleng was detained and killed by the Lebowa police. He was succeeded by the vice-chair, Louis Mnguni, a philosophy lecturer at the University of the North, who was a relative newcomer to resistance politics. The new vice-chair, Thabo Makunyane, underwent his initial politicization as a student in the 1970s in SASO (South African Students' Organisation), the standard-bearer of the Black Consciousness Movement. Like many of this student generation, he subsequently became involved with the ANC. In 1979, Makunyane was sentenced to five years for ANC activities. Upon his release in October 1985, he became active in the UDF. Makunyane was one of the few businessmen in the regional UDF leadership: he had some business interests in Sekhukhuneland and in the Pietersburg township of Seshego. Both Mnguni and Makunyane spent three years in detention without trial from 1986 to 1989.

Secretary of the regional executive was Joyce Mabudafhasi, a library assistant at the University of the North, who hailed from Venda. Mabudafhasi experienced her first spell in detention in 1976. From the late 1970s, she had been involved in organizing women's groups by initiating community activities such as gardening, soap making, and building clay ovens. Unlike the youth congresses, however, these women's groups did not grow into any kind of sustained organization. There were no systematic attempts to set up women's organizations in the Northern Transvaal. In April 1986, Mabudafhasi was seriously injured when a firebomb exploded in her house in Mankweng, the township adjacent to the university. Her house had become a hive of activists; the garage, nicknamed "Moscow," was taken over as a meeting place for comrades. In January 1989, Mabudafhasi joined with two other women to initiate a nationwide hunger strike by political detainees, which resulted in the release of hundreds of activists.[51]

Publicity secretary of the UDF Northern Transvaal was Peter Mokaba, whose stature as a youth leader was unrivaled among local youth. Like Makunyane, he belonged to the 1976 generation. During the student uprising he had been involved in organizing school boycotts in and around Mankweng and Pietersburg. He subsequently helped to establish local branches of COSAS and AZASO. In 1980, almost the entire executive of the AZASO branch at the University of the North, where Mokaba had enrolled as a student, went into exile to join the ANC. On his return in 1982, Mokaba and a fellow student were arrested and charged with activities for the ANC and MK. He was sentenced to six years, but he was acquitted on appeal and released in 1985. Immediately after his release he became involved in the regional interim structure of the UDF. Mokaba, who survived many attempts on his life, played a pivotal role in coordinating the youth organizations that were sprouting all over South Africa. When the long awaited national youth organization, the South African Youth Congress (SAYCO), was finally launched in March 1987, Peter Mokaba became its first president.[52] He was arrested in March 1988 on charges of MK activities in the Northern Transvaal. As had happened at a previous trial, once again state witnesses refused to give evidence, and Mokaba was acquitted in May 1989. This series of acquittals prompted allegations in the press that Mokaba had been working as a police informer. Mokaba was called to Lusaka for investigation. According to some reports, he was cleared by ANC headquarters; others maintained that grounds for suspicion remained. In spite of these spy rumors, Mokaba was elected president of the ANC Youth League, when it was reconstituted in 1990.[53] He was indispensable to the ANC efforts to establish a measure of control over youth militancy.

Thus, the central core of UDF activists in the Northern Transvaal had a clear and militant ANC profile. The charges of ANC and MK activities did much to enhance Peter Mokaba's standing among the youth but may have made more conservative sections of the population wary of the UDF. In 1992, when the time had come to placate other constituencies besides youth, Mokaba was presented in a very different capacity. ANC president Nelson Mandela introduced him to the million or more Zionist Christians who had gathered for their Easter celebrations at Moria, in the Northern Transvaal, as a member of the Zion Christian Church (ZCC). Mandela emphasized the overlap of ANC and ZCC membership and their "common objectives."[54] During the 1980s, the relationship had been less cordial. When Bishop Barnabas Lekganyane of the ZCC played host to President P. W. Botha at the Easter gathering in 1985, he exhorted his followers to practice "Love and Peace. The key to them is obedience to the laws of the headmen, the homeland governments and the government of the RSA."[55]

The UDF leadership in the Northern Transvaal was dominated by intellectuals and students. Trade union involvement remained limited. Overall, the trade union presence in these parts was weak. Most labor laws did not cover the homelands. The 1979 labor reforms, which had boosted the growth of the black trade union movement, did not apply in the homelands. Unions could not use the official disputes machinery to force employers to bargain. Nor could they hope to build a power base by sheer numbers. Unemployment was so high that those who joined unions could be easily replaced.[56] Since the policy of the Lebowa government precluded recognition of trade unions, most companies used homeland policies as an argument to refuse to deal with unions. Thus, unions found their sphere of operation in the Northern Transvaal largely limited to the mining areas and the conservative towns of "white" South Africa, outside the Bantustans.

A Pietersburg branch of SAAWU, the UDF-affiliated general union that played a central role in the Eastern Cape and the Ciskei, was set up by students at the University of the North. The main organizer was law student Alf Makeleng, who also served on the UDF executive. He was detained in June 1986 and died two years later in police detention.[57] Elleck Nchabeleng also worked briefly as a SAAWU organizer. The union gained a modest foothold in the commercial and catering sector and in the metal industry. The other trade union that became involved in the UDF was the metalworkers union UMMA-WUSA (a split from MAWU, the main black union for metalworkers) with a membership concentrated around the mining region of Steelpoort, south of Sekhukhuneland. The Steelpoort region was also one of the few areas where youth organizations made some attempts to link up with African workers on the white farms.

The UDF Northern Transvaal region was subdivided in six zones. Ideally, each zone should have coordinated the activities of affiliates in its area. In practice, organizations tended to link up vertically with their particular parent body, such as SAYCO or COSAS, rather than horizontally with organizations in the same area. The image of a proliferation of organizations is to some extent misleading, as a fairly limited number of activists were able to form the core of a range of organizations. Thus, Louis Mnguni was also chair of the Mankweng civic, formed in 1985, of which Joyce Mabudafhasi was the secretary and Peter Mokaba the publicity secretary. All three were also active in the Detainees Support Committee (DESCOM). Mabudafhasi was involved in the National Education Crisis Committee (NECC) as well as in the Human Rights Commission. Her son Raymond was chair of the Mankweng Youth Congress (MAYCO).

The absence of a regional office and of functioning subregions compounded the organizational problems. Thabo Makunyane later recalled how activists often used the name of the ANC or the UDF to legitimate a wide range of activities, from fund-raising to the burning of witches. People would produce letters with UDF letterheads to collect donations from local businesspeople or make pamphlets with a SAYCO logo, proclaiming that the aim of the organization was to recruit soldiers for MK. "Many affiliates took off in different directions, assuming a life of their own. Especially, this was the case with the youth. In many places, people were doing things in the name of ANC or UDF without these organizations even knowing."[58]

The old guard of the 1950s and the generation of the 1976 student revolt manned the organizational structures in the UDF Northern Transvaal. But the battles were fought by young men in their late teens and early twenties who were as yet inexperienced in the struggle.

Sources of Inspiration, Mobilization, and Organization

The UDF Northern Transvaal may have had meager facilities, but it did manage to latch onto institutions whose resources it could tap. The University of the North, also known as Turfloop, played a vital role as a center of communication, coordination, ideological direction, and recruitment and as a hiding place for activists on the run from the police. "The engine of building the structures was the University."[59] Nicknamed "Lusaka" in activist and police circles alike, the University of the North was, on the face of it, an unlikely place to become the planning center of revolution in the Bantustans. It was established in 1960 as a segregated institution for Africans from the various homelands in the Transvaal. In the 1970s, Turfloop was a bastion of the Black Consciousness Movement, but in the 1980s the UDF/ANC became the dominant force in student politics. Around 1980, the student organization AZASO, which had its origins in the Black Consciousness Movement (BCM), was taken over by Charterist students. In 1981, AZASO observed Republic Day with a daring feat: students replaced the South African flag at the Mankweng police station with an ANC flag.

The university itself remained largely under the control of the Broederbond. Lecturers were mostly conservative Afrikaners. Most of the black staff kept aloof from politics. Philosophy lecturer Mnguni and library assistant Mabudafhasi were rare exceptions. In some instances, students acted with success against right-wing lecturers who victimized political activists. "It could be a blessing in disguise when they were making racist remarks, then there is a reason to act against them; or when they are consistently failing students." Class boycotts resulted in the expulsion of several lecturers. The demand for the dismissal of law professor P. van Warmelo was put more forcefully: students poured acid over him.[60]

As AZASO worked its way toward hegemony on the campus, violent clashes ensued between AZASO and its rival, AZASM, the Azanian Students Movement, which remained true to BC ideology. AZASO managed to gain control of the student representative council (SRC) at Turfloop, thus obtaining access to the use of telephones, photocopy machines, meeting facilities, and occasionally cars for "student activities." Sport outings to other black universities and colleges were used for "spreading the gospel." Thus, student organization spread to the University of Venda, which originated as a branch of Turfloop. Through AZASO, the University of the North became the main resource center of the UDF in the Northern Transvaal.

In the early 1980s, both Charterist student organizations, COSAS (secondary students) and AZASO (postsecondary institutions), promoted student involvement in community affairs. AZASO took the initiative for the regional launch of SAAWU in the Northern Transvaal. AZASO's subcommittee for education assisted high school students in setting up SRCs. At its 1982 conference, COSAS had resolved to initiate the formation of youth congresses, so as to organize nonstudent youth. Student activists, both in secondary and in postsecondary institutions, saw it as their mission to build organizations in townships and villages. AZASO met regularly with members of the UDF

Regional Executive to plan rural campaigns. According to the students interviewed, the UDF and the ANC enc ̗uraged people to study at Turfloop rather than at the University of the Witwatersrand in Johannesburg because of Turfloop's central role in mobilizing the Northern Transvaal.

In 1983, the students from Sekhukhuneland met at Turfloop to discuss forming organizations in their home villages.[61] During holidays, students went to their villages to form youth groups. Afterward they would meet again at the university to exchange experiences. Among the core activists in Sekhukhuneland were several students from the University of the North. These were an important source of organizational know-how and of "political education." They taught youth how to conduct meetings and ran workshops on Marxism-Leninism.

However incongruous it seemed, a highly formal brand of orthodox Marxist-Leninist discourse became the language of village youth meetings. Thus, at a meeting in 1990 of the SRC at a teacher-training college in Sekhukhuneland, one could listen to students discussing their decision-making procedure in the context of "democratic centralism." Was it necessary to "consult the masses" of the student body about a request to lend a sound system to the local youth congress for a village meeting? Or did "democratic centralism" mean that "the masses" were in need of leadership, so that the SRC could take the decision now and report afterward to its constituency?[62] The drawback, however, of this organizational strategy was that many of the village-based organizations had little permanence: frequently structures collapsed or were left without direction when students returned to their campus.

In spite of intermittent police raids and closures of the university, students could organize relatively freely on the campus before the declaration of the State of Emergency on 12 June 1986. Meetings could simply be advertised. Academic programs were regularly disrupted by boycotts and demonstrations, but up until mid-1985 the university administration remained fairly tolerant of political activism. However, by mid-1986 the administration requested the South African army to patrol the campus because "safety of property and person could not be guaranteed, looting, malicious damage to property and physical violence became tools of student militancy."[63] About four hundred students were expelled. The SRC members went underground or into exile to join the ANC. Outside visitors were no longer allowed; students' movements were strictly controlled. Meetings on campus could be held only with police permission. But boycotts continued intermittently. After a boycott of lectures in 1988, which lasted several weeks, the university administration granted students the right to reestablish the SRC. The army presence on the campus lasted until 1989.

Student organizations of both secondary and postsecondary institutions and student contacts played a key role in initiating local youth congresses. The 1976 Soweto uprising had filtered down to some urban centers in the north but not to outlying areas such as Sekhukhuneland. Because schools in Sekhukhuneland and other rural districts remained quiet, parents in Soweto and other townships on the Witwatersrand began sending their children to school in rural areas, where they stayed with relatives or in boarding schools. These external linkages proved important: new ideas, such as student representative councils in high schools, music, magazines, and the latest township fashions were brought in by students from Soweto but also by high school students from Sekhukhune who spent the holidays with relatives on the Reef, looking for a temporary job. COSAS began forming branches in Sekhukhuneland in the early 1980s.[64]

Through COSAS, high school students began making demands for the introduction of SRCs in their schools, free books, and the abolition of corporal punishment. But COSAS was perceived as an urban organization. Among rural youth there is a clear feeling of resentment against the arrogance of township youth. Township youth used to refer to boys from rural areas as "*plaas boys*" (farmhands). Although some students became involved in COSAS, youth organization gained momentum only with the formation of local youth congresses, such as the Sekhukhune Youth Organisation (SEYO). COSAS was seen as "a thing from town," whereas SEYO was "our own organization."[65]

The Spread of Rebellion

Student unrest in the Northern Transvaal predated the formation of the UDF but escalated after 1983. Protest actions in schools in the vicinity of Turfloop and Pietersburg centered on the demand for SRCs and for an end to corporal punishment. The first youth congresses, set up to organize nonstudent youth, were formed in Mankweng and Seshego, the townships of Turfloop and Pietersburg. Mankweng was also the first township in the Northern Transvaal to have a civic. The civic was formed in 1985 in the course of a campaign by the Mankweng Youth Congress, which had forced the local town council to resign.[66] But initially, political activity outside the Turfloop campus and its immediate vicinity remained at a low ebb. UDF activists had initiated the Mankweng civic hoping that from there the civic movement would spread to other townships and villages. But while youth congresses spread like wild fire, the formation of civics took off only in 1990. In Lebowa's largest urban settlement, the Pietersburg township of Seshego, a youth congress was formed in 1984, but only after February 1990 did Seshego have its civic. The initiative then came from a group of young men who, by that time, considered themselves too old for the youth congress. The civic provided them with a new avenue for political involvement.[67]

The first casualty in the Northern Transvaal occurred on 16 June 1985, when high school student Shadrack Mafokoane was shot and killed by the Lebowa police when fights erupted after a commemoration of the Soweto uprising on the Turfloop campus.[68] In protest, the Mankweng civic organized a local boycott of the police. Shops selling to the police were targeted for a consumer boycott. The campaign to isolate the police was taken up by the UDF and spread to other townships and subsequently also to rural areas.

From July 1985 onward, many activists were detained and others forced into hiding. From November, several UDF affiliates organized consumer boycotts to demand the release of prisoners. In Mahwelereng, the township adjoining Potgietersrus, the youth congress instigated a ban on police entering hotels and shebeens, or taverns. Tensions escalated after the police opened fire on the youth and arrested 40 members of the youth congress. The youth retaliated with attacks on policemen's homes and government offices. The home of Lebowa's minister of education in Mahwelereng was destroyed in a firebomb attack. AZAPO activist Lucky Khumalo was beaten to death at the local police station.[69] In Motatema, a township near Groblersdal, battles between police and youth erupted in February 1986, leaving ten youth dead and scores of people injured or in detention. Six of these casualties fell when police tried to prevent youth from attending a funeral of earlier victims.[70] This funeral became one of the landmarks in the Lebowa uprising. Large numbers of young people from remote areas—including Sekhukhuneland—flocked to Motatema to attend the funeral. As elsewhere in South Africa, mass funerals played a vital role in the process of mobilization. Similar deadly cycles of violence were reported in the first months of 1986 from Seshego, where police went on a rampage against UDF and AZAPO members alike.

These months also marked the escalation of rebellion in Sekhukhuneland. In March 1986, thousands of youth all over this rural region poured out of their schools, commandeered buses and other vehicles, and drove in a convoy to the Lebowa capital, where they wanted to present their demands to the Lebowa government. But the convoy was stopped halfway by the Lebowa police. A battle ensued between police and youth, in which many youth were badly beaten or wounded by gunshots. Mass arrests inspired demands for the release of the students. Subsequent battles resulted in more youth being killed or injured. As in the townships, funerals of young activists "killed in action" became an important meeting place to make further plans.

By this time, open warfare had broken out with the police. Youth targeted property that they believed belonged to those sympathetic to the enemy, the Lebowa government. Local businesspeople, who depended on the homeland administration for licenses and contracts, were largely seen as belonging to the enemy camp. Buses, shops, and some schools were burned. Pressure was put on shopkeepers, shebeen owners, and taxi drivers to refuse their services to policemen.[71]

Beginning in mid-1985, the Lebowa government took harsher measures to stem the tide of radicalism. Public servants who were members of "subversive organizations," namely UDF and AZAPO, were threatened with dismissal. The assistance of the South African army was asked to help the Lebowa police force in combating the unrest. Chiefs were given more powers in school matters, including the right to prohibit admission of students from outside the area in which the school was situated.[72] The following year, the Lebowa legislative assembly passed an indemnity act, which granted indemnity to its officials and police force members for any action or utterance performed in curbing political unrest from 1 June 1985 up to 11 June 1986. After 11 June, a nationwide State of Emergency gave similar indemnity to all members of the security forces in the whole of South Africa. As a result, hundreds of lawsuits against the Lebowa government were frozen. Attorney Don Nkadimeng, for example, had to abandon 643 claims for assault, totaling two million Rand in damages, against the Lebowa minister of law and order. In 1988, the Lebowa Indemnity Act was nullified by the Supreme Court in Bloemfontein.[73]

The state was not alone in reacting violently to the spread of rebellion. Businessmen who became the target of boycotts, extortions, or hijackings joined forces with the police or formed vigilante groups on their own accord. In the newly built "capital," Lebowakgomo, youth threatened businesses to obtain money to bail out friends arrested for various offenses. In case of refusal, shops were looted or burned. Several businessmen paid 500 Rand or more to keep their shops open.[74] When requiring transportation to meetings or funerals, youth often commandeered cars or refused to pay taxi fares.

A particularly bitter hostility developed between young activists and members of the Zion Christian Church (ZCC) after President P. W. Botha's visit to the Easter celebrations. Pretoria's propaganda made the most of the respectful reception of the state president by two million law-abiding blacks, while Bishop Lekganyane condemned the violence in the townships. The traditional political neutrality of the ZCC members seemed already an anachronism in a "struggle culture" in which people belonged either to the "people's camp" or to the "enemy's camp." But Botha's visit to Moria had made the ZCC members positively suspect in the eyes of the youth. The following year youth organizations in several places demanded that ZCC members stay home at Easter and not make their customary pilgrimage to Moria. Zionists did not always turn the other cheek. Student periodicals reported several instances where groups of ZCC men, nicknamed the Moria Defence Force, invaded schools to teach the youth some "discipline."[75]

But organization and mobilization remained largely confined to youth. Not only the conservative sectors of African society—such as business, chiefs, or the African independent churches—were aloof or antagonistic to UDF actions; in addition, the UDF was largely unsuccessful in involving workers, supposedly the vanguard of the liberation movement. In some areas, however, notably in the mining regions of Phalaborwa and Steelpoort, students mounted joint campaigns with workers. The presence of an industrial workforce meant that youth activists could link up with union activists.

The Steelpoort Valley, south of Sekhukhuneland, is also one of the rare places where protest action by farmworkers was reported. In this area of forced resettlement, about 130,000 BaPedi displaced from the white farms have been resettled at Mampuru, inside Lebowa. The local chief in Mampuru, himself a victim of forced removals, was sympathetic to the UDF and allowed meetings to take place in his village. Some inhabitants commuted daily to the white farms in the Steelpoort Valley, making them more amenable to organization than farmworkers living on the farms. In 1986, farmworkers heeded a call for a stay-away from work on 1 May, which was most unusual.[76] At several farms, workers stayed away from work, demanding a daily wage of 5 Rand.[77] White farmers in the Steelpoort Valley complained about youth intimidating farmworkers, hijacking or firebombing their trucks, stealing from their lands, and burning buildings. They claimed that at roadblocks in Lebowa they had to buy an "ANC permit" for 1000 Rand to get safe passage. Armed farmers declared that they would shoot any youth found in their fields. "We eat barbed wire for breakfast and we are more right-wing than the AWB [Afrikaner Weerstandsbeweging, the Afrikaner Resistance Movement]"[78] They favored simple solutions to the insurgency: an electrified fence along the border with Lebowa and a blockade of food deliveries to Lebowa. When hunger would begin to bite, the "ordinary blacks" would evict the "comrades," after which life could resume as usual.[79]

These examples of linkages between youth and workers, however, were fairly exceptional and were limited to areas with a resident industrial workforce. The townships and villages of the Steelpoort and Phalaborwa region were not typical of rural Lebowa. In the rural parts of Lebowa, youth movements had little contact with migrant workers. Few workers showed an interest in political gatherings organized by youth. Asked about student-worker alliances, one student activist later recalled: "Actually, we had problems with people working and being union members in Johannesburg and Pretoria. They did not want to be involved in our struggle. Perhaps they were not politically motivated and just union members because they wanted better pay and job protection. The traditionally minded people complained that we were undermining the chief's position."[80] Migrant workers were generally seen by activists as "parents," not as workers with whom an alliance could be sought.

Through youth networks, the cycle of rebellion and repression, which originated in mid-1985 in the urban centers of Turfloop and Pietersburg, had reached the rural areas by the end of that year. By early 1986, rebellion had escalated to such an extent that it made the national newspapers. Reporting on the insurgency in the Northern Transvaal, the *Sunday Times* asserted that it reached "deep into the near-inaccessible rural areas of Sekhukhuneland," where "tribesmen are being introduced, sometimes violently, to the ideologies of the left."[81]

The Sekhukhune Revolt: The Actors

The roads of Sekhukhuneland are admittedly bad, but the description in the *Sunday Times* conjures up misleading pictures of a primeval wilderness inhabited by innocent tribesmen who are being infected by foreign ideologies. In reality, Sekhukhuneland is only a four- to five-hour drive from Johannesburg. Its inhabitants, who for the most part belong to the BaPedi people, have a long history of exposure to the outside world, largely due to a pattern of migrant labor that goes back more than a century to the early years of diamond mining at Kimberley. Even before the advent of the mining industry, young men from Sekhukhuneland went to work for cattle farmers in the Eastern Cape. Whereas migrant labor initially was a passing phase in the life of young men, lasting long enough for the purchase of a gun and perhaps some cattle, as the twentieth century progressed, migrancy increasingly became an almost lifelong necessity for many men and a growing number of women.

As previously described, migrant organizations played a vital role in the uprising of the 1950s when the NP government attempted to impose its Bantustan system on Sekhukhuneland. Nor were the people of Sekhukhuneland total strangers to the "ideologies of the left." Several leading figures in the migrant workers' organization Sebatakgomo, such as John Nkadimeng, Elias Motsoaledi, a trade unionist who was among Mandela's codefendants in the Rivonia trial, Flag Boshielo, and Peter Nchabeleng, were active members in both the ANC and the Communist Party. Although overt political activity was impossible during the 1960s and 1970s, the UDF in the 1980s could draw on a small nucleus of ANC veterans and on a collective memory of earlier episodes of resistance.

Students and Youth

The main actor in the Sekhukhune revolt was the Sekhukhune Youth Organisation (SEYO), which was not formally constituted until 1986. But from 1984 onward, local youth movements had been sprouting at the village level. The first Sekhukhune Youth Committee was formed in 1984 in the twin village of

Apel-GaNkoane, in the northern part of Sekhukhuneland. The major inspiration came from student organizations like COSAS and AZASO, while small nuclei of local ANC activists, like the Nchabeleng household in Apel, provided a link with local ANC traditions.

The Nchabeleng household was an important center of UDF activity in Sekhukhuneland. Several sons of the UDF president played a pivotal role in the youth movement, both on a regional and local level. People like Peter Nchabeleng and a few others kept alive something of an ANC tradition. Buried under the goats' kraal behind the Nchabeleng house was a collection of documents, including a tattered copy of the Freedom Charter. Some political discussions were held with his children and a few friends, but on the whole, political activity was low. Not many people dared to visit Nchabeleng's house because the police always came to interrogate visitors. Many villagers feared the household was a nest of terrorists. One youth activist recalled, "We were told that Peter Nchabeleng was a communist, that he had been trained by Russia and that he was coming with bombs to destroy us."[82]

Peter Nchabeleng survived several attempts on his life. In one instance in 1983, the principal of the local high school sent him a letter bomb in an envelope that allegedly contained the school report of his son Maurice. Because the envelope felt suspicious, Nchabeleng sent it back to the principal with Maurice and asked him to verify the contents. The principal refused. An expert analysis confirmed that the envelope did indeed contain a letter bomb.[83] Nchabeleng's eldest son, Luthuli, fed up with continuous harassment by police and schoolteachers because of his "terrorist" background, had crossed the Botswana border in 1982 to join the ANC.[84] In 1984, the second-born son, Elleck, returned home from Robben Island. Following the general instructions given by the ANC leadership on the island to departing prisoners, he became involved in various organizations such as trade union and youth movements in the Northern Transvaal, including a group of students in Apel. Initially, there was not much talk of politics: "The first meetings were with rasta kids who came to smoke dagga [marijuana]."[85] Later, when Elleck went to work with a community resource center in Johannesburg, he was instrumental in getting newspapers and other informational material and money for transportation costs to youth activists. Shops in Sekhukhuneland were afraid to stock newspapers, even such mainstream papers as the *Star, Rand Daily Mail, Citizen,* or *Sowetan.* Shopkeepers feared police harassment. "Lebowa police wanted to keep the rural areas isolated from the towns, so that people would not be aware of the revolt elsewhere in South Africa."[86]

In the remote village of GaMasemola, Nelson Diale, who was co-accused with Nchabeleng in the 1978 trial for terrorism, was also in touch with the local youth organization. Diale manned an advice office that became a nerve center of information and communication. This office was opened late in 1986 in Jane Furse, a village with a concentration of educational, medical, and commercial facilities. Many people were in the habit of coming to Jane Furse to seek help from the Lutheran Dean Mimiela and from Aaron Motsoaledi, a medical doctor, both of whom were sympathetic to the UDF. When repression became severe, with the police assaulting, robbing, and raping people, legal and other types of assistance was much in demand. Since there were no local lawyers, people had to travel to Pietersburg or Johannesburg to get legal advice. The advice office staffed by Diale and supported by the Lutheran Church and the human rights organization Black Sash was meant to provide for these needs. In its first years, however, the office could hardly function because of the continuous presence of police and the South African army.[87] Whereas most church ministers in rural areas were either hostile or indifferent, the UDF had a good relationship with the office of the Northern Transvaal Council of Churches in Pietersburg and with the Lutheran Church. The Lutherans, who benefited from fairly generous overseas funding, could perhaps afford a more courageous stand than churches that were dependent on local revenue. The Lutheran mission at Lobethal in Sekhukhuneland served as meeting place for a series of UDF meetings and allowed the use of its photocopy facilities.

The ANC input in the youth movement, while providing the youth with the powerful symbols of armed struggle, served to frighten off most of the older generation. "Many people were saying that the ANC was a bad thing. That is what they heard from parents and teachers. At first, old people were totally opposed to talking about the ANC. They warned us that we would land in jail."[88] However, it was not the old ANC guard but a burgeoning movement of youth, led by secondary and postsecondary students, that caused the Sekhukhune revolt. "In Jane Furse there was talk of SRC's for the first time in 1980–1981," recalled Philip Mnisi, who attended high school in Jane Furse and later worked as a student teacher in Apel. "COSAS was introduced at the same time. It was an idea that came from town, from the urban areas."

In Apel, COSAS was introduced in 1985. The demand for student representative councils ran into stiff opposition from principals and teachers. Overt organization in schools was not possible at the time; meetings were held in schoolyards. Some high school students became involved in COSAS, but when local youth organizations were formed, they became the dominant movement, absorbing most of the COSAS activists. "When SEYO came, then COSAS activity died. Because SEYO was our own organization. People now pursued the same issues in SEYO, and it were mostly the same people who were involved."[89] The SEYO constitution was obviously inspired by the COSAS concept of youth congresses: an organizational formula to accommodate both student and nonstudent youth and to link up with community issues. The SEYO constitution, modeled after that of the Soweto Youth Congress, states as one of the key objectives: "to mobilise and conscientize the youth for involvement in the struggles of their communities and to encourage the formation of community-based organisations."[90]

The villages of Jane Furse and Apel were the two main centers from which youth organization spread to other villages. Apel was locked in long-standing disputes concerning land rights with the neighboring village of GaNkoane.[91] Occasionally, these disputes had led to violent confrontation. This animosity had prevented any kind of joint organization or joint activities between the villages. "Sometimes your parents would beat you up if you were friendly with the other camp."[92] Rather than forming two organizations, youth leaders decided to form one youth organization for the two villages to demonstrate that "faction fights and division" could be overcome in the interest of unity in the liberation struggle. In 1985, Richard Sekonya of GaNkoane, a student at the Agricultural College in Tompi Seleki near Marble Hall (west of Sekhukhuneland) became the president of the Sekhukhune Youth Committee in Apel-GaNkoane, which subsequently became the local branch of the umbrella organization SEYO. He linked up with the youngest son of Peter Nchabeleng, Maurice, who attended high school in Apel. Another Nchabeleng son, Petrus, was a law student at Turfloop. The Nchabeleng house became a center of youth activity. As Sekonya recalled: "That old man was spending sleepless nights trying to help us and to solve our problems. Also he always involved us in solving our problems." From Apel, youth organization spread quickly to other villages. "People from all over Sekhukhune came to Apel to ask advice, because we were more advanced, we had the first branch and also the biggest." With the help of some funds provided by Elleck Nchabeleng from Johannesburg, activists from Apel traveled to other villages to organize branches of the youth movement. "We managed to organize many branches. For instance, Tafelkop exploded within a week after our visit. Our branch was well built."[93]

Contacts with the outside world proved important for the beginnings of youth organization in the villages, not only because the outside world provided an input of ideas and resources but also because by living in the villages of Sekhukhuneland one missed the politicizing direct encounters with racist teachers or employers and with the apartheid state. For firsthand experiences with apartheid, one had to go outside Sekhukhuneland. One activist recalled: "Political activity was very low. We were not politically active, we used to look down on people wasting their time on politics." His politicizing experience came in 1985, when he went to Pretoria to find a temporary job. "There I saw this long queue of men, some of them even old men, queuing for a job in a white man's garden. I saw apartheid alive in Pretoria; at home it was something you read about in the newspapers."[94] Encounters with the pass laws also proved a politicizing experience.

Richard Sekonya became involved in politics as a student at the Agricultural College in Tompi Seleki. Many staff members at the college were Afrikaners. Students from Turfloop assisted in forming an AZASO branch and a SRC, of which Sekonya became the general secretary. He described an incident that took place at the school in 1985:

> Oppression was at a peak that side, they could not even take a suggestion. We had objections against one black vice-principal and one white vice-principal. We sent a memorandum to the principal, but after a month there was still no reply. We resolved to take a school truck and load the possessions of the black vice-principal on the truck, to make clear that he had to move out. After we had put his things on the truck, we went to the house of the white vice-principal, but that was guarded by soldiers who fired warning shots. The white man also stood with a gun in his door. Students told him that they did not want him on the campus anymore. The soldiers would not allow us to take his furniture. We were angry because his house was guarded, while the black vice-principal's house had not been protected. We went to a filling station, made petrol bombs and bombed the house. The soldiers were shooting. Two persons were shot, they were injured.[95]

After this incident in September 1985, Sekonya was arrested but later released on bail. Since he had been expelled from the college, he could now become a full-time activist in Apel-GaNkoane, at least until November 1986, when he was sentenced to six years imprisonment, subsequently reduced to four years.

UDF documents mention a combined membership of the youth congresses of the Northern Transvaal totaling 120,000 members, making this the strongest youth movement in the country. When regional congresses linked up to form SAYCO in May 1987, the Northern Transvaal boasted about 150 local congresses, of which 40 were located in Sekhukhuneland.[96] But these figures are misleading. They suggest a signed up membership, while in actual fact they must be wild estimates. In reality, everybody who was considered to belong to the "youth" was also considered to be a member of the youth congress. "In the early years of SEYO, all the youth was considered to be a member. Sometimes force was used to get all the youngsters to attend the meetings. We would not permit the presence of any other organization in the village, such as the PAC. We threatened ZCC members that we would disturb their processions if they would not allow their children to attend our meetings. These days we are more democratic. But it is not always possible to start an organization without force."[97]

Youth organization in the remote village of Mphaaneng, which took off with help from Apel activists and AZASO members from Lebowakgomo, was run on the same principle. "We learned the lesson that you have to be united to make the country ungovernable. . . . There were weekly mass meetings on the banks of the Oliphants river. In five months time all the youth was organized."[98]

Such sentiments on the need for all-encompassing organization were quite in line with views of other UDF activists at the time. On the Turfloop campus, AZASO ran a recruitment campaign in 1985–86 under the slogan "every student an AZASO member," which aimed to exclude rival organizations from the campus. A UDF publication quoted with apparent approval another youth activist, who stated: "The call in the villages is to organise every person. Because those who are not with us can be used by the enemy against the people."[99]

SEYO's constitution put the age limit for membership at thirty-eight years, but most of the activists were between the ages of fifteen and twenty-five. In a sense, youth organization functioned as age groups: one did not join by choice—one was considered a member by virtue of age. Compulsory recruitment to age regiments was not a novel feature in BaPedi society. Delius and Mönnig have described how youth progressed from the status of *basemane* (boys) to *masoboro* (adolescent, uninitiated youth) and, after initiation, to adulthood. Initiation (*koma*) was held in the individual chiefdoms approximately every five years, and it was compulsory for all youth of the appropriate age—from early teens to mid-twenties—to attend.[100]

Initiation groups were formed into age regiments led by a son of the local chief. The process was designed to cement the loyalty of the members to the chieftainship and to reinforce bonds of solidarity and mutual cooperation between age mates. Masoboro ran their own courts to administer justice within the group. Group leaders emerged from switch-fighting competitions. Some of these features are clearly visible in the rural youth congresses of the 1980s. In Mapulaneng, another district of Lebowa, leaders of the youth organization were chosen by virtue of their physical prowess.[101] Youth organization exhibited the combination of unruliness and rough internal discipline typical for the masoboro. But insubordination went far beyond what was deemed acceptable in terms of custom. Not only did youth set the law for themselves, but they also aspired to set the law for the adult world. Youth groups administered rough justice to age mates and also passed judgment in adult matters such as domestic disputes between husband and wife, in matters that were the domain of the head of the family or, in more serious cases, the chief and his council.

Tribal ritual no longer served to integrate youth into BaPedi society. High school students identified "tribal custom" as a source of oppression. Boys objected to their forced recruitment to the circumcision school, which was seen as a means to subjugate them to the rule of the chief.[102] Stories of young men being drafted into initiation rituals against their will came from many parts of the Northern Transvaal, from Sekhukhuneland as well as from Venda.[103]

By opposing initiation and substituting in its place forced recruitment to the new rituals of liberation songs and toyi-toyi, the youth movement posed a fundamental challenge to authority and to the prevailing moral order. Political meetings were held on hills outside the village, traditionally the site of initiation school.

Thus the world of rural youth activists remained isolated both from the older generations in rural areas and from the UDF strategists in Johannesburg. SEYO publicity secretary Dewet Monakedi pondered a long time over the question of which UDF campaigns were taken up by his organization. He then came up with this answer: "We participated in the campaign to make the country ungovernable and to set up alternative structures. SEYO participated actively in the ungovernability campaign in Sekhukhune, but it was only the youth, not the parents."[104]

Parents was a key word in many interviews with young activists. While the textbooks prescribed a working-class leadership and student-worker alliances, in the mind of youth activists generation was a more important category than class. In theory, workers and peasants were allies in the struggle. In practice, as the youth revolt deepened into a general crisis of authority, workers and peasants were more frequently seen in their role as parents, belonging to the older generation that stood in the way of a new order.

Peasants in the local context meant mostly women. But women were seen as *mothers* rather than as potential allies in the struggle. Moreover, woman's position in rural society was even more subordinate than in town. In terms of both South African and customary law, African women were considered legal minors. It was, for example, highly unusual for women to serve on school committees.

Workers were mostly migrant workers. Unlike the townships, rural villages had no sympathetic intelligentsia to provide political direction. In the rural context, teachers and nurses were seen as the intelligentsia. But teachers and nurses were in the pay of the state, in this case of the Bantustan government. Teachers, moreover, faced a difficult job in the unpropitious environment of overcrowded rural classrooms. Lacking proper didactic material and training, they practiced a system of rote learning and maintained order with the *sjambok* (leather whip). Among the youth, teachers and nurses were reputed to be generally conservative and "highly reliable pillars of support for the regime."[105]

NOTPECO: "Workers" Are Parents

The Northern Transvaal was one of the few regions in South Africa where the UDF made a conscious attempt to organize migrant workers, drawing on the model of the migrant organization Sebatakgomo.[106] The Northern Transvaal People's Congress (NOTPECO) was formed as a UDF affiliate in August 1986 at a secret meeting in order "to further awaken rural people from political slumber," as the ANC-leaning weekly *New Nation* reported with a touch of urban arrogance.[107] NOTPECO aimed to set up a two-sided structure with an urban and a rural counterpart in order to address its twofold objectives: "to take up the demands of the communities from which we come and those of our members wherever they are; in hostels, compounds, maids' quarters, township etc."[108] On the urban front, NOTPECO was to form action committees, to be constituted by members coming from the same villages. These committees would then establish liaisons with village committees or civics in the home villages in the Northern Transvaal. This organizational setup was a direct copy of the structure of Sebatakgomo, which also combined hostel-based organization and village networks. Following the example of Sebatakgomo, NOTPECO organizers intended to use burial societies as building blocks for their organization. "Burial societies have been important, because people from the same village who are working in the cities often form burial societies together. We go to the burial society's meetings, and talk to all the villagers there. Then we go home to their villages, speak to the people there, and get them to join NOTPECO."[109] NOTPECO committed itself to fight "the violent and vicious system of apartheid and its Bantustan structures"—the migratory labor system, influx control measures, and hostel and compound systems—and to "replace them with the right to work and reside wherever we wish."[110]

Like Sebatakgomo in the 1950s, NOTPECO drew its membership mainly from Sekhukhuneland and the neighboring district of Nebo, with a sprinkling of members from Venda. It also established a foothold in the Lebowa district of Moutse: the Moutse civic belonged to NOTPECO. Its main urban stronghold was Tembisa, while it also had some presence around Pretoria, notably in Atteridgeville and Vlakfontein.[111]

From its beginning, NOTPECO had a strained relationship with the UDF. This was due partly to different perceptions of NOTPECO's role and partly to the controversial figure of its organizer and acting chair, Wilfried Monama. For the UDF leadership in the Northern Transvaal, NOTPECO's primary task was to provide a link between migrant workers in the hostels and community organizations in the townships. They were drawing the lessons from the 1976 Soweto uprising, when migrant workers in Soweto and elsewhere—allegedly incited by the police—had attacked protesting students. An organization of migrant workers was needed to get migrants involved in community issues in the townships; otherwise they would remain a reservoir of alienated men from which the police could recruit vigilantes to fight youth and civic activists. In the view of the UDF Northern Transvaal, NOTPECO's task was to form hostel committees to link up with civics.[112]

But in the eyes of the NOTPECO leadership, the migrants' organization was formed primarily to address issues back home, in the rural areas. "We formed NOTPECO committees in the villages, and also in hostels, like in Tembisa, and Dube and Denver hostel. The purpose of these committees was to organize the people in the hostels, so that they could address the problems in their home villages, like the problem with chiefs who demand a levy from migrant workers when they return home."[113] Combating Bantustans and involvement in home politics brought the NOTPECO leadership in open conflict with the chiefs, who were branded as being among "the worst oppressors and exploiters of the people."[114] The chieftaincy was obviously considered as an institution beyond reform. NOTPECO's organizers were not campaigning to make chiefs accountable to the villagers; they wanted to abolish chiefly rule:

> The administration of the villages must be run by the village committees. We are strongly against the chief and his royal council running the whole affairs of the village. The people benefit nothing out of this. The community must be actively involved in the way the village is run. The community will take over the chief's office to administer the village. A constitution will be drawn up by the whole community. This will be used as a guideline to run the village. The chief will be stripped of his powers over the community. So it won't be like in the past where the chief runs the village, and where people run bringing presents to the chiefs.[115]

Calls for the dismantling of tribal structures and the installation of elected village councils were certainly not inconsistent with mainstream UDF thinking in 1986.[116] However, UDF leaders contended that Monama hijacked NOTPECO in order to build the organization into his own fiefdom. They felt he then used this power base to wage his battles against chiefs and to interfere in faction fights involving competing claims to the chieftaincy, particularly in the festering dispute between the two half-brothers who contested the paramountcy of Sekhukhuneland. From Monama's point of view, this was not a diversion from NOTPECO's objectives; on the contrary, involvement in "home matters" was NOTPECO's very raison d'être.

Monama, in turn, replied that the UDF neglected the migrants. He complained that the UDF failed to send speakers to NOTPECO's meetings. It did not provide any funding nor assist with raising funds from other sources. NOTPECO did not raise membership fees, but it did manage to get some money from the South African Council of Churches, which it used to run an office in Johannesburg.

Wilfried Monama had a background in the ANC and Sebatakgomo as well as in township politics in Alexandra and Soweto. In the conflict with the UDF about the "correct line" of action, he therefore could invoke his own experience with the struggle and the rural-urban nexus. In spite of this background in national and township politics, Monama could not see it as NOTPECO's task to form a liaison with civics. Instead, NOTPECO's calling was to "fight against oppression at home," which involved fighting the Lebowa government and abuses by chiefs.[117] This view was shared by the NOTPECO secretary, Jepson Nkadimeng, who was otherwise highly critical of Monama's high-handed leadership. Nkadimeng, a Pedi migrant who was also an active trade unionist in Johannesburg, agreed that NOTPECO had no role to play in township politics. In his eyes, there was a division of labor: unions organize in factories, civics in the communities, and NOTPECO in the hostels. "Our work was organizing the people in the hostels, to tell them not just to give money to the chief whenever he asked for it, and to tell the people that they had a right to hold meetings. NOTPECO also called meetings in the villages, but organizing in the hostels was easier. There people are free from chiefly control, so there is no fear."[118]

The UDF leadership complained that Monama refused to be accountable to the UDF, that he tried to raise funds independently, that he called mass meetings without consultation: in short, that he tried to turn NOTPECO into an independent power base. Moreover, the UDF looked with suspicion at NOTPECO because its organizational setup in the towns was based on village networks: "It had some tribal connotations, it was organizing along tribal lines."[119] Organizations based on ethnic appeal did not fit in with UDF thinking. This taboo on ethnicity might in part be responsible for the UDF's failure to appeal to migrant workers, for whom ethnic networks provide a sense of identity and security in a hostile urban environment. Few organizations catered to specific migrant concerns. Trade unions organizing among migrant workers focused on pay and conditions in town, not on rural concerns. For the unions, "community involvement" meant involvement in the townships.

On the basis of the limited information available, it is difficult to judge NOTPECO's impact. None of the people interviewed could give any indication of its membership or support base. At one point, Nkadimeng, after long hesitation, mentioned a membership of "more than 10.000," but that seems highly exaggerated. The organization seems to have been effective in only a handful of villages. In Apel, there was no NOTPECO presence. NOTPECO's most active period was from 1986 to 1988. In 1989, Monama intended to run a campaign against chiefly rule, for which the questionnaires were already printed. But by then, attempts were underway to recruit chiefs into CON-TRALESA, an organization sympathetic to the UDF and the ANC. Although Monama had initially opposed the formation of CONTRALESA, he subsequently yielded to pressure from the UDF and abandoned the campaign.

The UDF attempted to get NOTPECO more into line by suspending Monama as acting chair and calling for new elections, while offering him a job as UDF organizer.[120] Although the constitution called for annual elections, the same leadership had stayed in place from 1986 to 1990. Monama, however, refused to call new elections and accused the UDF of meddling in NOTPECO's affairs. After the unbanning of the ANC, NOTPECO faded away, for no more activities were undertaken. NOTPECO could have become a useful vehicle to articulate migrant concerns, but it never realized its potential due to internal feuds and to a strained relationship with the UDF leadership, which on the whole remained quite remote from the world of hostels and migrants.

Some of the problems surrounding NOTPECO are reminiscent of Sebatakgomo's experience in the 1950s. At the time, some criticism was voiced of Sebatakgomo for being a tribally based organization. There was also the problem of loyalties divided between the imperatives of "the struggle," as interpreted by the political elite in the liberation movement, and migrants' primary loyalties to their home areas, which necessarily involved ethnic networks.[121] NOTPECO's significance in the 1980s was only marginal compared to the central role of Sebatakgomo in the 1950s. It is therefore difficult to draw parallels, but the central contradiction remained unresolved.

Monama and Nkadimeng gave conflicting views on NOTPECO's relationship with the youth movement. Monama saw it as part of his calling to bridge the generation gap in rural areas. Therefore, he said, youth were invited to attend meetings, although older people found this difficult to accept because it went against tradition. Nkadimeng stated that there were no joint meetings with the youth congresses. Possibly, such meetings centered around Monama rather than around NOTPECO. Among the UDF grievances is the complaint that Monama tried to recruit youth into his organization, thus trespassing on the recruiting grounds of another UDF affiliate, SEYO.[122]

From interviews with youth activists, it appears that there were some sporadic contacts. Significantly, both sides saw their relationship in terms of overcoming problems between youth and parents, not in terms of a potential student-worker alliance. SEYO publicity secretary Dewet Monakedi recalled having a meeting with Monama in 1986 "to discuss problems like parents who would not allow their children to attend meetings; parents not playing their role in the struggle. We tried to convince NOTPECO that they, the parents, should also play their part in the struggle."[123]

Other SEYO activists were completely unaware of these contacts. A group of SEYO core activists from Apel stated categorically that NOTPECO "never worked as it was meant to work, because of the leadership problem. These people also had no link with other progressive structures, they were just acting on their own."[124] The youth leadership looked upon migrants as adversaries rather than allies. "Migrant workers generally are conservative and traditionalist in outlook. They have little education and they feel inferior, coming from a Bantustan. They are hostile to people with education. They tend to be very sensitive towards things emphasizing their backwardness, they are very defensive. They don't want to lose authority."[125]

The Sekhukhune Parents' Crisis Committee: "Parents" Are Businessmen

If NOTPECO did not offer much prospect for linking the youth movement to a broader alliance, neither did the Sekhukhune Parents' Crisis Committee (SPCC). In name it resembled the Soweto Parents' Crisis Committee, which was formed by Soweto community leaders in 1985 to reestablish communication with the high school students, to find ways of addressing their major grievances, and to get them back to school. But the Sekhukhune version of SPCC was a different type of organization, formed by business owners who organized themselves against youth looting their shops, hijacking their vehicles, and extorting money. Businessmen in the Lebowa context meant mainly shopkeepers, taxi owners, and owners of the most lucrative business of all, beer halls and bottle stores. Small traders in rural areas found themselves in a vulnerable position. Obtaining a business license involved entrance into a local patronage network, usually a chief's council.[126] Sekhukhune business owners formed SPCC to protect their interests against unruly youth. As one youth activist later related: "During funerals, youth would go and get food from the shops and hijack buses and trucks. And then after being used, the vehicles were burnt. Youth, when needing transport, did not ask for a lift, just ordered the driver out and took over."[127]

SPCC secretary Morwamoche Makotanyane described similar experiences when explaining the origins of his organization: "The sole purpose of the SPCC was: to prevent violent activity of youth from penetrating into the business community."[128] The SPCC was formed in 1985 at the initiative of the Sekhukhune Chamber of Commerce after consultations among businessmen on the proper modes of defensive action. Some favored a violent response to ransacking youth, whereas others pleaded for consultation with youth leaders. "The problem with the youth was that they were very secretive; you would never know the names of the leaders."[129]

Peter Nchabeleng was invited to address a group of around fifty businesspeople and to explain the policies and activities of the UDF. He called for patience with the youth and consultations about their problems. Now that the majority position was in favor of pacification rather than confrontation, SPCC was formally established by the Sekhukhune Chamber of Commerce at a meeting in Magnet Heights. In effect, SPCC emerged as an alternative to right-wing vigilantism, not as an offshoot of the liberation struggle. About

150 businessmen attended the meeting to form SPCC and elected M. W. Makgaleng, a businessman in Apel, as SPCC's chair. The secretary was M. Makotanyane, a businessman from Mohlaletse, who was heavily involved in the dispute between the two half-brothers who contested the right to the Pedi throne.

SPCC then called a mass meeting for students and parents, "to ask the children what was their problem." The meeting was conducted in a highly charged atmosphere and was taken over by youth who demanded that policemen and members of the Lebowa parliament leave the venue so that the meeting could proceed. The police left. The Lebowa MPs had to sign a statement indicating that if they wanted to stay in the meeting, they would resign their seats. Two signed, but only one actually resigned subsequently. At this meeting a modus vivendi was worked out: the youth would no longer go around to collect money and food and would not go inside the shops; in turn, the business community agreed to provide a fund for bail for political activists.[130] Youth also pressured shopkeepers to refuse to sell any goods to policemen, for the campaign to isolate the police had spread from the townships to the rural areas.

On a few occasions, SPCC did venture beyond the concerns of businesspeople and into the role of an organization of concerned parents. An SPCC delegation attended a meeting in Durban in March 1986, called by the National Education Crisis Committee to discuss the crisis in the schools. There were occasional contacts with the UDF leadership, although SPCC was not a UDF affiliate. "At some point, the idea of forming a civic was discussed in SPCC, but it never materialized. Many people would rather rely on the army and police. People saw the comrades as their enemies. . . . Political activity became discredited."[131]

SPCC was not a bridge to reestablish contact across the generational divide. Youth leadership maintained at best an opportunistic relationship with businessmen who offered certain resources such as money and food—particularly for funerals—or the occasional use of their vehicles in exchange for protection. The deal seems to have worked fairly well for a while: lootings and burnings of shops diminished, as the youth leadership tried to impose some discipline on its unruly following. Plundering businesses was not a generally condoned practice. "Some comrades abused the names of the comrades and hijacked a van to take them to a funeral. Others hijacked a lorry with sweet potatoes at Jane Furse and took 2000 Rand from the driver. But other comrades brought the lorry back to the owner, an Afrikaner farmer, and they said that the thieves had abused the name of the comrades. Also, some time, comrades demanded liquor from the bottle store and went to another village to sell the stuff. But the comrades intervened and beat them up severely and brought the liquor back."[132]

But when the army moved into Sekhukhuneland after the outbreak of full-scale revolt, everybody who was remotely involved in anything resembling opposition politics became a suspect, including the SPCC leadership. In Apel, Makgaleng had to resign his position on the chief's council, and Makotanyane spent some weeks in detention. Attendance at meetings diminished, and SPCC ceased to exist in the latter half of 1986.

Limitations to Alliance Politics

The history of the UDF in Sekhukhuneland, and in the Northern Transvaal more generally, clearly illustrates the limitations to alliance politics. COSAS and AZASO strategy prescribed involvement of students in community affairs and close cooperation with community organizations. In the villages of Sekhukhuneland this strategy foundered due to insurmountable problems. There were no sympathetic organizations with which to link up. As the youth revolt deepened into an uprising against all authority, the older generation became even more alienated from political activism.

Following the example of the townships, the youth movement did make some attempts at community-oriented activities, but without success. The Youth Committee in Apel took up a bus campaign, demanding better transportation to Pietersburg. "It was difficult, very difficult to organize and to explain to people. People are afraid of organizing. We mobilized by having marches and chanting songs. People were frightened when they saw a march of chanting youth."[133]

This activity soon provoked the wrath of Chief Phasha of GaNkoane, and he pressured the parents to keep their children away from the youth movement. As the youth became convinced that the chief was intent on destroying their organization, "fighting chiefs" became one of the main objectives. "Our chiefs are part of the Pretoria government, they feared that we wanted to take over."[134] Several skirmishes ensued between youth and the chief's men, both in GaNkoane and in Apel. "In the evenings, we would sit on a big stone and sing freedom songs. A house owner nearby then went to complain to the chief, saying that the youth was singing songs insulting to the chief. One day, the chief came with his men, while we were singing, to attack us but we managed to turn this attack." Then the chief's men went to the home of one of the activists, where they broke the windows and the doors. The youth leaders were now furnished with a clear-cut issue. "We decided that we should organize our movement around local issues: we would resist the dictatorship of the chief."[135]

Chiefs became lumped together with other "enemy forces" in the campaigns against community councillors, Bantustans, police, and Members of

Parliament. In fact, many chiefs were MPs; sixty out of the one hundred members of the Lebowa Legislative Assembly were chiefs who were designated (not elected) members. In its most sophisticated form, the call on chiefs to resign meant that chiefs were not asked to abandon their positions as leaders of their tribes, but that they had to stop their "collaboration with the Lebowa government."[136] However, that is not how the call was generally understood: calls to make chiefs "accountable to the people," emphasizing the principle that *kgosi ke kgosi ka batho* (a chief is a chief by the people), gradually evolved toward demands to do away with chiefs altogether. "We intend removing the tribal chiefs as soon as possible. We have called on them to resign," youth leader Peter Mokaba of the UDF Northern Transvaal executive was quoted as saying in a newspaper interview. "Our ultimate intention is to allow the people to govern themselves. We have already established people's courts in some areas and are in the process of forming our own militia which will carry out the orders of the courts."[137] This amounted to a direct attack on the foundations of chiefly power. Faced with death threats and attacks on their businesses, several Members of Parliament from Sekhukhuneland resigned their seats. In the village of Driekop, Chief Marogo and three of his headmen were hacked to death.[138] The youth revolt reached its apotheosis in 1986, between March—when high school students staged their aborted march on the Lebowa capital—and May.

Confusion: The Breakdown of a Moral Order

In recounting this episode of youth power, young activists displayed ambivalent feelings. On the one hand, they had clearly enjoyed a sense of power and of pride in going it alone as vanguard forces of liberation, while the older generation was paralyzed by apathy and helplessness. As one activist said later, "The parents had lost confidence, but now the youth got many things done."[139] On the other hand, these activists felt a profound sense of insecurity and disorientation. The youth movement lacked sophisticated leadership and had no clear sense of direction. *Confusion* was the key word, popping up time and again in many conversations with young and old alike in Sekhukhuneland. The various "confusions" in the world of BaPedi youth are vividly described in a poem composed by a young activist in 1986:

From Confusion to Lusaka

There is a confusion between the father and the mother; there is a confusion
There is a confusion between the parents and the daughters; there is a confusion
There is a confusion between the parents and the sons; there is a confusion

There is a confusion between the tribal authority and the community; there is a
  confusion
There is a confusion between the principal and the teachers; there is a confusion
There is a confusion between the teachers and the students; there is a confusion
There is a confusion among the students; there is a confusion

There is a confusion between the employer and the employee; there is a confusion
There is a confusion between the poor and the rich; there is a confusion

But who is in Lusaka?
I have been in Lusaka, and I found the Zambians. And I know Kenneth Kaunda
  is their president but who is in Lusaka?
Is Lusaka the capital city of Zambia or Zambia the capital of Lusaka?
Is Kenneth Kaunda in Lusaka?
Yes I was never been in Lusaka.
Who is in Lusaka?

Many people have been in Lusaka!
Political leaders have been in Lusaka!
Student leaders have been in Lusaka!
Church leaders have been in Lusaka!
Infiltrators have been in Lusaka!
Hit squads have been in Lusaka!
Bantustan leaders want to go to Lusaka!
Ramodike[140] wants to go to Lusaka!
Even the people's enemy Mangosuthu Gatsha Buthelezi wants to go to Lusaka!
But who is there; who is in Lusaka?

Is Chris Hani[141] in Lusaka?
Is Umkhonto we Sizwe, the spear of the nation, Lerumo la Setshaba[142] in
  Lusaka?
Is it black, green and gold who is in Lusaka?
My poem will never be complete until I include my president Comrade
  O. R. Tambo
O for Organise
R for Regiments
and T for take over
Who is in Lusaka?
The African National Congress is everywhere.

Extracts from a poem by Mokibe Sydney Ramushu, Apel, 1986

How did young activists view the objectives of their movement? A common answer offered by interviewees was "fighting chiefs." Another answer frequently given pointed toward a more fundamental goal: "making revolution."

"Making revolution" implies a vision of a new social order. In the eyes of young activists, the old order was rapidly disintegrating. Moreover, the ANC and the UDF had called upon the youth to hasten the hour of death of the old order by making the country ungovernable. In early 1986, UDF pamphlets with the slogan "from governability to ungovernability" were circulating in Sekhukhuneland. But making revolution was a goal that clearly went beyond breaking down the already crumbling order. Amid the images of disruption and destruction, building a new society became the ultimate mission of the youth. Not only did they perceive themselves as the vanguard of the liberation struggle, implementing the call to make South Africa ungovernable, but they were also purging society of the forces of evil in order to construct a new moral community.

This pervasive sense of breakdown of the moral order is well captured in the poem above, composed in 1986 by Mokibe Sydney Ramushu, a high school student in Apel, who interwove verses by Mzwakhe Mbuli with his own stanzas. Mbuli, nicknamed the "People's Poet," was immensely popular among black youth, from Durban to Sekhukhuneland. Sydney Ramushu's poem "From Confusion to Lusaka" caught on among local youth. Years later, several young activists were reciting parts of the poem during meetings or evening strolls.

Confusion between Father and Mother

In their endeavors "to re-establish harmony and to effect reconciliation," youth activists took it upon themselves to solve domestic disputes.[143] Long periods of separation as a consequence of migrant labor contributed to a sense of family breakdown. Constructing a new order also required a reconstruction of family relations.

People's courts, in the form of either mass meetings of youth or a disciplinary committee of the youth organization, handled criminal cases such as theft, rape, or robbery and dealt with political matters such as "speaking ill of the organization." "Disciplining" deviant behavior usually meant administering a series of lashes with a sjambok. These youth courts also judged family disputes such as husbands beating wives, husbands who were not supporting their families, and cases of divorce. Divorce was considered a social evil that ought to be rooted out, so people's courts ordered couples to stay together.

Confusion between Parents and Daughters, between Parents and Sons

From the perspective of adults, people's courts usurped the functions of tribal courts and adjudication by elders, thus challenging the authority of parents and chiefs alike. It is unlikely that adults submitted voluntarily to courts run by youth. But faced with a mass of sjambok-wielding youngsters, they had little choice.

The generation gap was further accentuated by the recent upsurge in secondary education, which resulted in "educated youth" having different aspirations from their "uneducated" parents. In the past, rural people thought that "making revolution" was something for the Reef. But now, schools provided youth with a base for organization. Parents generally made considerable financial sacrifices to send their children to school in order to secure a better future, but they also resented the youth taking control. For student activists, the dividing line between educated and noneducated largely coincided with the gap between young and old. "The division in the community here is mostly between the illiterate old guard and the educated people. Most people who have not gone to school think that organization is only for educated people."[144]

The forced recruitment of youth into the youth organization was another major source of conflict. For parents, the sudden recruitment drive was a traumatic experience. "In 1986, the youth invaded our houses to take our children. They said all children must come; they were forced. There was no prior warning for this youth outburst. It took everybody by surprise."[145] Moreover, parents and teachers found it appeared to them as highly secretive and without a clearly defined leadership. The world of the comrades seemed beyond comprehension. "They are shadows in the night. Shadows we have all come to fear," the chief of Apel said to the *Johannesburg Sunday Times*.[146] The gap between youth activists and parents was further widened by a campaign that became known as "building soldiers." One activist described this crusade as follows:

Since the Boers were killing many people, there was a need to make more soldiers. The girls should abandon the preventions. So the youth carried out attacks on clinics, because at the clinics, contraceptives were given to the girls. And girls were forced out of their houses, to join the comrades. And then the girls would only come home the next morning. Most girls got pregnant in 1986. . . . The youth were saying: we need to make more babies to become soldiers, because the Boers were killing us. It caused much strain between youth and parents. The youth would go around the village singing and marching and collect the youth for a meeting. Girls were also forced to come. The parents could not complain or refuse to let their daughter go, because otherwise their house might be burned. At that time, the youth did not have clear direction; they antagonized the parents. . . . But these mistakes were also made because the youth had no one to turn to. There were few people around who could provide direction. The youth thought that the parents failed to solve any problem.[147]

The ideals of serving the community with a millenarian perspective of a better order blended with a reign of terror, which profoundly upset the relationship between parents and children. By early 1986, "there was a deep conflict with the parents. They saw us as terrorists. We could not sleep in our homes. . . . People were blaming us for wanting to be Jesus Christ, wanting to die for the masses."[148]

Confusion between Tribal Authority and Community

Chiefly rule was a major source of grievances among youth and adults alike. Since the chiefs were in the pay of the Bantustan administration, they no longer needed to maintain a significant level of legitimacy in their own village. A particular source of conflict was the control of the tribal authority over the school funds. In numerous instances, high school students wanted to call the chiefs accountable and demanded to inspect the books.

Women and girls were frequently ordered to plough or irrigate the chief's farm. As two female high school students complained: "This is called 'helping the chief's wife,' but of course the wife of the chief is never there. . . . Many weekends we are called to come and work. Sometimes only girls are called, sometimes only mothers are called. We don't get paid, we don't get food. This chief is not even aware of the discontent amongst us, because it is our tradition."[149] In these years of persistent drought, young men and women were regularly called upon to participate in rainmaking rituals and to perform certain duties. "The people in the village believed that the youth should go out in the mountains to catch a cobra. They believed that then the rains would come."[150]

But these old ways of "serving the community" did not fit in the scenario of the youth movement. Parents and chiefs were held responsible for forcing these rituals on rebellious youth. Young men protested against forced recruitment into the initiation school. Female students in particular seemed to find tribal customs repugnant and contrary to their status as "educated women." From their descriptions it is apparent that these rituals had lost all meaning:

> If a girl gets married, she has to run around the village half naked, with only a little transparent skirt. Or she has to run over the mountain, because she is told to chase a goat. . . . Girls are ill-treated and smeared with mud, after they get married. . . . They do funny things with you. . . . We think that the chief is responsible for keeping this tradition. It are the older women who make us do

these things. It is the tribal law. . . . This hurts our dignity. . . . We were not around when homelands and tribal authorities were introduced. We do not want their laws. We want nothing to do with that, and with tribal custom.[151]

Confusion between Principal and Teachers

The principal and the chief together were usually the dominating forces in the school committee that ran the school. Both would resist encroachments on their authority. One such attempt was the campaign by students to replace the old school committees with parent-teacher-student committees. Generally speaking, principals ruled the schools in an authoritarian manner; if teachers offered advice, they were branded as troublemakers. Principals were known to control the union membership of their teachers by employing the "stop order system": the principals deducted union fees from teachers' wages on behalf of the Transvaal United African Teachers Association (Tuata), which was known as a conservative union. Young teachers wanting to join the UDF-leaning National Educational Union of South Africa (NEUSA) could expect to run into trouble.[152]

The principal had to present the community with an annual financial state-ment on the school fund. Because of the high level of illiteracy in rural villages, principals wielded a great deal of power. School committees tended to rubber-stamp what the principals presented to them, as few members had the quali-fications to effectively monitor the principals' activities. If principals called meetings on weekdays when the migrants were away in the towns, it was likely that unacceptably high school-building taxes would be imposed.[153]

Confusion between Teachers and Students

Demoralized teachers in overcrowded and under-equipped schools resorted to rule by the whip. Students were struck with the sjambok for all kinds of shortcomings, such as coming late or not understanding the lessons. Humil-iating punishments, imposed for coming late, included "digging a hole so deep that you can stand in it without being seen" and being sent to the moun-tains to collect "a stone, as big as the size of a donkey's head." Teachers ordered pupils to run errands or perform jobs for them, even during school holidays. Girls had a particular difficulty. "Schools were a big problem. There was sex-ual harassment by teachers. If a student refused to make love with a teacher, then she would be lashed for not being able to answer a question. Or she would fail the test."[154] The abolition of corporal punishment became a central demand of the youth movement, along with the demand for free books and elections for a student representative council.

For the teachers, the outburst of revolt came totally unexpectedly: "On a certain day in 1986, after the morning prayer the children refused to come into the classrooms. They sat on the ground and threw stones on the roof. All the teachers ran for cover. Students then had no representatives, we did not know whom to talk to," related a high school principal. Subsequently, at this school in the village of Mankopane, an improvised SRC was elected to improve communication between teachers, the school committee, and the students. "But that made the parents very angry with the teachers. They did not want to discuss problems with children. Children should respect authority. Parents were also angry with teachers, for not enforcing discipline in schools. At that time, there was chaos, they were burning cars all over the place."[155]

A high failure rate in matric led to a buildup of frustrated students in this final year, with students often sitting repeatedly for the final exam before they either passed or dropped out. By that time, they were frequently in their mid-twenties. Among older high school students in particular, a sense of great frustration had been building up. Parents and teachers were not receptive to grievances. There was no one to turn to—at least until the youth organization came along. "It was only through SEYO that you could make your voice heard. . . . But now SEYO was powerful. People became motivated again, because SEYO could change things. The relationship with the teachers improved. In SEYO, awareness was the main thing. SEYO is a project within the ANC."[156]

Confusion among Students

However, confusion also reigned among the students. This was a multifaceted confusion; it involved differences between the politically motivated vanguard and those followers who were inclined to drift off into criminal activity. It also involved gender aspects.

At times, the dividing line between political activism and criminal activity became blurred, as shops were raided, cars hijacked, and money extorted in the name of the "struggle." Since all youth were considered members of the youth movement, it could be difficult for the politically motivated comrades to disassociate themselves from the thugs. In cases where the core leadership got hold of criminal elements, the scoundrels were often severely beaten up, and they in turn would try to take revenge.

Youth political activism involved mainly boys and young men. In the initial phase, a few girls and young women attended the meetings, but they found that the males were not inclined to take their contributions seriously. Issues of particular interest to women, including the unequal division of work between men and women, were not discussed at youth meetings. "The men do not help when it comes to fetching water, cooking, and sweeping." In this decade of drought, fetching water for the household had become an onerous burden, as it involved long walks and long waits to get a bucket of water.

Being overruled or shouted down by male comrades taught young women the lesson that a better forum in which to address their problems would be a women's organization. In Apel, the first attempts to form a women's group date from 1988, but only in 1990 did it become feasible to openly work toward a women's organization. Even then, a high school student in the neighboring village of GaMankopane who aspired to be a women's organizer found that she had to rely on men from the old ANC guard to call a meeting. She was somewhat more successful in trying to organize her own age group: "When trying to organize our own age group, I'll tell them that they are oppressed by their parents and their brothers. The oldest-born girl has to stay at home and do all the work, till she is 21, 22 years old. If this is discussed in an age group, then people realize the importance of organizing."

Tribal rituals for newly married wives were seen as degrading for women and were mentioned as another motive for women to set up their own organizational structures. By 1990, these attempts had not progressed much beyond some cautious initiatives by a few female high school students. They had no outside contacts to support their ventures and no links with the UDF-affiliated Federation of Transvaal Women (FEDTRAW), which centered mainly around the urban areas of the Witwatersrand. But traces of a feminist awareness had nevertheless trickled down to Sekhukhuneland. When asked about her motivation to work toward a women's organization, one of the interviewed high school students recited the classical formula of South African women's struggles: "Women are more oppressed than men. Women are oppressed by men, by national oppression and by class oppression." To this classical trio, she added a fourth source of oppression: "tribal custom."[157]

Male youth activists generally were of the opinion that the struggle was largely an affair for men. Females were seen as weak, unreliable, and easily intimidated or bought by policemen, who would seduce them with presents such as cheap jewelry or perfumes. "Some girls were involved in the early days, but not so much now. . . . But then the struggle became tough, we were detained, harassed and beaten. . . . Girls are afraid of the police, that is why they withdrew, they are cowards."[158] Gender aspects hardly figured in the SEYO version of the liberation agenda.

In early 1986, the problems among the students came to be overshadowed by one overriding concern, which is best summed up in the comments of a female high school student in Apel: "During 1985–86 we used to attend the meetings, but we did not know what it was about. Our political education only started in 1987. That time, '86, we got confused by witchcraft. . . . We were very occupied by witchcraft."[159]

Forces of Division: Tribalism, Witchcraft, and Capitalism

Who or what was causing all this confusion? Activists interviewed some years later tended to identify three elements as subverting society and sowing discord. The stumbling blocks on the road to a new harmonious order were *tribalism* (or factionalism), *witchcraft,* and *capitalism.*

Tribalism

Tribalism and factionalism were often used interchangeably: youth leaders believed that "faction fights" had to be overcome in order to reestablish harmony. Factionalism and tribalism were used in two meanings: these terms could refer to ethnic conflict and also to communal conflicts such as land disputes or conflicts involving succession to the chieftaincy.

When UDF leaders in Pietersburg or Turfloop mentioned the need to combat tribalism, they referred to the need to overcome ethnic conflict. For example, the UDF leadership had to deal with conflicts erupting between residents of Lebowa and Gazankulu, two Bantustans that each had chunks of territory around the white towns of Tzaneen and Phalaborwa. In the battle against Bantustans, youth organizations were encouraged by the UDF leadership to organize along nonethnic lines, so that people would not be fighting "the wrong battles."[160]

In Sekhukhuneland, similar motivations inspired the youth when trying to overcome communal conflicts and faction fights. But when they discussed the need to overcome tribalism and factionalism, they were generally not referring to ethnic conflict. They spoke about the long-standing feud between the neighboring villages of Apel and GaNkoane as a tribal conflict, although these were both BaPedi villages. The people of Apel, however, claimed that they were the first arrivals in these lands, and that the settlers in GaNkoane came later but kept encroaching on the land rights of the Apel residents. The villagers of GaNkoane did not dispute that those from Apel were the first arrivals, but they maintained that the original settlers did not establish themselves in the present village of Apel, which invalidated their claim to these land rights. Over the past decades, this dispute over land rights was fought both in court and in actual battles between the villages. In the 1970s, Peter Nchabeleng's father was killed in one such armed invasion from GaNkoane. In local discourse, the term *tribe* refers to a totemic group. The BaPedi were not labeled a tribe but an ethnic group. Petrus Nchabeleng explained: "The BaPedi have numerous tribes, each with his own totem. Like the Nchabeleng totem is a lion. They used to fight each other."[161]

Witchcraft

In the minds of young activists, tribal conflicts were associated with backwardness, with chiefly powers and tribal custom. In this age of modernity, these divisive practices had to be overcome. Youth intervention could at times solve the conflict, but it could equally serve to exacerbate tensions. In Mohlaletse, the village of the paramount chief, youth organization was split into two camps supporting the rival claims of the two half-brothers to the paramountcy. In Apel-GaNkoane, youth leadership made a conscious attempt to overcome this long history of faction fights by forming one youth organization for the twin villages of Apel and GaNkoane. In early 1986, when a conflict broke out in the neighboring village of Strydkraal, the youth of Apel decided to intervene. "The youth saw it as their mission to solve tribal conflicts, for example in Strydkraal and Mohlaletse. In Strydkraal the youth was not conscientized. Apel was more advanced. So we went to solve that problem."[162]

Since the people of Strydkraal fell under the authority of two different chiefs, a conflict had arisen about access to certain lands and the control of a school. Singing freedom songs, youth from Apel-GaNkoane marched to the kraal of Chief Masha in Strydkraal. They were met by the chief's men, who opened fire when the procession of chanting youth approached to "settle the faction fight." One of the bullets killed Solomon Maditsi, who thus became the first casualty of the Sekhukhune youth revolt. Other demonstrators were assaulted by the police and then locked in the same house with the dead boy. In February, the youth from Apel had a meeting with youth from neighboring villages to discuss subsequent action. It was decided to start a school boycott to demand the release of the detained activists. The youth marched to the Sekhukhune College of Education, a teacher-training college in Apel, where the students then joined the boycott. This march, however, ended in a confrontation with the police and with army units, leading to the detention of more youth. These clashes spurred the youth to further action—the formation of defense units, which went out to burn government property. Among the targets were tractors and buildings of agricultural cooperatives.

The funeral of Solomon Maditsi on 8 February 1986 became a milestone in the process of youth mobilization, drawing youth from many villages and infusing them with a sense of militancy and determination. According to some accounts, Chief Masha sent two delegates to the funeral and offered four cattle to apologize for the death of the youth.[163] Shortly after the funeral, a young activist was struck by lightning, which is commonly associated with witchcraft. The youth then took it upon themselves to establish who was responsible for this new attack on their ranks.

A mass meeting was called, to which the parents were also invited. In normal times, accusations of witchcraft directed against the community as a whole were dealt with by the chief's court, where only initiated men could attend the proceedings.[164] This gathering was called by the youth leadership. Chairing the meeting was twenty-year-old Maurice Nchabeleng, Peter Nchabeleng's youngest son. People who had information about the lightning incident were asked to come forward. Two youths recalled that at Solomon Maditsi's funeral they had heard an old woman complaining that the young men these days were behaving disrespectfully. She allegedly threatened to organize lightning to teach the youth a lesson. The accused woman was present at the meeting. According to the chair's later account, the woman admitted having said these words but denied any responsibility for the lightning. Calls were made to burn the woman. Chair Maurice Nchabeleng split the meeting into two groups: parents and youth each assembled in separate meetings to discuss the matter. The parents returned to the full gathering with a resolution to take "severe action." The youth had adopted a resolution that the woman must be burned immediately. It was then argued that there was not sufficient proof of witchcraft, so those in attendance decided that to obtain more certainty a *ngaka* had to be consulted.[165]

A delegation of the youth went out to consult a local ngaka, Ramaredi Shoba. After the proper ceremonies, during which the members of the deputation were given a medicine to drink, they saw the faces of the perpetrators of witchcraft appearing on a screen in the ngaka's hut. The suspected woman was not among the people who were identified as witches. The delegation returned to the meeting with a list of the people who had been found guilty of witchcraft. To obtain further proof, it was decided to ask a second opinion. One youth was sent to KwaNdebele, because the Ndebele *dingaka* had a reputation for being particularly powerful. However, the youth did not manage to find the ngaka he was supposed to consult. On his return to Apel, the young man found that the other youth had already burned the three culprits whose guilt had been established in the first consultation.

Some weeks later, lightning struck again. A delegation made another visit to the same ngaka, and afterward two women were executed. More suspects accused of witchcraft were hunted down. In about a week's time in the first half of April 1986, thirty-two people were burned to death: two in Apel and thirty in GaNkoane. The second spate of killings happened as a spontaneous outburst in a highly charged atmosphere, with the youth no longer bothering to follow traditional procedures. They decided not to waste any more time and money on consulting dingaka, reasoning that these people were just making profits, and that, anyway, "we all know who are the witches here."[166]

There is no long-standing history of witch burning in the Northern Transvaal, although ten years earlier two people had been burned to death in the same village, GaNkoane, which had a reputation for having "problems with witchcraft." Traditionally, those convicted of witchcraft were expelled or executed by other means such as hanging, stoning, or impaling. But the phenomenon of burning witches had been spreading throughout the Northern Transvaal since the early 1980s, although other means of execution also continued to be used. In 1984, the liaison officer of the Lebowa police said that the killing of witches had become a "national problem." In the past, there were two or three executions in each rainy season—when lightning strikes—but recently the numbers had increased. Previously, he explained, people accused of witchcraft were usually driven out of the village rather than being killed, but in the past ten years there had been a tendency to execute them.[167] The spate of witch killings in the first half of the 1980s is popularly attributed to the long period of drought. In the local belief system, an explanation was required for the misfortunes that befell the community: the crisis caused by the persistent drought was frequently attributed to evil machinations by witches.

In the initial rounds of witch killings in the early 1980s, the procedure usually involved identification of the guilty party by a ngaka and an authorization from the chief. Many mass trials were reported in 1983–84. One trial involved a chieftainess, or female chief, who was a sister of the Lebowa homeland leader Cedric Pathudi and 227 of her subjects from the village of GaChuene near Lebowakgomo. They were charged with the stoning to death of a woman who had been found guilty of striking a house with lightning in December 1983.[168]

But from the mid-1980s, several innovations were introduced as the youth usurped the powers of village hierarchies. The practice of burning social enemies had spread from the countryside to the townships, now taking the gruesome form of the necklacing of *impimpis* (suspected informers and other collaborators). Several of the alleged witches in Apel and GaNkoane were also subjected to a necklace execution; thus an urban innovation had come to Sekhukhuneland. Judging from the rather sensational press reports at the time, there seems to have been a mixed reaction among the villagers. Many were terrified at the sight of chanting youth carrying tires and rounding up witches to be necklaced on a stony mountain slope, but some voiced approval at the elimination of the forces of evil.

Family members of the victims were worried that those accused of witchcraft were not "smelt out by nyangas."[169] Some expressed total incomprehension, such as the relatives of the old and blind Mrs. Ramatsimela Sekonya: "Her death is something none of us understand—but then there is much happening now which we have yet to learn and understand. Now there is a great fear upon this place. At night we lock our doors and never go out into the dark. There is a devil here." The "rule of the comrades" instilled great fear in people who were at a loss to comprehend the collapse of the old order. "We hear these city words spoken by the youths. They talk of 'comrades' and the 'necklace.' We do not understand them, but we fear them deeply."[170] Many of the women interviewed at the time felt that the absence of men in the villages had complicated their problems and given the comrades a free reign. "If only our menfolk were here our mothers and grandmothers would not have been taken away and killed so ruthlessly."[171] However, other villagers were quoted as saying that "it is time that these people who ride on brooms and fly over other people's roofs at night are eradicated."[172]

After the witch burnings, the police and army moved into the village in full force. The youth fled to the mountains, but not without a battle. "By then, the youth had control of the villages. We were ruling ourselves and policing our-selves. The police could not just come in. It took them some days and then the Lebowa police came with support of the South African Police. The youth resisted. They fled into the mountains and wanted to fight the police."[173]

In the previous few months the villages had become no-go areas for the Lebowa police, to the extent that the Nchabeleng household, formerly a focus of close police attention, was harboring an MK fighter who had escaped from police custody. The week of witch burnings effectively ended the "rule of the comrades" in Apel. Armored police and army vehicles invaded the village while helicopters scoured the mountains to flush out the youth in hiding.

When the police came for Peter Nchabeleng's sons, they found only the father. Some villagers believed that Peter Nchabeleng, one of the few adults who was influential with the young activists, was behind the murders. In fact, Peter Nchabeleng had called a meeting with the youth to explain that the UDF was not there to deal with witchcraft; it was a political movement. Youth activists recalled that he was angry with them, impressing on them that the witch-hunts would give the police an excuse to intervene. They believe that without Nchabeleng's intervention, the burnings would have been more wide-spread. However, the Lebowa police suspected Nchabeleng of organizing the youth who were responsible for the murders. His wife, Gertrude Nchabeleng, later recalled the nocturnal visit on 11 April 1986 by the squad of about ten policemen who detained her husband. "They woke him up, saying, 'last time, it was Robben Island, this time we are going to kill you.'"[174]

The next morning police knocked again on the door, this time to tell her that her husband had died of a heart attack. For a while, the family remained uncertain about his whereabouts, until his body was located in a mortuary in Groblersdal. The inquest brought to light that Nchabeleng had died within twelve hours after he was taken to the police station in Schoonoord, the seat of the local magistrate. The postmortem report revealed that he had been severely beaten, causing subcutaneous bleeding that eventually caused unconsciousness during which he suffocated. At the inquest hearing the police officers admitted that their prisoner had appeared very sick, but they had made no effort to call a doctor. The officer in charge of the investigation in which Nchabeleng was arrested told the court, "A policeman may beat a person to death if he resists—but not intentionally."[175]

Several hundred youths were rounded up for questioning and for the beatings that had become part of police routine. Chief Richard Nchabeleng of Apel was also briefly detained and beaten up. Parents were ordered to bring their children to the chief's kraal, or homestead, where subsequently about 150 youth aged fifteen to twenty-one gathered.[176] The youth leadership managed to escape and went into hiding. Several youths hiding with student friends on the Turfloop campus were later arrested when the police raided the student quarters on the eve of the declaration of the State of Emergency in June. Maurice Nchabeleng and Silas Mabotha, chair and vice-chair, respectively, of the Apel branch of SEYO, were arrested on the Turfloop campus. Both were severely beaten and assaulted in the various police stations where they were kept for several months for interrogation.

By August 1986, charges were laid against 103 accused, but this number included youth accused of subsequent witch burnings. Including the thirty-two corpses found in Apel-GaNkoane, the number of victims of the Sekhukhune witch killings totaled forty-three. All of the accused were under thirty, and some were as young as fifteen. All except one were male.[177] Only in the first of the series of trials was evidence heard in court. In this initial case, the defense presented belief in witchcraft as a mitigating factor. In the case of nine of the accused, who pleaded guilty, this was accepted by the court. But two defendants, who denied such a belief and who maintained their innocence despite all the evidence accumulated against them, were sentenced to death. The sentences were later commuted to fifty-year prison sentences.

In subsequent trials the lawyers followed a different strategy. Once the accused had heard what had happened in the initial case, they were willing to confess their involvement in the killings. The lawyers would then attempt to strike a plea bargain with the prosecutor. It was agreed that some of the defendants would plead not guilty to the charges and would consequently be acquitted, while others would plead guilty to murder, provided that certain mitigating factors be recognized. The lawyers tried to get as many as possible of the younger defendants into pleading guilty. In the previous sentences, those under eighteen had received only a few cuts with the *sjambok,* while those over eighteen would be subject to comparatively severe prison sentences. Aware of Maurice Nchabeleng's record of political activism, the lawyer made sure that he and other political activists were not sacrificed in the plea bar-

4. The funeral of Peter Nchabeleng, UDF president in the Northern Transvaal, Apel, 3 May 1986. Photograph courtesy of Steve Hilton-Barber.

gaining. Both Maurice Nchabeleng and Silas Mabotha were acquitted. The court did not perceive the case against them as a political case.[178] Nchabeleng's own version of events is somewhat different. He claimed that the state had bought witnesses for 500 Rand to testify against him with a statement drafted by the police. The witnesses, however, informed the lawyer that they were being bribed, and when the lawyer raised the issue in court, the judge decided not to call these witnesses.

Not surprisingly, accounts of events in this fateful week are inconsistent and sometimes contradictory. The young men who held leadership positions at the time maintain that they, the "politically educated" leadership, had distanced themselves from the witch-hunts, as "the organization is not about these superstitious things." However, they were swamped by a mass of young newcomers, most of whom were around the age of fifteen. Those who had attended initiation school were allegedly the most zealous participants in the witch-hunts. Feelings were running high, and it was argued that anyone interfering to stop the burnings would have been killed also. Possibly this was the case, but this argument may be a rationalization after the event.

Several of the young men interviewed insist that the youth had been encouraged by older people, including Chief Phasha of GaNkoane, to go on

5. UDF poster of Peter Nchabeleng. Offset litho poster in black, red, and yellow produced by Mars for UDF, Johannesburg. Courtesy South African History Archive (SAHA); from *Images of Defiance: South African Resistance Posters of the 1980's/Poster Book Collective, South African History Archive.* Johannesburg: Raven Press, 1991.

with the witch burnings. The chief is said to have promised the youth four cows if they would "finish the job." But in a newspaper interview, chief Phasha was quoted as saying that if the killings did not stop, the parents would be organized to fight the comrades.[179]

There is no clear pattern as to the victims of the witch burnings. Most were elderly women, although several men and a young woman were also singled out. Several newspaper reports at the time interpreted the killings as the liquidation of suspected impimpis. This was definitely not the case. It was alleged that the victims were guilty of subverting the struggle, but they had done so in their capacity as witches, not as informers. Most of the victims were said to be "known witches." In some cases children even accused their parents of witchcraft. The evidence against them was that chimpanzees had been spotted around their houses and that they possessed herbs. Witches (*baloi*) are believed to make use of familiars (*dithuri*), such as monkeys, snakes, and owls. These familiars are used to perform evil errands for the witches. Witches, I was told, are capable of changing humans into chimpanzees. It was also widely believed that witches could transform people into zombies, who were then put to work. Some youths claimed to have found the proof of witchcraft in the houses of the suspects, who allegedly kept hands of little children in hidden places in their houses. This story refers to a widespread belief that the possession of certain human parts will bring good fortune.[180]

Among the victims were several dingaka, whose supernatural powers cause them to be both honored and feared. The ngaka and the witch make use of similar methods, but whereas the witch uses his or her powers for antisocial ends, the ngaka performs a necessary service for the community. This thin dividing line between good and evil magic makes it quite conceivable that a ngaka can turn a beneficial practice into a harmful one.[181] That indeed was the suspicion against the dingaka of Sekhukhuneland. Previously, the comrades had turned to the dingaka for help when the youth were involved in battling the police and the army. They had demanded a medicine that would turn bullets into water or, alternatively, into bees. When the dingaka proved unable or unwilling to provide this service, the comrades retorted that since the dingaka were able to make lightning and to kill people, it was evident that they did possess supernatural powers. It was now established that they used these powers not to support the freedom struggle but to inflict evil. Therefore, these dingaka were judged guilty of witchcraft. It was deemed necessary to root out this evil, which caused discord and division. Since the parents, once again, had forsaken to solve this matter, it fell upon the youth to rid the community of the causes of misfortune.[182]

The week of the witch killings marked both the apotheosis and the demise of the youth movement. In retrospect, youth leader Moss Mabotha believed that this was "a fateful event that caused the eventual crushing of the youth movement in Sekhukhune."[183] By this time the gap between the youth and the older generations had widened beyond repair. Youth rebellion had escalated into a revolt against all type of authority—against parents, teachers, chiefs, and dingaka alike. In the spate of witch killings in the first half of the 1980s, the procedure involved identification of the guilty party by a ngaka and usually an authorization from the chief. It was unheard of for youth to go and consult a ngaka; only adults could do that. By simply skipping the whole procedure for the later victims, the youth indicated that they were no longer interested in obtaining legitimacy for their actions from the established authorities. Having reached that peak of rebellion, the youth uprising was crushed in the inevitable crackdown by the security forces. On the mental map of young and old alike, the witch burnings mark a turning point. In numerous accounts of the Sekhukhune revolt given to me, events were told in relation to this fateful week: "this happened before the burnings," or "that took place after the burnings." The witch burnings, or more generally "Eighty-Six," is the landmark in people's memories. "After the witch burnings the people could no longer trust the youth. The youth went around hijacking and looting delivery vans. The older people could not understand what happened. They hated the slogans used by the youth since they sounded revolutionary."[184]

Although witch-hunts spread throughout the Northern Transvaal in the second half of the 1980s, there is only one other recorded incident that matches the scale of the witch burnings in Apel-GaNkoane. During April and May 1986, some 150 people in the Lebowa district of Mapulaneng were labeled witches and attacked. Thirty to forty people were killed by various means, including necklacing. Although Mapulaneng was equally part of Lebowa, it did not figure on the "mental map" of the BaPedi in Sekhukhuneland, from which it is separated by a mountain range. Most of the people I interviewed in Sekhukhuneland were not aware of the witch burnings in Mapulaneng, although a few had read newspaper reports. The antiwitchcraft movements in Mapulaneng are discussed by three authors who present rather different versions of events and different interpretations of the motives behind the witch-hunts.[185]

In spite of some dissimilarities, there is a common pattern in the accounts of the antiwitchcraft movements in Mapulaneng and Sekhukhuneland. In both cases, the necklace method of execution was used, and the established authorities—the ngaka, the headman, and the chief—were left out of the process. The older generation had lost control over the youth. Youth rebelled against a society in which they felt increasingly marginalized. Youth organization, for which student organizations and the UDF had provided the models and the legitimation, gave them a new place in society and a sense of power. The strongest manifestations of youth power were the witch-hunts. But power was not perceived as an end in itself: the community had to be purged of evil forces in order to achieve social harmony. As in Sekhukhuneland, the disintegration of society was blamed on witchcraft. "If it was not for witches we would be in Utopia. Everyone would know their place in the world and would

act appropriately. There would be perfect harmony. Witches are to black culture what the snake was to Eve."[186] Harmonious social relations could be
established, not by restoring the old hierarchical order, but by building a new
egalitarian society.

Criticisms from adults were mostly not of witch-hunts per se but of improper procedures used to identify witches and of exceptionally violent
methods of punishment. Because of this usurpation of the powers of tribal
hierarchies by youth movements, the witch-hunts in Sekhukhuneland and
Mapulaneng in 1986 mark a watershed. As previously mentioned, witch-
hunts were not a new phenomenon in the Northern Transvaal. But there is
both a qualitative and a quantitative difference between the series of witch
killings in the early 1980s and the witch-hunts that bedeviled UDF politics
in the Northern Transvaal beginning in 1985. Publications attempting to
explain the earlier spate of killings emphasize that accusations of witchcraft are
likely to emerge in times of rapid social transformation with increasing competition for scarce resources. Academics and activists alike pointed to the
power holders of the old order as those who used accusations of witchcraft to
bolster their position.[187]

That may have been the case, but beginning about 1985 the tables were
turned. Now the forces of change had taken it upon themselves to sniff out
the witches. The antiwitchcraft movements in Sekhukhuneland and Mapulaneng can thus underpin the thesis that witchcraft is not just an archaic phenomenon used to prop up the status quo in traditionalist societies. The idiom
of witchcraft can also be transformed into a reaction from below to challenge
the status quo and to provide a legitimation for modernizing strategies.[188]

The "new South Africa" inaugurated in 1990 did not mean an end to witch-
hunts. In the first half of 1994, more than seventy witch killings were reported
from the Northern Transvaal. Although youth activists were mostly in the
forefront of the witch-hunts, press reports also mention the involvement of
chiefs and dingaka in some of these proceedings.[189] Antiwitchcraft movements
were by no means limited to the Northern Transvaal, although this region had
a reputation of witch-hunts. In the historiography of the struggles of the
1980s, scant attention is paid to this phenomenon of witch-hunts, which
became more and more widespread in the second half of the 1980s and the
early 1990s.[190]

Far from being an exclusively rural phenomenon, witch-hunts also occur in
urban conditions, although they are not always labeled as such. In early 1986,
the youth organization of Mamelodi (MAYO), one of the Pretoria townships,
called upon the local youth to stop witch-hunting and burning suspected
witches. A crowd of several hundred people had set alight a local traditional
healer, who was suspected of having abducted a twelve-year-old child for

witchcraft purposes. Two elderly women had a narrow escape from a mob wanting to burn them for witchcraft. MAYO warned that witch-hunts did not enhance the freedom struggle. "These acts divide us from our parents, whose support we need to achieve our goals."[191]

What happened in Apel-GaNkoane in the aftermath of the witch burnings? Several months after this fateful week, some of the youth leadership trickled back to the village. They found their organization in shambles. Most fellow activists had either been detained or had gone into hiding. Schools in Sekhukhuneland began reopening in August 1986, but under strict army control. Many people were afraid even to talk to the youth leaders. The initial reaction of the villagers to the witch-hunts was the formation of vigilante groups, in which nearly all adult men participated for some time. Silas Mabotha, one of the local youth leaders, found his house surrounded by hundreds of men, who took him to the chief's kraal. There he was sentenced to fifteen lashes. However, after this punishment he did not experience any more harassment from the vigilantes. In Apel-GaNkoane, the vigilantes were a short-lived phenomenon.[192]

For a while youth activists felt isolated, pondering what had gone wrong. Toward the end of 1986, when the police and army presence became somewhat less pervasive, they decided to reorganize in underground structures. The model was Nelson Mandela's M-plan, devised in the 1950s to prepare for an underground organization based on small cells after the anticipated banning of the ANC as a legal, above-ground movement. One of the lessons drawn in this reassessment was the importance of strong grassroots structures, rather than relying on a handful of leaders and an unstructured mass following. Another lesson was the importance of political schooling, "to educate the members in politics and clear them up about witchcraft, because this thing had diverted our struggle from the real enemy."[193] The ANC had indeed called on youth to make the country ungovernable, but this call had been misinterpreted. The ANC wanted youth to burn government offices, not witches.

Not all activists were convinced that their organization had gone awry when they embarked on witch-hunts. Looking back, some still believed that "we have to clean our own house first, before we can attack the enemy."[194] They felt unjustly criminalized, for they believed they really had no choice. Not only was it necessary to eliminate evil, as bewitchment could undermine the struggle, but the witch-hunts were also meant as a positive service to the community. Killing the witches was a lesson learned from the parents, who on previous occasions had acted similarly against the forces of evil. True, in the past this had been done with the services of *dingaka* and a mandate from the tribal authority, but this option was no longer available. The opinions of the youth fell on deaf ears. They had no other choice but to take matters into their own hands—how could that be a criminal offense?

Many activists were vindicated in this belief by the publication of the book *Let Not My Country Die,* dedicated to the memory of two victims of the Sekhukhune witch burnings, Phadima Kupa and Ramatsimela Teka.[195] The book was written by Credo Mutwa, who is described on the back cover as a "High Witch Doctor," "Prophet of Africa," and "High Sanusi." Apart from these lofty distinctions, he is also the caretaker of a museum of African magic run by the Soweto Parks and Recreation Department, which is one the major tourist attractions on the guided bus tours of Soweto.[196] Mutwa launches a diatribe against the ANC and its communist friends "that seek to plunge my country and its people into the flames of Armageddon." He praises the memory of one of the victims, an old man with whom he once journeyed to a sacred tree in the Eastern Transvaal, "which must only be visited by those who have reached the highest peak of sanusiship." This book convinced many comrades that they had correctly identified the right persons as witches.

Capitalism

Although the belief in witchcraft lingered on, leading youth activists concluded that the focus on witches had diverted the liberation struggle. Arguments on whether or not witches exist were mostly deemed fruitless. Energies had to be redirected toward other battlefronts. The enemy had to be externalized: if people wished to believe in witchcraft, then it should be pointed out to them that "apartheid is the biggest witch." Under the State of Emergency, mass meetings were out of the question, but beginning in 1987, small-scale workshops were held to further the "political education" of young activists. The best antidote to unscientific superstitions was believed to be scientific socialism. Witchcraft beliefs had proved to be divisive, setting people against each other. Marxism, in contrast, provided useful knowledge, such as the scientific insight that lightning can be explained as a natural phenomenon. By separating beliefs from knowledge, Marxism helped to overcome the confusions and to establish unity: beliefs were divisive, but knowledge provided common ground.[197]

Here again, the link with student organizations at the University of the North proved important. University students possessed literature that provided the clue to understanding and to a new harmonious social order. Three volumes on dialectical materialism, written in the 1950s by Maurice Cornforth, an orthodox British Marxist, became the bible of the "politically advanced" activist. These volumes, entitled *Materialism and the Dialectical Method, Historical Materialism,* and *The Theory of Knowledge,* must have appeared like a book of revelation.[198]

Cornforth sets out to explain some key concepts of Marxism-Leninism, placing strong emphasis on its practical significance. Once readers have grasped the basic tenets of the philosophy, they are in possession of a revolutionary tool. Marxism, as Marx himself had stated, is "a philosophy which seeks to understand the world in order to change it."[199] This revolutionary theory "illumines the road by which the working class can throw off capitalist exploitation, can take the leadership of all the masses of the people, and so free the whole of society once and for all of all oppression and exploitation of man by man."[200]

Cornforth then points the way toward the discovery of "truth." People are prone to believe that if we genuinely seek the truth, then we must be strictly impartial and nonpartisan. "But the contrary is the case. It is only when we adopt the partisan stand-point of historically the most progressive class that we are able to get nearer to truth."[201] Unlike other classes, the working class has no interest in justifying its position and perpetuating its own existence, for its main interest is the establishment of a classless society. Therefore, the philosophy of the working class has a right to lay claim to the truth. As Lenin has stated: "The Marxian doctrine is omnipotent because it is true. It is complete and harmonious, and provides men with an integral world conception which is irreconcilable with any form of superstition, reaction or defence of bourgeois oppression."[202]

For young people, searching for guidance in a period of great upheaval and social disintegration, these were welcome certainties. Thus far, teachers and parents alike had endeavored to impress upon youth their impotence and ignorance. Now, from this marginalized position in South African society, they were suddenly thrust into the forefront of history and entrusted with a vanguard role in the impending revolution. "Materialism teaches us to have confidence in ourselves, in the working class—in people. It teaches us that there are no mysteries beyond our understanding, that we need not accept that which is as being the will of God, that we should contemptuously reject the 'authoritative' teachings of those who set up to be our masters, and that we can ourselves understand nature and society, so as to be able to change them."[203]

Marxism-Leninism presented itself to young activists as a tool of empowerment. It laid the theoretical foundations for people's power because it showed how ordinary people, once they had mastered socialist science, could become masters of the future. It provided the scientific evidence that truth, progress, and victory were on the side of the new order. According to Cornforth, man is about to embark on a new phase of evolution. He is on the threshold of "communist society, in which the whole social process will be brought under his own conscious, planned direction."[204] Here was the promised land with a new, harmonious social order. This goal could be reached only if one was prepared to make a clean break with the past.

Orthodox Marxism, teaching man how to understand society in a materialist way in order to "become masters of the future," was becoming the dominant ideology shaping the views of the youth leadership.[205] In the 1950s, rebellion was inspired by memories of a strong independent Pedi polity in the nineteenth century and images of a harmonious precolonial past. Neither the Sekhukhune rebellion of the 1950s nor the heroic battles of the Pedi armies against the Boers and British in the nineteenth century seemed to have played a prominent role in youth consciousness. Their ideal was not the restoration of peasant society but a victorious proletariat that would herald a communist social order. There is, however, a common strand between the glorification of a mythical peasant past and the idealization of a communist future: both types of societies were perceived as egalitarian and harmonious social orders. Visions of restoring the "primitive communism" of precolonial times could coexist with the idealization of the Soviet model as the guiding example for South Africa. The yearning for the communalism of olden times also inspired NOTPECO's vision of the future: "We agree with the Freedom Charter. The land shall be shared among those who work it. It is not that we want a situation where there are small farms and big farms. We want a situation where the people work the land collectively. The land must be returned to the people."[206]

Whether the call for land could have become a rallying cry to mobilize a broad alliance in the Bantustans is a matter of conjecture. On the rhetorical and emotional level, this call is sure to command wide support. In practice, access to land does not mean that one also has the resources to cultivate crops or keep cattle. Even in those rare years when the rains come to Sekhukhuneland, considerable expanses of land still lie fallow. Although there is a residual peasantry in parts of the Bantustans, a large part of the population is made up of rural proletariat, victims of resettlement and of the expulsion of black labor from the white farms. Access to urban areas and to urban support networks was likely to have a higher priority for many migrants than the maintenance of a rural resource base.[207]

These ideological discussions, however, were not of immediate interest to the rank and file of rural youth movements. Dialectical materialism is a rather complex topic. The workshops attracted only a limited number of activists. The mass of the youth lost interest. Many were demoralized after the experience of harsh repression.

The Charterist Movement in the 1990s: A Realignment of Forces

In Sekhukhuneland, the revolt was crushed in April and May 1986 when the South African army moved in. Villages were in a state of military occupation. People were forbidden to move in the streets with two or more other people.

Months of mass detentions, shootings, and beatings drove youth into submission, apathy, criminal gangs, or underground organizations. Some of the unemployed youth, many of whom had drifted along with the youth movement without much political motivation, were recruited into vigilante groups or the Lebowa police. This transformation of unemployed youth into vigilantes was seen as a serious threat by the youth movement. In 1987, the Northern Transvaal Youth Congress announced the formation of defense committees to deal with vigilante forces and committed itself to stop the recruitment of young people into vigilante groups. Money and the possibility of settling personal accounts were seen as the main motivation for becoming vigilantes.[208]

Although youth were the primary victims of both vigilantism and army and police repression, military occupation proved a harsh experience for the adult population as well. Soldiers and policemen behaved as an occupying force in conquered territory, robbing and beating people at random. It is widely believed that the SADF employed mercenaries from neighboring countries who had previously served in Namibia or in units of RENAMO (Resistência Nacional Moçambicana) in Mozambique. These foreigners, who did not speak any local language, had the reputation of being especially brutal.

In other parts of the Northern Transvaal, UDF activity still continued, although under increasing pressure. In protest against the murder of Peter Nchabeleng, the UDF Northern Transvaal had called a consumer boycott. Added to the protest were the demands that had become familiar features of consumer boycotts in the urban areas: an end to detentions, reductions of bus fares and rents, withdrawal of troops from the townships, and resignation of town councillors and members of homeland legislatures. By May 1986, consumer boycotts were affecting Pietersburg, Phalaborwa, Potgietersrus, and Tzaneen. The boycott was reportedly highly effective in Pietersburg, where the chamber of commerce admitted a 20 percent drop in sales during the first week.[209]

After the declaration of the nationwide State of Emergency in June 1986, most members of the UDF Northern Transvaal Regional Executive were detained, with the remainder going semi-underground or into exile. At this point the lack of a second layer of leadership became an acute problem. "The UDF never was a very strong organization," Thabo Makunyane said with hindsight. "What was missing, was a link between the structures. And then, the structures became static. No new leadership was coming up."[210]

Small nuclei of youth activists kept sporadic contact with SAYCO, which was formally launched at the height of repression, in March 1987. Activists who had fled to Johannesburg had occasional contact with the UDF Head Office, but there was hardly any framework for coordination and consultation between UDF organizations in the Northern Transvaal. Worst hit by the repres-

sion were Sekhukhuneland, Turfloop, and, beginning in 1988, Venda. To fill
the organizational vacuum, some new, semi-clandestine structures sprang
up. In 1987, a Far Northern Transvaal Coordinating Committee of the UDF
was formed, comprising Venda, the townships around Louis Trichardt and
Messina, and the northern half of Gazankulu. The far north had not experienced anything like the revolt in Lebowa, although the social basis of the UDF
was similar in this region. The UDF consisted of SAYCO, AZASO, and a few
sympathetic clergy. "Politics was youth politics. . . . The few adults who were
involved in the UDF were very isolated. They were regarded as terrorists."[211]
Only some sympathetic church workers could continue to operate openly,
although they also faced arrest and confiscation of documents. The Northern Transvaal Council of Churches continued its support work, providing
some income for the families of detainees and helping to find legal advice. This
assistance, however limited, proved important in the dark years of 1986–88 and
provided at least some sense of continuity and hope.

Most members of the regional executive were released in March 1989 after
having joined a hunger strike, but some were placed under restrictions that
did not lapse until February 1990. Finding that many organizations had collapsed and that surviving organizations were in a state of disarray, the executive members convened a consultative conference at which a task force was
elected to revive the UDF structures organization and to broaden it out
beyond youth organization by establishing more civics and women's organizations. Initially, progress was slow. The thaw in the political climate after
F. W. de Klerk's succession to the presidency was not immediately noticeable
in the harsh political landscape of the Northern Transvaal.

Confidence was partially restored with the UDF's Defiance Campaign in
1989 and the release of Walter Sisulu and other ANC stalwarts from Robben
Island in October 1989. But at the time of Sisulu's release, UDF organization
in the Northern Transvaal was still crippled so severely that the region could
not send an organized delegation to the welcoming rally in Soweto.[212] By
December 1989, however, organization had been sufficiently restored to assem-
ble a delegation to the Conference for a Democratic Future in Johannesburg.

Among the UDF activists in the Northern Transvaal who were trying to
pick up the pieces was the remainder of the SEYO leadership. They identified the centralized structure as one of the weaknesses of their organization
because it left the organization in disarray when the leadership was detained.
Reconstituting SEYO along federal lines, based on village units, would make
the organization less vulnerable. But by the time a SEYO congress was convened in March 1990, circumstances had changed drastically. In line with a
previous SAYCO resolution, SEYO decided to dissolve and to join the ANC
Youth League. In its concluding statement, SEYO resolved to embark on cam-

paigns for the dismantling of Bantustans and to give maximum support to the Congress of Traditional Leaders.[213]

When the UDF Northern Transvaal reported on the state of its affiliates as of January 1991, the UDF had not progressed much beyond its original youth and student basis.[214] Two new affiliates had been added to the list: the Northern Transvaal Civics Association and the Congress of Traditional Healers, an intriguing organization that was to have a life span of just a few months. The 1990 UDF financial statement also reveals a rather modest organization. The UDF Northern Transvaal had three organizers on its payroll, while the report on organizational assets mentioned four typewriters, two of which could not be used, one rhoneo (stencil) machine in the possession of an activist currently in detention, and a bakkie (van) that police confiscated in June 1986 and apparently subsequently sold.[215]

The challenge in this transitional period was to broaden the social base of the Charterist movement in the Northern Transvaal without alienating its youth constituency. While the UDF withered away, the ANC—in a transformation process from liberation movement to ruling party—attempted to gain control over the Bantustans. How did it cope with the legacy of this extraordinary period of youth mobilization?

In much of the Northern Transvaal, the UDF as such was not understood as a distinct movement with its own discrete symbolism and meaning. In fact, quite a few people whom I interviewed in Apel-GaNkoane had never heard of the UDF. If they belonged to the youth movement, that implied that they were part of "the organization." And "the organization"—that was the ANC. In this sense, the ANC faced no problem of legitimacy. After the unbannings in February 1990, it was a foregone conclusion in the Northern Transvaal that the UDF should disband in order to let the ANC take its rightful place. In other respects, however, the ANC faced a difficult start. It could not simply build on the foundations laid by the UDF, which in the rural parts of the Northern Transvaal had become largely identified with rebellious youth. In anticipation of the coming elections, the ANC needed to broaden its support base. Part of the ANC strategy was to win over Bantustan rulers, chiefs, businessmen—in general, the Bantustan elites who had been the adversaries during the 1980s. Much to the dismay of the youth congresses, Lebowa homeland leader Nelson Ramodike joined the ANC. Initially, this ANC strategy caused considerable tension between the Johannesburg-based leadership and local structures. The sight of Bantustan leaders wining and dining with the venerated old guard of the ANC leadership, while local ANC representatives were kept in the dark about what was going on, caused much bewilderment and resentment. In some instances, local activists even boycotted visits by ANC dignitaries. Much "political education" was required to explain to a youthful constituency that it was necessary to broaden out in order to "isolate De Klerk." The rapprochement with Bantustan leaders was as difficult to tolerate as the overtures to chiefs.

Here, CONTRALESA was available as a vehicle to guide chiefs toward the ANC. But before it could assist in establishing ANC hegemony, CON-TRALESA needed to be revived. After the initial excitement surrounding CONTRALESA's launch in 1987, not much had happened until 1989. Not surprisingly, organizing chiefs via youth organizations proved to be an unviable option. A new start was made with a conference in June 1989, attended by about 150 chiefs, at which the organization was restructured and a new executive elected. When interviewed in 1990, CONTRALESA official Samson Ndou claimed a membership of just over 1,000 chiefs, of whom some 350 had joined after 2 February 1990. He listed the CONTRALESA strongholds as Lebowa, Venda, KwaNdebele, and Gazankulu, all in the Northern and Eastern Transvaal.[216]

The formation of CONTRALESA allowed for consultations with the leadership of progressive organizations, but it did not always improve relationships at grassroots level. According to Ndou, clashes between youth and chiefs had worsened since February 1990, which he blamed on "agents provocateurs."[217] Activists rightly believed that chiefs joined CONTRALESA in order to entrench their position under a future ANC government. Enlisting chiefs as CONTRALESA members should have facilitated the formation of civic associations in homeland villages, as all could now find their own organizational home under the Charterist umbrella. But in practice, attempts to form civics frequently met with opposition from the chief, who wanted to keep control. The relationship was competitive rather than cooperative, as is evident from Nelson Ramodike's complaint that civics were competing for legitimacy and authority with the chiefs: "It is increasingly becoming clear that the major case in point is to have the Civic Association replace our Magoshi [chiefs]."[218]

Among CONTRALESA's most active members in Sekhukhuneland was Chief Masha from Strydkraal, where the deadly volley fired at the demonstrating youth in 1986 had done much to accelerate the process of youth mobilization. He worked as CONTRALESA organizer. One of the most enthusiastic members was K. K. Sekhukhune, who in 1991 became the officially recognized acting paramount chief after a Pretoria court had settled the succession dispute he had with his half-brother.

From 1990, CONTRALESA was seen as an important rural partner in the ANC's strategy to "isolate De Klerk" by drawing all kinds of disparate forces into a broad alliance under ANC guidance. Chiefs were seen as constituting part of the middle ground between the ANC and the government, hanging in the balance from which they could swing either way. The prospect of the ANC being swamped with yesterday's enemies elicited much criticism. On the other hand, in the conditions of 1990 it could not be taken for granted that the ANC would get majority support in the Bantustans. "We will be lucky if we get one third of the population organized on our side. A large part will be neutral, maybe sympathetic, but they can be swayed to the other side," was the assessment of an ANC veteran in Sekhukhuneland. To consolidate support, it was considered vital to recruit chiefs to the ANC's side: "We have to rob the government of this ground on which they can build."[219]

The dingaka had come to the same conclusion as the chiefs: forming an organization would diminish their individual vulnerability. In 1987, several dingaka approached UDF representatives to discuss problems related to the witch burnings. An attempt was made to affiliate with CONTRALESA, but since the dingaka were not chiefs, they did not qualify for membership. Subsequently, in 1990 applications were made to the ANC offices in Johannesburg and Pietersburg, from which they were referred to the UDF since the ANC could only accommodate individual members and not a group membership. The UDF leadership in Pietersburg sent two delegates, ANC veterans Nelson Diale and John Phala, to the initial conference of the Union of Traditional Healers in GaPhaahla (Lobethal) in Sekhukhuneland.[220]

At this meeting, held in January 1991, those in attendance drew up a statement explaining the reasons for the formation of the union. "Traditional healers must form their own union which will represent them in the new South Africa. Oppression must be abolished against traditional healers."[221] Much time was devoted to a discussion about membership fees and certificates. Proper certificates were considered of vital importance to convince western-educated medical doctors, customers, and comrades of the qualifications of the dingaka. "True proper certificates will show the difference between a healer and a witch." Oppression was obviously seen as coming from various quarters: from chiefs, who demanded money from healers when they were collecting herbs or healing people in the chief's village; from hospitals, which did not allow them access to their patients in hospital wards; from the government, which prosecuted healers for illegal hunting although it was the only way they could obtain the raw animal fat needed to mix with their medicines. This problem, the healers resolved, could be solved if the government provided them with free animal fat, to be supplied by slaughtering some animals in the Pretoria Zoo. There was also a prolonged discussion on the use of crocodile brain, and it was decided that since the brain was used only as poison, it should be prohibited. Perhaps the most compelling reason for the healers to join forces is summed up in the first paragraph of the statement:

Conflict between healers and comrades

(i) Healers were burnt to death by comrades reasons being that they bewitched people (no prove has been given)
(ii) There must be communication between Healers and comrades to end this conflict.
(iii) The reasons for this is to build to the new S.A.

The ANC was rather ambivalent about this venture. John Phala believed that is was wise for the ANC to support the healers' union for the same reason that support was given to CONTRALESA: "You cannot simply abolish them, you have to try and control them." By working with the dingaka, the ANC hoped to stop the witch-hunts. This, Phala thought, could be achieved by convincing the healers that they should no longer deal individually with accusations of witchcraft but should refer the matter to the councils of their unions.[222]

The dingaka agreed that the witch burnings ought to be stopped. In cases where the healers had provided their services to witch-hunting comrades, they claimed that they had done so under threat. They argued that both these matters—youth consulting dingaka and the burning of witches—went against the tradition. But those youth who had sought the services of healers had done so with the argument that "it is everybody's democratic right to come and consult a doctor." The dingaka now agreed on a procedure where they would still treat the victims of witchcraft, but they would avoid publicly naming the culprits. After having identified the perpetrator of witchcraft, they themselves would deal with such a person and prevent him or her from inflicting any more harm. The healers attending the meeting adopted a constitution, elected an executive, and issued a warning to the ANC that there would be no victory in the liberation struggle without their services.[223]

The healers' union, with its rather flimsy organizational base, proved to be short-lived. The driving force was Steve Mamaro, a young man from Sekhukhuneland who lived in Tembisa, on the Reef. When Mamaro disappeared shortly after the Lobethal meeting, the union collapsed. Efforts were made to revive the organization, now under the name of CONTRADOSA (Congress of Traditional Doctors). CONTRADOSA issued membership certificates but seems not have conducted many activities beyond that.[224] Most union members were unaware that their organization had affiliated with the UDF, for outside contacts were conducted by Steve Mamaro. Most youth activists in Sekhukhuneland were equally unaware of the existence of the "comrade dingaka." Although many of them recognized the political expediency of working with chiefs, they reacted rather scornfully to the idea of working with dingaka, who were seen as profiteers making a lot of money from poor and ignorant people. Their practice was "unscientific" and thus could not easily be reconciled with the progressive cause, which entailed fighting superstitions. In the beginning of the 1990s, scientific socialism continued to be seen as the more obvious remedy for unscientific superstitions.

Sekhukhuneland Revisited

What was the legacy of "the times of the comrades" in Sekhukhuneland? My first visits to Sekhukhuneland took place between July and September 1990. Calm had returned to the rural villages, but the atmosphere was somewhat unsettled. On the one hand, there was the uncertainty about De Klerk's intentions: Was all of this really irreversible? On the other hand, there was insecurity about the future: Would the ANC deliver on its promises? Or would the leaders settle comfortably as the new ruling elite? In smoke-filled shebeens, young men discussed the contradictions inherent in "negotiating the seizure of power." Was the ANC on the point of "selling us out"? How many concessions were going to be made? To local youth activists, it seemed that the ANC leaders were too worried about their shiny Mercedeses to venture on the bumpy gravel roads of Sekhukhuneland. But the festive relaunch of the South African Communist Party in a Soweto stadium in July 1990 inspired great excitement in Apel-GaNkoane. A bus had been hired and filled to capacity—and more—to take local youth to this memorable event. Joe Slovo and Chris Hani, leaders of the SACP as well as MK, had assumed almost mythical dimensions among Sekhukhune youth, even more than Mandela and Sisulu. After all, the armed struggle had not been waged from Robben Island.

Maurice Nchabeleng tried to persuade villagers to sign up as ANC members. One hundred members were required for the formation of an ANC branch. It was not easy. "Even now," he conceded, "we have no links with our parents." Apart from building the ANC, the greatest challenge in these months was the formation of a civic association. The two villages of Apel and GaNkoane were going to have a joint ANC branch but two separate civics since the civics would deal with village matters. This required intricate rounds of consultations between youth, ANC veterans, the chief, teachers, principals, and businesspeople. Members of all these groups could often be found in the bottle stores, shebeens, and beer halls: here at least was common ground. Mr. Makgaleng, formerly the chair of the Sekhukhune Parents' Crisis Committee, was in favor of forming a civic but warned youth activists against too much singing of freedom songs. Youth, he told them, should try and keep a low profile, as some people still associated comrades with the burning of people.

This advice went unheeded. When the GaNkoane civic association was launched on a hot Saturday in September 1990, the dusty schoolyard was alive with wildly shuffling feet of toyi-toying schoolchildren, freedom songs, *viva*'s, and *amandla*'s (power-to-the-people salutes). A jarring sound system blasted a pop version of Nkosi Sikelele. The invited dignitaries had indeed come: Paramount Chief K. K. Sekhukhune, Chief Phasha of GaNkoane, Louis Mnguni, representing the ANC and UDF leadership from Pietersburg, and a COSATU delegation from Johannesburg. They were all welcomed by a guard of honor, formed by young men and women in various fantasy uniforms adorned with ANC colors and SACP symbols.[225] There were the combative slogans of the 1980s: "Long live the spirit of no surrender, long live the spirit of no compromise" and "Viva proletarian internationalism." But there were also new slogans, blending the spirit of the 1980s with the quest for new allies: "Long live the classless society, long live progressive chiefs." Louis Mnguni, speaking on behalf of the ANC, reassured the dignitaries who were seated behind a table under a makeshift shelter: "We of the ANC love our chiefs and have never undertaken anything against chiefs." But the representative of the newly formed Northern Transvaal umbrella structure of civic associations sounded less inclined to honor chiefly traditions. Civics, he explained, should form committees to look after education, social welfare, pensions, health, and building activities. He complained that the government had forced the people to go through the chiefs to address problems, but now the civics should deal with the issues directly.

The address of Chief Phasha, who had not yet been officially installed after succeeding his father, was delivered by a spokesman. Things had changed, said the spokesman, but in the past they had been afraid of the youth. They were aware that their youth liked politics, but education should come first, for lack of education causes bad things, like stealing and poverty. If all people were educated and rich, there would be no need to steal items like cold drinks from the shops. He ended with an exhortation to the youth "not to take action, because that will frighten us." Although Chief Pasha's spokesman and other speakers were rewarded with a polite applause, the arrival of SAYCO president Peter Mokaba caused a frenzy. Mokaba had a clear message, not of moderation and "back-to-school" calls, but of familiar battle cries: the people should be armed to fight Inkatha and the Boers and to repossess the land.

The meeting was a success in that all the prominent guests, from the paramount chief to the ANC delegation from Pietersburg and the COSATU delegation from Johannesburg, all made the journey to the dusty schoolyard in a homeland village. But the main invited guests were absent: the adults of GaNkoane. The vast majority of the several hundred people in the schoolyard were schoolchildren, most of them young, many under twelve. There was a sprinkling of elderly women and old men, including some old ANC activists from the 1950s. But people in the age group between twenty-five and sixty were conspicuously lacking. The civic never took off. Chief Phasha insisted that the civic should meet in his kraal, in order for him to keep control over the proceedings. The executive insisted on meeting in the school. Without the chief's support, the civic could not function.

The ANC branch for Apel-GaNkoane was indeed established. Within a year, it was firmly under the control of teachers, who had taken care to assure their positions in the "new South Africa" by joining an ANC-leaning teachers' union. Most of those elected to serve on the executive were teachers, plus there were two principals and one or two businessmen. It was explained to me that one needs a businessman as treasurer: "If he eats the money, it can at least be reclaimed from his shop."

Youth political activity was now mainly confined to the ANC Youth League. One of the original student activists conceded his marginalization with a mixture of resentment and resignation: "The youth has been demobilized." The disbandment of SEYO and SAYCO aroused mixed feelings among Sekhukhune activists. In spite of their loyalty to the ANC, they clearly felt the channeling of their movement into the reconstituted ANC Youth League was a loss of autonomy, making youth organization subservient to the "mother body." The "old men" were taking control again, telling the youth to go back to school. How could the "old men" understand that the youth of Apel and GaNkoane were in urgent need of a disco?

Youth power was not consolidated. As the constitutional negotiations dragged on, many young activists felt increasingly marginalized. Their venerated leaders, who had urged them on as shock troops of the revolution, were now preaching the virtues of patience and moderation. Among the beneficiaries of the constitutional negotiations were not only the chiefs, who obtained official recognition of their role and status, but also the Bantustan officials, who won a promise that all civil servants would continue to be state employees after the abolition of Bantustans. Their pensions were guaranteed. Many youth activists found it difficult to accept that their former enemies fitted so comfortably in the new order.

But village youth emerged from this decade with more organizational experience and a stronger self-confidence. Corporal punishment was not abolished but was greatly curtailed. Principals and teachers were generally willing to deal with student representative councils. Rural youth had forcefully put themselves on the national agenda. They had appropriated the modes of political action from the townships and the Marxist discourse from the university campuses, and they blended these into their own brand of millenarianism, combining the battle for political power and a better place in society with a zest for moral renewal.

I returned to Sekhukhuneland in April 1994, on the eve of the elections.

Talk among local ANC activists centered on the lack of development in rural areas and the comfortable deal secured by their former adversaries, such as chiefs and Bantustan officials. Much indignation was aroused by the ANC decision to put Lebowa's prime minister Nelson Ramodike on the ANC list. He was forced to step down at the last minute when local ANC structures in the Northern Transvaal sent the message to headquarters that this was over-stepping the limit of what they were prepared to tolerate in the interest of "unity." Otherwise, local interest seemed at a low ebb. Where would we find a place to watch the much trumpeted television debate between De Klerk and Mandela? In Nelson's Place, a shebeen frequented by youth, only about ten boys and young men had assembled to witness this historic event. They watched mostly in silence, grinning gleefully at the thought that De Klerk would be serving as vice-president under Mandela. But why the lack of inter-est? Where were the other comrades? "People are tired of politics. Mandela is the messiah. He will help us."

Chief Richard Nchabeleng of Apel, now a member of CONTRALESA, was equally indifferent about the "independence elections." What would the elec-tions mean for the village and the position of chiefs? He kept rubbing his eyes, sighing that these were difficult questions. Only one topic could arouse any passion on the part of Chief Nchabeleng. "Those GaNkoane people must be stopped." A new conflict between the two villages had arisen over a piece of land. GaNkoane residents had torn down a house that belonged to one of Nchabeleng's subjects. If only those people would be arrested, the trouble would be over, the chief felt. But nothing happened because the civil ser-vants of Lebowa were on strike. In the Lebowa administration, civil servants indulged in an orgy of promotions and went on strike when Pretoria refused to foot the bill. The police strike was now over, but at the magistrate's office nobody was working—therefore nobody could be arrested. But after the elec-tions, Chief Nchabeleng intended to "take the law into my own hands" and settle this thing once and forever.

The talk of the village was the resurgence of the old animosities between Apel and GaNkoane, not the impending historic elections. Those from Apel had launched a consumer boycott against shops in GaNkoane after the destruction of the house. The revival of "tribal conflict" was of no consequence for the elections. Like those from Apel, the people of GaNkoane would vote for the ANC, for there was no alternative. While by far the majority of the roughly 350 members of the Apel-GaNkoane branch of the ANC lived in Apel, membership in the ANC Youth League was spread more evenly between the two villages. Young activists made house-to-house visits to educate the vot-ers. Some of the old people were still afraid of the youth, explained an eld-erly woman who served on the local ANC executive: "They are saying 'the youth will kill us?' They remember what happened in 1986. But those were not the comrades. Those youth smoked dagga and they came from GaNkoane. GaNkoane, that is a different place. There they burn witches when lightning has hit. Those GaNkoane people don't know sympathy."

Thus the generational conflict that marked the witch burnings of 1986 had been reformulated to express the most salient conflict of the present. Otherwise, not much had changed in Apel-GaNkoane over the past four years. Education was still a shambles. In most schools, teachers were on strike because salaries had not been paid over the past months. Since the beginning of the school year, students at the teacher-training college had been boycotting classes in support of their demands that more students be admitted to the college. Because of the civil servants' strike, pensions had not been paid for two months. Now Radio Lebowa announced that officials from the Transvaal Provincial Administration would take over from the Lebowa civil servants. In Sekhukhuneland, pensions would be paid out at the magistrate's office in Schoonoord and the police station in Apel, which had been built in 1990. Thousands of elderly men and women converged on the police station, queuing patiently to await the arrival of the officials. Hundreds of people had already arrived the evening before payday, fearing that the money would have run out if they came late.

"Remember Sydney's poem?" asked Maurice Nchabeleng as we drove away from the police station, where hundreds of old men and women sat huddled together to spend a long, cold night in the open. "Remember all the confusions? They are still here. Except for one. There is no more confusion between the parents and the children. The parents no longer fear their children."

CHAPTER FOUR

"Yah, God Is on Our Side":
The Krugersdorp Residents
Organisation and Township Revolt

> For once, God. . . . has given us that spirit to do it just right.
> Yah, God is on our side.
>
> *KRO chair phoning the secretary of the civic*

Civics and Popular Mobilization

TOWNSHIP-BASED ORGANIZATIONS of residents known as civic associations or civics made up an important part of the UDF's membership. During the 1980s, civics vacillated between different roles: watch-dog bodies representing the interests of all township residents; political bodies aspiring to construct Charterist hegemony at the local level; brokers taking up individual problems and grievances of residents; organs of people's power; front organizations for the ANC, preparing to grab local power in the event of a seizure of power by the liberation movement. Sometimes a civic was formed as an end in itself, namely to provide residents with a vehicle to address township issues such as rents, transportation, crime, electricity. Sometimes a civic was a means to an end: activists launched a civic in the belief that campaigns around rents or washing lines would provide a low-threshold starting point from which residents could gradually be drawn into wider political struggles against the apartheid state.

The rise of the civic movement predates the formation of the UDF. Community organizations, which became known as civic associations, began to emerge toward the end of the 1970s, partly prompted by the installation of community councils in a number of townships. These councils took over some of the functions of the state administration boards, notably the collection of rents and the allocation of houses. Rent increases generally accompanied the installation of the community councils. Opposition to rent increases became

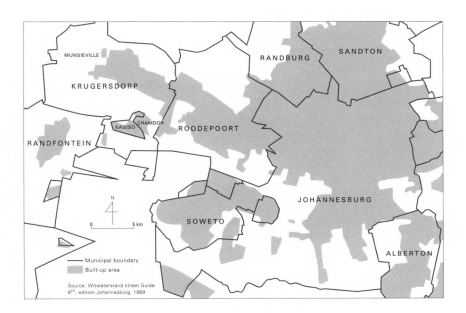

2. The West Rand. Map by Nel van Bethlehem.

a prominent feature of civic struggles in the 1980s, as the community councils and their successors, the town councils that were established under the 1982 Black Local Authorities Act, unsuccessfully attempted to make ends meet with frequent increases in rents and service charges. Among the first civic organizations were the Soweto Civic Association (SCA) and the Port Elizabeth Black Civic Organisation (PEBCO), both of which subsequently served as models for community organizations in other townships.

During the 1980s, most civics affiliated with the UDF, but some remained outside the Charterist fold. The Soweto civic was initially reluctant to join because it included AZAPO activists. In some townships, UDF-affiliated civics had to compete with Black Consciousness organizations or those community organizations leaning toward the PAC (Pan Africanist Congress), while a number of civics in the Western Cape adhered to the Trotskyite doctrines of the New Unity Movement. Civics in the African townships were not a vital concern to the UDF in its early phase, as the campaign against the tricameral parliament centered on the Indian and colored communities. But with the outburst of township revolt in September 1984, civics sprang to national prominence.

Community organizations were formed on the assumption that township residents shared a community of interests, by virtue of the fact that they lived in the same place. This assumption often proved true when the inhabitants felt beleaguered from outside—for example, by the police or the army. Joint action against a common threat may engender a community spirit, but this is rarely a lasting phenomenon. As with "the people," the widespread "community" discourse obscured the fact that the inhabitants of a certain place share some interests on some issues but may have divergent interests on other issues. As townships began to show more economic differentiation, the assumption of common interests became less self-evident. But in the African townships of the 1980s, increasing economic differentiation had by and large not yet resulted in clearly class-based political organization and action. Under conditions of repression and disenfranchisement, mobilization was less likely to occur along the lines of social class.

Among the Transvaal civics, the Krugersdorp Residents Organisation (KRO) in Kagiso had the reputation of being a strong, well-organized civic.[1] The story of Kagiso modifies the image of township revolt as it was transmitted by the mass media. Images of almost unbridled militancy and near anarchy dominated media coverage of rebellion in the townships. Kagiso presents a picture of reluctant rebellion: residents were not eager to plunge into militant mass action, and when they finally did, they were not intent on promoting chaos and anarchy. On the contrary, their appreciation for the civic was predicated on its capacity to deliver a certain amount of law and order. Within the Kagiso civic, different perceptions of the proper role of a civic organization coexisted, partly because of the different backgrounds of civic activists. Should the civic leadership give priority to mobilizing residents in mass campaigns and then use the momentum to build strong organizations? Or should organization precede mobilization, in order to avoid the risks of undisciplined actions and ill-considered ventures?

What kind of people were the driving force behind the Krugersdorp Residents Organisation? What motivated them, and how did they try to mobilize their fellow residents? Who was included in "the community," and who remained excluded or on the margins? What were the issues that galvanized the people of Kagiso into collective action? What was the impact of the UDF on township organization? The story of the rebellion in Kagiso is preceded by a discussion of the structural conditions and an introduction of the actors.

Structural Conditions: A Profile of Kagiso Township

Kagiso—the name means "peace" in Tswana—was a medium-sized township on the West Rand, some fifteen miles west of Johannesburg. The township, established in 1956, was designed to serve the white town of Krugersdorp and the adjoining Chamdor industrial area. To the northwest of Krugersdorp was another, much smaller and older township, Munsieville. During the 1980s, Munsieville residents were threatened with the destruction of their homes and removal to Kagiso to make room for the planned extension of the white residential areas of Krugersdorp.

In the mid-1980s, Kagiso had between 60,000 and 70,000 inhabitants. Around 20,000 people were living in Munsieville.[2] Two hostels in Kagiso housed about 5,000 people. Another 10,000 people were without conventional housing and lived mostly in backyard shacks. On average, one dwelling accommodated 9.2 people.[3] In terms of age and gender, Kagiso's population was fairly evenly distributed. The ethnic composition was mixed, with a dominance of Sotho and Tswana speakers.

Sprawling squatter settlements on the outskirts of the township sprang up only in the late 1980s. Kagiso had thirteen primary and two secondary schools. There was no secondary school in Munsieville, so those high school students attended school in Kagiso. At the edge of the township was the fairly large Leratong Hospital, which also served as a training institute for nurses. Living conditions were roughly comparable with other PWV townships, and the new housing extensions built in the 1970s and 1980s compared favorably with the older settlements.

Kagiso consisted of two parts: Kagiso I, one of the older townships in the region, and Kagiso II, a much bigger extension, built mostly in the 1970s and 1980s. Kagiso I became the stronghold of the civic organization. Only the main roads were paved, and electrification was slow in reaching the area. At the beginning of the 1980s, only about 10 percent of the houses had electricity. Since the early 1980s, residents had been paying a monthly fee for the electrification of the township, but only 14.5 percent of the homes had electricity by the end of the decade.[4] Nevertheless, in spite of these monthly fees, families applying to have electricity connected to their homes still had to pay a fee of 2000 Rand.[5] This was an outrageous amount, compared to the tariffs in the adjoining white city of Krugersdorp. Throughout the 1980s, electricity remained high on the list of civic concerns. Numerous residents complained about extremely high electricity bills, which gave rise to the suspicion that the council tampered with the electricity meters.

During my visits to the township in 1990, I found Kagiso residents in the midst of a boycott of rents and service charges. The town council had reacted by halting several services, such as garbage collection. The streets of Kagiso were lined with enormous piles of rotting garbage. On days with heavy rains, garbage mixed with overflowing sewers and rain to create torrential streams, damaging the poorly maintained roads. Roads deteriorated further as a result of the inventiveness of residents, who dug gullies in the road to extend electricity cables to houses that were not formally connected. Improvised wiring also crisscrossed from electricity poles through windows of houses. The electric company ESCOM had complained that it had a monthly loss of 300,000 Rand and threatened to cut off electricity.

Next to the hostel in Kagiso I was a block of burned-out houses, which were deserted after Inkatha fighters in the hostel had launched an attack on the neighborhood in August 1990. The battle between Inkatha and the Kagiso residents erupted in the context of the township war in 1990, when Inkatha ruthlessly attempted to establish a foothold in the Transvaal while the ANC tried to safeguard its hegemonic position in the Transvaal townships. At the time of my visits, the two hostels had become no-go areas for township residents. Most of the original inmates had fled the violence, and the hostels had been taken over by Inkatha. The original dwellers had sought refuge in the township or in a nearby squatter camp. But this was a new situation. During the 1980s, the two hostels were on the margins of township life but were not out-of-bounds for the residents.

Most residents of Kagiso and Munsieville worked in Krugersdorp and the Chamdor industrial area, while some found employment in Roodepoort or Randfontein and in Johannesburg. As several activists pointed out, the Chamdor industries, which included chemical enterprises and a brewery, paid their taxes to Krugersdorp and spilled their pollution in Kagiso. As elsewhere on the West Rand, trade union presence in Kagiso was fairly weak. At the beginning of the 1980s, only the Food and Beverage Workers Union (FBWU), an affiliate of the Council of Unions of South Africa (CUSA), was organizing in Kagiso. The general union GAWU (General and Allied Workers Union), an affiliate of the UDF, recruited some followers during the 1980s, whereas the Metal and Allied Workers Union (MAWU) established a presence in this region only in 1987.

The recession of the first half of the 1980s had an uneven impact on township residents. Income distribution became more uneven, with a simultaneous growth of an upper-income group and a very low income group. Unskilled workers and casual labor generally experienced falling wages. Skilled workers, on the other hand, could look forward to fairly substantial wage increases, partly thanks to the increasing bargaining power of their trade unions. At the same time, African urban areas witnessed the growth of a middle class as new opportunities opened up in retailing and transportation, such as the booming taxi business.[6] The increasing social differentiation in the townships manifested itself in a greater variety of housing. This development, made possible by the greater security of tenure, which was introduced as part of the reforms of the Botha government, was clearly visible in Kagiso. Private developers built new neighborhoods with fairly comfortable homes next to the all too familiar "matchbox" township houses. But even the so-called elite estates had unpaved roads.

Before 1971, townships formed part of the municipal area of the white towns. Soweto, for example, was part of the municipality of Johannesburg, while Kagiso was part of Krugersdorp. Townships and towns had a common fiscal base, so the municipality could provide township services from local tax revenue on business and property. This state of affairs changed in 1971, when townships were taken away from the municipalities and put under the control of the Bantu administration boards. The government introduced the principle that Africans must pay for their own administration. Since the boards received no money from the municipalities, local government for Africans came to depend on income from rents and site rents, service charges, the sale of houses in leasehold schemes, and the boards' monopoly on liquor and beer sales. Restrictive regulations against business in the townships meant that for a long time no viable business sector could emerge, which could have helped alleviate the fiscal crisis. Township residents continued to spend the bulk of their income in white areas. In the scheme of Grand Apartheid, townships were designed as dormitory towns for a temporary labor force whose ultimate destination lay in the homelands.

The town councils, established under the 1982 Black Local Authorities Act, were faced with financial disaster. Many councillors were aware that the new system of local government lacked a financial base. They demanded the inclusion of industrial areas within township borders. They argued the case for government subsidies on municipal services and claimed access to income from municipal traffic licenses and traffic fines. But none of these requests were granted. The town councils also lacked the traditional source of black township revenue: beer and liquor sales, which had provided 70 percent of the income of the administration boards. The boards retained the revenue from sorghum beer sales in the beer halls, and most other liquor sales were privatized. Thus the new councils' income from alcohol was restricted to fees obtained from distributing licenses for liquor stores. These licenses were much sought after, and the mayor and councillors generally saw to it that the income from liquor outlets lined their private pockets. Fourteen out of fifteen liquor outlets in Lekoa, in the Vaal Triangle, were reportedly in the hands of mayor Esau Mahlatsi or members of his family.[7] Similar patterns prevailed in other townships, where mayors and councillors ensured that the lion's share of the required licenses for bottle stores, gas stations, supermarkets, and other shops went to themselves or their relatives. Faced with a lack of income and full of ambitious plans for the improvement of township infrastructure, the town councils set out to increase rents, in many cases by substantial amounts. In the 1970s, as was the case in the 1980s, people's resentment was aroused not only by financial hardship but also by the total lack of communication between the local administration and the residents.

Kagiso went through its first experience with township revolt in the 1976 uprising. In spite of some evidence of underground activity by the PAC in 1977, Kagiso seemed politically calm at the beginning of the 1980s. In the 1981 elections for community councils, Kagiso had a relatively high turnout of 48 percent of registered voters, which amounted to 7,700 voters. Three years later, in the 1983 elections for the new Black Local Authorities, Kagiso again showed a relatively high poll of 36.6 percent of the registered voters.[8] Although the council hailed this turnout as an "outstanding success," this percentage is misleading, since only 4,008 inhabitants had bothered to register on the voters' roll. The "registered voters" were only a small portion of the eligible voters. Elections were held in three wards only, as the candidates in the other wards were uncontested. The actual number of votes cast was definitely less impressive: 1,445.[9]

The Actors: The Krugersdorp Residents Organisation

As in many other townships, rent struggles provided the impetus towards the formation of a civic association in Kagiso. In 1980, house owners in a new extension refused to pay their water bill in protest against a steep rise in the monthly bill for the repayment of the loan, interests, and service charges. Initially the council threatened to cut off the water supply. But after the local Action Committee formed an alliance with members of COSAS (Congress of South African Students) who promised to bring water in drums, the council gave in and reduced the monthly bills.[10] Later that year the mayor of Kagiso announced in a newspaper advertisement an increase in rents in the older part of the township. The matter was discussed in an informal gathering of youth, most of them in their early twenties. Their anger was directed not only at the rent increase but also at the arrogance of the community council for making an announcement in the press without bothering to inform the people of Kagiso.[11] A core group of perhaps five young men discussed plans for a campaign against the rent increase. They envisaged more than an ad hoc protest: their goal was to involve people in Kagiso in building an independent organization of residents, following the example of PEBCO and SCA.

Their strategizing sessions were inspired with new ideas by the arrival of a newcomer, Bafana Seripe, who had worked in the Western Cape as an organizer for the Young Christian Workers, a remarkable organization that is discussed in more detail later in the chapter. Seripe told his friends in Kagiso about the civic movement in the Western Cape: how they were conducting door-to-door campaigns and using media to organize people. More youth were contacted, including members of AZAPO and members of a Christian youth club that had been established at the initiative of a local pastor, Frank Chikane. By this time, about fifteen young men were involved.[12] These men conducted house-to-house visits and discovered that people were unaware of the impending rent increase. In their discussions, many other issues came up. "The activists were sometimes greeted with suspicion and taken for tsotsis, and on the other hand sometimes welcomed with tea or coffee. The activists became convinced that the time was ripe for the formation of a civic organisation."[13]

Their style was apparently not confrontational. The house-to-house campaign "even stretched to the houses of ordinary policemen, who took the issue solely as a rent problem and merely as a civic matter."[14] The activists met frequently to evaluate the progress of the campaign and to plan the next stage. The core group had grown to about thirty people, and the idea of forming a residents organization took more concrete shape. "But most of us were still young, and then older people would be reluctant to get involved, because the youth had the image of being radical."[15] In further discussions, "it was decided that the organisation would need a mature experienced leadership, which would be elderly people."[16] Among the people approached were a local trade unionist, Joe Makgothlo, who was in his forties, Lettie Nzima, a middle-aged woman who was active in church-based social work, and Frank Chikane, the pastor of the Apostolic Faith Mission.

The launch of the civic took place in February 1981, in a venue made available by the Catholic Church in Kagiso I. As it happened, the residents elected the executive committee from among the people who delivered speeches at the meeting. Makgothlo was elected chair, and Ike Genu, a worker in his late twenties who was active in Chikane's youth club, became vice-chair. One of the youth activists, George Moiloa, found himself elected secretary, rather to his surprise. The meeting was characterized by a joyous mood: "It was for the very, very first time, the people of Kagiso felt and enjoyed an experience of organisation which they themselves set up and named."[17]

The same sense of embarking on a historic mission permeates the preamble to KRO's constitution:

We the Residents of Kagiso, having noted over years:
That there was no Leadership In Kagiso of the people by the people for the people except government created institutions or bodies to further its oppressive and exploitative machinery;
That this community of Kagiso, like any other black community in South Africa, has been and is brutally subjected to the inhuman, discriminatory unjust laws of the white racist regime and forcefully deprived of any say in the enacting and execution of the said laws;
That thus most of the residents have no houses, and some denied the right to. Many are unemployed, resulting in poverty stricken families and persons in the Land of Gold;

That further noting that our children are forced to go through an unacceptable form of education;

therefore RESOLVE to found the Kagiso Residents Organisation based on
the following Constitution.[18]

The day after the launch of KRO the Kagiso council decided on the immediate suspension of the rent increase. With the most pressing issue apparently
solved, many inhabitants lost interest. Subsequent mass meetings were not
well attended. "It appeared people felt there was nothing to worry about any-
more. It also appeared like people felt that the committee was elected and had
to do everything for the people."[19]

The fledgling civic went through a lull until the rent increases were rein-
troduced in August 1981. Organization building was to prove a slow process,
with many ups and downs. In spite of the varying fortunes of KRO, there was
a remarkable continuity in the civic leadership. Although several new people
were co-opted to the executive in subsequent years, no new elections were
held until the end of the decade.[20] This continuity allowed for an accumula-
tion of organizational experience, but at the same time may have impeded the
development of new local leadership. When the executive was detained, there
was no second-layer leadership to take over.

Although several older townships residents were to play leading roles during the 1980s, the inception of the civic association in Kagiso was the work
of the Soweto generation. "In each and every township, there existed a core of
youth which remained deeply politically motivated." Whereas before 1976
friendships developed around football and "other frivolities," now youth was
brought together by the desire to come to grips with the issues of "real life,"
noted a group of students—themselves part of the 1976 student generation—
in their oral history paper on the Kagiso civic.[21] Around 1980, there were at
least three politically motivated youth groups: the Young Christian Workers
(YCW), the Interdenominational Youth Christian Club (IYCC), and the Congress of South African Students (COSAS).

Membership was to some extent overlapping, but before the formation of
KRO there was no intensive contact between the three groups. Nevertheless,
there were obvious common strands in youth consciousness: a religious inspiration, drawing on Christian values but frequently combined with distrust of
the established churches; a legacy of Black Consciousness (BC), which could
coexist with adherence to Charterist principles; strong anticapitalist sentiments and a belief in socialist and communal values; the strong conviction that
they were fighting for a just cause; and a sense of mission to work toward of
a new, egalitarian society. All these elements are eloquently expressed in poetic
form in the diary of one of the graduates of the Soweto revolt, Lawrence
Ntlokoa, who was to play a key role in civic life in Kagiso.

The Kagiso civic could draw on a wider range of experience than just current and former high school students and young workers. Several local leaders developed links with national political organizations. A Roman Catholic nun, Sister Mary Bernard Ncube, who was closely involved with youth groups in Kagiso, became president of the Federation of Transvaal Women (FEDTRAW), an affiliate of the UDF. Frank Chikane became vice-president of the UDF Transvaal region. Several Kagiso activists had links with the ANC, either directly or through their family background. The KRO chair was an active trade unionist, as were several other civic activists. What motivated the people who became leading civic activists?

Religious Leadership

Two Christian institutions played a pivotal role in promoting community organization as well as in stimulating youth involvement in community affairs. Sister Mary Bernard Ncube, a short, middle-aged nun who exuded unfailing energy and a natural authority, and her small congregation of nuns in a convent in Kagiso I provided meeting facilities and a network of contacts outside the township.[22]

Sister Bernard was arrested in March 1983 and later sentenced to twelve months for possession of banned literature. Among the publications found in her possession was a photograph of ANC president Oliver Tambo and a copy of an article in the ANC magazine *Sechaba* containing a speech by Tambo.[23] Among other documents later confiscated and produced by the state in the KRO trial was a letter to her from Nelson Mandela in Pollsmoor Prison. In the course of the 1980s, she was detained repeatedly, including three months spent in solitary confinement due to terms of the 1986 State of Emergency. When Sister Bernard was banned from Kagiso in 1987, she went to live in Soweto and took up employment with the Institute of Contextual Theology in Johannesburg.

One other church-based center of inspiration and resources was the Apostolic Faith Mission of pastor Frank Chikane, who was appreciated by youth activists as "a very powerful person." In his autobiography, Chikane describes how, at a young age, he became involved in the life of this church, which was marked by grassroots participation, mutual support networks, and a holistic form of spirituality. In Chikane's view, the spirituality of his church fitted with the African world view. In both, there was no conception of a dualistic world of the spiritual that was different from the world of the social. "Africans' total life experiences were understood and interpreted in relation to their God." God was not a spectator in the war that was raging between the evil spirits and the spirit of righteousness—God, Chikane felt, must be involved. But in hindsight, he saw a basic problem in the church's acceptance of the sociopolitical status quo in South Africa. He realized that "whereas this grassroots form of holistic spirituality addressed our spiritual and social needs, it did not address the source of this country's social abnormalities. It was more of a survival strategy of the victims of society than a strategy to end victimisation."[24] According to Chikane, the missing link in his church was "a direct confrontation with the forces of evil within this struggle between evil and goodness in the world." The task that Chikane now saw before him was to reappropriate the Bible and to oppose the use of Christianity for the legitimation of evil systems.[25] He started work in Kagiso barely a week or so before 16 June 1976, beginning his ministering in an intensified conflict situation. In the months after 16 June, Chikane helped to trace members of the community who had suddenly disappeared. He was detained in June 1977, badly assaulted for six weeks, and released only in January 1978.

Following Chikane's arrival in Kagiso, several social and youth projects had been set up around his congregation. The Interdenominational Youth Christian Club (IYCC), combining evangelical work with social projects, proved a training ground in leadership and organizing skills for numerous young men and women in Kagiso. Ike Genu, one of the young congregation members and later vice-chair of KRO, recalled his first encounter with what later became known as liberation theology: "Frank then began preaching this new philosophy and that was what made us aware."[26] Genu became chief deacon in the parish and stayed with his family in the mission house. The driving force behind the social project, known as the Kagiso Self Help Scheme, was a middle-aged woman, Lettie Nzima, who in 1981 became one of the members of the KRO executive. The church premises became the focus of police attention, while the church establishment warned Chikane against involvement in politics. Because of this pressure from his church, he declined the request to become chair of the civic organization in Kagiso. In an informal capacity, however, he participated in the formation of KRO. Subsequently, in August 1981, Chikane was provisionally suspended by his church. The family was evicted from the church premises and moved to Soweto. After another spell in detention, Chikane went to work with the Institute for Contextual Theology in Johannesburg. Freed from the constraints of the church, in which he could no longer be a pastor although he remained an active member, he became vice-chair of the Soweto Civic Association. From 1983 to 1985 he was vice-president of the UDF Transvaal region. As one of the accused in the Pietermaritzburg Treason Trial, he was out of circulation for most of 1985, but he nevertheless played a key role in initiating the Kairos document, which stated that the seed of a "prophetic theology" had been sown and which demanded that Christians participate in the liberation struggle.[27] In 1987, Frank Chikane succeeded

Dr. C. F. Beyers Naudé as secretary general of the South African Council of Churches (SACC). In 1990, he was fully reinstated in the Apostolic Faith Mission.

Although they represented different church traditions and different generations, there are marked similarities in the religious and political visions of Sister Bernard Ncube and Frank Chikane. Both were influenced by the call of Latin American theologians to take sides in the "struggles between the forces of righteousness (light) and unrighteousness (darkness) to be able to develop an authentic theology. . . . To be part of the liberating work of God, you have no choice other than to take sides with the poor, the downtrodden and the weak."[28]

For Sister Bernard as well as Frank Chikane, both capitalism and apartheid belonged to the forces of unrighteousness. In his autobiography, Chikane counterposed "those who live at the expense of the blood, life and sweat of others" to the "classless society which could be compatible with the ideals of the Kingdom [of God]."[29] This egalitarian vision of the Kingdom of God was shared by some influential young activists for whom religious inspiration remained important in spite of their scorn for the church establishment. Several found an organizational home in the Young Christian Workers, a remarkable international movement that produced a synthesis of Christianity, Marxism, and militant social action.

The Young Christian Workers

Unlike COSAS or BC-inspired youth groups, the Young Christian Workers (YCW) rarely made the headlines. The movement emphasized organizing at the grassroots level and was rather scornful of organizations that sought a high public profile, such as the UDF. YCW never became a UDF affiliate. But this youth organization deserves more attention than it has thus far received in newspapers and history books, because it has produced a remarkable crop of highly motivated and talented activists. After their years with YCW, many moved into leading roles in the trade union movement, the civic movement, or, to a lesser extent, the UDF itself.[30] YCW was an urban-based organization. There were no traces of YCW in the Northern Transvaal Bantustans, but both in the Johannesburg area and in the Western Cape a substantial number of interviewees traced the beginnings of their political involvement to the YCW. Several leading activists in Kagiso had a background in the YCW; some came to represent the "workerist opposition" in the civic. YCW also offered youth the opportunity to keep in touch with other townships and to exchange experiences.[31]

The Young Christian Workers organization owes its existence to a Flemish priest—later cardinal—Jozef Cardijn (1882–1967), who in the 1920s began organizing young workers in the industrial town of Laken in Belgium. After World War II, in which Cardijn was imprisoned in a German concentration camp, the organization grew into an international movement, the Young Christian Workers.[32] In South Africa, YCW was introduced by Eric Tyacke, who in 1970 was also instrumental in the formation of the Urban Training Project, a service organization for African trade unionists. In the 1950s and 1960s, YCW was a broad, church-based movement, but in the 1970s, YCW became more specifically involved in workers' issues, such as advising on workers' rights and addressing the problems of young domestic workers. Although the links with the Catholic Church offered some protection, the YCW leadership jealously guarded the autonomy of the movement against the church establishment. The image YCW sought to portray was that of worker militancy rather than religion. Many YCW members were in fact unaware of its links with the Catholic Church, but a militant Christianity remained a source of inspiration. As Lawrence Ntlokoa told his police interrogators, YCW stood for the theology of liberation rather than for charismatic Christianity.[33]

Indeed, the 1975 Declaration of Principles of YCW expresses strong anti-capitalist sentiments and pledges "to bring about complete change, a new organization of the structures of society in the cultural, social, political and economic fields. A society that will ensure the complete fulfillment of man as a HUMAN being, i.e. a classless society."[34] In this struggle for a better world, YCW projected itself in a vanguard role, aspiring to be a living example of what this new society ought to be like. Lawrence Ntlokoa, who as a nineteen-year-old was appointed YCW organizer for the Transvaal in November 1976, claims that he was told in his training course that the YCW in South Africa strove to bring about change by means of revolution, "but under the condition that the proposed change in South Africa must be obtained by the working class and not by a so-called bourgeois system. . . . To achieve this political aim under Black Majority rule and to retaliate against military action by the government, the YCW, the trade unions and the Roman Catholic Church, to a certain exten[t], will accept the support of armed forces irrespective of their origin and ideologies, from outside South Africa."[35] A YCW chaplain showed him how to tune in to the ANC's Radio Freedom. During YCW seminars youth learned about the history of the banned liberation movements. Ntlokoa was told that the ANC and YCW shared the vision of a classless society, for which Tanzania stood as a model.

After his conviction for public violence on charges of stoning a bus and setting afire a delivery van of the Afrikaans newspaper *Rapport,* Ntlokoa became thoroughly disillusioned with YCW. During his spell in detention he received no salary and no other support, as YCW policy did not condone the use of violence. The Roman Catholic hierarchy most likely fostered a different vision of the Kingdom of God and of the road leading toward this destination. Detention was followed by a banning order, which gave Ntlokoa the distinction of being the youngest banned person in South Africa. Due to this banning order, Ntlokoa could not openly participate in civic activities, but he was in touch with several leading activists, and Frank Chikane allowed him the use of the facilities of the IYCC. During most of 1981 and 1982, he was in prison on various convictions for violations of his banning order. After the lifting of his banning order in 1983, he became secretary of the Kagiso civic.

Ntlokoa was bitter about the YCW "oligarchy" and skeptical about church institutions, but his political ideals remained inspired by a mix of Christianity and socialism, as is evident from his diary and from a letter written in 1980. Rereading the Bible during the long months of his banning order, he discovered that "Salvation history is totally on the side, objectively and subjectively, of the poor, the oppressed. . . . Faith then, brings with it new dimensions of the liberation struggle."[36] The following fragments from Lawrence Ntlokoa's diary, written in Kagiso in 1985, illustrate how Christianity and socialism continued to inspire Ntlokoa's world view, even after he had left YCW.[37]

Goodbye 1984

Just the year before you
I was a banned man
The newspapers said I was
The youngest banned in S.A.
I was banned because I believed
I believed in goodness
I believed in the Bible
And I was a Christian
1984 let me tell you about
the self of mine

So the Rastas say
They spent no trial six months
At a prison called the Fort
and guys inside call it No. Four
A prison I once visited
I also visited Groentpunt
And Leeukop Maximum
And also a prison in Benoni
They call it Modder Bee
I don't know what Modder means

It sounds like Afrikaans to me
. . . .
I also saw the eyes of the church
the good I praise
the evil I criticise
I reserve my soft words
for the workers
the working class
also for beggars
who are the slaves of misery
while prices mount up
like waves of the sea
ah—each wave stronger

Who among us can fight waves
except Jesus Christ the only begotten
Christ the friend of the workers
who died for their cause
who was tortured in detention
and died in pain
hanged on the wooden cross
who once said to his comrades and the masses
"do you suppose that I am here
to bring peace on this earth
No, I tell you.

But rather dissension
why do people pretend to be godly
when they are filthy inside
only the sharks survive the waves
there is no peace
and never can be peace
without change
without revolution
but he was sold out
by a sell-out—Judas
. . . .
most of the people really did hear what the
preacher man was saying
the brother said

"God blesses only those who suffer
who suffer with resignation"
If the brother saw

Children eating leftover food
sometimes rotten
given by a corrupt system
which creates hunger
he would stop talking about resignation
and rebel
rebellion comes from bitterness
but the brother is too fat
and a shark
to can care about people in hunger
how can he say that
. . . .
Not even a cent
it is not backwardness
or the colour of a man's skin
that causes poverty
it is capitalism
Unity of struggle
of the two opposites
the oppressed on the one hand
the oppressor man
the class contradiction between
workers and capitalists

capitalism exploit workers
and workers are exploited by capitalists
a fusion
an illusion
remake the world
too many people are sad
too little people have everything
too many people have nothing
. . . .
Let's bring it right
let's make the conditions necessary for free
and democratic South Africa

. . . .
when the colour
black or white
means nothing more than the colour of a man's eyes
. . . .
From the Diary of Lawrence Ntlokoa, Kagiso, 1985

Ntlokoa dropped out of school in the sixth standard, or grade, but he had always been an avid reader, and he continued his education by correspondence courses. From his YCW experience he kept an analytical approach, an interest in revolutionary theory, and an awareness of sociopolitical struggles in other parts of the world. Among the publications that the police confiscated in 1983, when he was charged with the possession of banned literature, were many articles on the Sandinistas in Nicaragua. At the time of the formation of KRO, Ntlokoa had broken off contact with YCW. But YCW was to provide another core of young activists who played a leading part in civic activities in Kagiso.

Like the Federation of South African Trade Unions (FOSATU), YCW decided against affiliation with the UDF. A position paper stressed the role of YCW as an autonomous organization of working-class youth that should not engage in joint action "with non-class based organisations as this can cause problems during actions and regarding the aims and direction of actions."[38] The paper objected to the UDF's formula of representation, in which large trade unions would not carry more weight than a service center employing just a few people. "YCW wanted to keep its prophetic mission, it did not want to be swallowed in this broad movement."[39] With its emphasis on building strong working-class organizations with proper channels of accountability, YCW was bound to be suspicious of the UDF's tactics. From its "workerist" position, it criticized the populist politics of both the UDF and the civics, which tended to move from one protest campaign to the next without building a solid organizational infrastructure. There are valid points in these criticisms, but the YCW's puritanical clinging to its "class base" hampered its effectiveness. In Kagiso, for example, YCW activists contributed significantly toward the formation of a civic. But subsequently they left the fledgling civic to its own devices because YCW wanted to be "class based," whereas a civic was a "populist" organization.

The YCW's organizing method was to start from daily experiences in people's lives. Small groups would hold weekly meetings and discuss strategies for change, beginning with very concrete actions. Factory workers would discuss a strategy to get management to give overalls to the workers or to improve safety conditions. High school students devised a way to approach the bus company with a request to fit the bus schedule to the school hours. These actions would then be evaluated and, if necessary, followed up. As people gained more confidence, they moved on to tackle bigger issues. But this step-by-step approach was rather out of tune with the spirit of immediacy in the mid-1980s. YCW activists were generally critical of consumer boycotts of white-owned shops, since they usually lacked clearly defined goals, were enforced in an undemocratic way, and could result in the loss of jobs. In many cases, shopkeepers in the townships took advantage of the boycott to raise their prices. One activist commented on how YCW was somewhat out of step:

> People were also romanticizing the armed struggle at that time. There was this mood that the seizure of power is imminent. YCW lost many people to MK. We were told to stop analyzing and to come and fight, because liberation is around the corner. People got impatient with the YCW's method of analyzing and strategizing. It was the time of easy slogans. . . . Also, the inter-organizational rivalry badly affected the YCW. In YCW were people both from UDF and from AZAPO. YCW was preaching political tolerance, but that went against the mood of the time. Some YCW members in the Eastern Cape were almost killed by the UDF because they did not want to side against AZAPO.[40]

Thus, although it had made a significant contribution to the development of talented leadership for trade unions, student organizations, and civics, in the fray of the mid-1980s YCW was increasingly forced to the sidelines. Toward the end of the decade, YCW membership stood at a low ebb. The unbanning of the ANC caused a new discussion about YCW's future. The 1991 YCW national executive remained convinced that the organization still had a role to play: "The YCW has to look beyond immediate political goals; you need to have a vision, a vision of a better society, the Kingdom of God."[41] YCW as such was not among the main actors in the mid-1980s. The organization nevertheless deserves to be taken into account in any assessment of this episode, because of its importance as a training ground for youth leadership.

In Kagiso, YCW deserves mention in at least two capacities. Several leading activists had an YCW background, while a core of YCW activists came to present the local variant of a "workerist opposition" in the heady months of people's power in 1985–86. The young man who introduced a group of Kagiso youth to YCW was Bafana Seripe, who had been working for YCW in the Cape. He became YCW organizer for the West Rand in 1981 and served as YCW national president from 1982 to 1984. His audience was duly impressed. "Most of us had much problems with Christianity, but the YCW was dealing with our concrete problems. It dealt with issues like SRC's, corporal punishment, problems of unemployment, the importance of unionization, the different strands in unionism, like workerism and populism, with worker problems like health and safety, long working hours and with community issues like the corruption of town councillors."[42] Seripe's YCW group then

linked up with Frank Chikane's IYCC and some AZAPO activists to conduct
house-to-house visits to inform residents about the impending rent increase
and to prepare the ground for the formation of the civic.

Other civic activists in Kagiso with a YCW background were the brothers
George, Tizza, and Busang Moiloa, and Serge Mokonyane. At the time, the
YCW group consisted mainly of young workers and unemployed youth, not
high school students. George Moiloa, who in 1981 was elected secretary of
KRO, recalled a certain ambivalence in his YCW group toward his civic activities. "The emphasis was on workers' action. People in the YCW would be
somewhat scornful of community work such as in KRO." The "heavy guys" of
the YCW favored work floor action and regarded community work as a "soft
option." They were rather dismissive of all the campaigns, rallies, and commemorations that tended to become an end in itself. "It was more noise than
substance, it did not change anything."[43]

COSAS, ANC, and Trade Unions

Since they are much better known than YCW, the Congress of South African
Students (COSAS), the ANC, and the trade unions need less introduction.
Kagiso had a fairly active COSAS branch in 1979–81. One of the COSAS
activists in 1980 was Vusi Gqobi, who also served on the COSAS national
executive. He was in touch with Chikane's IYCC, where he met Lawrence
Ntlokoa. In 1981, when Ntlokoa, thoroughly fed up with his banning order,
unemployment, and police harassment, wanted to flee the country, he contacted Gqobi, who was a student leader of some stature. Gqobi arranged
transport to Swaziland for Ntlokoa, his girlfriend, their baby boy, and one
other young man. But Gqobi was apparently working as a police informer.
The car was halted at a roadblock by policemen who knew all the details about
its occupants. Ntlokoa landed in jail for 14 months for contravening his banning order. Meanwhile, Gqobi skipped the country but was subsequently
arrested by the ANC in Mozambique.[44]

This incident led to the breakdown of the COSAS branch in Kagiso. Later,
in 1984, the branch was reconstituted by a new crop of high school activists,
but it remained weak and ineffective. "There was too much harassment. We
could not have meetings, not in the schools and not in the churches. Only
later, in 1985–86, then it was possible to have meetings."[45] The absence of an
active COSAS branch partly explains why Kagiso remained quiet in 1984–85,
while riots spread through the Vaal and the East Rand townships.[46] Although
the YCW branch in Kagiso seems to have produced only male activists,
through COSAS some young women became involved in civic matters. One
of them was Nomvula Mkhize, who after having completed matric became an

active trade unionist and a civic activist with a strong interest in women's issues. She emerged from this turbulent decade as a dedicated member of the South African Communist Party (SACP), serving on the SACP Transvaal leadership in 1991.

The ANC was virtually unmentionable in the early 1980s. George Moiloa and his brothers never discussed politics at home but discovered the ANC on their own: "We began listening to Radio Freedom around 1973. We used to kind of steal my father's radio. When he came home after work, he would unlock his cupboard and I would take the radio out and take it to school. One time he caught me. I told him that we were listening to Radio Freedom and he was absolutely furious. Eight years later I found out that he been an ANC member all along."[47]

At the time of the formation of KRO, ideological loyalties were not clearly crystallized. George and his friends worked with AZAPO members and generally considered BC organizations to be allies rather than adversaries of the ANC. The extent of ANC underground organization in Kagiso is difficult to gauge. My interviews were conducted in 1990–91, when many people claimed that they had been working in the ANC all along. Ike Genu, the vice-chair of KRO, mentioned himself and Sister Bernard as members of an underground ANC cell in Kagiso.[48] He saw it as his responsibility to ensure the primacy of the ANC in township politics and to guard against tendencies to build the UDF or the civic leadership as an alternative organization. For example, he distributed banned ANC literature during civic meetings.

Trade union organization was rather weak in Kagiso, but the civic leadership included some active unionists. KRO chair Joe Makgothlo acquired organizational experience in the Food and Beverage Workers Union (FBWU). He worked as an overseer for South African Breweries (SAB) in Chamdor and was actively involved in the FBWU and in its umbrella organization CUSA (Council of Unions of South Africa), as well as in the Lutheran Church. Unlike FOSATU, CUSA favored involvement of its union membership in community issues. Makgothlo agreed with that position: "If I get a pay rise, and the rent goes up, then I lose again. I am the same person on the factory floor and in the township." He found that the organizing and negotiating skills learned in his union activities were helpful in his civic work. Trade unions and the Soweto Civic Association served as a model when members of the KRO sat down to write a constitution for the civic.[49]

Another active trade unionist in the KRO executive was Serge Mokonyane, who lived in Munsieville and worked for an engineering company in Krugersdorp. He was a voluntary organizer for GAWU (General and Allied Workers Union) before he became a full-time employed GAWU organizer in 1983. Not only did the civic benefit from people with union experience; conversely, the unions could make use of civic channels. "The West Rand had a low level of trade union organization. The civic saw it as significant to popularize the unions, to give workers advice, to distribute pamphlets with information on various trade union offices. Kagiso became a GAWU stronghold."[50]

With these various inputs, KRO could benefit from wide-ranging experiences and organizational expertise. Leading activists were linked into an extensive network of contacts with other organizations and other townships. Sympathetic church leaders provided meeting facilities. The civic could draw on the experience of older, respected township residents and on the energies of highly motivated and articulate youth activists. It had the potential to become a broad-based organization.

KRO's First Phase, 1981–1983

Of the ten people who were elected to the executive of KRO in February 1981, only four or five actually took up their positions. Active involvement in civic matters meant taking risks, and the KRO leadership was acutely aware of this. When George Moiloa accepted his election as KRO secretary, he decided to resign his job as distributor of the West Rand Sorghum Beer Board. He expected to be victimized if he combined civic activism with work for a state enterprise. Moiloa, who had completed high school in 1978, decided to look for a factory job instead. But he remained unemployed for nearly a year, during which he worked as a full-time activist. He then managed to get a well-paid clerical job at Hoechst in the Chamdor Industrial Area, with prospects for further improvement. But the police used to follow him around the plant, and he was detained several times until he lost his job because the management found the police presence embarrassing. Immediately after Moiloa was fired, the police came to fetch him and made it clear to him that he would never find a new job. He remained unemployed until 1983, when he was appointed organizer for the Young Christian Workers.[51]

After the suspension of the rent increase, the immediate cause for the formation of KRO, many residents lost interest. It proved difficult to staff the various subcommittees. The original plan for a signed-up, fee-paying membership, as outlined in the constitution, did not materialize. Initially, only the Catholic Church and the Apostolic Faith Mission were willing to provide accommodation for meetings. Other churches refused because of objections by the community councillors, some of whom were also church elders, and out of fear for the security police. The KRO executive arranged a meeting with all the churches in Kagiso, explaining that "the churches do not belong to the security police, but to the people."[52] But it was only after KRO approached the South African Council of Churches in Johannesburg that churches in Kagiso were made available for civic meetings.

Interest in the civic was revived when the council decided to reintroduce the rent increase in August 1981, and the bus company announced a raise in fares from 30 cents to 32 cents. Also at this time, the council decided to go ahead with the construction of a large hostel for migrant workers, a project that had been planned back in 1976 but that remained unknown to the inhabitants of Kagiso until work on the building actually began. Not only KRO but also the board of Leratong Hospital and a training center at Chamdor protested against the erection of a 20 million Rand hostel that was to accommodate about six thousand men. The hostel, much larger than the existing migrant workers' barracks in Kagiso I, was to be built between Leratong Hospital and Kagiso II. The proposed hostel was branded "a danger to the community" and a threat to "the morals of the people."[53]

In a newspaper interview, Frank Chikane explained that the planned hostel would "injure the morals" and break up family life in the township. Thousands of married men would be forced to live together in this huge complex. Hostel dwellers, however, were portrayed not only as menaces but also as victims of the system. "Hostel-dwellers are only human. They are forced to live in circumstances that force them to misbehave." The site of the hostel caused fear among student nurses at Leratong Hospital, who would have to pass it on their way to work. Residents quoted in newspaper interviews were generally of the opinion that hostels did not belong in townships altogether, in view of the attacks by hostel dwellers on residents in several sections of Soweto after the 1976 unrest.[54]

KRO also linked the building of a unisex hostel to the perpetuation of the migratory labor system and noted that, whereas the labor was required by white industrialists, the black township was saddled with the social consequences of the migrant labor system. Moreover, the township had a severe shortage of housing, as was evident from the proliferating numbers of backyard shacks and the overcrowded houses, which parents had to share with their married children. The solution proposed by KRO was to build the hostel in a white residential area and to provide houses for township residents on the proposed hostel site. The Kagiso council, which had initially approved the hostel complex, now reversed itself and supported the demand to build two thousand houses instead. The issues were discussed at a public meeting attended by about a hundred residents. The council argued that the rent increases for Kagiso and Munsieville were long overdue, for rents in other West Rand townships had already been raised back in 1979.[55]

KRO called a mass meeting at which those attending decided not to pay the rent increase. Instead, they would stage a boycott against the Greyhound bus company and would march to the West Rand Administration Board office in order to see the mayor. The marchers were met by police wielding sjamboks and firing tear gas. Some violent incidents took place, such as stoning buses and setting afire some buildings.[56] The mayor refused to see the petitioners, arguing that most of the marchers were children. After the march, three members of the KRO executive were detained for over two weeks on accusations of holding an illegal meeting, but the charges were eventually dropped. Ten others, arrested on charges of public violence, were later acquitted.

The campaign was partially successful. The hostel project was not abandoned, but it was scaled down to a smaller size, and new housing projects were undertaken. But the rent increase was implemented, although KRO made another attempt at stopping it by engaging a lawyer who argued that the measure was unlawful since it had not been officially announced, as legally required. However, rents were simply announced in retrospect.[57]

A new rent increase in 1982 brought a new protest meeting. This time, at two meetings organized by KRO, petitions circulated calling for the resignation of the council, the scrapping of the Community Council Act since "it was not approved and accepted by the Black people of Krugersdorp" and the recognition of KRO as "our sole representative organisation established according to a constitution made and accepted by the Black people of Krugersdorp."[58] This was going one step beyond protests and petitions: now the civic declared the council illegitimate since it was based on legislation in which Africans had had no part. Thus, even before the formation of the UDF, civics linked local issues such as rents with the disenfranchisement of Africans.

Information on the relationship between KRO and the migrants in the hostels—a relevant matter, particularly in view of the events in 1990—is rather sketchy. Representatives of the older hostel in Kagiso I were invited to the 1981 meeting protesting the construction of a new hostel. According to Sister Bernard, they joined residents in rejecting the new hostel.[59] George Moiloa recalled several not very successful attempts to involve the hostel people in civic matters. At one point, the civic tried to address hostel issues when hostel dwellers approached the civic with a complaint about the lack of hot water. "We were willing to look at their problems . . . but there was no follow up. But we were already struggling with organizing the residents, that was our first priority. It was a difficult time, people were scared, it was very depressive. . . . Hostels fell outside the scope of KRO; squatters mostly, too."[60]

The inmates in the hostels were not affected by rent increases in the townships, since their fees were set under different regulations. Backyard tenants, living in shacks in the backyards of township houses, would be indirectly affected, as the landlords would generally pass on any increase in rents and service charges to their tenants. However, tenants were in a more vulnerable position that did not allow for collective action. Township residents in council houses could diminish their individual vulnerability by engaging in a collective rent boycott, but backyard tenants could not link forces and were afraid of eviction in a time of acute housing shortages. Another raise in service charges came in 1983, but KRO succeeded in getting the increase in rates reduced by petitioning the minister of cooperation and development.[61] This was the year of constitutional reform, with a concomitant relaxation of repression in the colored and Indian communities, the main targets of the government's co-option strategy. For Kagiso, however, 1983 was a year of fear.

In March, Sister Bernard, Lettie Nzima, and Ike Genu were detained on charges of possession of banned literature and, in the case of Genu, ANC membership. When other members of the executive were called as state witnesses, the KRO leadership became divided on whether or not to give evidence. After consultations with a lawyer, chair Joe Makgothlo did give evidence but without further incriminating Genu. George Moiloa and Lettie Nzima refused to testify.[62] Moiloa was detained in August 1983, together with two others, on charges of furthering the aims of the ANC, charges that related to the celebration of National Women's Day in 1982. The state alleged that in the past this event had been commemorated by the ANC Women's League. Therefore, if the accused had now marked this occasion on the same date, they were guilty of furthering the aims of the ANC. After a trial lasting more than three months, all three were acquitted.

In the case against Genu, the public prosecutor produced some T-shirts in green, yellow, and black with texts such as "Mayibuye" and "Back to God" and a copy of the ANC magazine *Mayibuye.* One of the T-shirts sported the words "Viva Mandela," a text obviously puzzling to the court clerk, who noted in the proceedings: "Mandela who is on Robben Island. Apparently a prisoner."[63] The judge noted that Genu had no previous convictions and that he had already spent over half a year as a remand prisoner, but he considered ANC membership a "very grave crime." Genu was sentenced to eight years. Testimony in the court case against Genu appears to indicate that he had been openly propagating the ANC, bringing ANC flags to civic meetings in church halls, pointing out the radio frequencies for Radio Freedom, and telling people that KRO was fighting civic issues under the banner of the ANC.[64]

This harsh sentence, based solely on the use of ANC symbols, was more severe than had been customary at that time. In the trial against Moiloa, the state produced ANC publications that he claimed he had never seen before. "They also brought in an ex-ANC fighter to testify in camera. This scared everybody to death. People were thinking that we were involved in underground activity." He interpreted the court case as an attempt to take the KRO leadership out of circulation and to warn residents not to associate with these "terrorists." The political trials served their purpose. Many residents were thoroughly intimidated, and the civic leadership became weakened by internal division. Suspicions had been sown by a seemingly arbitrary policy on the part of the public prosecutor as to which persons were issued with a subpoena to testify in the case against Genu. George Moiloa, although called as a state witness, was not subpoenaed in the case against Genu. This had the usual effect of causing rumors and speculations: Why would the police have decided to leave Moiloa alone? Moiloa was critical of Genu's "populist" style, which aimed at popularizing the ANC rather than building grassroots support for the civic. "I did not want this very high political profile. People began to freak."[65] Shortly afterward, Moiloa left Kagiso where his "opting out" was not taken kindly by the remaining civic leadership. However, he did not drop out of activism but, rather, chose to operate in a new environment: he went to work as YCW organizer in Soweto.

By late 1983, KRO had seriously declined. Attempts to revive the civic produced no concrete results. "KRO had reached a state of exhaustion."[66] The lapse into inactivity can be partly explained by repression. An important part of the leadership was removed from civic life by trials that dragged on for months, while the Kagiso community was intimidated by the severe sentence against Genu. It has also been argued that KRO had a weak structure, relying too much on single-issue campaigns rather than on organization building.[67] Moiloa had a somewhat different assessment of KRO. In accordance with YCW principles, he believed that concentrating on the concrete local issues of everyday township life was the best strategy for building solid organizations. But confidence in the benefits of collective action would grow only only if it could be shown that the action produced concrete results. Delivering the goods generally required dealing with relevant authorities. He blamed KRO's relative ineffectiveness on the strong focus on protest and the lack of negotiating skills. "KRO believed very much in protest action. You would have meetings and blast the councillors as sellouts. . . . We limited ourselves to protest, we got ourselves arrested, we scared people off, and we could not deliver anything for fear of engaging in reformist action."[68]

This verdict seems overly harsh: KRO was not adverse to dealing with authorities. On several occasions its campaigns were at least partially successful. KRO's leadership was not out of touch with residents who preferred nonconfrontational tactics over radical posturing. Illustrative of this is the fact that KRO only called for a boycott of the rent increase; residents continued to pay the original amount of rent. In the insurgent atmosphere of the mid-1980s, many civics, including KRO, went through a process of rapid radicalization. But before radicalization set in, from 1983 until 1985 KRO first went through a phase of decline and revival.

KRO's Decline and Revival: 1983–1985

For South Africa, 1984 was marked by the introduction of the tricameral parliament, the successful election boycott spearheaded by the UDF, and, beginning in September, the eruption of township revolt in the Vaal Triangle. But in Kagiso not much happened. In late 1983, KRO affiliated with the UDF but did not take an active part in UDF campaigns. Another rent increase failed to galvanize protest. The Kagiso civic had now joined forces with the Munsieville Development Committee. Renamed as the Krugersdorp Residents Organisation (KRO), it represented both the Krugersdorp townships. Up until this time, the committee in Munsieville had been fairly ineffective, limiting itself to the occasional organization of charities or assistance with funerals. Nevertheless, some important changes occurred in this period of inactivity. Beginning in 1985, youth became more prominent in civic activities, while KRO also experienced a partial change in leadership.

Lawrence Ntlokoa's banning order was lifted in July 1983. The severe terms of this order, which forbade him from receiving visitors without prior permission, had precluded any active involvement in civic matters. Unable to find a job, he completed his high school studies through a correspondence course. In December 1983 he was attacked and stabbed by a group of balaclava-clad men. During a three-week stay in the hospital he did some hard thinking about the next phase of his life. He first wanted to get a job. He did indeed manage to find a position as stock-controller with Hoechst in the Chamdor industrial area and joined the Chemical Workers' Union, later becoming shop steward. In June 1984 he was co-opted to the executive of KRO and appointed secretary of the civic. In the somewhat milder political climate of 1984, having a regular job and holding a leading position in a civic were apparently no longer incompatible, as they had been in the days of George Moiloa. Ike Genu was acquitted on appeal and returned from Robben Island in August 1984. He resumed his position as vice-chair of KRO.

Ntlokoa, now in his late twenties, embarked on an evaluation of KRO's performance with the use of methods learned in his days in YCW. While the civic was still trying to get on its feet, the townships of the Vaal Triangle erupted in a violent conflagration of rent protests, attacks on councillors, and police repression. "We were then drawn into events, like the other civics. There was no time for a thorough reorganization."[69] In support of the Vaal townships, KRO launched a consumer boycott against white businesses. It was a purely local boycott, not linked to similar initiatives elsewhere, and it fell flat because of poor organization. Later that year, an attempt to boycott Greyhound buses in protest against a rise in fares also failed.[70] The two-day stayaway in November of that year, also called in protest against repression in the Vaal townships, was equally ineffective in Kagiso.

Strategy and tactics receded to the background when KRO became caught up in unfolding events. But the strategy document drawn up by Lawrence Ntlokoa in late 1984 still makes interesting reading. Under Lenin's adage "without a revolutionary theory there can be no revolution," he criticized the absence of social cohesiveness and the lack of political education.[71] Civic activists, claimed Ntlokoa, met only at meetings. They did not attempt to involve their families or friends, and they had no other joint activities, which the author blamed on bad ways, womanizing, excessive drunkenness, negative attitudes, and bad company, among others. "It is because some people (activists) are not wholly revolutionary are opportunists who are in struggle for what they can get out of it, e.g. information (to be passed on to the enemy) popularity that the individual gains and material gains. That is why they don't try to conscientize those close to them." After this rather stern moral judgment on his fellow activists, Ntlokoa lamented the lack of political education, resulting in spontaneous action without proper organizational foundations and without a clear sense of direction. This amounted to taking "advantage of spontaneity without sowing the seeds, so the struggle can be a class-conscious struggle. Now that things are happening in Vaal, East Rand, Evaton and other places we feel left out and without proper planning we want to jump the wagon." He pointed to the absence of an organized fee-paying membership. KRO was based on the assumption that every resident in Kagiso was a member and that anyone attending meetings was an activist. This resulted in loose structures and lack of funds to finance further activities. "There is no political hegemony and coherence. The organization since its launching has been working loosely. There was no political education of the activists at all, let alone of the masses." Building a "community of activists" required more social activities and also a more service-oriented approach—for example, by setting up a burial society and a food cooperative that could provide low-priced groceries because of bulk-buying. Ntlokoa aspired to build a "political community" in Kagiso, rather than an issue-oriented civic with limited goals. In spite of the revolutionary headline, the focus was on organization building rather than on confrontation.

In spite of these discussions on how to reorganize the civic and how to widen its base and its scope, not much happened. Another analysis of KRO, presented at a committee meeting in May 1985, again noted that KRO had "the potential of becoming an effective organisation," but that it was hampered by limited participation and inadequate communication "with the masses." "We tend to talk too much at meetings but our talking never produces any action and deeds."[72]

Meanwhile, KRO was apparently sufficiently revamped to engage in a successful battle on familiar terrain: a rent issue. In March 1985, residents had

6. Silkscreened poster in black and yellow produced by KRO Ad-Hoc Committee, Johannesburg, 1985. Courtesy South African History Archive (SAHA); from *Images of Defiance: South African Resistance Posters of the 1980's/Poster Book Collective, South African History Archive.* Johannesburg: Raven Press, 1991.

received notices from the council claiming rent arrears ranging from 22.50 to 900 Rand, in some cases dating back to 1981. No explanations were offered. Instead, mayor Edward Moeketsi had added a message that read: "Thank you for your loyal support of my council and for keeping Kagiso calm in these troubled times."[73] Two mass meetings, organized by KRO in Kagiso and Munsieville, were attended by about two thousand people. At these meetings, it was resolved that a KRO delegation should meet the town clerk to demand an explanation for these arrears, since many residents could produce their receipts of rent paid since 1981. It was also resolved that until the matter was solved satisfactorily, residents should pay only their normal rents. Those attending the meetings also called on the town councillors to resign.[74] One resident raised the question whether KRO could meet with the council, but this apparently was not a cause for much debate. The minutes simply state that "it was explained that it is possible."[75] A KRO delegation met town clerk B. J. Vorster, who explained that a mistake had been made with a change in administration. It was all blamed on the computer. All arrears accumulated before July 1984, the date on which the Kagiso council became a local authority under the new system of local government, were written off.[76]

The call for the councillors to resign had been made repeatedly in previous months, with KRO warning that it would call for a boycott of shops owned by town councillors if they did not heed the call to step down. Mayor Moeketsi had retorted that "for the sake of peace in the township," KRO should "not try to emulate what our contemporaries in other areas are doing." He gave a curious justification for wanting to serve on the town council: "We are equally involved in the struggle. Even scavengers play a significant role in the struggle because without their help, diseases could spread."[77]

Although KRO successfully intervened in the rent dispute, this action did not lead to a revival of sustained civic activities. In the same period, a housing seminar had to be canceled due to lack of attendance.[78] A transportation dispute, which arose in early 1985, was resolved between the Kagiso Taxi Association and the town council, apparently without intervention by KRO. The Greyhound Bus Company, which ran intertown bus lines on the West Rand, had introduced a new system of minibuses that operated in the township and between Kagiso and Krugersdorp, charging five cents less than the local Black Taxis. The Kagiso Taxi Association, representing about eighty taxi owners, was angry about the perceived unfair competition that threatened to put local enterprise out of business. The council, which had not been informed by Greyhound about the new minibus service, sided with the taxi owners.[79] The taxi owners obviously saw no need to turn to KRO, since they were assured of a sympathetic hearing by the council. It was common for town councillors to have an interest in the Black Taxi business, either through direct ownership or through front men.

Nor was KRO involved in a limited rent protest in Riverside, an elite housing section in Kagiso, where residents protested against high rentals of over 100 Rand for poorly built houses. The Kagiso town clerk admitted that houses in Riverside were expensive, but added that nobody was forced to live there.[80] The localized protest action by these relatively well-off residents was apparently conducted without involvement from KRO.

One long-standing issue, the threatened demolition of Munsieville to make way for an extension of Krugersdorp, seemed resolved when Gerrit Viljoen, minister of cooperation, development and education, stated that no community would be moved by force. The Kagiso Council warmly welcomed the announcement, which cleared the way for the upgrading of Munsieville. It also meant that land in Kagiso, which had been set aside for Munsieville residents, could now be allocated to private developers for a new housing division.[81] KRO, however, remained suspicious of the suspension of forced removals.[82] They had good reason: the demolition of Munsieville would be contemplated again in 1986.

The Role of Women

Meanwhile, KRO made new but largely unsuccessful attempts to broaden itself from a single-issue organization to other spheres of township life. In February 1985, KRO held a special "Mothers Mass Meeting" to discuss problems of pensioners and "specific mothers' issues at house, community and at work."[83] But attendance was poor. At a subsequent meeting, the KRO executive resolved that a women's organization needed to be formed to establish cooperation with the Federation of Transvaal Women. It was decided that "Sister Bernard should co-opt some women."[84] It is noteworthy that KRO chose to address its potential female constituency as "mothers," which indicated limitations both to the range of women addressed and to the scope of envisaged activities. In Kagiso as elsewhere, women's issues were frequently marginal to the civic's central concerns.

The young men who laid the foundations of KRO "did not consciously think about involving women." They reasoned that the "mass consultation process was done at night. It was thought that only men would be able to move around the township at night."[85] After the formation of KRO, women did play a role, with Sister Bernard and Lettie Nzima, both middle-aged women, being the main exponents. Prominent women like Albertina Sisulu and Amanda Kwadi were invited to address civic meetings, and KRO also participated in the commemoration of Women's Day on 9 August. But women's involvement remained problematic. Women were reluctant to assert their position; men generally believed that a woman's place was in the home. "Initially, women were unable to participate in civic activities," recalled Nomvula Mkhize later. "One reason was the insecurity of the streets at night. But another reason was that men would not allow their wives to be involved in these activities. It was a general thing; no attention was given to women's issues."[86] She herself became involved in politics through COSAS and church youth activities. But not many young women took an interest in politics. Mkhize's interest in politics was raised because she used to hang around with the boys on her street. She commented further on the complications women faced:

> There was the combined problem of age domination and gender domination: as a young girl you could not raise issues like sexual abuse, women's problems, female unemployment etc. Men usually did not take these issues seriously. For instance, if the husband dies, then the house—the ownership or the rent contract—goes to the oldest son, not to the wife. Women are in a dependent position. There are also the problems with health care. There are no proper clinics in Kagiso. The clinics that are there focus mainly on contraception. That is very humiliating for women, because if you are seen going to such a clinic, the men will point at you and say, hah, she is taking contraceptives, she must be having a boyfriend.

The women's group in Kagiso, formed in 1984, later became a branch of FEDTRAW (Federation of Transvaal Women). But even in 1984 "it was still very difficult to get women to come to meetings, because the men left many responsibilities to the women, household work, looking after children. They thought that women should stay at home; even men who were themselves political activists would take that position. Because it would have consequences for themselves, they would have to share in household work. Taking women's issues seriously is very threatening for men."[87] Nomvula Mkhize came to represent the women's organization in KRO, where she tried without much success to get women's issues on the agenda.

The problems encountered in Kagiso were fairly typical of women's organizations in the Transvaal townships, as is evident from a report on a workshop held in 1984 by the Federation of South African Women (FEDSAW), which was also attended by representatives from Kagiso.[88] The various women's groups described how they organized women around everyday concerns: high prices, high rents, low wages for women workers, child care, a bulk-buying scheme to provide cheaper groceries to members, mutual aid schemes, day-care centers. These were low-threshold concerns likely to engage ordinary women. Politics and matters specifically relating to the oppression of women, such as rape and other forms of sexual violence, proved more difficult. The Soweto group reported that many grassroots women were apprehensive of joining because of the high political profile of the group. Elsewhere, women had even accused the organizers of "hijacking them into politics." Other members had become "confused" about women's organizations after reading about the "women's liberation" movements in England and the United States.

The participants discussed extensively why women, although active in trade unions, student organizations, and civics, rarely got elected to leadership positions. This problem was blamed not only on men who believed that women were inferior but also on women who had internalized the established role patterns: "We are told that we are weak and we believe this." This lack of confidence enables "our male comrades to take us for granted." They "don't always show us respect. They also tell us what our women's groups should be doing." However, from these proceedings it is clear that even women activists hardly contemplated a redefinition of roles. Although tradition, culture, and churches were blamed for perpetuating the belief that women are weak, and although it was emphasized that women needed to take part in the broader struggle, the women's organizations basically limited their concerns to family and household obligations: "As women we have to look after the children and the house. This means that we have to deal with all the financial burdens, the rising prices, GST, increases in community services. We also have to see to the education of our children. So we are the ones who take all the responsibility— we are the sponges at the bottom absorbing all the shocks."

Even in discussing how women should be involved in the political struggle, it was still taken for granted that women should play this role in their capacity as mothers: "We, as mothers, are the first teachers of our children. We are the ones teaching future generations. . . . Without getting this knowledge for ourselves, we cannot hope to educate our children in a responsible way nor will we be able to teach other women."[89] Both political culture and religious ethics, even in the variant of liberation theology, militated against women's involvement as women. A document entitled "Black Woman's Theology" stressed that men and women were absolutely equal in personal and fundamental values, but that women fulfilled different functions that were not competitive but complementary to those of men. It then pronounced a divine sanction over women's role as mothers: "The primary function, the lofty goal, and the sublime mission which God himself has set a woman is motherhood."[90]

Politically active women were often inclined to subordinate women's interests to the national liberation struggle. Amanda Kwadi of FEDSAW, who held the women's portfolio on the UDF Transvaal executive, harbored deep suspicions against *feminism:* "The idea of feminism goes hand in hand with capitalism and imperialism, something which the Women's Federation in South Africa denounces. Maybe, as time goes on, there'll be clarification, but at the moment when we get deep into feminism it goes so much against African tradition that it is totally out. We're in the middle of a liberation struggle, but women's liberation is not necessary at this stage. We are far more concerned about total liberation; and automatically our own liberation will follow."[91]

Not only men but also women invoked "tradition" or "human nature" to justify patriarchal gender relations, even though actual practice was often far removed from the supposed traditional ideal type. After a slow start, the women's organization in Kagiso grew to about two hundred members in 1985–86. Members tended to see their organization as a discussion group for mothers' problems, such as undisciplined children, juvenile delinquency, and housing problems. Funds were raised by selling secondhand clothes. Members did not see their group as a lobby to put women's affairs on the agenda of the civic, for "they were dealing with separate issues."[92] Overtly political action was taken only when repression mounted, and women saw their children beaten up by the police. Thus, when in early 1986 the women marched to the police station in Krugersdorp to protest against police harassing their children, they were acting in their role as mothers. The march was welcomed by the civic leadership and still was mentioned in the interviews with KRO leaders as one of the feats of township resistance in Kagiso.

This example of repression inducing a radicalization of women is at odds with Jeremy Seekings's suggestion that the shift to violent conflict in the mid-1980s contributed to the exclusion of women. In seeking to explain why women were less prominently involved in township politics than in the 1950s, he points to the tensions between "the politics of organisation and the politics of confrontation." Escalating confrontation brought a growing influence of former or potential gang members, with their machismo group culture in which women were more likely to be seen as "rewards and trophies" than as equal participants.[93] This may well be the case, but it would not be a reason for women to keep clear of civic activities. Many civics became actively involved in improving public safety, an issue to which women gave high priority. In Kagiso, the civic and the youth congress owed much of their popularity among women to their anticrime campaigns.

Youth Organization: A Slow Start

Attempts at organizing women in the context of the civic had a slow start. More surprisingly perhaps, setting up a local youth congress also proved difficult. Like elsewhere, high school students in Kagiso were impatient with the pace of events in the adult organizations: "The youth is more fast thinking."[94] But transforming youth consciousness into youth organization was not a smooth operation. About two hundred people had been invited by KRO to a workshop in May 1985 to discuss the feasibility of forming a local youth congress, but only eleven people showed up. The participants believed that there was a potential for a youth organization, "but lack of organisation is having a role of frustration and confusion." Politicized high school students, the most likely youth to take the initiative, were being "victimised at school level."[95] After the COSAS branch had collapsed in 1982, attempts had been made to reconstitute a Kagiso branch. An interim structure had been formed in 1984, but schools did not permit COSAS meetings on the school grounds.

In Munsieville, "youth interest groups" had been established in late 1983, organized to take up general issues such as the lack of facilities for youth but also to tackle matters of public safety such as stabbings and rape.[96] In May 1985, a committee was formed by youth from Kagiso II. KRO discussed whether the International Year of the Youth could provide a suitable framework for a local youth organization to get off the ground. The range of possible activities discussed sounds surprisingly apolitical: drama, music, reading, tennis, cinemas, meetings, football, poetry, boxing, horse racing.[97]

The nationwide banning of COSAS in August 1985 provided another impetus for the formation of a youth congress in Kagiso. Church youth groups and sports clubs were approached as youth began to assert a distinct role for themselves in township politics. The Kagiso Youth Congress (KAYCO) was formed around July or August of 1985.[98] Meetings were held in the Catholic Church near Sister Bernard's convent. Surprisingly, KAYCO leaders saw their main responsibilities not in addressing specific youth issues but in maintaining public safety. The high death rate in Kagiso, as a consequence of crime, stabbings, and excessive drinking, was singled out as the most pressing concern.[99] The first major campaign undertaken by KAYCO was the anticrime campaign in December 1985.

Violent protest in Kagiso began on 16 June 1985 with the commemoration of the 1976 student revolt, in spite of KRO's efforts to ensure a peaceful day of remembrance. The Taverners' Association had agreed to KRO's request to close the shebeens, or taverns, on the weekend of 16 June; shops would close down from 10 a.m. to 5 p.m. No special observance of the day was demanded from the Taxi Association.[100] Violent incidents erupted when police fired tear gas into the crowd after the service in the Methodist Church. [101] The shop of town councillor Goodman Mabasa was set on fire although he had obeyed a call to keep his shop closed. Shortly afterward, Mabasa and another councillor resigned their positions on the council and were applauded by KRO for doing so. Violent incidents intensified during July and August. Houses of councillors and police vehicles were pelted with stones, and a supermarket was plundered and set on fire. Most incidents involved youth, with schools—both primary and secondary—being the main centers of violent protest. In several instances police fired teargas or rubber bullets.[102]

An attempt by the civic to enforce a consumer boycott in August 1985 fell flat, and several KRO leaders were detained for a hundred days.[103] Ike Genu would remain in detention until March 1986. Unrest in the schools simmered on after the events of 16 June, which had led to the arrest of several students. One of the causes of unrest was the death of a pupil from the Junior Secondary School, who was allegedly shot by his uncle, a shopkeeper, during an argument over gasoline. Youth plundered the shop and later set afire the shopkeeper's house. In September, firebombs caused 300,000 Rand of damage in the Senior Secondary School. Student demands included the introduction of democratically elected student representative councils (SRCs), an end to corporal punishment, improvement of the library, and the release of fellow students who had been detained in June.[104]

Violent incidents, including more attacks on the houses of town councillors, continued until December. But compared to many other townships in the PWV region, Kagiso remained fairly quiet. The partial State of Emergency, declared on 20 July 1985, included Soweto and several other West Rand townships, but not Kagiso. Only in December 1985 did Kagiso enter a phase of mass mobilization and widespread rebellion and repression. Before looking at KRO in that phase of township revolt, we examine the changing context in which the civic was now operating.

Local Politics and National Liberation

Why was it that Kagiso, and other townships like Soweto and Mamelodi, remained relatively quiet until late 1985, while the Vaal townships erupted in September 1984? Why do people not revolt?[105] If rebellion was a natural state of life for oppressed Africans, as the liberation movements proclaimed and as many authors have assumed, why then was it that most of the time most people did not revolt? If civics formed part of a UDF/ANC conspiracy to overthrow the South African government in a violent revolution, as the state argued in numerous political trials, why then was revolt so very uneven, both in time and in place? The idiom of the *struggle,* in which all the *oppressed* are lumped together into the *underclass* or the *fighting masses,* paints an exaggerated picture of the homogeneity of black South Africa and of the revolutionary fervor of ordinary black South Africans. It ignores the cleavages—economic, social, cultural, ethnic, generational, and gender—within black society. At least part of the rebellion of the mid-1980s was a generational revolt, challenging not only the white oppressors but also African patterns of authority.

The picture that emerges from this chapter thus far is that most people in Kagiso were not waiting impatiently to plunge themselves into a revolutionary onslaught on the state—not because they were contented helots but because most of the time the perceived risks of collective action outweighed the perceived benefits. Township revolt in Kagiso was a reluctant rebellion. Kagiso residents were driven toward revolt when violent repression interfered with their daily lives to a point where it could no longer be ignored.[106] While the UDF head office in Johannesburg and the ANC headquarters in Lusaka undoubtedly aspired to steer and coordinate events, most outbreaks of revolt, in Kagiso and elsewhere, were spontaneous and local. Local incidents provided the spark that set off the explosion into revolt. But the existence of the

UDF made the sparks into a bushfire that began to resemble a general insurrection. Struggles against local governments became linked to a challenge to
the central state. As most civics affiliated with the UDF, they entered into a
broad network allowing for consultation and coordination and providing
access to new resources.

In the first one and a half years of its existence, the UDF was strongly
focused on national politics. After a reassessment in 1985, linking local grievances to the strategic issue of state power became central to the UDF mode
of operation. The UDF could stage massive protests. But—with boycotts as
a centerpiece of its strategy—could it also point toward concrete improvements obtained as a result of mass action? How could the UDF negotiate
improvements without falling into the "reformist trap"? How did KRO deal
with the local town council? What did affiliation with the UDF mean for civic
activities?

For KRO, the replacement of the old community council by the new town
council, established under the Black Local Authorities Act, seemed to make little difference. Sometimes confusion could arise, for some former responsibilities of the administration boards were transferred to the town councils.
Complaints of incompetence and corruption continued as before. For years
on end, residents kept paying a monthly fee of 2.50 Rand for the electrification of the township without seeing any progress. Councillors were widely
accused of giving out trading concessions, liquor licenses, and building sites
for bribes. The mayor himself was a shop owner, and one councillor reportedly had allotted nineteen trading sites to himself. In the view of KRO, councillors were a self-serving clique of shop owners "who only get themselves
voted into the council only to get business."[107]

KRO dealt with the town council while at the same time calling for the resignation of the town councillors. Meetings with the council were arranged
to discuss the riots in June 1985 and again in early 1986, at the height of township revolt, shortly after Mayor Moeketsi's house burned down. In the same
period, a KRO delegation went to meet the commander of the Kagiso police
station to discuss what could be done about escalating violence and unruly
youth burning delivery vehicles.[108]

The KRO chair, however, made a clear distinction between dealings with
local authorities and contacts at the level of national politics. Although contacts on a township level were unavoidable in order to function as a civic
organization, dealings at a national level would amount to usurping the position that rightly belonged to the liberation movement.[109] KRO had no principled objection to dealing with the town council, but the leadership preferred
to deal with the "whites who are controlling the council," in this case the town
clerk.[110]

Joining the UDF made no difference for KRO's contacts with the town council. Civic activists maintained a largely pragmatic view in which obtaining results outweighed a principled rejection of contacts with "puppet structures." Affiliation with the UDF was discussed and approved late in 1983 at two KRO meetings, attended by a total of perhaps five hundred people. But affiliation with the UDF was initially not perceived as making a distinct political choice. Leading civic activists had an image of the UDF as a service organization providing support and better coordination for civics. Only later did it transpire that the UDF was a national political organization with a clear political identity. When the UDF assumed an overtly Charterist profile, some saw this as a betrayal of the original idea behind the Front, which was to unite "all the political groupings of the oppressed. . . . It was intended that the Front would incorporate the Black Consciousness Movement and what was known as the progressive non-racial democratic movement and church groups."[111] Others put the blame on BC-oriented groupings for opting out, thereby making the UDF adopt a Charterist position.

A KRO representative attended the monthly meetings of the UDF West Rand Area Committee, which functioned, in fact, as a kind of civic forum to coordinate activities and exchange information between the civics of Kagiso, Munsieville, Azaadville, and Mohlakeng. Exchanging information was particularly useful because all these townships had to deal with the same administration board. Lawrence Ntlokoa, who usually served as KRO representative on the UDF Area Committee, had a less favorable assessment of the UDF General Council. In this body representing all the UDF affiliates in the Transvaal (beginning in 1986 it represented only those in the Southern Transvaal), KRO apparently felt somewhat marginalized: Johannesburg- and Soweto-based activists called the tune. "Cliques and cabals were building their own power-base, trying to gain control over resources. People based in Johannesburg had a much stronger position in terms of resources. The Soweto Civic Association had three offices and full time staff. We were working from our houses and from the convent. The SCA had nationally well-known personalities, like Dr. Motlana, Winnie Mandela, Curtis Nkondo. They got funds from overseas. When people overseas think of South Africa, they think of Soweto."[112]

Tizza Moiloa, who later served as chair of the UDF West Rand Area Committee, equally believed that the UDF was useful but that it did not make much difference for KRO. KRO activists helped with the distribution of *UDF News,* but otherwise there was only limited participation in UDF campaigns.[113] The UDF provided a plethora of media, either through its own workshops for media skills or through sympathetic service organizations. KRO representatives attended some workshops, but they believed that the

UDF had only a modest bearing on the functioning of the civic. UDF T-shirts and publications, however, did find their way to Kagiso, and certainly the leading activists kept well informed about events elsewhere in South Africa.

The UDF, of course, made a difference in one crucial aspect, although this would only gradually transpire: through the UDF, the Kagiso civic became linked to national politics. Taking up the UDF demands on the level of national politics inevitably made KRO more of a politically aligned organization, incurring a loss of support from non-Charterist residents. In the early 1980s, people from various political tendencies, including AZAPO and PAC sympathizers, had worked together in civic activities. The antagonistic relationship developed only in the second half of the 1980s. In the beginning of the decade, the ideological borderlines were not yet clearly drawn. Civic activists interviewed generally agreed that AZAPO or other BC activists occasionally turned up at meetings, but when it came to the door-to-door campaigns, "they did not really do their bit."[114] In the eyes of residents with Africanist sympathies, KRO indeed functioned initially as a nonpartisan organization, catering to all residents. But then KRO was "hijacked by certain elements" into the UDF, thereby giving "certain elements now access to resources, while others had no access."[115] Robert Mangope, regional organizer of the PAC-leaning AZANYU (Azanian Youth Organisation), attended the meeting where affiliation with the UDF was discussed. In his view, KRO stands accused of using what he considered a classical ANC tactic: swamping the meeting by inviting a multitude of organizations—youth, students, women's league, trade unions—which all served as a front for the ANC. Opponents would then be overruled and intimidated by the singing of revolutionary songs. As a representative of AZANYU, which was labeled a "political formation" rather than a "mass formation," Mangope was ordered to leave the meeting. AZAPO activists had not bothered to come to the meeting.

With Charterist hegemony established in KRO, Africanists decided in 1984 to form their own organization, the Kagiso Civic Organisation. KCO was mainly based in East Park, one of the new neighborhoods where rents were much higher than in the old section of Kagiso. In style with this middle-class profile, KCO took a highly legalistic approach, engaging lawyers to take up rent issues and other matters. It avoided mass demonstrations, boycotts, and other forms of popular mass action. It had no qualms about dealing with the town council. The Africanists' stated belief was that civics should not have a political profile but, rather, should act as a nonpartisan lobby for civic matters. They even considered it irrelevant who ran the township, as long as proper services were delivered. Political affiliation by a civic was seen as hampering efforts to address the basic needs of residents. Although there is some substance to several of the KCO criticisms on the performance of KRO, this alternative civic organization seems to have limited itself largely to censuring their more successful rival, rather than coming up with alternative action. In common with many Africanist and BC activists, KCO leaders produced perceptive comments that could easily lapse into armchair criticism. Some of their swipes at KRO are clearly a caricature. The claim that the KRO executive was dominated by youngsters who "still live under parental care" is without substance.[116] KRO obviously owed its fairly wide base of support at least in part to the leading roles played by respected older residents like Joe Makgothlo and Sister Bernard. Apart from ideological differences, a battle over control of resources seems to have been at the center of the antagonistic relationship.

KRO, as a UDF affiliate, managed to impose Charterist hegemony on opposition politics in Kagiso because the Africanists and BC proponents withdrew or were forced out. After this description of KRO through its ups and down in more or less quiet times, we now examine how in late 1985 Kagiso was drawn into the general pattern of rebellion.

Mobilization and Mass Protest, 1985–1986

The consumer boycott, launched in December 1985, brought Kagiso into the maelstrom of township revolt. Previous efforts to link up with nationwide or regional mass campaigns—like the November 1984 stay-away and the August 1985 consumer boycott—had largely failed. Now Kagiso moved into the next phase, from limited local protests to challenging the power of the (local) state. Escalating state repression as well as extrastate terror attacks were decisive factors in this process of mobilization and radicalization, which assumed a dynamic of its own once it got underway.

Boycotts aimed at white businesses and at shops owned by black collaborators originated in mid-1985 in the Eastern Cape. The idea behind this new tactic was twofold: business could be pressurized to address some of the local grievances and could intercede with the Pretoria government in support of some of the national political demands. The Eastern Cape boycott was highly effective and resulted in a working relationship between local businessmen and local civic and UDF leaders, notably in Port Elizabeth. This became a model for boycott campaigns elsewhere, but the successes of the Eastern Cape—which had the reputation of being the most militant and the best organized region—were not easily matched.

It is not quite clear what made KRO decide to join the boycott at this particular moment. It was probably the temporary lifting of the consumer boycott on the Reef that prompted KRO to join in when the boycott was reimposed. In Soweto and other Reef townships, consumer boycotts had been in force since the end of August, with varying degrees of effectiveness. On 29 November, the boycotts were lifted for eight days, to be reimposed on 8 December. Two reasons were given for the suspension: consumers needed an opportunity to make purchases in white business areas, particularly those goods not available in township stores, and the Transvaal Consumer Boycott Committee (CBC) needed a break "to sort out the confusion of the past three months and give the campaign a new direction."[117] Serious problems had been encountered in enforcing the boycott, since Soweto and the East Rand townships had numerous routes that people could take to white shopping areas. Monitoring the boycott was the preserve of youth. Although their participation was indispensable for the success of the boycott, even the boycott organizers acknowledged that their often violent methods easily antagonized people. Stories of excesses by monitors who forced boycott breakers to drink fish oil or eat soap powder circulated throughout the townships. A third problem was that many township businesses took advantage of the boycott by raising their prices. Because of these previous experiences in the same region, KRO must have been well aware of the potential problems when it embarked on a consumer boycott.

The CBC called for a "Black December," which was to last from 8 December until 31 December, in support of demands for the army to pull out of the townships, the release of all detainees, the lifting of the State of Emergency, and the resignation of town councillors. Residents were also asked to boycott all businesses owned by councillors, to refrain from excessive drinking, and to abstain from birthday and graduation parties and lavish weddings. Various festivals and shows, including the Black Miss South Africa beauty contest, were canceled or postponed.[118] Any hopes that white businesses might have had for an early end to this boycott by making arrangements with the organizers were quashed when CBC members were detained. The renewed boycott call for the Christmas season was not universally popular, as the CBC realized. Ill-conceived campaigns, lack of adequate consultation and information, and various degrees of coercion and interference in people's lives had made many residents wary of boycotts. Apologizing for the behavior of some overzealous monitors, a CBC spokesperson pointed out that "it is not our intention to drag people kicking and screaming towards independence. We would be happier if they willingly got involved."[119]

Although the Kagiso boycott was called after consultation with the CBC, it remained a locally run campaign that would last much longer than the boycotts in other townships on the Reef. KRO activists told conflicting accounts about the initial degree of support for the boycott. Some activists were critical of the inadequate groundwork, of the mixing of national political demands with local issues, and of insufficient attention to the adverse effects of a boycott on certain groups of workers. KRO also held a meeting with the Kagiso businesspeople, who became closely involved in the boycott. The critics allege that the businessmen ended up almost running the boycott, since they stood to gain most.[120] Information on boycotts elsewhere also came through newspapers, which reported in considerable detail about the successful campaign in the Eastern Cape.

A local consumer boycott committee was formed in Kagiso, the Krugersdorp Consumer Boycott Committee (KBCB), on which KRO, the women's organization, the youth organizations, KAFCOC (the Kagiso African Chamber of Commerce), and others were represented. The committee appointed boycott monitors, most of whom were youth. Aware of abuses occurring elsewhere, KRO leaders told the boycott monitors to "educate the people" and to explain that the boycott had been called in protest against the detentions and the presence of the army and police in the townships. If withdrawal of the security forces was the aim of the boycott, then for Kagiso it had an adverse effect. It was the boycott that for the first time brought a massive, heavy-handed, trigger-happy police force into the township. As Makgothlo stated later, before the consumer boycott no one had ever been shot by the police, but after the boycott it happened regularly.[121] As township violence flared up, tear gas, bullets, batons, and sjamboks became a regular feature of life in Kagiso.

The Consumer Boycott

Whether or not preparations had been adequate, the consumer boycott in Kagiso made a false start. In the first week after 9 December 1985, there was widespread harassment, intimidation, and "generally unruly behavior by youths, acting against adults whom they believed to be breaking the boycott."[122] As one Kagiso resident told a reporter: "Youths as young as 14 years stop taxis and private cars coming from town. They destroy groceries found in the vehicles and in some cases assault those who refuse to hand over their goods. Where in the world have you seen youths as young as 12 years making decisions?"[123]

Youth were in the forefront of the boycott monitors, who had erected barricades at the entrance routes in the township, where taxis were stopped and passengers searched. Yet the first resident shot dead by police while he was searching people's groceries was not a *youth*. Steven Rooi Mashigo, shot in the stomach after being confronted by policemen who accused him of intimidating and destroying people's groceries, was thirty-four years old and a father of three children.[124] This incident illustrates the ambiguous nature of the category of *youth,* a label that was often equated with unruly behavior. Adults who engaged in unruly behavior—in other words, who behaved as youth— frequently came to be labeled *youth.*

During the rest of the month there were several more casualties among boycott monitors. Most died at the hands of the police; one was shot by a local businessman. During the second week of the boycott, at least fourteen Kagiso and Munsieville residents were detained because of the consumer boycott. At the same time, spokespeople for KRO and KCBC were obviously worried about excesses. One of the problems was how to distinguish between genuine monitors and people intent on robbing in the name of the struggle. A KRO spokesperson told the *Star* that the civic leadership disassociated itself from "acts of hooliganism and criminal behaviour perpetrated by people claiming to be monitoring and enforcing the boycott, but whose intention is to rob black people." He emphasized the nonviolent nature of the boycott, which he saw as a peaceful way of "indicating our abhorrence of the apartheid regime. We want white businessmen to take up our grievances with the Government, which must realise that we are also human beings and that our demands should not be suppressed." He said that fifteen knives and other weapons had been confiscated from people posing as members of the boycott committee.[125] Criminal elements who robbed motorists, shebeen owners, and taxi drivers in the name of the struggle had been punished and later lectured on what the boycott meant. Hundreds of rands in cash and goods that false monitors had seized were recovered.[126]

Nor was it always clear to residents what the boycott entailed. Could her husband go to town and buy a lawn mower and new planks to fix the ceiling, without fear of being confronted by the comrades? a resident inquired in a phone call to Sister Bernard. Sister Bernard explained that the boycott applied to foodstuffs only, not to hardware.[127] There was, of course, no guarantee that the boycott monitors would apply the same criteria; there were conflicting interpretations of what the boycott entailed.

Precautions had been taken to prevent windfall profits by local business owners in Kagiso. Shops owned by town councillors had already been forced to close down as a result of previous boycotts and attacks. Mayor Moeketsi's shop also had to close. KRO held talks with local business owners, asking them to lower their prices as they would now get more customers. KAFCOC reportedly agreed that its members would reduce the prices at their shops by 25 percent.[128] Boycott monitors would also see to it that local shopkeepers were not exploiting the situation. The Krugersdorp Consumer Boycott Committee was fairly broadly based. The rival Kagiso Civic Organisation was not officially involved in the boycott committee, although KCO activists did attend meetings in an individual capacity. Although some of their ideas found a receptive ear, they were at the same time labeled a "reactionary organization." "If you did not go along with a mass meeting's decision, you were labeled a sell-out. There were songs like: neighbor, you are a sell-out if you oppose the people."[129] Although KCO supported the consumer boycott, differences developed over the mix of national and local demands and over the duration of the boycott. AZANYU called off the boycott in January, to allow parents to buy school uniforms and schoolbooks, but KRO's boycott lasted until the end of February. During that month, serious skirmishes reportedly took place between AZANYU and KRO activists.

The beginning of the boycott campaign also marked an upsurge in violent attacks on councillors. The three-year-old son of councillor Anthony Zulu died after a firebomb attack on his house. Zulu, who suffered injuries, vowed not to resign, for that would amount to showing weakness. The councillor, who was also an Inkatha official, suspected that the people who wanted him to resign from the council would likewise want to force him out of his four businesses in Kagiso. Two other councillors, including the deputy mayor, resigned shortly afterward. Another councillor was said to be on the run after his house in Munsieville was firebombed.[130] A week after the consumer boycott started, a meeting was called by the women's organization and the Kagiso and Munsieville Youth Congresses to discuss the excesses. Participants decided that intimidation had to be curbed, and the burning of delivery vans was ruled out. Another item on the agenda was how to combat crime.

The anticrime campaign was to become one of the major feats of the youth congresses, for which they were widely praised. Township violence declined after the youth went from shebeen to shebeen asking customers to surrender their knives. A huge pile of knives was subsequently stored in the convent. Apart from confiscating weapons, the youth activists also ordered youngsters out of the shebeens. As with the monitoring of the boycott, the anticrime campaign raised the issue of who was a *comrade*. "Some people would harass drinkers and shebeen owners, but they are not moving with the comrades themselves. If shebeen owners came to complain to KRO, we did look into it." Makgothlo traced the origin of the use of the term *comrades* to COSAS, but then others took over the name, doing "very bad things in the name of comrades. So a hooligan today calls himself a comrade."[131] But Makgothlo remained outspoken in his support for the "original" comrades: "It are the comrades who bring some order in the townships." Excesses did not disappear, but subsequently intimidation by youth enforcing the boycott seems to have diminished, although the burning of delivery vans continued for months.

The anticrime campaign won wide support for KRO and the youth organizations. Both in court statements and in interviews, numerous residents mentioned this campaign as a useful function performed by these organizations. "As a result of these actions there are no more tsotsi's carrying knives in the area and Kagiso is now as a result thereof a safer place to live."[132] Although the festive season usually brought a fair share of drunken fights, Christmas 1985 is remembered as the most peaceful Christmas in Kagiso's history: "Leratong Hospital reported not a single casualty of violence, no stabbing, nothing."[133]

One problem with enforcing discipline among young activists was the weak state of youth organization. KAYCO (Kagiso Youth Congress) and MUYCO (Munsieville Youth Congress) were formed after the banning of COSAS in August 1985. Accounts of the exact date of the formation of the youth congresses vary, but it is clear that they did not come into their own until the December campaigns. These campaigns attracted many new recruits, most of whom had little or no "political education"; likewise, the youth leadership was equally lacking in experience. The chair of MUYCO joined the youth congress in December 1985 and was immediately elected chair. MUYCO claimed a membership of about three hundred, while KAYCO was said to have seven hundred members.[134]

On New Year's Day, the Krugersdorp Consumer Boycott Committee called mass meetings in Kagiso and Munsieville to announce the end of the boycott. Others, however, argued that the goals of the boycott had not been met, so the residents resolved to continue the boycott of white-owned shops for an indefinite period and to extend the boycott to the Greyhound Bus Company. The boycott organizers were now overtaken by a ground swell of militancy. The boycotts in Kagiso were no longer part of a nationwide campaign—the Transvaal Consumer Boycott Committee had called off the boycotts in the Pretoria townships, Soweto, the Vaal Triangle, and the East Rand.[135]

A series of mass meetings, usually disturbed by police firing tear gas, had now become a regular feature of civic activities. Previously, one meeting would be called for all Kagiso residents. But in this phase of popular mobilization, no hall was large enough to accommodate all the interested residents. In one week in January, seventeen meetings were held in various church halls; all were packed, with over a thousand people attending each meeting.[136] Issues discussed at these meetings included the township crisis, the education crisis, the consumer boycott, combating crime, and keeping young children out of the shebeens.

The Bus Boycott

On 6 January 1986, the West Rand townships of Bekkersdal, Kagiso, Munsieville, and Mohlakeng embarked on a boycott of the Greyhound Bus Company. Greyhound saw the move initially as simply a part of the general consumer boycott, but there were specific grievances against Greyhound. The company was accused of insensitivity to people's problems. As Ntlokoa explained to journalists, Greyhound had refused to make buses available for funerals, had allowed police to use its buses to carry vigilantes who assaulted members of organizations, and had not invested any of its profits in the community in the form of bursaries or improvement of educational facilities. Greyhound had also neglected to erect bus shelters.[137]

The bus boycott began as a great success. Residents walked to work or took taxis. KRO chair Joe Makgothlo went on foot to work at Chamdor, to show others that it could be done. One can sense the feeling of exhilaration in his phone conversation with Lawrence Ntlokoa, when he describes how the boycott took off. After all the trials and tribulations of failed previous boycotts and the rather messy start of the consumer boycott in December, Ntlokoa felt that the struggle had now been vindicated:

> For once, God. . . . has given us that spirit to do it just right.
> Makgothlo: Yah, God is on our side.[138]

The boycott was hailed as the weapon of the powerless, as one of the few remaining options for nonviolent resistance. But the boycott was not unproblematic. Enforcing the boycott entailed various degrees of coercion. The role of youth in monitoring the boycott was not always readily accepted by older residents, who resented being subjected to questioning and searches. And residents were differently affected by the boycott: for some, it simply meant an inconvenience, for others, it put their livelihoods at stake. People employed at stores in Krugersdorp risked losing their jobs when employers began retrenching workers for lack of business. Others were obviously directly benefiting from the boycott, notably local shopkeepers and the taxi business. At the time, the taxi fare was only five cents more than a bus fare. The Taxi Association agreed to charge half price for students. Taxi owners had their own grudges against Greyhound, as the company was believed to have opposed their license applications and to engage in unfair competition.

In the second week of the bus boycott, Greyhound was ready for talks. The company would no longer oppose taxi license applications, would provide free travel for pensioners on days when they received their money, and would act on requests for free buses or reduced charges for special occasions according to their merit. But by now several boycott leaders had been detained, and their release was made a precondition for talks with the bus company. Police harassment resulted in increased community support for the bus boycott. Taxis were stopped by police for being overloaded; private cars carrying people to work were stopped, and drivers were fined because they had no taxi licenses. In this second week of the boycott, police used bird shot to disperse youth who were helping people to form queues for taxis at taxi stands. Many were injured—one youth had more than 130 bird shot pellets lodged in his body—and a number were arrested.[139] By this time, revolt in Kagiso had escalated to the point of drawing national political attention. Adriaan Vlok, deputy minister of law and order, paid a visit to the township on 22 January to discuss the unrest and the consumer and bus boycotts with the local authorities. The day after Vlok's visit, traffic officers, police, soldiers, and local road transportation board officials carried out a blitz on taxis. Residents claimed that police and soldiers forced them to board buses. Private car owners were charged fines of up to 300 Rand for carrying passengers. Taxis had long delays as police meticulously checked the safety of the vehicles and searched the passengers. This type of police harassment continued for months, during which time many residents continued to walk to work at Chamdor, Luipaardsvlei, or Krugersdorp, a distance of between three and eight miles.[140]

In February, the boycott organizers received a letter purportedly from Greyhound employees urging the boycott committee to hold talks with Greyhound management, saying they feared loss of their jobs if the company had to close down certain bus lines. A spokesperson for the boycott organizers doubted the authenticity of the letter and dismissed it as "another attempt by Greyhound management to confuse residents."[141] The next day the Transport and Allied Workers' Union denied any knowledge of the letter and distanced itself from the letter's contents.[142] Whatever the merits of the letter, Greyhound employees obviously had ample reason to be concerned. For the bus drivers, who had experienced frequent stoning of buses since mid-1985, work had become positively dangerous. In the eyes of township youth, bus drivers operated on the side of enemy forces. The police unrest reports for early 1986 registered frequent complaints of stoning and arson from Greyhound employees who were living in the Kagiso hostel.[143] When after ten months of boycotts Greyhound decided to withdraw its bus services from the West Rand, over a hundred workers were dismissed.[144] KRO contacted the Transport and Allied Workers' Union. The demand that Greyhound employees should not lose their jobs as a result of the boycott was included in the list of demands. But otherwise the dismissal of Greyhound workers was seen as inevitable: "If they lost their jobs, that was the work of the police, who was creating divisions, not of KRO."[145]

When meetings were called to discuss the consumer boycott at the end of February, residents agreed to suspend the boycott until 7 April 1986 to give people a chance to stock up. But when it came to a discussion of the bus boycott, people voted for continuation. Greyhound was now seen as siding with the police and the South African Defence Force (SADF) and therefore as sharing the responsibility for the loss of lives and for numerous injuries.[146] According to KRO chair Makgothlo, the Kagiso bus boycott stood largely on its own. There was no coordination with bus boycott committees in Randfontein and Bekkersdal.[147] In early April, KRO applied for permission to hold a mass meeting in the Kagiso stadium in order to discuss the bus boycott. Permission was granted, and on Sunday, 5 April, about five thousand people assembled in the stadium. They were in an angry mood. On Saturday, Kagiso had buried another fourteen-year-old victim of the unrest. Political funerals had now become an almost weekly routine. According to the police version of events, young Modiri Mmesi was shot dead and three of his friends were injured when a policeman opened fire after a beer hall in Kagiso was attacked with firebombs. But according to an eyewitness, the boys were nowhere near a beer hall: they were playing in the garden of Isaac Genu's house.[148] Police interfered with the funeral and opened fire on a group of youth near the cemetery. Four youth were reported to be in critical condition in the hospital. Speaker after speaker called for a resumption of the consumer boycott since the demands had not been met. The boycott was presented as the weapon of the powerless. "They have the guns, we have the buying power." The crowd replied with *"asithengi edolobheni"* (we do not buy in town). It was resolved to resume the consumer boycott and to continue the bus boycott. KRO was mandated to present "the people's demands" to Greyhound management; until these demands were met, residents would continue the boycott. The list of demands was now further extended to include an end to apartheid in buses, paving of roads, scrapping of plans for the minibuses, rehiring of dismissed Greyhound workers, free buses for funerals, and an obligation to consult the civic on future fare increases.[149] After these decisions were made by residents, the police pounced with renewed vigor on residents traveling in taxis and private cars in a new bid to break the boycott. As before, police explained the roadblocks as an exercise in crime prevention.[150] Eventually a meeting between Greyhound and KRO took place, with the bus company agreeing to most of the demands. Greyhound would offer normal bus service beginning 1 July. The deal was scuttled by the proclamation of a nationwide State of Emergency on 12 June and by the detention of the entire civic leadership. The agreement had been reached before this date, but under emergency regulations KRO could no longer hold meetings to put the deal to the residents. With the KRO leadership in detention or on the run, the bus company no longer had a negotiating partner. A similar situation prevailed in other West Rand townships. At the end of October 1986, Greyhound decided to withdraw its bus service from the West Rand townships.

Although residents were obviously affected by the boycotts in different ways, one group deserves special attention: the migrant workers in the township. In view of the bloody battles in 1990 between hostel dwellers and residents, the question arises whether the seeds of confrontation were sown in this period of boycotts. Unfortunately, information on the experiences of hostel dwellers in Kagiso is scarce. Those among them who were Greyhound bus drivers had obvious reasons to resent the boycott, but they cannot have been numerous. I was unable to interview people who had been living in the hostels in 1985–86. Accounts by KRO activists vary, with some civic leaders admitting that the hostels were largely neglected, whereas others stated that there were regular consultations. Varying accounts can be explained in part by the different positions of the two hostels. The old hostel in Kagiso I seems to have been more involved in civic matters than the new, much larger and better equipped hostel in Kagiso II. Some KRO meetings were conducted in the old hostel. The civic took up some of the grievances of the hostel dwellers, such as the lack of electricity and hot water and the provision of proper beds rather than cement bunks. The hostels were included in the cleanup campaign in early 1986. Efforts were made to get sponsors for the hostels' football team. Trade unionist Serge Mokonyane recalled that he addressed many meetings in the hostel, "and I would go in my UDF T-shirt, there was no problem about that."[151] Civic activists generally asserted that there was a good relationship, certainly with the hostel in Kagiso I. It remains unclear how the migrants themselves viewed the position, taken by KRO, that the migrant labor system and the hostels needed to be abolished altogether. From the scant studies of migrant life, it is clear that many migrants retained strong links with their rural homesteads and had no ambitions of becoming permanent city folk.

The School Boycott

From mid-1985, schools in Kagiso experienced intermittent boycotts, as pupils protested against the detention of fellow students or campaigned against corporal punishment, the shortage of textbooks, overcrowded classrooms, or underqualified teachers, or in support of their demand for student representative councils. Beginning in December, school boycotts were called in support of the consumer boycott. Teachers in Kagiso schools were generally regarded as conservative. They did not actively participate in civic activities. Efforts to set up teacher-parent-student committees to manage the school crisis were unsuccessful. KRO made some attempts to fill the void. A KRO delegation attended the conference organized by the Soweto Parents' Crisis Committee in late December in Johannesburg. This initiative then led to the formation of the National Education Crisis Committee (NECC), which played a prominent role in attempts to solve the school crisis.

The meeting in Johannesburg resolved that children should return to school on 28 January 1986. This date was chosen in an attempt to reach consensus with student organizations: the official date for the opening of the new school year was 8 January. Boycotting students, on the other hand, were reluctant to go back to school before their demands had been met.

KAYCO had called a meeting on 27 January in St. Peter's Catholic School to discuss the back-to-school call. While the meeting in the school hall was in progress, two armored police vans—nicknamed *hippos* in township parlance—drove toward one side of the school, while a third hippo and a police van parked on the other side. Some KRO leaders who were attending the meeting—among them Ntlokoa—walked to the gate to ask the police why they had come. Before any discussion could take place, police fired tear gas at the hall. While the children scrambled out of the hall, police started shooting bird shot at the doors. About twenty policemen had taken up positions near the main exit. Desperately trying to escape, children broke the windows and jumped out at the other side of the hall. Some were bleeding from cuts. Seeing that children were jumping out of windows on the other side of the building, police ran around the hall to start shooting there as well. Some students were sjambokked while running away. Several children fell, and most ran off in different directions. Police rounded up about a hundred pupils and began loading them into police vans. Alarmed by the shooting and shouting, parents rushed to the schoolyard to protect their children. Ntlokoa and Sister Bernard made another attempt to talk to the police and were greeted with "Shut up, kaffir" and "Fuck off, girl," respectively. After some discussion, the children were released. But when the pandemonium was over, fourteen-year-old schoolgirl Maki Legwate was found lying on the school grounds, bleeding profusely. She died soon afterward. The girl had been killed by police bullets.[152] In spite of this incident, children in Kagiso went back to school the next day, demonstrating that they were disciplined students who followed the call of the leadership of the struggle.

More than any other single event, this incident had a profoundly politicizing effect on ordinary townships residents. People who previously had been wary of militant youth disrupting township life now became united against a common enemy, and getting rid of the murderous presence of the security forces became their number-one priority. Tennessee Maleke, who subsequently became active in the women's organization, recounted how her political involvement began on this very day: "We simply had to protest. . . . My involvement in the organization started then and there. Before, many people were scared, or they thought that the youth was to be blamed for throwing stones. But then it was so evident that the police was wrong."[153]

The school crisis, of course, was far from over. The next focal point was Kagiso Senior Secondary School. Pupils demanded that their principal resign either his position as a town councillor in Mohlakeng (the township of Randfontein) or his position as principal. Until he had given up one of these posts, they refused to go back to school. The principal refused to resign but promised to go on leave to quell the explosive situation.[154] At this point, police invaded the school and detained numerous students. This was the sign for a new round of school boycotts, demanding the release of the comrades in detention. For a few months, "the students were in power." Former student activists recalled that principals became willing to consult with them and to concede the recognition of student representative councils (SRCs). "There was almost mutual understanding." When the principal indeed disappeared from the scene and the students were released, it was decided to resume classes. But the roles would soon be reversed. After the imposition of the State of Emergency, the principal returned to the school, and many students were detained anew. He refused to readmit students who had been in detention. Students tried enlisting the help of parents, but this produced no decisive results. Parents above all wanted to see the situation in the schools return to normal. "In the end, the students forced themselves back to school. Then the principal had to let them stay."[155]

At Kagiso Senior Secondary the relationship between pupils and principal was clearly antagonistic. A similar situation prevailed at Matsoepe High School, where the principal refused to recognize SRCs and expelled many students. His house was firebombed just before Christmas. But more sympathetic teachers were also at a loss when they had to handle a situation in which their pupils set the law for themselves. The phone conversations tapped by police allow a glimpse at their problems, as in the case of a school teacher phoning Sister Bernard about her predicament. Five boys had come to her house, saying that her students complained about her. She told her visitors that the students were mannerless; that is why she had been telling them to behave themselves. She regarded herself as being "in the struggle," and she wondered how the comrades could behave as if only they were in the struggle. She felt that the pupils must humiliate and despise her since they had gone to the point of reporting her. After having listened to this emotional outburst, Sister Bernard, a fellow educator, offered words of encouragement.[156] Although not all student demands were won, some victories proved durable: SRCs were still functioning five years later. Corporal punishment had not been abolished, but teachers resorted less readily to the use of the whip.

Persuasion and Coercion

Boycotts were generally hailed as "the community's peaceful weapons of resistance." But in spite of their Gandhian pedigree, the enforcement of boycotts could involve considerable degrees of coercion. Kagiso activists derived at least part of their inspiration from the press reports on the Eastern Cape boycotts. But local conditions in Kagiso were rather different from the Eastern Cape. Krugersdorp was dominated by the Conservative Party. Business owners in Krugersdorp made no attempts to negotiate with the boycott leaders; nor, it seems, did KRO leaders take the initiative and contact Krugersdorp businessmen.

One advantage of the boycott tactic was that it allowed for participation by ordinary people. KRO activists indeed saw it that way: "The methods we used also helped narrow the gap between the activist and mass element. Every person actually felt they were playing their proper role and participating."[157] But KRO never developed the tight web of street committees that was recognized as the foundation for people's power. In fact, these elaborate structures with street committees were largely limited to the Eastern Cape townships and a handful of townships in the Transvaal. Alexandra, an old freehold township located in the heart of white Johannesburg, assumed a symbolic role as a model of people's power. But Alexandra was atypical.

KRO intended to rely on persuasion, and it opposed intimidatory tactics in the enforcement of boycotts. But even persuasion could involve the loss of hard-earned goods. "For those who break the boycott, the activists explain the issues to them and take the stuff to the pensioners and the needy."[158] In spite of attempts by KRO and the Consumer Boycott Committee to run the boycott by persuasion rather than coercion, violent incidents kept flaring up. The burning of delivery vans was initially blamed on "agents of the system," since the vigorous crime prevention campaign had supposedly eliminated "the menace of the so-called comrade tsotsis."[159] Obstructing delivery vehicles was obviously at cross-purposes with the boycott: if residents were to buy in the township, township businesses needed to receive provisions. But attacks on delivery vehicles continued, and KRO apparently had no control over the perpetrators. Speaking to journalists, a KRO spokesperson emphasized that these attacks ran against KRO policy: "We warn these people—we do not know where they come from—that disciplinary action will be taken against them."[160] In spite of all the warnings, the burning of vans and hijacking of cars continued. Firms in Krugersdorp that phoned Sister Bernard or Ntlokoa found that the civic could offer little help. In some cases, firms requested KRO to send a group of comrades to protect deliveries against thugs. Ntlokoa firmly rejected the offer of protection fees: "Oh no well, we don't work on those basis. We just don't feel its right." But at least one youth leader, named Thabo, apparently approached firms with an offer of protection for money.[161]

Several stores in Kagiso itself were equally under threat. The local bottle store, property of the town council, was apparently considered fair game. A woman in the bottle store phoned Sister Bernard to ask for help when the brewery truck arrived. The previous day, a truck had been burned while the driver was trapped inside. "We are now scared and we don't know where we should direct our complaint," said the woman. Sister Bernard could offer, or would offer, no help.[162] Others resented the arbitrariness of the rule of the comrades. A supermarket owner complained that "the UDF boys" had closed his shop and told him it would remain closed until the end of the boycott. Three reasons were offered: he was charging high prices; he had tried to prevent youth from burning a delivery truck with Coca Cola; and "when they wanted to burn those youths who were helping with the delivery truck, we protected those youths."[163]

Such violent behavior that was clearly out of line with KRO policy was often blamed on "outside elements." This claim is not altogether unlikely: youth from several townships kept close contact and paid frequent visits to each other, particularly during weekends with funerals. Kagiso was one of the few townships around Johannesburg where the State of Emergency did not apply. It was not exactly a free haven, but it might have offered militant youth somewhat more room to maneuver. But unruly elements outside KRO's control also came from Kagiso itself. The *tsotsis,* or township gang members, who supposedly had been flushed out during the December anticrime drive, had made a comeback posing as comrades. They used the name "the United Front," or simply "the United." This gang of about thirty to forty people, aged between sixteen and thirty, emerged as an organized force in January. "They were very active, but they had no history of political involvement; they just took advantage, confiscating shopping, looting and burning delivery vans, hijacking cars."[164] Without exception, the KRO leadership, when interviewed later, was full of praise for KAYCO and blamed the excesses and the violence on the United Front. KAYCO, which boasted a membership of about seven hundred, was credited with stopping crime and spreading the word about the consumer boycott by going house to house. The United were particularly active in manning the roadblocks where vehicles coming from outside were stopped and searched for goods from white shops. Rivalry and animosity between KAYCO and the United at times resulted in violent encounters. As two KAYCO activists later explained:

> There were different approaches to the struggle. Some wanted to politicize the youth. Others wanted to burn cars. So the United boys made a mistake. They thought they could burn the cars because the cars belonged to the bourgeoisie. And many youths were very angry because of the daily killings. And they were also responding to Tambo's call to make the country ungovernable. That is why they went out burning cars. . . . Some youths moved away from organizational politics. They were tired of all this talking and wanted action. We introduced workshops to discuss strategy and tactics, but not everybody would come to those meetings.[165]

This type of workshop, conducted in English, was likely to highlight the division among youth between the politically aware high school students, who could conduct meetings and express themselves in English, and the dropouts, the uneducated lumpen proletariat who lacked the background, the skills, and the patience to participate on an equal footing in these sessions. The lumpen element chose the battlefield where they felt most at home: the streets.

Lawrence Ntlokoa and Sister Bernard, who worked with KAYCO, did not manage to come to grips with the United boys. The note of despair in some phone conversations among civic leaders indicates that the gang's activities had become very disruptive. In mid-March 1986, after another hijacking of *combis* (minibuses), Sister Bernard told Ntlokoa that she was losing hope.[166] Toward the end of April the problem was still unresolved, as indicated in the following conversation between Makgothlo and Ntlokoa:

> Makgothlo: Those youngsters! I told them that it is the last time we will hold a meeting of this kind. . . . Ja, because they think as they can terrorise people, the people are scared of them. . . .
> Ntlokoa: We don't want to be bullied by eleven guys.[167]

As Sister Bernard explained to the lawyers in the KRO trial: "Let me say plainly that they are a tsotsi element, people that don't go to school and kind of really rough—a crime element. We would tell them that is not really necessary that you should be killing one another and getting drunk, being kind of useless. They are unemployed people roaming around. . . . Most are ill-educated, drop-outs, they are angry and bitter youth."[168] Moreover, they had their own network with other gangs of *comtsotsis,* or comrade gang members, in Soweto, Alexandra, and other townships, keeping each other informed of events in all townships. Groups visited each other and exchanged information, especially during vigils and funerals. One dispute between KRO and the United involved a most common source of division in township politics: money. Access to resources could be a divisive matter. Rumors circulated that South African Breweries had donated 18,000 Rand to KRO and that Lawrence Ntlokoa was driving a car donated by the brewery. Another rumor had it that KRO had taken money from Greyhound. In actuality, the car had been provided by KRO's lawyers in the court case against the minister of law and order to facilitate collecting evidence and witnesses.[169] KRO had no regular income, as it had no registered fee-paying membership. It did not have a bank account. Civic leaders used their own resources, such as Makgothlo's car. And from time to time, the civic asked for donations. Makgothlo mentioned churches, businessmen, and South African Breweries—where he worked as overseer—as sources of contributions.[170] Attempts at collecting money were also conducted by various groups or individuals during funerals, "but it was not a KRO activity and we discourage that very strongly."[171]

The Role of Repression: Police and Vigilantes

Police presence in Kagiso had significantly increased in December 1985. Beginning in early January, police became particularly brutal after two white policemen from Krugersdorp had been killed by miners in a nearby mining compound. Police claimed that they had to operate heavily armed because of this attack.[172] After the start of the bus boycott, police action became especially vicious. Kagiso now entered into the deadly cycle that already prevailed in other townships. Victims of police violence were carried to their graves by large and angry crowds. Police turned out in equally massive numbers, provoking the funeralgoers. A political funeral frequently produced more martyrs. At the funeral of schoolgirl Maki Legwate, police fired tear gas, sjambokked mourners, and detained seven funeralgoers. A prayer service in the Methodist Church for Maki Legwate was disrupted by police throwing tear-gas canisters into the church and then storming the building. Scores of schoolchildren where injured as they scrambled through broken windows.[173]

At the end of February, a campaign of social isolation was called against town councillors, black policemen, and black soldiers. "Nobody will talk to them," Ntlokoa announced to the press, "they will not be allowed in any shebeen or shop and those who stay in backyards will be told to leave because the community has decided that we don't want these people."[174] Indiscriminate police violence and brutal nightly patrols by white vigilantes from Krugersdorp strongly contributed to the process of political mobilization in Kagiso. In a community under siege, many residents closed ranks behind the civic leadership. "Before 1986 the system had targeted the leadership only, and the residents were mostly left alone. But in 1986 the police started shooting at random, and that is what made people more militant. It is the system which really managed to mobilize the people."[175] Genu's view of the role of the police in the process of politicization is borne out by numerous statements by residents in the KRO trial. "I only became a member of the Kagiso Youth Congress after having been beaten up by the police. This happened as a result of being taken to meetings held by the Kagiso Youth Congress by a friend. Before I was not really concerned about politics in the township."[176] Police presence became all-pervasive, demonstrating a total disrespect for people's privacy. They were "walking into people's bedrooms in the middle of the night."[177]

At least six people were killed in January 1986, with scores of people having to be treated in the hospital for gunshot wounds or for injuries caused by sjamboks and batons. Residents also alleged that the security forces were raping women.[178] Faced with this escalation of state violence, KRO decided to seek an interdict from the Supreme Court to restrain the security forces. With the help of lawyers, KRO collected 118 affidavits detailing the allegations of brutality committed by the security forces against the residents of Kagiso and Munsieville.

In February, vigilantes from Krugersdorp unleashed a reign of terror. The leader of the Afrikaner Resistance Movement, the Afrikaner Weerstandsbeweging (AWB), Eugene Terreblanche, had called on AWB branches on the West Rand to form vigilante groups.[179] Residents of the Krugersdorp suburb Dan Pienaarville, which borders on Munsieville, held an urgent meeting in late January, following the firebombing of a house in the suburb and allegations that blacks from the townships were planning to burn down white schools. The Krugersdorp Town Council and the security forces promised to build a security fence between Dan Pienaarville and Munsieville and to secure army protection for the schools.[180] Residents in Dan Pienaarville lived in fear of firebombs and kept buckets with sand and water on hand during the night. Over ten thousand town residents signed a petition demanding that Munsieville residents be moved to Kagiso within a year. The people of Munsieville reacted angrily to this petition. Older residents had already experienced removals before they were resettled in Munsieville in the 1940s. Several Munsieville residents said that they had lived in the area long before the whites settled in Dan Pienaarville and that if whites objected to being neighbors, then they were the ones who should leave.[181]

Dan Pienaarville was an extension of Krugersdorp built in the early 1980s. People who bought houses there did so in the belief that the squalid township next door was going to be demolished. They felt cheated when the government announced in October 1985 that Munsieville was not going to be moved but would be upgraded. The Krugersdorp Action Group was formed to contest this government decision. While police and town authorities turned a blind eye, the Krugersdorp Action Group formed an armed vigilante group and announced its intentions in the local newsletter: "We intend to take drastic action if we feel the situation warrants it, and it can be left to the police to come and fetch the bodies."[182] In February 1986, the Krugersdorp Town Council unanimously rejected the government decision and demanded the removal of Munsieville as soon as possible. Council members called Munsieville "a cancer that needs to be removed. We have to protect our white skins. We will remove it, true as God."[183] Nightly raids by masked whites, sometimes accompanied by blacks believed to be policemen, were a regular occurrence in both Munsieville and Kagiso. The *Sunday Star,* having interviewed dozens of township residents, painted a grim picture of "an orgy of destruction."[184] Whites with balaclavas descended on the townships nearly every night, shooting residents and beating them up with truncheons, pickax handles, sjamboks, and rifle butts. One twenty-two-year-old man, Stephen Matshogo, was so horrendously beaten that his corpse was hardly recognizable. A township doctor said he treated people who were pulled from taxis and cars and were beaten up by men dressed in what were thought to be police uniforms. One night alone two doctors reported seeing at least fifty-two victims of violent attacks, all of them with massive bruises and cuts. Among the victims were young children. Medical reports, submitted as evidence in the court case, present a picture of indiscriminate violence. The victims were between ten and sixty-seven years of age and included both men and women.[185] A local priest, Bishop William Kunene, told how masked men would beat little children playing in front of his church with sjamboks and rifle butts. The men threatened to burn the bishop's house, since the comrades had been burning policemen's houses. Not only people but also the people's parks, arranged by township youth, were the targets of attacks. The parks were ruined by the invaders.[186] The South African police denied any allegations of misconduct, blamed Matshogo's death on faction fights, and claimed that police units were carrying out a crime prevention action in Kagiso on 24 February. This was the most violent day in a series of vigilante raids. Among the victims was a local black policeman who was severely sjambokked by six white policemen and one black, although he indicated to them that he could identify himself as a police constable.[187]

With temperatures rising in both the townships and in Krugersdorp, the issue of Munsieville had become a symbol of South Africa's racial polarization. Since the vocal right-wing activists in Krugersdorp belonged to the camp of the Conservative Party and the AWB rather than to the National Party—they had called for the resignation of their NP member of parliament, Leon Wessels—the Botha government had little reason to woo the angry whites. Toward the end of March, President P. W. Botha announced that Munsieville would not be removed. Instead, the government had opted for a patrolled buffer zone with a road, safety fences, and high streetlights between Munsieville and Dan Pienaarville, which was soon dubbed the "Berlin Wall" solution.[188] This left both sides dissatisfied. Militant whites felt betrayed because the state had reneged on earlier promises to remove the township residents, while the people of Munsieville did not relish the thought of being fenced in. The stipulation that Munsieville could not expand beyond its existing borders made residents doubt whether the promised upgrading of their township would amount to anything substantial.

Besieged by Krugersdorp vigilantes and a vengeful police force, the people of Kagiso and Munsieville tended to close ranks behind leaders who shared their anxieties and who took concrete action to try and protect them against arbitrary violence. When KRO leaders pleaded their case in court, they were confident that they represented the overwhelming majority of Kagiso residents. Living under siege had contributed to the forging of a political community.[189] The court application was supported by three ministers of religion in Kagiso and backed up by 118 affidavits containing allegations of police brutality. In view of the "particularly grave" nature of the allegations, Judge R. J. Goldstone ordered the affidavits to remain private and confidential until the ministers of law and order and of defense had an opportunity to reply. While not admitting any of the allegations, the minister of law and order undertook to pass on instructions to the police on the West Rand prohibiting them from committing unlawful acts.[190] But serious incidents involving the police continued.

The funds for the litigation were provided by the South African Council of Churches (SACC) and the Commission for Justice and Reconciliation of the Catholic Church. When the court proceedings opened in April, the minister of law and order, the minister of defense, and the divisional commissioner of police on the West Rand all denied the allegations. They stated that the allegations had been made to further the aims of the ANC and to create "liberated" areas in the townships.[191] The army, however, acknowledged the validity of the claim that on several occasions SADF officers had thrown rubber snakes into passenger cars at road blocks. This was meant as a "practical joke" to defuse tensions, and according to the SADF, it was appreciated as such by most residents.[192]

When the case proceeded in open court with well-documented charges against the police and with accompanying media publicity, it became a matter of increasing embarrassment for the state. The proclamation of a nationwide State of Emergency in June 1986 provided the state with an opportunity to put the lid on it. On 11 June, the entire executive of KRO was detained under the emergency regulations, as well as a whole range of other activists from Kagiso. Later the members of the executive were detained under section 29 of the Internal Security Act, which allowed for unlimited detention without trial for the purpose of interrogation. They had no right to see a lawyer, which meant that the court case against the minister of law and order could not proceed.

The widely supported court case of KRO against the minister of law and order was a manifestation of Kagiso as a political community. The concept of Kagiso as political community, with strengths and limitations, is further explored in the conclusion of this chapter. The next section deals with another civic activity that contributed to the shaping of this political community: popular justice.

Popular Justice

The Kagiso Disciplinary Committee (DC) had its origins in the December anticrime campaign and in efforts to curb abuses in the enforcement of the consumer boycott. It was constituted in January, when it became obvious that things were getting out of hand. "People were just generally burning things without having a clear direction as to what is happening."[193] Around this time, a group of people who would later become involved in the DC went to see the commander of the Kagiso police station and Mayor Moeketsi to discuss the problem of escalating violence, notably the burning of delivery vehicles. This attempt at joint action by calling a mass meeting to discuss the problems came to nothing, perhaps because shortly afterward the house of the station commander burned down.

The DC, chaired by KRO executive member Bongani Dlamini, was composed of young activists in their twenties.[194] The DC heard cases of people found with knives and confiscated their weapons. Formally, the DC was "not an organ of KRO, but KRO would have consultations with it."[195] At the same time, elderly men founded an organization with the same goal of "controlling the tsotsi element."[196] Significantly, it was called the Fathers' Congress. There is no unanimity on the origins of the Fathers' Congress. According to Serge Mokonyane, it was an attempt on the part of KRO to get elderly men involved in community affairs. "Some fathers were fairly conservative; they did not want their wives to attend meetings. So we thought to solve this problem by organizing the fathers." But apart from an attempt on the part of the civic to organize the more conservative elements, it was also an attempt by these elderly men to regain control over a terrain that they traditionally considered their own preserve: administering justice was seen by some as "exclusively a fathers' domain." They invoked African tradition and the practice of township *makgothla* (informal courts conducted by elderly men) to support their stance that this was a matter for fathers only. Here was a potential source of generational conflict, but it was solved within a couple of weeks as the scope of the DC widened to include mediation in disputes between neighbors and domestic problems. Mokonyane commented on the involvement of the elders:

> But people said they could not present domestic problems to these youngsters. You cannot discuss problems like barren wives or husbands who cannot provide sexual satisfaction because the husband is always drunk, with a group of youngsters. This type of thing could turn against KRO. So we purposefully took a decision to get parents involved in the DC. Initially, it took a great deal of convincing, because the people thought they were not educated enough to conduct these things. Some people came forward in meetings, they offered themselves to sit on the DC. These people had various backgrounds, there were no set criteria. At the other hand, the youth had some problem to let go their handling of disciplinary matters. But in the end they were convinced to hand over to older people.

The role of youth was now limited to summoning people to the meetings of the DC. Most members of the DC, which counted about ten members, were elderly men. Women and youth had some input, but their influence was clearly limited, for "most fathers thought that women had no business on the DC, since they ought to be at home and attend to household things."[197] The Munsieville DC, however, had one female member, and in Kagiso, women were sometimes involved when the DC dealt with domestic issues. The new chair of the DC was a man of about fifty years in age, Morgan Montoedi. He exercised this function for only two months. In March, his wife, three children, and one grandchild were burned to death when firebombs were thrown into his house. Montoedi himself was badly injured. KRO blamed the attack on "agents of the system."[198] The house of another member of the DC, George Xolilizwe, was also firebombed.

Soon after the personnel change from youth to "fathers," the committee found itself dealing with all kinds of petty crime, domestic matters, and jealousies. The DC did not consider itself fit to deal with serious crime such as murder, rape, or assault with grievous bodily harm. But KRO claimed that this type of crime did not happen during the months that the DC functioned. "There was very little crime, until we were all detained. Then crime soared."[199]

Marriage problems were apparently among the main issues before the committee, with both men and women phoning Sister Bernard at the convent to complain about wives not sleeping at home or not looking after the children or about husbands who ran off with their pay envelopes to sleep with other women. Both parties to the conflict were summoned to the convent to present their case to the Disciplinary Committee. From the phone conversations, it seems that women were generally in a weaker position: if a husband went off with his pay to another woman, the party to be "disciplined" was apparently the other woman, not the unfaithful husband. The DC saw it as its duty to counter divorce. "We would tell the couple to solve their problems and stay together. For example, a husband chasing his wife out of the house and taking his girlfriend in. We would talk to that man and tell him that he cannot do that since he is a married man."[200] According to this committee member, the DC was successful in solving marital problems. "There was no more divorce at that time."

Interestingly, the jurisdiction of the Disciplinary Committee in these matters seems to have been widely accepted. Tapped phone conversations, recorded by police, include calls with the local leader of the Zion Christian Church, generally regarded as politically conservative. From his reply it appears that the sessions of the DC had his full approval and that he referred marital conflicts to this committee.[201] But there were also limitations to the legitimacy of the court. Residents who adhered to AZAPO, AZANYU, or the PAC refused to accept its jurisdiction. The rival civic KCO opposed the DC as a "kangaroo court," although it supported the anticrime campaign. While many people apparently regarded mediation in domestic conflicts as a useful social role, the Africanists were opposed to meddling in their family affairs. "None of the AZANYU members or their families were ever touched by the courts. We had made it clear that we would not allow that. They avoided people with AZANYU or PAC links."[202]

One harrowing case involved a woman who—fearing the DC as much as she feared her boyfriend—attempted to commit suicide by drinking a bottle of detergent when she was summoned to a meeting. She no longer wanted to live with her boyfriend in his backyard shack because there were quarrels with the owners of the house. At a previous session, the DC had told the woman to submit to the authority of her boyfriend: if she left the place without his permission, she was to get five lashes.[203]

In many of the cases brought to its attention, the DC fulfilled a useful role as dispenser of justice, but there were obvious limitations. The role of youth in summoning people to DC meetings was considered improper by many older residents, and the taboo on invoking police assistance put people in an awkward position when they tried to claim what was legally theirs. Punishment meted out by the DC was on the whole moderate: the emphasis was on reeducation rather than on punitive sanctions. If children were found guilty of misbehavior such as stabbing, stealing, or assault, the DC would call in the parents. After explaining what the children had done, the DC would ask parental approval for the punishment to be administered. The average punishment was five lashes, with a maximum of ten. Some KRO activists maintained that only children were flogged and that matters between adults were settled without physical sanctions, but there is room for doubt.

Although the DC undoubtedly served a useful function, and the civic widened its support base by allocating the function of popular justice to elderly men, the DC also had its critics. It was, after all, a new venture, and most members lacked experience. The most common criticism was that the DC neglected its educative functions because "some members thought that all problems can be solved by administering a couple of lashes."[204] Activists in the Young Christian Workers, who had campaigned against corporal punishment in the schools, were inclined to oppose the use of the whip. This was for principled reasons but also because in YCW they had learned to weigh the consequences before jumping into action. "So we were critical of the handling of the lumpen proletariat by the People's Courts. If you beat them up, they might side with the police."[205] Another YCW activist was critical of the lack of accountability, experience, and "political direction" of the members of the DC. In principle, both parties could present their own side of the story; but in practice, the DC had often already made up its mind. Apart from the lack of a fair hearing, the DC was also used to settle all kinds of scores. "People dragged their neighbors to the court to settle some old feud. The civic was not equipped to deal with this kind of thing. I saw a group of comrades arriving to fetch someone in a house next to mine. He did not want to come and they beat him up on the spot, quite severely."[206]

Moreover, even loyal critics of the proceedings of the DC were acutely aware that the court would not take kindly to criticism. Several interviewees mentioned the case of one activist belonging to this "workerist opposition" who had been critical of the consumer boycott and of the "kangaroo courts." He was summoned before the DC, ostensibly because of some domestic issue, but in reality because the DC members wanted to teach him a lesson for his criticism. The case, however, was settled without resort to the whip.

The Emergence of a Political and Moral Community

To what extent was Kagiso in 1985–86 transformed into a political community? A community, not in the sense of residents sharing the same geographical space, but of people sharing a common purpose. In interviews with many civic activists from Kagiso, a clear sense of nostalgia transpired for the heady days of people's power. It was, on the one hand, a period of fear and heightened repression; but on the other hand, residents shared a feeling of solidarity and a sense of purpose that was not experienced either before or after this episode. Forging active political communities was a key element in the strategy of the UDF and many civics, as can be seen from Ntlokoa's 1984 strategy document, in which he laments the lack of social cohesion.[207] A civic, in his view, had to move beyond a single-issue interest group of residents toward building a political community. One feature in the shaping of these political communities was a sense of a shared destiny: a vision of a future society that was prefigured in attempts to establish an alternative hegemony.

The most visible manifestation of the emergence of an alternative hegemony in Kagiso was the way in which youth tried to remodel the world of the township. Once the youth became organized in the congresses, they provided various services to the community. Help with the organization of funerals was generally appreciated, although some parents, grieving over the loss of their children, resented youth hijacking the burial ceremony from the family and the church leadership. Youth also conducted cleanup campaigns and thought of various means of embellishing the township. Apart from the practical purpose of winning community support, these campaigns also served an ideological goal. People's parks, baptized Nelson Park or Biko Park and adorned with car tires painted with the names of fallen heroes, represented an effort to reclaim ideological ground from the state. Graffiti proclaimed that the future would belong to the youth: "We are the world, we are the children" or "We are the future and nothing can stop us."[208]

Funerals offered an obvious platform for symbolic manifestations. This, in fact, was one of the arguments advanced by police against KRO during the trial. Police spokespeople claimed that KRO took over the funerals, with slogans, banners, speakers, and crowds of funeralgoers wearing political T-shirts. For the police, displaying these symbols of the struggle meant that KRO disrespected the solemnity of a funeral. KRO explained that this was not at all disrespectful, as people dress in a "uniform" according to the occasion. If the deceased was a member of a football team, the other team members would attend the funeral in football T-shirts. If he was a trade union member, the other members would come in union T-shirts.[209]

Police imposed strict restrictions on funerals, arguing that black youth exploited funerals to promote lawlessness and violence and to advertise the banned ANC and SACP with flags, banners, and slogans. Funeral processions on foot were banned. The ceremony was to be limited to the church and the churchyard, with funeralgoers transported in motor vehicles. Political speeches were banned; the use of loudspeakers was not allowed. The number of mourners was limited, usually to four hundred, while nonblacks were banned from participation altogether. The restrictions on numbers and the ban on walking processions were frequently ignored, as in the case of the funeral of seventeen-year-old Joseph Mono, which was attended by about fifteen hundred people.[210] Mono had been shot by police during the march of Munsieville mothers to the police station while he was helping several women who had been tear-gassed by police. Many funeralgoers were subsequently detained, including two Catholic nuns, Sister Bernard and Sister Christina.

The ideological meaning of these symbolic manifestations was not lost on outside observers. The Afrikaans Sunday paper *Rapport* reported how children as young as twelve or thirteen had unleashed a reign of terror, applying Maoist revolutionary principles. They manned street blockades, checked on taxis, prescribed to businessmen how to run their businesses, and cleaned the streets. A striking feature of this reign of terror was the "ominous quiet and order." "The children clean the rubbish, keep the streets clean. The fairly neat parks are named Biko Park, Nelson Mandela Park and 'The Fallen Heroes.' The stated goal of all these activities is to make clear that they are more effective than the town councils."[211]

Efforts to establish an alternative hegemony were apparently far more threatening to white domination than sheer anarchy. The people's parks were thus interpreted as elements in the alleged total strategy of the UDF and the ANC to create "liberated zones." The reporter spotted the ominous presence of car tires not only in the parks but also in front of certain homes, notably at the house of a town councillor in Munsieville, where they obviously served a purpose of intimidation. The report then went on to quote policemen and politicians who equally emphasized the discipline that is apparent in this "revolutionary onslaught." Leon Wessels, the National Party MP for Krugersdorp, believed that white South Africans could no longer claim to understand the black man. "A new breed of black people has grown in South Africa, people who do not fear death and who are prepared to die for what they regard as freedom."[212]

What made KRO into one of the more effective civics in the PWV townships? Within its limitations, it managed to some extent to deliver the goods. It preferred a nonconfrontational strategy, thus minimizing the risks to which township residents were exposed, and it combined political radicalism with some socially conservative features, as shown in the section on popular justice. Rather than espousing calls to make the townships ungovernable, the civic endeavored to create some order with the anticrime campaign and the provision of some kind of justice. Therefore, it performed socially useful functions. In affidavits for the court case, many ordinary residents declared their support for KRO.[213] They described the civic as "an organisation which is chosen by the people and not appointed by the government," and one that enjoys legitimacy among township residents. Also, the civic performed effectively as a pressure group: "An example of this the last time when there was an intended rent increase, they approached the authorities and negotiated with them as a result of which there was no increase." Residents also expressed support for KRO's political role, striving toward "a more just society" in South Africa. This fits well with Makgothlo's own view of KRO's function. He explained KRO's strategy in a meeting with KRO lawyers, who asked how he would reply to the state's charge that civics were conspiring with the ANC to make South Africa ungovernable. KRO's strategy relied on mobilizing large numbers but was not averse to dealings with authorities, who, after all, were needed if the civic wanted to function. KRO took up issues "by having mass meetings . . . and making a hell of noise. Because of the pressure, things sometimes changed; there was the instance of a new hostel, and we said no hostels before people had houses, and because of that pressure then houses started springing up. . . . Houses are low quality with high rentals, but at least the hostel came much later, after all these houses had been built, and then later on we said all right, let's talk."[214]

Makgothlo disputed that Kagiso was ungovernable. "People still go to the offices, they still pay for their services, water and light, rent is still being paid, rubbish is still being collected." As further evidence, he added that unlike Alexandra, Kagiso had not become a no-go area for the police. Out of a total of sixty police homes in Kagiso, only three had become the target of arson. The attacks were carried out against specific policemen, such as the one who was held responsible for the death of a child. Thirty-five black policemen were still living in Kagiso, while by this time police in Alexandra had been forced to evacuate their houses. Rather than promoting ungovernability, KRO saw itself as providing some useful services and maintaining some semblance of order. Consumer boycotts were seen as a nonviolent tactic to seek redress for grievances. While the local authorities were clearly seen as illegitimate, KRO took a pragmatic position when it came to dealing with them.

It is a tribute to the responsible leadership of KRO that Kagiso was spared some of the excesses, like necklacing, that bedeviled other townships. Winnie Mandela made her notorious "matches and necklaces" speech in Munsieville in April 1986. Speaking to about five hundred people in the Pentecostal Church in Munsieville, Mandela exhorted the people of South Africa to join forces to overthrow the government: "Together, hand in hand, with that stick of matches, with our necklaces, we shall liberate this country."[215] Although she was at this time still held in wide esteem, this particular piece of advice was not taken up in either Kagiso or Munsieville.

On the other hand, one should not underestimate the insecurity and bewilderment felt by ordinary residents who were subjected to "revolutionary discipline." Resentment against arrogant and unruly youth transpires clearly from many phone conversations between residents and Sister Bernard, as well as from several affidavits and interviews. An illustration of this "balance of fear" was given by a Kagiso woman in one of the affidavits: "I do fear the comrades but only in the sense that they mete out punishment after decisions have been taken by people's courts, if people have been acting anti-socially. I however fear the police more than I fear the comrades." Others professed that they found cops and comrades equally frightening.

The construction of a political community was not just the work of the civic leadership. Only under conditions of beleaguerment was Kagiso transformed into an entity that can be regarded as a political community, closing ranks against an external threat. Another necessary ingredient was a dose of ideological inspiration, in order to give a wider meaning to the bread-and-butter concerns of everyday life. Local concerns obviously were the key issues in recruiting support for the civics, but most of these issues could not be solved on a local level: it was unavoidable to address the vital issue of control over central state power. Moreover, the sense of belonging to a nationwide movement was a vital element in the shaping of political communities. Organization and ideology, key factors in the making of a political community, needed to reach beyond the bread-and-butter issues of rents and transportation.[216] By virtue of belonging to the UDF and sharing its vision of a more just and egalitarian society, the civics provided an ideological underpinning to otherwise largely parochial concerns.

The term *political community* perhaps overemphasizes the political dimensions. Turning back to Kagiso, I would suggest that the forging of a political community can also be seen as the making of a moral community. Because of the prevailing liberal and Marxist paradigms, the role of religion as motivating force and source of legitimacy is often overlooked. As Chikane explains in his autobiography, the dualistic world view in which the spiritual world is separated from the social world does not accord with the African world view. Not only were the people of Kagiso involved in a battle against an oppressive state; they were—in Chikane's words—taking part in the "struggles between the forces of righteousness (light) and unrighteousness (darkness)."[217] The anticrime campaign, the cleanups, and the social isolation of the police and the town councillors all fit in with the endeavor to cleanse the township of evil forces. The anticrime campaign was described as "cleansing the township of thuggery. . . . We have actually ridden the township of youth drunkenness and irresponsibility."[218] By reaffirming family and community values, the Disciplinary Committee served as moral beacon in these times of confusion.

Lawrence Ntlokoa's diary provides a good illustration of the envisaged moral order. While he observes that Christianity is used to preach resignation, he is not going to abandon the terrain of religion in order to fight a secular political battle. On the contrary, he sets out to repossess the spiritual forces from the fat clergy who have betrayed the cause of the poor. Christ is "the friend of the workers, who died for their cause." It was not only a political ideology but also a religious belief that provided a source of legitimacy for the civic leadership. This became evident on the first day of the bus boycott, when the overwhelming success of the boycott was experienced as a moment of redemption: "Yah, God is on our side."

The envisaged moral and political order was egalitarian in terms of race and class. There is considerably more ambiguity with regard to gender and generation. Women at this time played a somewhat more prominent role in the township than in the early 1980s, when they were not even taken into account by the youthful activists who embarked on the first campaigns against rent rises. But women remained largely confined to their role as mothers: a redefinition of roles was not really on the agenda. The DC enforced existing patriarchal relations. In this sphere, although the committee provided an avenue for women to call men to account, the DC operated as a conservative institution, guarding an entrenched system of social and moral values. Youth had conquered new terrain for themselves, but they met the boundaries of their newfound power when it came to dealing with the domestic matters of adults. The DC was formed precisely to take over from the youth the function of dispenser of popular justice.

The youth who constructed the people's parks and the elderly men who dispensed people's justice did not, in all likelihood, share the same vision of a future society. From the story of township revolt in Kagiso, it has become obvious that there were limitations to the consensus that supposedly under-lay this political or moral community. People with Africanist leanings did not recognize the authority of the Disciplinary Committee. Dissidents from the workerist opposition were excluded from the decision-making process. YCW members who were critical of the consumer boycott and who approached the KRO executive with the proposal to confer about an alternative course of action were told that there was to be no discussion. "If you disagreed, it meant that you were not supporting the struggle."[219] Critics were excluded from the Consumer Boycott Committee. They questioned not only the wisdom of the consumer boycott, which involved a considerable degree of coercion, but also the process of decision making and the lack of accountability. The civic lead-ership made decisions, which were subsequently endorsed in mass meetings. These emotional meetings did not provide a platform for discussion or minor-ity positions. Critics, even when loyal to the cause, were promptly labeled reac-tionaries: "It was simply not possible to disagree with majority decisions."[220]

Criticism was also voiced about the ill-considered goals of the consumer boycott: the demands were a rather haphazard mix of local and national issues, some of a short-term nature and others, long-term. Following the YCW tac-tics, they would have preferred to concentrate on winnable issues as a means of slowly building a more confident community. These critics believed that civics ought to concentrate their efforts on civic matters, not on national pol-itics. Only by focusing on the direct everyday concerns of residents could civics hope to grow into strong grassroots organizations. The boycott in Kagiso was called for an undetermined period without a chance of demands being met. As a result, the campaign fizzled out without any demonstrable victory. The bus boycott did not result in an improved bus service but in Greyhound stop-ping the bus service altogether. The civic leadership underestimated the poten-tially divisive character of the boycott. The political community proved a fragile construction, which did not survive the detention of the civic leader-ship. For the workerist critics, the phase of Kagiso's transformation into a political community was a period in which they preferred to lie low. Several of them were to play a leading role again when the civic was reconstituted along somewhat different lines in 1989.

Collapse and Resurrection, 1986–1991

From June 1986, KRO effectively ceased to function. The entire leadership was in detention and would remain entangled in legal procedures for years. After the Supreme Court declared their detention illegal in 1987, some members of the executive were indeed released. But the day after the release, both the released leaders and those still in detention were charged with subversion and sedition. The released KRO leaders chose not to go into hiding but appeared in court. The state asked for the defendants to be re-detained, but the judge granted bail since the KRO leaders had demonstrated that they would keep themselves available. The terms of bail, however, entailed serious restrictions. Some members of the executive were restricted to the magisterial district of Krugersdorp, and others were not permitted to enter Kagiso or Munsieville until 1988, when the charges against them were finally dropped. Some KRO activists were not released until 1989. Some years later, an out-of-court settlement was reached in which the state agreed to pay substantial damages for unlawful detentions.

In addition to the members of the KRO executive, youth and student leaders were taken into custody. According to KRO secretary Ntlokoa, more than three hundred people were detained at some point during the State of Emergency. Others went underground and left the area or the country altogether. "Under the emergency, everything was immediately put down. As soon as somebody raised his head, the police would swoop in. The violence died down when the emergency was declared."[221]

7. Sister Mary Bernard Ncube meets a well-wisher on her release after sixteen months in detention, 19 October 1987. Photograph courtesy of Eric Miller.

For Kagiso's political community, conditions under the State of Emergency led to a "reversal of gains. Crime re-emerged very strongly. Now the comrades—those who had not been detained—were afraid of the gangsters."[222] In the schools, teachers and principals reasserted their authority, although the student representative councils survived the State of Emergency. For the boycott campaign against the town council elections in 1988, some trade unionists from Johannesburg were enlisted to help with the distribution of pamphlets. Only nine people were engaged in this campaign, trying to cover a township of about seventy thousand inhabitants.[223]

With the UDF effectively banned, COSATU moved to fill the void in the political arena. The COSATU Third Congress in July 1989 resolved to rebuild the Mass Democratic Movement around the "strategic alliance" of COSATU and the UDF. The congress called on union members to be active in strengthening and rebuilding structures at national, regional, and local levels and emphasized the need to build street committees.[224] It was this trade union initiative that led to civic revival in Kagiso. NUMSA (National Union of Metalworkers) officials and shop stewards in Krugersdorp formed the Chamdor Industrial Area Committee, which included six COSATU unions and two NACTU (National Confederation of Trade Unions) unions.[225] The area committee soon found itself involved in classic civic activities. In June, the Kagiso Town Council announced a substantial increase in rent and service charges. A week after this announcement, the area committee drew up a petition opposing the rent increases and appointed a delegation to present the petition to the town council. In July, about three hundred residents gathered in the hostel in Kagiso I to hear a report-back on the delegation's meeting. The hostel dwellers were active participants in the area committee.

Meanwhile, the Chamdor Industrial Area Committee attempted to resolve a conflict between activists of KRO and the Kagiso Civic Organisation (KCO), which had launched protest action against rent increases in the new neighborhood of East Park/Joshua Doore.[226] For a short while, the rivaling civics worked together in the Kagiso Interim Co-ordinating Committee (KICC), but this broadly based committee did not bring an end to the divisions. KRO activists resented KCO calling separate meetings and making separate attempts to meet the town council.[227] KCO, as a minority partner, worried about being swallowed by "a multi-structural body" such as KICC, which represented unions, students, and youth. It suspected that NUMSA acted as "an organ of the ANC" and had been assigned the task of reviving civics in order to establish Charterist hegemony. Plans to form one joint civic organization foundered on long-standing distrust, personal rivalries, and the inability to agree on a system of representation.[228] The attempt to establish one civic for all Kagiso residents finally faltered when KCO withdrew from the KICC.

When the protests failed to stop the increases of rents and service charges, those attending a meeting called by KICC on 30 July resolved to embark on a rent boycott. After three subdued years, 1989 marked the revival of defiance. In December 1989, residents staged a protest march to present their demands to the city council. The list included a demand for the resignation of the Kagiso Town Council and for a new system of municipal government with a single tax base and a single administration for Krugersdorp and the townships.[229] The boycott of rent payments and service charges was implemented in December, after the council had turned down a KICC proposal for a flat rate of 45 Rand for all houses. Some residents paid the flat rate, others stopped paying altogether. This was the first organized rent boycott in Kagiso: previous protests were limited to a refusal to pay the increases. As a result, Kagiso was faced with further deterioration of services in 1990. Garbage collection was suspended, while the electricity company ESCOM threatened to cut off electricity now that residents had stopped paying their bills. The rent boycott presented the civic with a new problem: the main occupants of houses stopped paying rent but were still charging rents from their subtenants. Most landlords charged their backyard tenants around 30 Rand. The housing shortage had become even more acute after the abolition of influx control in 1986, and the number of subtenants had increased spectacularly. Ike Genu estimated that in 1990 over half the inhabitants of Kagiso were backyard tenants. The civic decided to issue a guideline for the subtenants' rents to be halved.[230] Whether the guideline was respected is, of course, an open question.

Another familiar issue that posed itself before the fledgling interim civic was transportation. Taxi owners, who had a monopoly after the cessation of Greyhound bus services, had forgotten their earlier promises about reduced fares for students and pensioners and consultation with the community about fares. In mid-1989, the fares had again been increased, making taxis now substantially more expensive than buses. When a meeting of KICC with the taxi associations produced no result, those attending a meeting of Kagiso residents decided on a taxi boycott. However, this boycott never took off. KICC found that the bus company PUTCO (Public Utility Transport Corporation), which also serviced various parts of Soweto, was willing to open a bus service between Kagiso and Johannesburg, but the town councils of Kagiso and Mohlakeng (the Randfontein township) refused permission for the bus service. The town councillors presumably had an interest in the taxi business, either directly or through front men, and had no desire to undermine the taxi monopoly.

In March 1990, one month after the unbanning of the ANC, KICC was transformed into a new civic organization, now called the Kagiso Civic Association (KCA). It included some old KRO activists but also a significant element of KRO's former "workerist" critics. Because of the trade union influence during the revival process, the civic now had "more of a working class perspective. . . . There is much emphasis on working with a proper mandate from the residents. It is less of an activist-led organization."[231] Ike Genu, who had the most clear-cut ANC credentials, was the new chair. Tizza Moiloa became vice chair, Serge Mokonyane general secretary, and Lawrence Ntlokoa vice general secretary. Other long-serving civic activists such as Joe Makgothlo and Ben Ntsimane were chosen as members of the executive.

KCA did not become a UDF affiliate, but it joined the Civic Associations of the Southern Transvaal (CAST), which now operated as an umbrella for civics, planning to join with regional umbrella organizations elsewhere into a national platform for civic associations, while the UDF was phasing out. The new civic had more elaborate structures than its predecessor. The new leadership was critical of mass meetings as a forum for the decision-making process. Mass meetings now served only an informative function. For purposes of decision making and consultation, Kagiso was divided into seventeen blocks, with each block having a representative on the KCA Central Committee. This committee, which was to meet every week, was the decision-making body. Apart from the seventeen block representatives, the membership of the central committee included two delegates from each hostel and two delegates from every affiliated organization such as student and women's organizations, taxi associations, and local business associations. In the new setup and in a context where the ANC was heading for negotiations, the youth were no longer at the center of civic activity. The emphasis on report-backs and mandates resulted in a fairly cumbersome procedure, with block representatives conveying the majority opinion of their block. The decision by the KCA Central Committee was then taken back to the block meetings, where it could be either confirmed or overturned. The KCA constitution prescribed a registered and paid membership, but this had not yet been implemented during my visits in 1990–91.[232]

Although South Africa was now heading for peace talks, the year 1990 was the most bloody episode in Kagiso's history. The township became engulfed in the wave of violence that swept through the Transvaal when the power battle between Inkatha and the ANC was exported from the green hills of Natal to the industrial heartland of the Witwatersrand. Patched together from newspaper reports and interviews with several KCA leaders, the story of the hostel war in Kagiso is roughly as follows. In August 1990, a fight between Zulu and Xhosa migrant workers erupted in the hostel in Kagiso I, with Zulu reinforcements being bused in from outside. Three hostel dwellers were killed. KCA made an unsuccessful mediation attempt. Inkatha then took control over the hostel and drove out the Xhosa and Sotho workers. The civic came to their assistance, providing food and shelter in church centers. This was interpreted

by Inkatha as a hostile act. The Kagiso residents were obviously siding with
the Xhosas and were therefore on the side of the ANC. Nocturnal attacks from
the hostel on neighboring houses left between forty and fifty people dead, the
majority of them ordinary residents without any political affiliation.[233] With
most of the original inmates driven out, both Kagiso hostels became Inkatha
bastions. Civic activists in Kagiso were adamant that the bloody events in
August 1990 had nothing to do with tensions between residents and migrants
but were planned and executed by outsiders. They claimed that violence from
Natal had spilled over to the Transvaal townships and was not the result of tensions that had been building up locally.

In May 1991, a new wave of violence engulfed Kagiso when more than a
thousand armed hostel residents attacked the recently established squatter
camp Swanieville in a predawn raid. A total of twenty-seven people were
killed, and thirty more were injured; eighty-two shacks were burned down.
A one-day stay-away called by KCA to commemorate the victims was about
70 percent effective.[234] The motivation for this attack was vague, but it seemed
to involve a dispute between the squatters and the owner of the farm (a
Mr. Swanepoel) where the settlement had sprung up. Initially, squatters had
been paying site rents to the farmer, but the allocation of sites had been taken
over by a squatters' committee, which then also began to collect rentals.
Rumor spread that the owner had enlisted the help of hostel dwellers to drive
the squatters off the land.

Police stood accused of collusion in this attack. The day before the massacre, a curfew was declared in Kagiso, although the township was perfectly
calm. On the same day, police raided the camp and confiscated weapons.
Newspapers posed the question of how nearly a thousand armed men could
walk about five miles from the hostel to the squatter camp without being
noticed by police, yet immediately after the attack a large police force with
armored vehicles was on hand to escort the attackers back to the hostel.
Inkatha admitted responsibility for the attack, claiming it was done in retali-
ation for the kidnapping of two Inkatha hostel dwellers.[235] Out of an estimated one thousand attackers, only seven accused stood trial, and they were
acquitted for lack of evidence. While South Africa headed for a negotiated settlement, Kagiso buried more victims than during the height of township
revolt in 1986. The hostels were the main source of violent conflict, but not
the only one.

For the first time, rivalry between ANC and PAC went beyond rhetorical
acrimony and an occasional skirmish. Two deadly encounters left much bitterness on both sides. In 1990, fights erupted between ANC youth and PAC
youth in Munsieville. The conflict originated as a dispute between two boys
about a girl, but the brawl soon attracted numerous youth. The fight left one

person injured and one young man, an ANC adherent, stabbed to death. Then all hell broke loose, and PAC followers were forced to leave Munsieville. In 1991, when ANC and PAC agreed to work together in a Patriotic Front, peace talks were conducted in Munsieville. It was agreed that the PAC followers could return to their homes. Fresh problems erupted when members of the ANC youth found out that peace had been concluded without their involvement. Meanwhile, the PAC apparently celebrated the agreement as a triumph and reportedly boasted about their weapons, whereupon ANC youth decided on an expedition to seize those weapons, leading to another ANC-PAC fight. This time a PAC member was stabbed to death. Cooperation between KCA and KCO was becoming even more unlikely after this incident.[236]

A new boycott campaign in 1991 exposed new fissures in the community. The civic had called a boycott against a fancy new shopping mall, which contrasted sharply with the increasingly squalid conditions in the township. The complaint was that the investor in this shopping center, the insurance company Old Mutual, had not consulted with the civic and that tax revenues from the mall were flowing to Krugersdorp and not to Kagiso. The boycott had a multifarious array of supporters and opponents. Among the ardent supporters of the boycott were small traders in Kagiso, who feared the competition from the big chain stores at the mall, and the taxi associations, which feared losing customers if people would shop at the new mall rather than travel to Krugersdorp. But the mall also had its advocates. People from Kagiso who found work at this shopping center saw their jobs threatened by the boycott. Some residents were attracted by the lower prices and the greater variety of goods. Unemployed youth provided a ready reservoir for the recruitment of thugs by various parties involved. Several civic leaders received death threats, and at least one was physically attacked. In different accounts, the death threats were said to be emanating either from unemployed youth or from members of the ANC Youth League. No longer at the center of political life in the township, youth felt sidelined and marginalized. Some of the core activists of the 1980s were also disillusioned, resenting the takeover of the civic leadership by some of their former critics. In 1990, Lawrence Ntlokoa was no longer in the forefront of civic activity. In 1991, he was running two shebeens.

Kagiso: A Reluctant Rebellion

The story of Kagiso's reluctant rebellion shows certain similarities, but also stark contrasts, with the youth rebellion in Sekhukhuneland. The civic had a broad social base and a fairly representative leadership. Unlike the Sekhukhune youth, KRO had the capacity—albeit limited—to provide useful services. It could build on organizational experience acquired in church work, trade union organization, and youth organization. Its leadership was well educated, but not necessarily well-off. Some were employed; others were full-time activists. Business was not represented on the civic executive, but KRO was not antagonistic toward local businessmen. It singled out just those businesses which were owned or run by the town councillors.

Generational frictions came to the fore on numerous occasions, notably in the complaints about excesses by youth in enforcing the consumer boycott and in the initial stage of popular justice. But these are not as central in Kagiso as in the story of the Sekhukhune revolt. On the whole, youth activity—with the exception of the tsotsi element—was fairly integrated into overall civic activity. KRO demonstrated that local issues provide a useful starting point for popular mobilization, but its history also illustrates that issue-oriented local mobilization does not easily result in sustained organization. Most of its demands were marked by moderation. It is striking that Kagiso residents kept paying rents throughout the 1980s, whereas most of the Soweto residents ceased paying rents in 1986. If residents protested against rent increases, they only refused payment of the increase. Radicalization of township politics was a product of the general atmosphere of insurrection and, in particular, of the indiscriminate police brutality in the first months of 1986. But even at the height of revolt, Kagiso did not behave as a "liberated territory": it had recourse to the courts of the apartheid state to restrain the security forces. In this court case, the state alleged that community organizations such as KRO were being used as tools in the liberation struggle in order to make the townships ungovernable, to set up liberated areas, and to establish an ANC presence. By 1986, KRO leaders indeed perceived the civic movement as part and parcel of the liberation struggle, but their concern was not to make the township ungovernable. On the contrary, they owed much of their popularity to their efforts to establish a new order, deriving its legitimacy from a mixture of old values and new ideals.

As in Sekhukhuneland, socialist ideals of a classless society inspired an egalitarian ethos. Unlike Sekhukhuneland, Christianity also proved an obvious source of inspiration and legitimation. By 1990–91, the civic movement in Kagiso was struggling back on its feet, preparing itself for a new role under changing conditions.

The debate on the future of civics took off in the context of a renewed interest in the importance of autonomous organs of civil society. After the fall of the Berlin Wall, this was a lesson repeatedly stressed by several leading ANC and civic activists: civics and other organizations such as student representative councils ought not to be used as conduits for the ANC or in the future as simple transmission belts for the ruling party. Civics were now being cast in a developmental role and simultaneously in a watch-dog role, to ensure that the ANC members who were in power would not neglect the concerns of ordinary people. At the same time, the temptation to use civics to build the ANC on a township level was great. Civics seemed to provide a more or less ready-made network of grassroots activists, while the ANC experienced great problems in setting up organizational structures. Proponents of the autonomy of civil society seemed to dominate the debate. But in reality, the fate of the ANC and the civics was inextricably linked. Ideally, civics should have experienced a new boom in the more open and hopeful climate of the early 1990s. In practice, many civics virtually collapsed, as the "organs of civil society" were emptied into an ANC that now had to staff positions in government and parliament at the national level, as well as at the regional and local level.

CHAPTER FIVE

Grassroots:
From Community Paper to Activist Playground

> We had the spontaneous awakening of the working masses,
> their awakening to conscious life and conscious struggle, and
> a revolutionary youth, armed with Social-Democratic theory
> and straining towards the workers.
>
> *Lenin*

Media and Movements

IT USED TO BE SAID JOKINGLY that the United Democratic Front in the Western Cape was more media than movement. Media policy was central to the UDF's overall strategy, but the Western Cape was most prolific in the media it generated. This chapter explores the role of a pioneering initiative in the sphere of alternative media, the community paper *Grassroots* in the Western Cape.

A tabloid with a somewhat irregular cycle of publication, *Grassroots* might at first sight appear rather inconsequential. It hit the streets about once a month. Under its red masthead appeared a bold headline, exposing a scandalous deed by the government or celebrating a heroic victory by the people. "They'll starve us to death," exclaimed the story about a rise in the bread price. "Afdakkies to stay," assured an article that explained how "the people" had forced the town council to give in to their demand that residents be allowed to build corrugated iron extensions onto their houses. On the inside pages, it offered advice on pensions, divorce, and the prevention of diaper rash, it celebrated Charterist heroes of the 1950s; and it featured the everyday struggles of ordinary people. But a lot of strategic planning and thinking preceded the production of these pages. *Grassroots,* launched in 1980 as "the People's Paper," was South Africa's first community paper of this type. It became a model for numerous publications elsewhere in the country, where a *Grassroots* staff member often rendered assistance in the initial phase. Most other community papers were short-lived ventures, but *Grassroots* survived until 1990.

Community issues were central to the raison d'être of the alternative press, but addressing community issues was not an end in itself. Housing, transportation, and jobs were more likely to awaken an interest in the average township resident than the Freedom Charter or Marxist classics. But these bread-and-butter issues were a means to an end, stepping stones in a mobilization process against racial and class oppression. The *Grassroots* staff members did not perceive themselves primarily as journalists but as media workers with the mission to promote and sustain collective action. While the commercial press presumably anaesthetized its readership with "sex, sin, and soccer," the alternative media meant to empower their readers through promoting organization. Once organized, people would be able to exert control over their own lives.

Who are "the people" and "the communities" in whose name the alternative papers fought their courageous battles? The problematic nature of these concepts has been explored in previous chapters. In the Black Consciousness

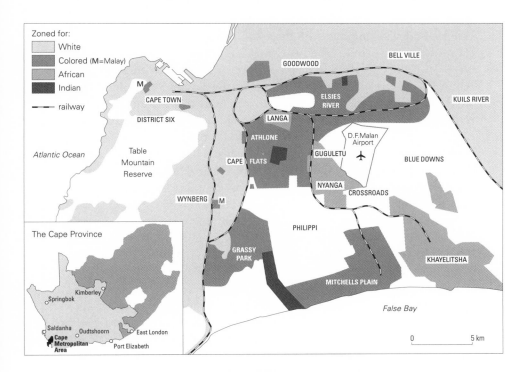

3. Cape Town and surroundings. Map by Nel van Bethlehem.

phase, these concepts were rather straightforward: they included all "oppressed" or "disenfranchised" people and excluded those who had chosen to work on the side of the oppressor. But when following a Marxist analysis, as became current in the 1980s, the conclusion that the oppressed did not necessarily share the same class interests was inescapable. Media activists in the 1980s vacillated between these two positions. On the one hand, political loyalties remained a crucial criterion, with a sharp dividing line between "us" and "them." "Sellouts"—such as Indian and colored members of parliament, African town councillors, or policemen—were not considered to be part of "the community." On the other hand, many media workers aspired to infuse their readers with a working-class consciousness. Apart from its inherent virtue in terms of Marxist doctrine, promoting class consciousness promised an additional benefit in the conditions of the racially segmented Western Cape: Africans and coloreds would find common ground if they identified with their position as workers. However, building alliances across racial divides proved difficult. *Grassroots* was not successful in trying to bridge the gap between coloreds and Africans.

The community papers targeted their audiences both in terms of "residents" or "communities," and in terms of "workers." Middle-class elements were encouraged to join forces with the working class and to accept "the leadership of the working class," on the assumption that the interests of the two classes were compatible. The issues that bound these communities together were primarily negative in nature: opposition to rent increases, forced removals, bus fare increases, police brutality. By developing a culture of resistance, the left-wing media were able to articulate these struggles in positive terms.[1] The young intellectuals who invested such an extraordinary amount of energy in the alternative media strove to lift their working-class audience beyond narrow parochial community concerns toward the class struggle. But the class consciousness of the activists themselves was often a rhetorical facade for youth protest against prevailing patterns of authority. Their media products, more often than not, amounted to youth culture posing as class culture. Moreover, for a "community paper" to foster "class consciousness" is a rather problematic proposition. As explored below, *Grassroots* had for a number of years a rather tense relationship with the main progressive trade unions in the Western Cape.

In theory, the mission of the alternative press was clear: empowering people to fulfill their part in the struggle for national liberation, and—in the eyes of many media activists— to prepare for a socialist transformation as well. Most of the alternative papers preferred to look beyond the anti-apartheid struggle, taking the premise that racial conflict was merely a convenient camouflage for the real divide in South Africa: the class struggle.

What, in practice, happened in the dilapidated buildings where media activists and volunteers struggled to bring their paper more or less regularly to the streets? Was "the community" willing to devote their free Saturday afternoons to discussions about the most effective way of portraying rent struggles and the wider ramifications of the battle for more washing lines? Or would they rather indulge in "sex, sin, and soccer"? Following the pattern of the two previous case studies, this chapter first sets the scene with a brief description of the structural conditions prevailing in the Western Cape. Then it introduces the agent which is central to this case study: a newspaper as a collective organizer.

The Western Cape: Conditions and Actors

Although *Grassroots* was considered the model of a successful community paper, the communities it meant to serve are among the least homogeneous of South Africa. In apartheid terms, the Western Cape was to be the unofficial "homeland" of the colored people. Some 40 percent of the roughly three million colored people lived in the Cape Peninsula. The introduction of the Coloured Labour Preference Policy in the mid-1950s aimed at reducing the size of the African population. Under this policy, which was not abolished until 1984, employers were obliged to give preference to colored labor. African workers could be hired only if no coloreds were available. Africans were therefore relegated to the most poorly paid and unskilled jobs. The construction of family housing for Africans was virtually stopped. Since Cape Town itself was to be a white city, its colored and African inhabitants were forcibly resettled on the uninviting sandy plains of the Cape Flats, with the most notorious example being the destruction of the multiracial heart of the city, District Six. The Group Areas Act, designed to purge the cities of their black inhabitants, caused enormous social and psychological dislocation. The social fabric that held District Six together disintegrated when its inhabitants were scattered over the Cape Flats, where a high crime rate went hand in hand with high unemployment. For the Cape coloreds, the Group Areas Act was perhaps the most hated piece of apartheid legislation.

As influx control began to collapse in the early 1980s, the size and composition of the Western Cape population, and of the Cape Peninsula in particular, underwent a drastic change. With a population increase of 26.4 percent between 1980 and 1985, the population of the Cape Peninsula grew at a much quicker pace than in South Africa as a whole (16.5 percent), due to an influx of Africans. The "legal" African population had decreased, but the "illegal" African population had increased considerably. Most Africans were Xhosa speakers from the Eastern Cape, but the Africans themselves were far from a homogeneous "community." The settled urban population with secure residence rights in the African townships of Langa, Nyanga, and Guguletu was in a very different position from the newcomers who settled in sprawling squatter camps, continuously subjected to police raids.

Although coloreds continued to be by far the most numerous population group, by 1985 they had ceased to be an absolute majority. In 1980, coloreds accounted for 54 percent of the Cape Peninsula population, but by 1985 this had shrunk to 46 percent. Whites decreased their share of the population from 32.5 percent in 1980 to 25.6 percent in 1985. In other words, the Cape Peninsula went through a process of Africanization that gained momentum in the beginning of the 1980s and continued at an accelerated pace into the 1990s.

The majority of the colored population belonged to the Dutch Reformed Mission Church (Nederduits Gerformeerde Sendingkerk, or NGSK), a mission offshoot of the main Dutch Reformed Church (Nederduits Gerformeerde Kerk, or NGK) that was closely allied to the National Party and that provided ideological legitimation for its apartheid policies. With Afrikaans as their primary language, many coloreds were oriented toward Afrikaner culture. Coloreds suffered from discriminating legislation, but they were not as severely restricted as Africans. Compliance with white rule held the promise of social upliftment, while identifying with the cause of African liberation promised severe repression and an uncertain future. Colored advancement usually took the route of the teaching profession, church service, or employment with central and local government.

A minority among the Cape colored people, the Cape Malays—descendants of the Malay slaves of the Dutch East India Company—were followers of Islam, although they, too, had adopted Afrikaans as their primary language. Better educated and more isolated from Afrikaner institutions than the wider community of Christian coloreds, the Islamic Malays boasted a tradition of learning, entrepreneurship, and political radicalism. Much of this political engagement, however, remained confined to left-wing fringe politics, which had only tenuous and intermittent links with the mainstream movement of African nationalism. The UDF, with its structure of local and organizational affiliates, opened new avenues for involvement in a broader protest movement. The Malays played a prominent role in the UDF Western Cape. The Call of Islam, a religious-political association originating among the Malays, became a UDF affiliate.

The peoples lumped together under the label *colored* in terms of apartheid legislation were, in fact, highly diverse. The Group Areas Act defined coloreds as a "rest" category: "any person who is not a member of the white group or the native group." With this intermediate position in the racial hierarchy and the absence of a common history and culture, colored people were prone to a sense of insecurity and a crisis of identity, often internalizing negative white stereotypes of coloreds as being impotent, subservient, irresponsible, and inclined to violence, crime, and drunkenness.

These highly diverse communities formed *Grassroots*'s target audience, bundled together behind a common label as the "oppressed and exploited majority," an opaque phrase that refers to the African, colored, and Indian population. Although these three groups could all be considered oppressed, they were differentially affected by apartheid legislation. Separate legislation gave rise to separate forms of organization; for example, organizations of colored and African students or residents had to deal with different regulations and authorities in the field of education or housing. As state policy in the 1980s was geared toward co-optation of coloreds and Indians, they enjoyed more freedom of expression and organization than the Africans, who continued to be excluded from state power. Because of the demographic concentration of coloreds in the Western Cape, the UDF had more room for maneuvering than, for example, in the Transvaal. But the UDF and *Grassroots* were only partially successful in evolving formulas to bridge the racial divides. The problem was compounded by the left wing's taboo on issues of identity and ethnicity.

Adopting a working-class approach in order to find common ground in a racially divided environment proved no solution, as the Western Cape's working class was itself highly segmented. Apart from the docks and the construction industry, heavy industry was virtually lacking. The economy was dominated by light manufacturing—mainly textiles and food processing—services, and commerce. Sizable numbers of both coloreds and Africans worked as farm labor on the white farms of the Western Cape, but since these were located outside the Peninsula, they fall outside the scope of this chapter.

In terms of labor struggles, the Western Cape stands out as the least militant region in South Africa. Most strikes involved African workers. The largest colored unions remained in the grip of a conservative, white-controlled trade union bureaucracy almost until the end of the decade. However, a few radical independent unions emerged in the 1970s, of which the General Workers' Union (GWU), the Food and Canning Workers' Union (FCWU), and, to a lesser extent, the Cape Town Municipal Workers' Union were to play an important role in radical politics and debates in the 1980s. The FCWU, which had roots in the Congress tradition, had a clear Charterist profile, with two former SACTU (South African Congress of Trade Unions) leaders, Oscar Mpetha and Liz Abrahams, playing leading roles.

The General Workers' Union was a general rather than an industry-based union, but it followed a more cautious policy than its compeer SAAWU (South African Allied Workers Union) and concentrated on building workers' organizations rather than seeking direct confrontation with the state. The

GWU had a mainly African membership, with colored workers accounting for at most 10 percent of total membership. Colored workers were unlikely to feel at home in a union that had become imbued with African culture. Xhosa was the commonly used language in the GWU, while Afrikaans was the language of the colored working class.[2] Conversely, African workers believed colored workers to be unreliable when it came to industrial action.

One consequence of the Coloured Labour Preference Policy was the lack of opportunities for African advancement. Most African workers were unskilled or semiskilled; many were migrants. While organizations in the African townships of the Transvaal could draw on a reservoir of professionals and an educated working-class leadership, the African townships of the Peninsula had a limited potential for providing African leadership for trade unions, community organizations, and the UDF itself. The UDF Western Cape was dominated by coloreds—including many students—and white intellectuals.

If the African population of the Peninsula did not figure prominently in the UDF leadership, it does not follow that militancy was lacking. The African townships had the reputation of having far more staying power when it came to bus boycotts, consumer boycotts, or strikes. The Africans in the squatter camps became international front-page news, with their courageous resistance against the state's deportation schemes. But the squatters, most of whom were illegals, were fighting different battles than the colored students or even the settled African township population. The squatters fought a battle for survival. Their first priority was to gain the right to stay in the Western Cape and not to be deported to the poverty-stricken villages of the Transkei. Squatter struggles took place in isolation.[3] Trade unions and the left-wing intelligentsia had other priorities. The launch of the UDF provided new opportunities to link up with squatters and to place the demand for residence rights on the political agenda. But since the UDF leadership had few contacts in and little knowledge of the squatter communities, they were uncritical in choosing their new allies. Squatter leader Johnson Ngxobongwana was welcomed as a progressive leader, although in his home base—the squatter camp Crossroads—he had already become notorious for his extortionist practices and his violent suppression of any opposition to his leadership. Later, Ngxobongwana's men would turn against UDF supporters.[4]

Although labor militancy was generally weak, the colored intellectuals produced more than their fair share of ultraleftist ideologies. ANC traditions have historically been weak in the Western Cape. The Coloured People's Congress, which represented the coloreds in the Congress Alliance in the 1950s, was small in numbers and weak in organization, in contrast to the much more influential South African Indian Congress (SAIC). Some of the political energy was channeled through the Labour Party, which hovered between participation and nonparticipation in state structures, until its 1982 congress finally decided in favor of participation in the tricameral parliament. But a sizable part of the colored population kept aloof from politics. Social conservatism and the religious orthodoxy of the NGSK were more characteristic of large sections of the colored population than political radicalism or working-class consciousness.

The Western Cape, however, is unique in its long tradition of Trotskyite socialism, represented by the Non-European Unity Movement (NEUM), which in the 1980s was revived as the New Unity Movement (NUM). Other ultraleft organizations such as the Cape Action League (CAL) and the Western Cape Youth League operated in the same ideological vein. The birth of the UDF met with a mixed reception. "The UDF = a betrayal of the working class," ran the headline of a pamphlet issued by the Western Cape Youth League. The Unity Movement was traditionally opposed to the "pro-capitalist, anti-working class nature of ANC bourgeois social democracy" and the "unprincipled Stalinism of the SACP."[5] Although the Unity Movement remained a small core of colored intellectuals, it left an indelible imprint on resistance traditions in the Peninsula. A sizable part of its membership were colored teachers, who thus had easy access to new disciples in the high schools. The Unity Movement's basic argument with Charterist organizations concerned the issue of alliance politics. It was hostile toward multiclass alliances. Its position on nonracialism denied the validity of any concept of racial or ethnic differentiation or group or minority rights. The Unity Movement was therefore opposed to the multiracial concept of the Freedom Charter and the multiclass nature of the United Democratic Front. Its guiding principles of boycotts and noncollaboration with ruling-class agencies led the Unity Movement into a cul de sac of splendid isolation. Its sterile ineffectiveness is frequently blamed on the fundamentalist interpretation of the principle of noncollaboration.[6] Close to the Unity Movement's ideological position but more critical of its abstentionism was Neville Alexander's Cape Action League, which in the early 1980s was active in community struggles over rent and housing, as well as in the election boycott of 1984.

From 1981, Charterist political organizations and ANC symbols began to reemerge. However, when colored activists began discovering the ANC in the early 1980s, they were mostly discovering the ANC in exile rather than the ANC tradition that had survived in the African townships. In the 1980s, the ANC tradition would replace Black Consciousness as the dominant ideology among colored high school students and on the campus of the University of the Western Cape (UWC), originally established as a college for coloreds. UWC students were active in community organizations, in UDF campaigns, and in *Grassroots*. The university also provided legitimizing ideologies for the renewed popular resistance: Vice-Chancellor Jakes Gerwel advertised his university as the "intellectual home of the left." The distinct ideological flavor of the Western Cape was often noticeable in wider UDF gatherings, where the complicated arguments on noncollaborationism forwarded by the Western Cape delegation were generally greeted with a mix of impatience and amusement.

Mobilizing and organizing the community was the task that *Grassroots* and later the UDF had set for themselves. In order to weld a cohesive community, ready to engage the apartheid state, the divisions discussed above needed to be overcome. A series of mass campaigns around 1980 convinced local activists that this could be done.

The year 1979, which was also the year that *Grassroots* was conceived, has become something of a legend in Western Cape history. A strike at the Fatti's & Moni's pasta factory marked the beginning of a new phase in trade union struggles and alliance politics. African and colored workers joined forces. Community activists came out in support of the strikers and organized a seven-month nationwide consumer boycott of the factory's products. Students were drawn into a workers' struggle; workers became more politicized. Some became involved in the new community organizations that began to emerge toward the end of 1979. The strike ended in victory for the unions, which won the reinstatement of dismissed workers. It was equally important in opening up new possibilities for alliances between trade unions and community organizations and in building nonracialism. Another strike, called by the General Workers' Union in the meat industry in 1980, ended in defeat. Few colored workers participated in a solidarity strike with African workers. The union sought community support to generate financial support and to support a boycott of red meat. The red meat strike showed the limitations of alliances across class and racial divides. Whereas the African butchers maintained a boycott for six weeks, the colored butchers started selling red meat again after three days. Although the union lost the strike, community support for the strikers stimulated the union to adopt a more positive approach toward cooperation with community organizations.[7]

Adding to the atmosphere of popular mobilization was a boycott of colored high schools. Black Consciousness had given a new identity to colored students. They were no longer seeking to emulate whites and instead wanted to identify with the Africans in the liberation struggle. *Coloured* increasingly became an objectionable name, only to be used between quotation marks or preceded by *so-called*. The preferred term was *black*. This newfound identity was now being injected with a dose of Marxist analysis. The new generation of student activists was guided by ideals of nonracialism and working-class leadership. Student struggles were no longer fought in isolation. Students attempted to involve parents and teachers and to link up with trade unions and community organizations. In the same year, a bus boycott was organized in protest against a rise in tariffs. The boycott was effective both in African and colored areas, although the African townships showed more staying power.

The year 1980 was also a landmark in the growth of community organizations. The parent-student action committees that had been established at the time of the school boycotts were transformed into civic and residents organizations, where previously there had been little organization in the colored areas. A rent increase in colored areas led to the formation of the Cape Areas Housing Action Committee (CAHAC). The CAHAC constitution was clearly inspired by the Freedom Charter. Community organizations held their first mass campaign in Mitchell's Plain, a colored working-class area. In protest against a rent increase, mass meetings and house meetings were held, and activists went door-to-door collecting signatures for petitions.[8] Not only civics but also youth organizations sprang up around these boycotts and undertook overtly political programs. Young people who joined were given a crash course in the history of the ANC and the SACP, provided with leadership training, and brought into more theoretical discussion groups on dialectical materialism. *Grassroots,* launched in 1980, was meant to play the role of catalyst in initiating and strengthening community organizations.

To coordinate opposition to the new constitutional proposals and the Koornhof Bills, community organizations and trade unions combined to form a Disorderly Bills Action Committee (DBAC), which was more broadly based than Charterists only. This committee became notorious as an ineffective talk shop, bogged down in ideological and personal differences. DBAC, nicknamed the Disorderly Committee, fell apart when the UDF was set up. CAHAC members, including Trevor Manuel, had attended the anti-SAIC conference in Johannesburg in January 1983, where it was decided to work toward a nationwide United Democratic Front. In May 1983, all major progressive trade unions and numerous community organizations attended a conference to discuss the formation of a Western Cape UDF. But when the Western Cape region of the UDF was formally constituted in July, the unions were absent.

By the time of the launch of the UDF, the honeymoon between progressive trade unions and community organizations in the Western Cape was already over. The strikes and boycotts of 1979–80, which had generated a community of activists, had played an important role in the formation of community organizations. The unions benefited from community support, while the community activists became even more convinced of the benefits of alliance politics. But in the aftermath the unions were left with some questions. How would they keep workers' control over workers' struggles? Was the boycott a good strategy (since it allowed community organizations to demand similar support for their struggles)? If community organizations insisted on reciprocity, unions risked being dragged into "populist struggles" over which they had no control. For some Congress activists, supporting union campaigns was a means toward an end. Their final goal was entrenching Charterist hegemony, while trade union leaders worried that the still fragile unions would be undermined by adventuristic strategies. In turn, community activists reproached the unions for soliciting community support when it suited them but providing little manpower in support of community struggles.

For the emerging unions, two elements were vital for trade union organization: worker control and internal democracy. Union leaders were somewhat skeptical about community organizations led by activists, and posed the question whether community organizations were inherently undemocratic because their "mass base" was at a distance from the activists, who were accountable only to themselves. The General Workers' Union and the Food and Canning Workers' Union (FCWU) decided against joining the UDF. They gave priority to working toward a trade union federation. The GWU did not withdraw from the political arena: it played a role in the opposition against the Koornhof Bills, which—if implemented—would further increase the insecurity of Africans without permanent residence rights. The union objected particularly to the lack of internal democracy in the UDF and to its multiclass nature. UDF affiliates did not have the same strong tradition of membership participation and leadership representativeness as the GWU had. If the GWU joined the UDF, its members could be swept into campaigns and struggles over which they had no say because the structure and practice of the UDF would not allow them to play a meaningful part in the decision-making process. Second, UDF affiliates were mostly multiclass organizations, whereas the union was a working-class organization. Therefore, there was a danger that working-class interests could be subordinated in the struggle for democracy against the state.[9]

When the GWU decided not to affiliate with the UDF, it fell from grace with *Grassroots* and the community organizations. The South African Allied Workers Union (SAAWU), a general union that had joined the UDF, was then held up as the model of a progressive union, highly politicized and waving ANC flags. SAAWU's self-appointed vanguard role was not appreciated by other unions, which resented the lack of consultation.

Apart from the general dispute over the relationship between community organizations, which were primarily interested in engaging the state, and the trade unions, which viewed capital as their main opponent, some of the old fault lines in the Western Cape may have contributed to the later problematic relationship. The GWU and, to a lesser extent the FCWU, counted many migrant workers among their members, while township-based community organizations such as the Western Cape Civic Association (WCCA) were dominated by Africans with permanent residence rights. The UDF Western Cape was generally perceived as dominated by coloreds. The dominant role of youth in the UDF also contributed to the sense of alienation on the part of many migrants, for youthful activists showed little sensitivity for their traditional values. While the relationship between unions and community organizations was a subject of open debate in the UDF, other dividing lines in the social makeup of the Western Cape were mostly obscured by the community ethos and the struggle rhetoric. There was no strategy to address the differential concerns of migrants, residents, or squatters.

The strongest taboo was on the relationship between coloreds and Africans. Although there was public debate on the desirability of whites—"members of the ruling class"—in the struggle, there was hardly any mention of the divide between coloreds and Africans. The constant drumming on the theme of nonracialism certainly had its virtues, for it instilled nonracialism as the accepted norm. But some ideologues were such eager consumers of this particular piece of propaganda that they failed to acknowledge the considerable gap between norm and practice.[10] The old fault lines would resurface periodically during the 1980s and after. Civics in colored areas and in African townships did not succeed in initial plans to form one single umbrella organization. The civics in the colored areas joined together in CAHAC, whereas the African civics worked under the umbrella of the Western Cape Civic Association. Similar problems beset the women's organizations, until they finally merged in one organization, the United Women's Congress. The launch of the Cape Youth Congress (CAYCO), prepared by colored activists, was saved only at the last minute when a compromise formula was devised to accommodate youth from the African townships. At the outset of the 1990s, divisions between coloreds and Africans continued to be a central feature of Western Cape politics.

How did *Grassroots* as a community paper deal with this profoundly divided Western Cape community? Before following *Grassroots* on its course through the 1980s, we first explore the strategic concept behind the paper.

A Newspaper as a Collective Organizer

More than the UDF activists in the Northern Transvaal or the West Rand, the university-trained activists who stood at the cradle of *Grassroots* had a cosmopolitan outlook. Their background in student activism and academic learning had equipped them with knowledge of social movements elsewhere and with a network of contacts that could be tapped for both ideas and funding. Inspiration came from Latin America, Britain, and prerevolutionary Russia. The much vaunted slogan *POEM*—Popularize, Organize, Educate, and Mobilize—was an acronym derived from Latin America; it stood for methods of "communicación popular" that were developed for rural areas and city slums. Another important source of inspiration could only later be openly revealed. From the beginning, some of the core activists had a clear model in mind: Lenin's project for a newspaper. But as they had never seen the *Iskra* model, transplanting Lenin's recipe for a newspaper as an organizing tool to a different continent and a different age left ample room for improvisation.

Writing in 1901, Lenin described how the urban workers and the "common people" were ready for battle, but the intellectuals were not fulfilling their role: there was a lack of revolutionary organization and guidance. This organization would be built around a newspaper: "A newspaper is what we most of all need."[11] Without a regular newspaper it would not be possible to spread principled all-round propaganda and agitation on a systematic basis. The frequency and regularity of the publication would serve as a barometer for the state of organization. The newspaper would not only serve to instill a socialist consciousness in the workers but would also broaden the horizon of revolutionaries who were totally immersed in parochial local concerns. A newspaper was needed to link local organizations to the common cause. The role of this newspaper would not be limited to spreading ideas, political education, and winning political allies. "A newspaper is not only a collective propagandist and a collective agitator, it is also a collective organiser."[12] Around this paper would grow an organization that would deal with local issues and also with general political developments: it would give meaning to the struggles of the people. In one of his most famous writings, "What Is to Be Done?" Lenin argued that workers cannot develop a socialist consciousness on their own: "The history of all countries shows that the working class, exclusively by its own effort, is able to develop only trade-union consciousness, i.e. the conviction that it is necessary to combine in unions, fight the employers and strive to compel the government to pass necessary labour legislation etc. The theory of socialism, however, grew out of the philosophic, historical and economic theories elaborated by educated representatives of the propertied class, by intellectuals."[13]

Left to their own devices, said Lenin, workers would succumb to bourgeois ideology and forsake their long-term socialist aspirations for the short-term gain of a few kopeks' pay raise. Likewise, local organizations would fail to see their struggles in a broader political context. The spontaneous growth of the workers' movement and the theoretical doctrine of social democracy, which had originated independently, now had to come together. Needed was a catalyst: the task of running a newspaper would create a revolutionary vanguard that could channel and direct the revolutionary proletariat and infuse the workers with the socialist consciousness that was not the concomitant result of proletarian class struggle but that could come about only on the basis of profound scientific insight.

Reading these texts in the late 1970s, Western Cape activist Johnny Issel could not fail to draw the lessons. Workers in the Western Cape were manifesting an unprecedented militancy with a wave of strikes and boycotts. Students were involved in school boycotts and proved receptive to Marxist-Leninist recipes prescribing a student-worker alliance. But there was no organization to channel all these struggles into one coordinated attack. Issel later recalled:

> There was a lot of confusion as to how to advance politically. . . . We had no organization to support the workers. We wanted to mount a support campaign by boycotting Fatti's and Moni's products, but organization was lacking. . . . You should see the emergence of *Grassroots* in the context of the 1980 student strikes, involving the setting up of parent-teacher-student committees, the red meat strike, the bus boycott. In 1980 we consulted local resident organizations and other organizations: altogether 54 groups were consulted. The news-gathering meetings served as a forum to bring organizations into contact with each other.[14]

On 3 January 1980, Johnny Issel became the first *Grassroots* organizer, a job that he soon had to give up because of a banning order. At the time of the launch of *Grassroots,* thirty-three-year-old Issel regarded himself as a professional activist. Interviewed ten years later, he still regarded activism as his lifelong career. He had a background in student politics at the University of Western Cape, community work, and trade union activities. Like many others, he became disenchanted with Black Consciousness after 1976: "From 1976 to 1979 was a time of withdrawal, of repression, and reflection. It was an introspective period. We began reading much wider than BC literature. I read Lenin: 'What is to be done?' And I discovered the trade union movement. BC centered mainly around a group of intellectuals and petty bourgeois, students, teachers, etc. But we had to involve the masses. That could be done through civic movements, youth movements, and trade unions."

Detention in May 1980, followed by a new banning order in October, put an early end to Issel's public career as a media activist. However, he managed to secure another base from which he could work at the formation of a revolutionary vanguard: the Churches' Urban Planning Commission (CUPC), created by the Western Cape Council of Churches to train church workers for work in the displaced colored communities that had been scattered around Cape Town after the destruction of District Six. Issel put the resources at his disposal to a new use. "We turned it into a training ground for political activists. The churches did not like that, but it was very effective."[15] In addition, he was closely involved in the formation of the youth movement.

Because of his series of banning orders, Johnny Issel's public profile was not as prominent as that of some other Western Cape activists. But throughout the 1980s he remained a key figure, versed in a conspirational type of politics that aroused both suspicion and admiration. Behind the scenes, he also remained closely involved in running *Grassroots.* "He had a tremendous influence in the Western Cape," recalled a former youth leader, "but he is also a controversial person. Many admire him, others hate him. . . . He was a fiery speaker; he could magnetize an audience. He could also tear people apart if they had not fulfilled their assignment. He demanded total loyalty; he did not tolerate dissent."[16] Many felt attracted to Issel's magnetic personality but were also uneasy about his ulterior motives. Issel played a central role in the persistent factionalism that plagued the UDF Western Cape. This factionalism was caused by ideological and tactical differences as well as by rivalry between leading activists who were each building their own power base, competing for followers and funds.

For *Grassroots,* the controversies surrounding Issel proved a mixed blessing. One of the key activists in the UDF Western Cape held that the effectiveness of *Grassroots* was limited because it was identified with one faction within the UDF. If you were not part of that faction, you had no access to the paper. "*Grassroots* was seen as Johnny Issel's thing. And you could not engage in any direct discussion with Johnny, because he had a banning order. He did not hold any position, he could not be challenged, he was not accountable."[17]

His successor at *Grassroots* was herself no stranger to Leninist recipes on the use of media. Leila Patel, a sociologist with a background in theoretical Marxism, worked as the *Grassroots* organizer from 1980 to 1983. Like Lenin, she asserted that a paper was needed to give meaning to the struggles of the people in the battle for hegemony between the state and the forces of revolution. Without a local newspaper, nine-tenths of the significance of localized struggles would be lost.[18] Some of the discussions around the birth of *Grassroots* echoed the polemics between Lenin and some revolutionary contemporaries about the dialectics between media and organization: Which should come first?

The starting point for *Grassroots* was to mobilize people around everyday concerns such as rising bus fares or poor housing. This tactic led to the criticism that *Grassroots* was "worshiping" grassroots organization as a goal in itself. This, it was believed, would result in the development of a trade union or economistic consciousness. In focusing strongly on local issues, *Grassroots* elevated the local, economistic struggle to class struggle and thus misplaced its task of developing the political consciousness of its readers. *Grassroots* was blamed by these critics for focusing only on building local organization while ignoring the vital importance of linking these organizations to a national political movement. *Grassroots* retorted that one could not mechanically transplant Lenin's *Iskra* model onto local conditions in the Western Cape.[19]

While the *Grassroots* founding fathers recognized the tactical advantages of mobilizing people around everyday grievances, they were equally aware of the long-term strategic perspective: they were the ideologically trained vanguard called to lift community struggles to a higher level. The link between local and national struggles, between rent struggles and the struggle for national liberation and socialist transformation, was frequently emphasized. The ultimate ambition behind *Grassroots* was to grow into a nationwide newspaper project.

Although some media activists were arduous students of Lenin's classics, it is obvious that not all of the *Grassroots*'s workers were committed Leninists. Some discovered Lenin only in the course of time, moving from practice to theory rather than vice versa. Saleem Badat, the *Grassroots* organizer in 1983–86, depicted the paper as a product of "spontaneity": "Through its own experiences and quite aside from any theory or model of media, it began to define a role for itself as a community newspaper and elaborate its distinctive contribution in national liberation/socialist struggle. When Lenin's writing on *Iskra* as agitator, propagandist and collective organizer did become available and was read, there was a sense of it being a second reading."[20]

Mindful of the prescriptions of the two-stage strategy of national liberation and socialist transformation, the media activists were not bent on an undiluted proletarian revolution. In the South African context, fighting apartheid was an obvious priority. Here another source of inspiration was of paramount importance: the ANC. For obvious reasons of survival, both Lenin and the ANC had to be hidden from public scrutiny. "In 1980, the ANC was unmentionable. ANC links was not something you could discuss. Many of us who went into *Grassroots* felt part of the ANC, although we did not know that the others had similar sympathies. There were not formal links, but we saw ourselves as fulfilling ANC objectives."[21]

Early issues of *Grassroots* had no overtly political profile, but soon *Grassroots* was to play a role in establishing Charterist hegemony in the Western Cape. As the ANC unbanned itself in the course of the 1980s, ANC slogans and leaders figured more prominently in the columns. For the Marxists on the *Grassroots* project, one central question was the extent to which the Freedom Charter entailed a socialist program. Badat recalled a lot of debate among the *Grassroots* staff about interpretations of the Freedom Charter. "What does it mean: 'the land will be shared'? Are we talking about collective systems or are we going to divide the plots and create a peasant class?"[22] But these debates were limited to the ideological vanguard and did not spill over into the newspaper columns.

This activist elitism stands in stark contrast to another source of inspiration behind *Grassroots:* the participatory and egalitarian ethos of the 1980s. The central principle behind the *Grassroots* operation in the early 1980s was "the paramountcy of democracy," not only in the content of the paper but also in the structure, the organization, and the production cycle. An elaborate process of deciding on the contents, collecting stories, and writing was aimed at involving as many people as possible. The organization of the production and distribution was also calculated to enhance participation.[23] This model of direct democracy had its price in terms of efficiency, but for many it was an important learning experience. At *Grassroots,* people learned how to run a democratic organization, "how to take minutes, how to put up your hand if you wanted to speak, how to chair a meeting. Here I got the confidence for actively participating in meetings. Without *Grassroots,* there would not have been such a wide range of organizations."[24]

Everybody had to be involved in everything. *Grassroots* employed a staff of three or four workers, who all received the same minimal salaries. The egalitarian ethos manifested itself also in a collectivist style. The paper had no editor; the stories had no bylines. Not individuals, but organizations were highlighted. Staff would not present themselves as professionals or journalists, since these categories belonged to the world of the petty bourgeoisie. They were media activists for whom news was not an end in itself, but a means to promote organization.

The ideal type of operation was represented by the Electricity Petition Campaign, which was later to become the subject of nostalgic reminiscences. The Electricity Petition Committee was formed in 1981 by some residents of Mitchell's Plain to get the due date for the electricity bills changed to the end of the month when workers received their salaries. "The campaign reached its peak when 200 Mitchell's Plain residents—the people themselves—marched on Civic Centre to present City Council with a memorandum containing their demands and a petition signed by 7,500." In the jubilant story of "People Power from the Plain," in which the term *People* is consistently spelled with a capital *P, Grassroots* explains that in this campaign a "new concept of leadership" had emerged. Should the petition to the city council be handed over by a delegation from Mitchell's Plain? "No! The People would be their own leaders. They would ALL go to Cape Town and hand in copies of the memorandum. . . . Before they boarded the buses it was decided not to have a spokesperson or persons. The People would speak for themselves. Each and everyone was fully acquainted with the issues at stake. It didn't matter which individuals eventually spoke. The People were One."

The emphasis on collective leadership and the rejection of specialization that would exclude the uninitiated are typical of this concept of democracy. *Grassroots* was not bothered by the question of the extent to which this manifestation of people's power was actually representative of the residents of Mitchell's Plain. "The People" were portrayed as uncompromising heroes, not to be intimidated by officials or security police. When a security policeman was spotted in the gallery during the discussion with the deputy town clerk, they objected to his presence. "'Go!, Go!, Go!,' the People thundered. And the security police, in the gallery and in the doorway, left." Later a man posing as press photographer was identified as another security policeman. "Out! Out! Out!," the People roared and he was bundled out of the hall." The victory eventually gained by "the People" of Mitchell's Plain is not the major thrust of the story. The Cape Town City Council agreed to grant residents a month respite to pay their bills.[25]

The newspaper's role in promoting organization was not limited to the coverage of these glorious events. Half a dozen members of the Electricity Petition Committee came together to write the story and devise a cartoon, which was then submitted to the full committee for approval. The Sunday morning after *Grassroots* came out, Mitchell's Plain volunteers gathered as usual to sell the paper door to door. They had been briefed beforehand about the electricity issue so that they could draw people's attention to the story and invite them to a meeting. In this way, some three thousand copies of *Grassroots* were sold, and one thousand people attended the meeting.

This focus on "the People" and "the Community" reflects a populist approach in which class divisions are obscured in order to underline the joint effort for the common good. This "unity of the oppressed" is a constant theme in UDF discourse. But the *Grassroots* staff was itself somewhat uneasy with the concept of a community paper: they not only aspired to promote popular struggles but also made deliberate efforts at building a worker consciousness.

From Colored Identity to Worker Consciousness

In addressing its readers, *Grassroots* used both a popular and a class appeal. Building working-class unity required instilling a worker consciousness that would also serve to overcome the division between African and colored workers. If workers would identify with their position as workers in a capitalist economy, then the divisive legacy of apartheid could be overcome.

A graphic example of how *Grassroots* tried to guide its readers from colored consciousness to worker consciousness is a comic strip featuring Mrs. Williams, a middle-aged clothing worker from Manenberg, as the heroine (see figure 8). Mrs. Williams is first introduced in the August 1984 issue, where she is watching Labour Party leader Allen Hendrickse giving his election talk on television. She is marveling at how wonderful it is that "we coloureds are getting the vote at last," until a UDF activist knocks on the door to explain that the New Deal will benefit only a handful of sellouts, while more hardship and oppression is in store for the majority of the people. Rents and prices will go up in order to pay for the newly privileged colored and Indian Members of Parliament; the Group Areas Act will remain intact; colored sons will be conscripted into the army to be sent to the border in order to defend apartheid; Africans will become more vulnerable to deportation to the homelands. At the end of the first comic strip, Mrs. Williams has made up her mind not to vote in the tricameral elections.

half a year later , , ,

8. Comic strip, featuring a rapid transition from colored consciousness to worker consciousness. Reprinted from *Grassroots,* August 1984 and February 1985.

Half a year later we find Mrs. Williams at her workplace, where the boss is giving her hell because she is fifteen minutes late. She is late because she stopped on the way to buy a *Grassroots* "with this 'Freedom Charter' thing in it." During the coffee break, the old cleaner—presumably an African—explains the origins of and the ideas behind the Freedom Charter. From a marginal non-person, the old man suddenly becomes a fountain of wisdom, which he derived from his participation in the campaign in the 1950s to draw up the Freedom Charter. Bright pictures of the workers' paradise of Cuba appear in the strip while the old man relates that employment is not a favor but a right: "in countries where workers make the laws, everybody has a job." At the end of the story, while the boss again yells at her for exceeding the break, Mrs. Williams has truly imbibed a proletarian consciousness. She is pondering about a bright future, when "we'll make the laws one day, we'll control the factories. And your days of rudeness and bossing will be over."[26] This is a rather sudden conversion from colored compliance to worker militancy: it is doubtful whether a real-life Mrs. Williams from Manenberg could identify with the comic strip heroine.

In trying to guide its readership from colored consciousness to both non-racialism and worker consciousness, no concessions were made to accommodate colored identity. Many activists at the time would have been adamant that there was no such thing as colored identity. While the struggle against the apartheid state was being waged, no cracks could be allowed in the facade of nonracialism. Only in the more open political climate of the early 1990s could ethnicity be recognized as a relevant issue on the agenda of progressive organizations and publications. In this respect, *Grassroots* mirrored the UDF Western Cape at large: it offered a political home for colored people, but at the price of denying or effacing their cultural baggage.

Interviewed in 1991, Jonathan de Vries, publicity secretary on the UDF Western Cape Regional Executive Committee, made a critical assessment of this one-dimensional view of people and politics: "We were all Marxists, then. We were building the workers' revolution; we were going to perform the socialist transformation of South Africa. People were important only in so far as they were useful in this process. There was an enormous lack of humility. People were a means to an end."[27] Looking back, De Vries acknowledged that for working-class people, it was difficult to be involved in the UDF. Many never came to meetings because they were not fluent in English, they could not follow the latest political or ideological argument, or they were not well versed in the activist jargon. Their days were filled with work, with considerable time spent on travel between home and work, on household work, on looking after the children, and so on. "So the UDF became the playground for young people, many with a university education, many having cars so that they were mobile; they became the operators of the UDF." In spite of De Vries's criticism, in which he did not spare his own role in political power games, his overall judgment of the UDF remained positive. One of its most important achievements in the Western Cape was that—for the first time—it gave coloreds a political home, "which they did not have before, it gave them a sense of belonging." But he was also acutely aware of the price that had to be paid for becoming part of mainstream resistance. In this political home, there was no place for "coloreds" as such, but only for "blacks." In order to be accepted as black, colored identity had to be forsworn. Years later, De Vries still became emotional about the negation of colored identity, about the taboo that made it impossible to refer to coloreds. "I am not a very colored colored, I have moved away from my background, I have traveled abroad, I make music with whites and Africans. But from this now somewhat more detached perspective, I do believe that there is a 'colored identity,' and that the UDF should have tried to accommodate that identity, rather than denying it. But the liberation culture was an African culture; the songs were either military songs or church hymns. There was no incorporation of colored identity in the UDF. That could not even be discussed."[28] He regretted that the UDF and *Grassroots* had not tapped the creativity of ordinary people but, rather, had sought to mold them into a unitary culture that would facilitate the imposition of a new hegemony. Colored culture, De Vries believed, required a kind of carnival atmosphere. The military style alienated ordinary people.

Colored identity, of course, was not shaped by carnivals alone. Church and religion were other important ingredients, but the young Marxists at the helm of the UDF and *Grassroots* were not inclined to pamper the religious sentiments of their basically conservative church-going constituency. They were building a secular movement: the youth were seen as taking the lead in breaking the stranglehold of the church. "The Youth . . . who have been bearing the frustrations within their denominational and ecumenical church youth groups very patiently for a long time broke with these and set out to build secular movements which would articulate, in no uncertain terms, there [sic] bottled-up political grievances."[29]

Grassroots had little time for the church leaders who were such a prominent feature of UDF propaganda. Allan Boesak made international headlines, but he is hardly mentioned in the columns of *Grassroots,* which preferred to portray "working-class leaders." Only in the *Grassroots* rural editions and in its rural offshoot for the Southern Cape, *Saamstaan,* was much attention given to Boesak and other religious leaders. In announcing the launch of the UDF on the West Coast where Allan Boesak would be the prominent guest speaker, *Grassroots* resorted to a religious discourse: "We read everywhere in the papers how people try to tarnish this man's name. We ask those people: how can you tarnish the name of someone who is the spiritual leader of 700 million Christians?"[30]

"A world leader speaks" ran the reverential headline announcing Boesak's visit to Oudtshoorn.[31] *Saamstaan* has indeed been instrumental in building the UDF in the South-West Cape, where organization was nonexistent before the paper was launched. Local leadership here was mainly provided by church people, not by students or young academics. The paper was largely produced in Afrikaans, with some sections in English and Xhosa. Repression in this conservative rural district was harsher than in the Cape Peninsula. *Saamstaan* had to be printed in Cape Town; the copies were frequently confiscated by police before they arrived in Oudtshoorn. In contrast to its urban model *Grassroots*, *Saamstaan* was more inclined to stick to local issues rather than be carried away by high politics. While the *Grassroots* staff was justifiably proud of the success of *Saamstaan* in such a difficult environment, they also had some critical comments on the contents. *Saamstaan* tended to address problems at people's homes rather than at their work. Coverage of an important sector of the rural population, the farmworkers, was far too limited. With progressive trade unions virtually absent, worker organization was seen as a long-term objective. *Saamstaan* believed that a community paper ought to highlight mostly civic issues.[32] In other words, *Saamstaan* was too much of a community paper; it did not instill a worker consciousness in its readers.

Religious arguments and dignitaries were seen by the secular Marxists of *Grassroots* as most suited to mobilize the not-so-sophisticated colored people in the rural areas. They were most prominent in the 1984 campaign to persuade coloreds and Indians to boycott the parliamentary elections. Interviewed by *Grassroots* in Laaiplek on the West Coast, colored Dutch Reformed minister Nico Botha gave religious arguments for his boycott decision: "This decision is based on the gospel of Jesus Christ."[33] Overall, the *Grassroots* radical activists seem to have been more enticed by the third-world militancy of the Cape's Islamic leaders than by the vanguard of the Nederduits Gereformeerde Sendingkerk.

Interviews with numerous *Grassroots* activists reveal that they did agree on one characteristic of "colored identity": colored people did not have much confidence in themselves, nor in collective action: "Colored people cannot stand together."[34] This was a negative trait, one that had to be overcome. Bridging the divide between Africans and coloreds was perceived as a one-way street. Coloreds needed to be persuaded to accept the "leadership of the African majority." No allowance was made for bringing coloreds into the

Charterist fold by appealing to the distinct traits of the Cape colored community: its strong sense of religion, the carnival-like festivities, the fact that Afrikaans was the mother tongue of most colored people, in particular in working-class and rural communities.

The language issue was hotly debated during the whole decade. Should "unity of the oppressed" be promoted by adopting a single unifying language? Or should one start "where the people are," addressing readers in their mother tongue? The initial choice was for the whole newspaper to be produced in English since this was seen as the most unifying language. Opinions differed as to whether this choice would exclude part of the intended audience. Some argued for the inclusion of articles in Xhosa and Afrikaans; others believed that although people spoke Afrikaans and Xhosa, they tended to read in English. "The view was also very strong that language in our society has been used to divide our people. And that the paper should at all times promote unity."[35]

In subsequent years, the staff experimented with various compromise formulas, such as translating some stories or inserting supplements in Afrikaans or Xhosa. With the recurrent language debates, *Grassroots* was ahead of its time. During the 1980s, the progressive orthodoxy held that English was the language of the struggle and the instrument of unity. General open debate on language policy began only in the 1990s. On the language issue, the *Grassroots* staff proved fairly flexible, experimenting with various formats. But in many other instances, accommodating diversity could not be reconciled with the overriding concern for unity. And building unity was one of the features that distinguished the alternative media from the commercial press. The commercial media were seen as divisive, while "our role was to bring people together."[36]

An appetite for debate and diversity was not compatible with Leninist recipes for the use of media. In "What Is to Be Done?" Lenin fulminated against the freedom to criticize, which he felt permitted unprincipled opportunists without a coherent theory to undermine the strength of socialism with their eclecticism. Once the ultimate truth had been established, there was no more need for discussion: "'Freedom of criticism' means freedom for an opportunist trend in Social-Democracy, freedom to convert Social-Democracy into a democratic party of reform, freedom to introduce bourgeois ideas and bourgeois elements into socialism. . . . Those who are really convinced that they have made progress in science would not demand freedom for the new views to continue side by side with the old, but the substitution of the new views for the old."[37]

Defining the class interest of the proletariat could not be left to the workers. This was the duty of the intellectual vanguard with the proper theoretical background. Similar thinking prevailed among the activists who ran *Grassroots* and later the UDF in the Western Cape. As Andrew Boraine, treasurer of the UDF Western Cape, later recalled: "There was a lot of vanguardism, with many activists distrustful that the working class could make the right decisions, when left to its own devices." He also referred to the language issue to illustrate his point. Meetings were generally conducted in English, but if the leaders had really wanted to involve ordinary people, it would have been necessary to have translations in Afrikaans and Xhosa. By way of reciprocating their exclusion, the Africans would sometimes resort to a similar strategy: if UDF meetings were held in the townships, they would sometime deliberately speak only in Xhosa and not provide translations.[38]

Grassroots was instrumental in building a network of activists in the Western Cape, thus laying the foundations for the UDF in this region. Nearly everyone who became involved in the UDF had at one time or another been working on *Grassroots*. But the activists tended to get intoxicated by an activist subculture that was rather remote from the concerns of ordinary people. Commented *Grassroots* volunteer Rehana Rossouw:

> When we became activists, with our workshops in Marxism-Leninism and Gramsci, we lost touch with ordinary people. We were also rather patronizing. We thought that debates were not relevant for ordinary people; they would only get confused. Debates were for activists. The activist culture was too remote from ordinary middle class and working people. We became a subculture. We all looked like Che Guevara's. . . . We were into reggae, not disco. We called each other comrades, we embraced African comrades. And we took for granted that nonracialism, socialism, etc., were accepted by "the people."[39]

In the early part of the 1980s, lack of participation by ordinary people was usually blamed on the false consciousness instilled by the dominant powers. But with interest for and participation in *Grassroots* declining sharply toward the end of the 1980s, the activists began questioning their own performance. Earlier in the decade, they mobilized protest in the Western Cape to unprecedented heights. But when the wave of protest ran out of steam and crumbled under the weight of repression, the weak foundations were revealed. The activists had built numerous organizations, but many of these were not firmly rooted. After more than ten years of involvement in organizing civic associations, CAHAC chair Wilfred Rhodes, one of the civic activists who had a working-class background as a weaver in the textile industry, gave a mixed verdict. As he recalled, the initiative to build community organizations came from students at the University of the Western Cape and other postsecondary institutions: "The problem with the activists is that they did not take the people along with them. That is a problem when working with students, they want to be where the excitement is. . . . When the activists moved on, they did not leave much behind. There were no people to take over the work."[40]

Grassroots in 1980–1983: The Mobile Revolution

The idea to launch a community paper in the Cape Town area was first proposed in May 1976, a month before the 16 June uprising, by a group of colored academics, professionals, businessmen, and community leaders who linked up with the Union of Black Journalists (UBJ). The wave of bannings, detentions, and repressive legislation in the post-1976 years led the project promoters to conclude that at that time there were no realistic prospects for a widely circulated, professionally produced independent black newspaper. But government restrictions could be circumvented by starting a paper that was inexpensive, would not require registration, and could be circulated through a ready-made distribution channel provided by community organizations.[41]

Initially, the publication would avoid a high political profile. It was hoped that the paper would be financially self-sufficient after one year. The newsletter would be distributed free of charge. Money would be raised from advertising and subscriptions by sympathetic individuals and organizations. The *Grassroots* initiators expected to raise half the newspaper's total costs from its own income. Meanwhile, *Grassroots* went in search of funding for the remaining 50 percent. Local South African funding organizations such as the Urban Foundation were judged unacceptable because they were seen as basically supportive of the prevailing system. Some money was made available from church funds in South Africa, but the bulk was to come from overseas sponsors, notably WACC (World Association for Christian Communication in London) and ICCO (Interchurch Organization for Development Cooperation), a funding organization that was run by the Protestant churches in the Netherlands. From a visit in 1980 by Mac Maharaj, a member of the ANC executive and a prominent SACP member, ICCO learned that the ANC backed the promotion of an aboveground, radical press inside South Africa. The ANC had confidence in *Grassroots* but wanted to see more grassroots involvement in the paper by involving civic associations and volunteers who could go from house to house to discuss local issues with the people. Thus, unknown to most of the people involved in the *Grassroots* project, the ANC had encouraged ICCO to adopt the newspaper project from the beginning. One of the few people who were aware of the contacts between the ANC and ICCO was Essa Moosa, a Cape Town lawyer who was chair of *Grassroots.* Wide consultations were held before the launch of *Grassroots,* including external consultations with the ANC. Talks with the ANC were conducted by people who made overseas trips to Europe anyway. Another way of staying in touch with the ANC outside of South Africa was through NGOs that would send representatives to visit projects, often passing through Lusaka on the way.[42]

By 1982, there was no more mention that *Grassroots* could shortly stand on its own feet with help of local funding sources. ICCO committed itself to funding *Grassroots* for a period of three years. For the rest of the time that *Grassroots* was in existence, ICCO would remain the main financial supporter, occasionally urging *Grassroots* to explore other sources of funding and to generate some income of its own. By 1985, ICCO had become the only foreign sponsor. The annual costs of the *Grassroots* newsletter amounted to about 100,000 Rand, of which two-thirds came from ICCO and one-third was earned by *Grassroots*. As repression mounted after 1985, the newspaper's survival became a goal in itself, a beacon of hope signaling that resistance could not be smothered altogether. ICCO then felt obliged to maintain the financial lifeline, and questions about the long-term viability of *Grassroots* became of secondary importance. The fact that *Grassroots* still managed to continue publication was considered as a moral boost for the besieged anti-apartheid organizations.[43] In view of its puritanical advertising policy, *Grassroots* was unlikely to become a self-financing enterprise. The publication scorned advertising from multinational firms: "All content of news items and adverts should only promote businesses and other organisations that are acceptable to the community. . . . Our news and advertisement content should only promote the organizational activities of democratic bodies controlled by the community."[44] Moreover, it held little attraction as an advertising medium. In 1982, 30 percent of the costs were covered by advertising revenues. But businessmen saw advertising in *Grassroots* as a donation to the cause rather than as a commercial investment. By 1983, production costs per copy were calculated at 40 cents, while copies were sold for 15 cents.

As the original idea to produce a newspaper with only volunteers proved unviable, three more full-time paid positions were created, in addition to the permanent organizer. A news and production officer, an administrative officer, and an advertising and distribution officer were appointed in 1981. In the first annual report, lavish praise was heaped on the sacrifices made by staff members: "It was a policy of the organisation to equalize the salaries of the staff and we managed to do this over the last few months. Although the staff can earn more elsewhere, they regard their work as a labour of love, rather than as a means to earn a good salary."[45]

But by 1983 a more sober note prevailed. Having to work with underpaid staff was now seen as a problem: "In the running and staffing of the project we cannot have any romantic notions of political struggle."[46] Poor remuneration hampered the hiring of professionally qualified people. Journalist Ryland Fisher, who worked as a volunteer convenor of the Saturday mornings newsgathering sessions, initially resisted the pressure to join the *Grassroots* staff. He had just been promoted to senior reporter at the *Cape Herald,* a commercial paper directed at a colored readership. Going to work for *Grassroots* meant going to one-quarter of his salary and consuming his savings. He saw the cut in salary as a much bigger problem than the political risks: "Police harassment and all that was part of life in the 1980s."[47]

Grassroots had a difficult start. While experimenting with methods of community participation, the project suffered from disorganization as a result of the banning of Johnny Issel. "We ended up with the worst of both worlds: no efficiency and no democracy."[48] By mid-1981, *Grassroots* was fairly well on its feet. "Grassroots is now very firmly rooted in the community and is being acclaimed not only in this country but in media circles throughout the world."[49] But a detailed analysis presented at the same meeting is less self-congratulatory. It questioned whether *Grassroots* was perhaps "too sleek and too professional" and thus inhibited participation of its readers. The report stressed that, in order to reflect the interests of the community in the paper, the links between *Grassroots* members, who were mainly intellectuals, and the community had to be strengthened.[50]

Various methods were explored to enhance popular participation. The decision-making body of *Grassroots,* the General Body, set out the major policy guidelines at an Annual General Meeting (AGM). It was composed of member organizations such as the civics, trade unions, women's organizations, and youth clubs. Apart from determining policy, member organizations also took part in making the paper. From the general body, subcommittees were formed to carry out the news gathering and production, distribution, fund-raising, and workshops to train people in media skills. In terms of content, format, and methods of production, *Grassroots* wanted to distinguish itself from the commercial papers, where "decisions are taken at the top and filtered to the bottom. At Grassroots, all decisions are taken democratically by all the community people and organisations involved."[51]

The paper was produced in a five-weeks cycle. At the first news-gathering session, all worker and community organizations were invited to send representatives so that "the new issue can grow from the very grassroots of the people." A list of stories for the coming issue was discussed and approved, and the assignments were divided among the participants. Three weeks were available to complete the stories, during which time another meeting was held to check on progress. If organizations were involved, the stories were submitted for their approval. Meanwhile, the Advice Committee, consisting of professionals with a background in law, medicine, child care, or social work, contributed articles for the "advice page." These articles also had to be approved by the news-gathering committee. On printing day, about fifty youth volunteers gathered for the collating and folding of the paper. Distribution was also seen

9. Frank Chikane addresses the Annual General Meeting of *Grass-roots*. Photograph courtesy of Jimi Matthews.

as an important link in the operation. Civics were the most important outlet: civic activists used *Grassroots* to go from door to door and to gain entry into houses by starting a discussion about local issues. But from this point, the media activists lost sight of the operation. "While Grassroots is reaching the communities, we still do not know whether the paper is being read."[52] Not only did *Grassroots* receive little feedback from the distributors, it also received little revenue. Collecting the sales money from the distributors proved a major headache.

The second AGM, held in 1982, marked a peak in popular participation. It was attended by 150 delegates representing 101 organizations. Circulation had risen from five thousand copies for the first edition to twenty thousand in early 1982.[53] It was becoming clear that operating a paper as "an organizing tool" was more of a dialectical than a unilateral process. The level of active involvement in *Grassroots* depended on the strengths of community organizations. The *Grassroots* raison d'être was somewhat rephrased: *Grassroots* was a product of the level of organization in communities, its growth was dependent on the growth of community organizations, and it could not grow independently from organizations. This also became the explanation for the newspaper's poor performance in the African townships: *Grassroots* was weak because the state of organization was weak.[54]

This way of producing a newspaper ensured a wide participation, to such an extent that it became difficult to give everybody an active part. But it also resulted in a considerable degree of uniformity. "Our stories follow the same formula," noted the news-gathering committee in 1982, "a victory through community action is usually the thrust of the story. . . . We do not address ourselves to problems experienced and mistakes made by organisations. Instead we glorify their actions."[55] By 1983, the AGM was still grappling with the overemphasis on victory. It was resolved that the contents of the paper should become more critical and educative and should stimulate debate.

Democracy Turning "Democrazy"

The discussion on the balance between democracy and efficiency was also taken up in the newspaper columns. This debate provides some interesting insights in shifting notions of democracy, evolving from an emphasis on mass participation, with everyone being involved in everything, to a phase where specialization set in and the emphasis shifted to concepts of mandates and accountability.

A good example of the first phase of mass participation is the story of the people of Mitchell's Plain and the Electricity Petition Campaign. In this phase, the message driven home was the importance of organization, of standing together to achieve common goals. Conditions could be changed, if people were properly organized. Repenting scabs were to be welcomed into the ranks of striking workers. The emphasis was on the importance of winnable goals and standing by one's organization—hence the focus on the battle for washing lines and more flexible rules for the payment of the electricity bills. Rent struggles proved more difficult to sustain. Although people might be willing to take the risk of having their electricity cut off for a while, they were less likely to risk eviction. In 1982 a campaign by CAHAC against rent increases had to be called off without the demands being met. The lesson drawn by *Grassroots* was that stronger "democratic people's organizations" were needed: "Sometimes people took militant decisions but were not able to carry this out." In the volatile political climate of 1980, protest campaigns persuaded the authorities to postpone rent increases. But by 1982, the authorities again felt confident enough to hold their ground.[56]

Much space was devoted to explaining the general notions of democratic organization, such as how the elected officials were at all times responsible to the general membership, voting procedures, a quorum, motions and resolutions, and taking minutes. In the initial phase of promoting democratic organizations, democracy meant popular participation. In order to stimulate participation by ordinary people, specialization and individualism were to be avoided. But when participation became an end in itself, it began to have a paralyzing effect on popular action. "Are we all going democrazy?" asked a contributor to *Grassroots* in May 1983: "Democracy is running wild within our organisations. It is sweeping like a wind through all our sub-committees, leaving us all exhausted. When we are about to make a decision, it rears its head and reminds us that to be democratic, we have to ensure that more people participate in making that decision. We cannot decide and act upon that decision without further consultation. All members of our organisation must be party to the discussion. . . . But what does it matter? The struggle is still long. We have all the time in the world. Don't we?"[57]

Responding to the criticism in its next edition, *Grassroots* basically stuck to the concept of general involvement, avoiding a division of labor. The characteristics of democratic organization were explained in contrast to the way in which a factory was run. Interestingly, the defining feature making a factory "undemocratic" was not that the boss was the owner of the means of production, but that the managers monopolized knowledge and insight. The managers were the "thinkers" who planned, organized, and controlled the workers. The other work was divided into specialized jobs, so the workers became familiar with only their particular part in the production process. "People at the top of the factory have important information. They do not share it with the workers. In any organisation to make the right decisions all the information is needed." By contrast, in democratic organizations "all members are workers and managers. Everyone has a say in planning, organising and controlling what happens. All share in the thinking and doing. Everyone in the organisation makes the rules. . . . People learn as much as possible about running the whole organisation. People who have special information share it with others. People are helped to get the skills so that they can do the whole job."[58]

The defining characteristic of democracy was popular participation, not pluralism. In practice, the vision of popular participation proved an elusive ideal. In *Grassroots,* as in many community organizations, the tone was set by intellectuals, leaving ordinary working people with a feeling of being excluded. A letter to the editor complained about too much intellectual talk at the *Grassroots* meetings: "An unnecessary throwing around of big words. . . . It looks more like a University lecture than a grassroots meeting. Why don't they speak in a way that people can understand."[59]

Did the *Grassroots* stated objective to stimulate debate mean that attention could be paid to diverging views, conflicts of interests, or malpractices within progressive organizations? This was to prove a contentious issue. Already in 1980, organizer Leila Patel had raised the question of whether coverage could be given to splinter organizations. If there were two women's organizations active, or two civic associations operating in the same area, could *Grassroots* write about both of them? Should tensions between trade unions and community organizations be exposed? Should tensions among the different unions be exposed?[60]

At several AGMs pleas were heard for more debate in the paper. But debate was easily seen as divisive. The rare examples of debates in the newspaper— one instance was the coverage of conflicting views on the visit by Senator Edward Kennedy—were criticized at subsequent AGMs. Among themselves, activists held many discussions on all kinds of issues, such as the merits of boycotts or participation in the tricameral elections. But these debates were not brought to the attention of the *Grassroots* readers. "The level of political maturity at the time was appalling. If you even suggested such a idea for a debate in *Grassroots,* you were likely to be branded a sell-out. So there were debates among ourselves, but few in *Grassroots.*"[61]

The extensive and sometimes bitter debates preceding the formation of the UDF in the Western Cape were not covered in the pages of *Grassroots.* Sometimes there was a hint of dissenting opinions, but no effort was made to present the arguments. A conflict within CAHAC—one of the core organizations in *Grassroots*—was treated cursorily on the letters page, without *Grassroots* providing any further explanations. After much discussion, it was finally agreed to publish part of a letter from three civic associations, announcing their breakaway from CAHAC.[62] The dissenting civics were in the camp of the UDF's left-wing critics. They accused CAHAC of championing middle-class interests with its demand that workers ought to have the right to buy their houses. By contrast, the dissidents claimed to represent the interests of the worker-tenants. *Grassroots* readers were left in the dark about the wider ideological battle behind the civic conflict, although at the time both sides to the conflict produced statements explaining their views.[63]

Whatever the merits of the dissidents' case, this conflict basically revolved around the issue of alliance politics, which was central to the debate within progressive organizations at the time. Although *Grassroots* purported to have the broad progressive movement as its constituency, it pointedly ignored the whole debate in order not to "confuse" its readers. Significantly, all interviewees vividly remembered the affair, which must have been the subject of much heated debate. "*Grassroots* took its line from organizations. It followed the ANC line, or what people thought was the ANC line. So in the case of the civics which disaffiliated from CAHAC, their problems could not be discussed because those splitting away were to the left of the ANC. . . . There was a clear political line. We would ignore everything that was not the ANC line."[64]

Establishing an Alternative Hegemony

Avoiding a high political profile was a fairly constant policy for *Grassroots* in its first three years, in order to avoid inviting state repression and frightening off readers. Political issues such as political funerals, trials, and raids on ANC bases were covered only when they were tied to local or national organizational efforts. If a campaign was launched to appeal for clemency for six ANC men sentenced to death, *Grassroots* would cover it. But if there was no organization involved in the issue, it was deemed not expedient to cover the story.[65]

In the first three years of publication, *Grassroots* dealt with local issues involving rents, housing, and transportation, stressing the importance of building organizations in the community and in the workplace to tackle problems. It also addressed general matters such as inflation (explained as a consequence of bosses making excessive profits), wages falling far short of the poverty line, child labor, pensioners' problems, evictions of Africans from squatter settlements and deportations to the Transkei, and "sports for the oppressed." The advice pages provided information on health and nutrition, growing vegetables, securing unemployment benefits, workers' compensation for injuries at work, and pensions. Among the more political matters raised were the implications of the constitutional proposals.

By 1983—the year of the birth of the UDF—staff began to question whether the time had come for the paper to assume a more overtly political profile. "Are we lagging behind the people? Should *Grassroots* become more 'political' and less 'issue-oriented'?" The proposed change of direction meant that the political content of the "lessons of struggles" needed to come out more clearly, "linking present struggles around rent, higher wages and so more directly to Apartheid and capitalism." Also questioned was the current organizational setup, implying that *Grassroots* could not move at a quicker pace than the organizations that made up *Grassroots*. In order to provide political direction—in other words, to fulfill its vanguard role—the newspaper would need to have a measure of independence from its affiliated organizations.[66]

Beyond the battle for washing lines, a larger project loomed. To outsiders, *Grassroots* might have looked like a fringe publication of little consequence, but in the mind of the core activists the alternative media were important weapons in the battle for hegemony between two competing world views: the dominant view versus the people's view. This is clearly indicated in Leila Patel's speech at the *Grassroots* AGM in March 1983. "We find ourselves in a position of two competing views of the world—a competition for the hearts and minds of the masses. That is, a dominant view as it is played out in the media of the status quo, and alternative media, which put forward a people's viewpoint of the world and life in our society." In Patel's view, the state and capital are closely intertwined in their joint efforts to instill a false consciousness in the people. "Through the mass media, the state and its allies have a vital source of control over the masses, politically, economically and ideologically. . . . And, I don't have to tell you how great their control is. For those of us who are organizing in communities, there are many nights that we have had to compete with Dallas and Night Rider for people at our meetings. The People's Press, and we see Grassroots as part of this, is the voice of 80 percent of the silent majority."[67] The task of the ideologically trained vanguard was to make people aware that their troubles were not caused by fate, but by apartheid and capitalism.

In attempting to establish a counter hegemony, the battle lines between "us" and "them" needed to be clearly defined. "Them" included the government, the bosses, and the mainstream media. "Their" propaganda was mendacious; "ours" was truthful:

> Propaganda tries to make people think and act in a certain way. Not all propaganda is lies. Government propaganda tries to get people to accept the system as it is—racism, national oppression, sexism and capitalism exploitation. Propaganda from the people however, has a very different message. It aims to get people to support and join the struggle for a non-racial and democratic South Africa where men and women are equals and where there is no exploitation. Our propaganda and their propaganda is definitely not the same.[68]

With this emphasis on its propaganda mission, *Grassroots* served its readers a rather monotonous menu. Within its core, there certainly was an awareness of the dilemma. More practical minds like Ryland Fisher, who had a background in journalism, argued that the paper should become more lively in order to keep in touch with ordinary people. *Grassroots* was acquiring a reputation as a "problems paper." People were well aware that they had problems; they wanted to read a paper not only for their information and education but also for entertainment and excitement. But the ideologues were not inclined to make concessions to "false consciousness." The gap between activists and ordinary people was a consistent feature in the history of *Grassroots*. "It was difficult to reconcile the political aims with sports stories and horse racing. . . . Activists would criticize the 'gutter stories.' The activists won the day; in the end they were the only people reading the paper."[69]

Two elements occupied a central place in the construction of this counter hegemony: Charterism and socialism. From the beginning, *Grassroots* had been dominated by Charterists, a number of whom were in favor of an open editorial policy, covering all kinds of issues of importance. But since the newspaper came to be seen as a Charterist mouthpiece, organizations outside the Congress fold did not bother to attend meetings or to submit news items. And since the non-Charterists did not take part in the more tedious work, such as distribution, activists felt that if others did not put in any work, their activities did not merit coverage in the paper. This attitude became more pronounced after the launch of the UDF. It was felt that coverage of activities outside the UDF camp would involve promoting rival organizations.[70] By the mid-1980s, the *Grassroots* chair frankly admitted that the paper was not serving as a platform for anti-apartheid resistance in a broader sense: "It was always the policy of Grassroots Publications to serve as a broad forum—to give expression to progressive political views prevailing in the oppressed community. It is clear that this policy was not implemented in practice."[71] Although the problem was recognized, it was not being addressed. With "unity of the oppressed" under Charterist direction as the overriding concern, there was little room for divergent views in the counter-hegemonic project.

Building Alliances: Colored Areas and African Townships

There was no ideological background to the rivalry between two progressive women's organizations, which for years bedeviled the UDF Western Cape. Both Women's Front (WF) and the United Women's Organisation (UWO) had adopted the Freedom Charter. The differences had to do with racial divides and with a sociocultural gap. WF was based in the townships, where it was seen as a revival of the Federation of South African Women (FEDSAW), an ANC-aligned women's organization in the 1950s. UWO had an African membership as well but included white and colored women, many of whom were students or academics. From the point of view of the townships, these were people from "the other side of the railways," with "branches in Cape Town, academic members, more resources, and also pushing some feminist issues like rape."[72] Other women's issues taken up by UWO included the legal position of black women as minors, maternity leave, day-care centers, equal pay for equal work, and the enforced use of contraceptives.

Women's Front was a more traditionalist organization, dominated by old ANC stalwarts from the 1950s for whom women's issues were of secondary importance in the national liberation struggle. The emphasis was on commemorations, petitions, demonstrative funerals, and protest meetings. "The idea was that the people from exile and from jail would come back, take over the leadership and tell us what to do. They would solve all problems. But we had to learn to think for ourselves. We could not always look back to the 1950s."[73] In contrast to the sober meetings of WF women, UWO meetings were often conducted in English and enlivened with all kinds of festivities, music, and banners. Feminist discourse, emanating from the universities, found its way into UWO but not into WF. Although WF had already in 1982 called for a joint campaign involving civics, youth, and church groups against the Koornhof Bills, it was initially not welcomed into the UDF. UWO had already affiliated with the UDF and was represented on the UDF Regional Executive. Only after an intervention from UDF Head Office was WF accepted as a UDF affiliate. But much bitterness remained between the two organizations. The division among the women affected other groups in the townships, notably youth. After much goading from UDF Head Office and even from the ANC in Lusaka, WF and UWO finally decided to merge in 1986. The younger women in the organizations then proved more flexible. After a difficult start, in which positions on the executive had to be parceled out equally between representatives of both organizations, the antagonism died down.

How did *Grassroots* deal with this division within the ranks of its own constituency? It did not address the issue since Women's Front had no access to the paper. UWO was represented on the *Grassroots* board and provided the input for stories on women's issues. "Women's Front," according to one of its leaders, "had no people with media skills, no resources. It did not go to the press with its stories. . . . We felt that others were deliberately ignoring Women's Front and letting us die a natural death by starving us from resources. The *Grassroots* attitude was: 'if we don't write about them, then they don't exist.'"[74]

Grassroots focused exclusively on UWO, which was presented as the only women's organization. The two African women who worked as the *Grassroots* township organizers were both UWO members. Several interviewees indicated that the split between the women's organizations deeply affected township politics, but the issue was completely ignored in *Grassroots*. The newspaper identified with and depended on UWO. Within Women's Front, it was believed that Johnny Issel was behind efforts to get WF to disband.

Similarly, *Grassroots* completely ignored the problems that accompanied the formation of the Cape Youth Congress (CAYCO). The initiative to launch

CAYCO came from the colored areas, where the formation of a regional youth movement had been under discussion since 1981. Local youth groups were engulfed in their own organizational problems, which had to do with the degree of centralization in the proposed organization and with personality clashes. This process did not involve the African townships. Before CAYCO's launching conference some contact had been made with youth in the townships, who responded that they were not yet ready to join. On the eve of the CAYCO launch in May 1983, African youth arrived in great numbers, claiming to represent eight CAYCO branches. Their arrival posed an acute problem. The colored youth activists were not prepared for them and had met to distribute leadership positions among themselves. The African youth did not want to put forward some candidates of their own to be included on the executive; they demanded open elections. "It took a somewhat ugly turn, with coloreds voting for coloreds and Africans for Africans."[75] In its first two years, CAYCO was plagued by tensions along racial lines. These divisions lessened, and in 1984, an African youth, Roseberry Sonto, was elected CAYCO chair.

These were important learning experiences for movements trying to build nonracial organizations. Yet there is no mention of these developments in the pages of *Grassroots*. Although there could be some public mention of the controversy surrounding the involvement of the white student organization NUSAS (National Union of South African Students), the much deeper divisions between colored and African youth were apparently unmentionable in the alternative media.

The third important component in the *Grassroots* project, the civics, experienced similar problems when attempting to organize across the racial divide. Initially, the emerging civic bodies in the African townships and the colored areas worked toward forming one umbrella structure, but in 1981 the civics of Langa, Nyanga, and Gugulethu went their own way. In 1982, two umbrella organizations were formed: the Western Cape Civic Association (WCCA), which united the civics in the African townships and a number of squatter settlements, and the Cape Areas Housing Action Committee (CAHAC), which had an initial membership of fourteen civics in colored areas. Both events and subsequent activities by WCCA and CAHAC are duly covered in *Grassroots*. But the unsuspecting reader found no clue as to the raison d'être of two umbrella bodies. "New Umbrella civic body," ran the headline over the story announcing the formation of the WCCA. But there was no indication that its members came exclusively from African areas and no explanation for the breakaway from CAHAC. From later interviews I gathered that the African civics had advanced two reasons: they had a language problem at CAHAC meetings, which were conducted in English and Afrikaans; and they had to deal with different authorities since African and colored areas fell under different administrations. Civic activists in CAHAC were unconvinced and suspected racist motivations on the part of the African civic leaders, who resented colored domination of CAHAC.

The history of *Grassroots* itself also provides a clear illustration of the problems encountered in attempts at bridging the divide between coloreds and Africans. *Grassroots* had originated as a colored initiative without active involvement of Africans from the townships. It never became solidly rooted in the townships. "Numerous attempts to arrange meetings with people [from the townships], to get community representatives to attend Grassroots general and news-gathering meetings, to be represented on our broad general body, and to build a strong distribution network in the townships had not proved very successful."[76] After this frank admission, the analysis of this weak spot is rather disappointing: "We believe there could be many reasons for this, the main one being the many problems in the townships."

The weak state of organization in the townships is often mentioned as explanation for the poor performance of *Grassroots*. But this was firmly denied by Zollie Malindi, one time president of the UDF Western Cape, who believed that organization in the townships was much stronger than in colored areas: "People in the townships are more politicized, because of pass laws and so on. Coloreds had less problems. The government always differentiated between coloreds and Africans. It is more difficult to organize coloreds; some are petty bourgeois; they aspire to be like white people."[77] Malindi believed that *Grassroots* was not widely read because it was not a township-based publication and because it lacked Xhosa speakers on its staff. Malindi and youth leader Roseberry Sonto were involved with another publication, *Township News,* which was launched in the mid-1980s. *Township News* was written in Xhosa and therefore accessible to people with only a few years of primary education. It worked in cooperation with *Grassroots,* sometimes translating stories from *Grassroots* and making use of its workshops for media skills.

Some progress in gaining a foothold in the townships was reported after the appointment of an African as township organizer in August 1982. By March 1983, circulation in the townships had reportedly increased from 200 to 1,500 copies.[78] A change in language policy was implemented in 1984, with more stories being written in Xhosa. But the secretarial report for the April 1985 AGM noted that sales in the townships had dropped from 2,000 to 750.

African participation in gathering the news and distributing the paper remained poor. *Grassroots* was still seen as a colored paper. "When you went to the *Grassroots* office, you did not see an African."[79] News was not coming forth from township-based organizations: the township organizer had to go out to gather news. The most concrete contribution of *Grassroots* to furthering interracial contact was perhaps the collating and folding of the paper. Groups of youth from the townships and colored areas were brought to the printer, where a party was held as they folded the newspapers. Here colored youngsters learned African freedom songs and *toyi-toyi* dancing.

When she resigned in 1985, Hilda Ndude, the first township organizer for *Grassroots,* summed up her experience as "a hard one, with little assistance from the [Grassroots] office and also little assistance from people in the townships."[80] She did not get along with the news and production staff, who in turn contended that she did not do her job. Her successor as township organizer was Velishwa Mhlawuli, who made the headlines when she survived an assassination attempt in 1988 in which she lost one eye. Her relationship with the *Grassroots* staff was somewhat better. She believed that *Grassroots* became more popular in the townships after 1985, when a Xhosa edition of the paper was produced. "People now understood the paper better. They wanted to read about their struggles and their victories in their own language."[81] The *Grassroots* news organizer was less convinced of the central importance of the language issue. He blamed the paper's poor performance in the townships on the township organizers, who used their *Grassroots* salary and facilities to further their other political interests, which centered mainly on the women's organization. The job was not assigned on the basis of any particular qualities. Organizations in the townships named people who needed to be rewarded with a job because they had been detained, or they had children and were in need of money. If someone did not show up for weeks and went off to the Transkei without offering any explanations, *Grassroots* had no possibility of sanctioning the negligent worker. "You could not halve her salary, or dismiss her. That would upset the townships. We had a weak foothold in the townships, and we could not jeopardize that."[82]

Apart from the image problem of *Grassroots* as a colored paper, media were apparently not a priority for township activists, who relied more on word of mouth to organize meetings, boycotts, or demonstrations. Township activists did not believe that the paper was of much benefit to them, and after 1983, the UDF would absorb much of activists' energies.

Building Alliances: Community Organizations and Trade Unions

The first year of publication for *Grassroots* coincided with the high tide of euphoria about joint worker-community action. The paper's editorial for December 1980 hailed the newly emerging alliance in glowing terms: "The Fattis & Monis dispute, the supportive action which followed, not only formed a landmark in the Trade Union movement, but shows a turning point in the struggle of the mass of the suffering people in South Africa. Community supportive action, as we have not seen for many years, has taught the

oppressed a new form of struggle. Unity in action, the basis of the Fattis &
Monis episode, is the requirement for an unfree people to achieve their goal."[83]

But the 1980 experience had created unrealistic expectations about the
involvement of the unions in overtly political campaigns and community
struggles. An article written by the Food and Canning Workers Union
(FCWU) for *Grassroots* drew a sharp distinction between unions and community organizations, both in terms of constituency and leadership. "What is
important is that the members of a trade union are workers, and that a union
should be led by workers. A trade union brings together workers who are
divided in so many different ways, because they are an oppressed class and
share a common oppressor." Community organizations, on the other hand,
"are open to workers and non-workers. In most cases the leadership of these
organisations are intellectuals or people with more education. At this point,
community organisations do not have a strong base of worker members. The
workers who do participate do not always feel that they have a major part to
play in such organisations."

The FCWU contested the concept of a community as a homogeneous body,
claiming that there could be no lasting alliance between workers' organizations
and community organizations unless it is clearly understood that "there are
class divisions among the oppressed." The article concluded with the statement
that unions must be allowed to determine their own priorities.[84]

Class divisions within "the community" were indeed mostly ignored by
Grassroots. A story on the plight of domestic workers provided a rare glimpse
of the class divisions within the community. The story denounced the appalling
conditions for domestic workers in the colored areas: presumably both the
exploiters and the exploited were colored. There was no mention of race in
this article. It quoted an official from the Domestic Workers' Association, who
accused employers of kidnapping practices. "So many times people go and
fetch children on farms without telling their parents. Sometimes the children
go home pregnant and with no money. We feel we need to do something
about this. This is almost a daily problem."[85] While this presumably is an
example of "class oppression" within the colored community, there was also a
widespread practice among somewhat better-off colored households to hire
African domestics. But while *Grassroots* paid regular attention to the plight of
domestic workers, this aspect was never mentioned.

Mindful of Lenin's scathing critique of the narrow "economism" of trade
unions, *Grassroots* was firmly on the side of the community organizations and
the "popular democratic struggle." When discussing the unity talks between
the independent trade unions—one of the unions' priorities that made
involvement in community struggles take second place—*Grassroots* identified

itself with the general position of community organizations, arguing that "a narrow economic view must be criticised in the strongest terms. The struggle is not only between workers and bosses, it is also a fight against the state for political power."[86] To underline the point, the newspaper held up the shining example of SACTU (South African Congress of Trade Unions), which had concluded an alliance with the ANC in the 1950s, thus extending its struggle beyond the workplace to the community. From the perspective of independent unions, SACTU's experience was a lesson to avoid: by allowing itself to be dragged into all kinds of ANC campaigns, SACTU had hastened its own demise.

The relationship between community organizations, *Grassroots,* and the trade unions became more problematic with the formation of the UDF. The independent trade unions GWU, FCWU, and FOSATU (Federation of South African Trade Unions) decided against joining the Front but announced that they would support the campaign against the new constitution. That marked the end of the honeymoon with the independent trade unions. "For us, everybody at that time who was not in line with the ANC was lumped in the camp of the detractors. Unity Movement, trade union people who insisted on independent worker organization. . . . We saw them as opponents of the ANC. The ANC was our holy cow; we had finally found a home."[87]

But tensions had already arisen before the formation of the UDF. As David Lewis, former GWU secretary pointed out later, there were conflicting perceptions of "communities." In the *Grassroots* concept, the community equaled the workers, while unions were questioning whether worker interests really coincided with community interests. Unions such as the GWU were at the time much concerned with establishing "worker control" in the unions, while community organizations were seen as organizations of activists. In community organizations, there was "not much involvement of the rank and file. Unions were much more concerned with their membership, with the whole tedious business of mandates, briefings, accountability of leadership. Activists are concerned with 'leading the masses,' but they have only very fleeting contact with people."[88]

Although civic activists and youth activists, when interviewed, were convinced of the importance of *Grassroots* in the early phase of organization, Lewis did not believe that the newspaper made any significant contribution to union organization. Initially, GWU designated people to attend the news-gathering meetings. "But it was a very cumbersome job . . . , it took most of your free Saturday." Media were not a priority for the unions, and moreover, *Grassroots* lacked credibility. "People were not keen to get a copy. It never portrayed the problems of organizations, it was very triumphalist. Also, we did not necessarily share the same interests. Unions then were working on national unity. *Grassroots* was much more parochial, focusing on local community organizations." He questioned the validity of promoting unity by plastering over problems: "The left media have never properly understood what was their job. For instance, when we had these difficult unity talks, the commercial media would cover all our disunity, exploiting the differences. But our own media did not cover the problems. Here we could have dealt with the problems and explained what were the issues. But the left media think it is their job to smooth over the problems, leaving it for the commercial press to exploit the disunity."

The lack of credibility was exacerbated by an image problem. Not only was *Grassroots* seen as a colored paper that did not appeal to the GWU's largely African membership, but it was also seen as a platform of the youth. GWU's main constituency was among hostel dwellers, who had been involved in bitter conflict with youth in 1976. The migrants, many of whom were quite conservative, regarded the youth, and by implication *Grassroots,* with much suspicion. GWU found participation in *Grassroots* too time-consuming and chose to stay clear of political quarrels between community organizations of different ideological backgrounds.

In response to problems with news gathering, *Grassroots* decided in 1983 to form "interest groups," notably a women's group and a labor group. News from the organizations in these fields was not forthcoming. Ideally, these interest groups would involve the organizations in these fields. That became the mode of operation for the women's group that was formed by members of the United Women's Organisation. The labor group, however, did not include any trade union members, for the unions felt that they could not spare their members for media activities.[89]

Grassroots kept battling with the issue. Ideological recipes prescribed a working-class leadership, but in real life this proved elusive. Although the paper found a receptive audience among student youth, it did not manage to involve working youth. The skills required for producing a newspaper meant that it remained a preserve of well-educated people, in spite of continued efforts to spread skills more evenly. Training in media skills thus far focused on activists, stated the secretarial report in 1983. "We hope 1983 will see Grassroots equipping more working class people with the necessary skills to prepare them to assume leadership positions in our association."[90] Young workers would have to produce the leadership needed "if we are to end racial oppression and capitalist exploitation in our country." In 1985 *Grassroots* apparently began to despair that one paper could serve the divergent interests within the community: the organizer proposed to investigate the possibility of a "young workers' magazine to help raise the consciousness of this constituency."[91]

In this respect, the predicament of *Grassroots* resembles that of CAYCO, whose basic constituency was high school students and students from post-secondary institutions, with a sprinkling of young workers and unemployed youth. "The whole atmosphere would not attract young workers, because students dominated the discussion. And we were using English, the struggle language, while many workers would speak Afrikaans. Oh yeah, we had endless discussions about the leadership of the working class and the leadership of the African majority. But our leadership came from mostly middle-class areas, from the more affluent families, university students. But we were involved in working-class issues. 'Organizing the working youth' was always on our agenda, but it never got off the ground."[92]

Grassroots in 1983–1985: Linking Up with National Struggles

The launch of the UDF presented Grassroots with a new challenge. Linking local issues to the struggle for national political power—a central tenet in UDF strategy—fitted eminently with the newspaper's editorial policy of drawing out the political content of community issues. With its history as an organizational tool, it was natural for *Grassroots* to see its task as building the UDF. Beginning in 1983, the UDF occupied a prominent place in its pages. But it was only from 1985 onward that *Grassroots* fully became a mouthpiece of the UDF.

With a special issue covering the UDF's launch, *Grassroots* plunged enthusiastically into the campaign to build the UDF. The new constitution and the tricameral system provided useful targets for *Grassroots,* since they could be tackled from many angles. In the run-up campaign to the tricameral elections in August 1984, many organizations came out in support of boycott calls. This provided a good opportunity for broadening out, notably to include religious organizations. Spokespeople on behalf of the Muslim Judicial Council called for an election boycott, warning that those who would run for election would automatically be expelled from the organization.[93] Muslims also launched their own organization, the Call of Islam, to mobilize against the constitution. Christian-inspired resistance was more prominently featured in the *Grassroots* rural editions in Afrikaans, as in the story on the UDF and the election boycott in the Southern Cape. Here a colored *oom* (uncle) gives a religious motivation for his refusal to vote: "I stood at the ballot box. I brought the bible and the voting together: there was a gap. Then I brought the UDF and the bible together; and there was contact. Then I walked past the ballot box."[94] But once the elections were over, few efforts were made to relate to religious sentiments.

For *Grassroots* as a community paper, the UDF presented both a new challenge and a liability. "Before, we were fighting for high wages, low rents, equal education. Now we see how they are all part of the same struggle. As we see how the new constitution will affect our daily lives, so our bread and butter struggles have been united in a bigger struggle against the new constitution and apartheid, against exploitation and oppression in all its forms."[95] But how should *Grassroots* relate to these highly political campaigns? This question was addressed at an assessment meeting in October 1983, where *Grassroots* secretary Lynn Matthews hailed the new challenges but warned against getting completely caught up in the politics of the UDF: "We know that the people in our communities still struggle because there is no work. There is no food and no homes. In Crossroads today, people are calling for support in their fight for the right to live and work where they choose. In Kewtown the maintenance fight continues, and in Bellville, Lotus River and Belhar the fight for electricity still goes on. Grassroots cannot forget the day to day struggles of the people. It cannot overlook their need to build strong democratic organisations."[96]

The rapid growth of the UDF also posed a dilemma for the local affiliates, which felt that building the Front happened at the expense of consolidating their own still weak organizations. After the UDF anti-election campaign, CAYCO reported a widespread feeling that the "UDF anti-election campaign destroyed our organisation as well as others and that we should never allow it to happen again."[97]

For *Grassroots* and the UDF Western Cape as a whole, this strong focus on the constitution and the election boycott meant that coloreds were the main target audience. Since the New Deal aimed at the incorporation of coloreds and Indians, colored people needed to be dissuaded from voting. With this offensive against the constitution and the "dummy institutions" for coloreds, issues in the African townships took second place. Squatter struggles, a prominent feature of resistance in the Western Cape, also received scant coverage. Only when open warfare—clearly instigated and promoted by the police—erupted between various factions in Crossroads and its satellite camps, did *Grassroots* begin to deal with the issue. The UDF in the Western Cape was equally aloof and largely ignorant of the political dynamics in squatter communities.[98]

With the formation of the UDF, it was natural for *Grassroots* to widen its scope, but it is questionable whether the newspaper could take the bulk of its "grassroots" readership along. In going for "hard politics," it may have alienated ordinary readers. Stories about national political issues tended to be fairly abstract, which prompted repeated calls for *Grassroots* to become more popular. "Were we appealing to an activist and student readership whilst leaving others behind?"[99]

The UDF in general experienced similar problems when launching solidarity campaigns with other parts of the country. UDF leaders found that although activists were readily able to identify with national political issues, ordinary people in the community were unable or unwilling to make such a link. "Lots of people in the community say what has that [repression in the Ciskei] got to do with us. . . . You have got to make the link . . . that has been very hard."[100]

Although the UDF was based on highly local organizations, its meetings were dominated by national politics. "The UDF did not strike a proper balance between bread-and-butter issues and national politics. . . . Yes, civics did handle things like rents and they were UDF affiliates. But when civic representatives came to the meetings, they put on a different cap and talked politics. The more they got sucked into national politics, the more they got out of touch with their own constituency."[101] This verdict by Jonathan de Vries is shared by Joe Marks, the 1983–85 vice-president of the UDF Western Cape, who later became one of its most outspoken critics. Marks, a jovial gray-bearded vegetable vendor with a history of political involvement dating back to the Coloured People's Congress and the South African Communist Party in the 1950s, was known for his propensity to deviate from the politically correct line. Boasting about his working-class background and his daily contacts with ordinary folks as a street vendor, he was scornful of the activists who pretended to "lead the masses." Marks believed that *Grassroots* lost its popular appeal once it became caught up in "hard politics." After the launch of the UDF, he commented,

> *Grassroots* was no more the people's paper. It had become the instrument of a political elite. When *Grassroots* was addressing bread-and-butter issues, rents, electricity, refuse removal, street lights, then people saw it as their paper. . . . But the people here, they get scared when they see *polatiek*. When they see Mandela's portrait and Mbeki's portrait, they start shivering. Rents is an issue people want to discuss, but they want to stay clear of politics. Our people want a nonpolitical paper. . . . What do people want to read about? That the rapist who got hold of the neighbors' daughter is caught and that problems surrounding electricity bills can be worked out. . . . The "People's Issues" is how to combat robbery, not high politics. Surely, we would like people to be interested in a nonracial unitary South Africa, in discussions about economic policy. But unfortunately, the people here don't give a damn.[102]

This, of course, was a recurrent problem in the *Grassroots* editorial policy. Should the newspaper start from where the people are? Or, rather, should the paper give direction, prefiguring where the people ought to be? Although there were differences of opinion regarding means and methods, there was consensus on the basic direction among those producing the paper: *Grassroots* ought to prepare the way for the ANC in the Western Cape.

Popularizing Charterism and Socialism

In the early phase of *Grassroots,* promoting the ANC was done mostly indirectly—for example, by using slogans from the Freedom Charter such as "There shall be houses, security and comfort." With the launch of the UDF, *Grassroots* and its core member organizations, such as CAHAC, assumed an overtly Charterist profile. CAHAC adopted the Freedom Charter in 1984 as "a basis for the establishment of a just and democratic order in South Africa."[103] *Grassroots* featured do-it-yourself instructions for producing ANC or Free Mandela buttons.

Initially, the people who worked on *Grassroots* had reminded themselves periodically of the need to broaden out and to encourage debate, but then the paper began to follow a clear-cut political line. What exactly was the ANC line could be established by scrutinizing ANC publications, such as Oliver Tambo's annual New Year message on January 8. "In those days, you would not question the directives of the movement. That was the style of politics. We also had to convince ourselves that the ANC was the best organization. In the process of convincing ourselves, we could not allow any doubts. So in the process we ignored other organizations. The organization was 'correct at all times.' That explains the political purity. Very strong emotions were involved where the ANC was concerned."[104]

The authoritative interpretation of the ANC line came to be a major topic of discussion. "Some of us, who had been abroad and who actually met ANC people, were aware that ANC people were also human and that the ANC had many problems. But you could not come home and tell that [to] the people here; they simply would not believe that. If you would disagree with something the ANC did, you would only discuss that with very close friends who shared your political loyalties."[105]

But the strategy for *Grassroots* was twofold: to establish Charterist hegemony and to promote a workers' consciousness. What did it mean: The People Shall Govern? That the ANC would take over the state? Or that the workers were going to control the factories? Or both? In covering various events, *Grassroots* projected a "leading role of the worker" as the correct political line. It ran features on worker leaders from the 1950s who were closely associated with the ANC or SACTU, such as Oscar Mpetha, Liz Abrahams, or Dorothy Zihlangu. In its extensive coverage of student affairs, it hammered the message home that students could not go it alone: only worker-student alliances could bring victory. Student organizations and student activists duly rehearsed the correct line: not they, but the workers were to lead to struggle. But "the line" could easily be appropriated to mean that the students—being of working-class background—were after all the engine of the struggle.[106]

Promoting socialism on a more abstract level was easier than coming to grips with the much vaunted need for worker leadership of the struggle. *Grassroots* began articulating "a more explicit indictment of capitalism" and added a workers' supplement that "tried to provide a vision of a new society and articulated the meaning of working-class leadership."[107] Unemployment, rising prices, recession, housing shortages, and inadequate health facilities were routinely blamed on the capitalist system. Recessions and unemployment would stop only "if the workers decide what should be made and how much should be made."[108] The same message was trumpeted in glowing portrayals of socialism in other countries, with a clear preference for third-world models. Cuba was the example of a country in which there was no unemployment, since "workers make the laws."[109] The education systems in Cuba and Mozambique were claimed to serve "the needs of all the people, and especially the workers," while in South Africa "education only serves the need of the government and the bosses."[110]

With more and more people being drawn into various kinds of UDF activity, involvement in *Grassroots* declined, for the paper was no longer the only progressive game in town. Participation in the Saturday news-gathering sessions, which previously would attract sixty to seventy people, had dwindled to a handful. The initial idea of democratic newspaper production collapsed, as activist energy was now directed elsewhere.[111] Declining popular participation necessitated changes in the mode of operation. *Grassroots* was now being produced just by staff members without the involvement of organizations. Similar problems were experienced with the distribution. The average circulation dropped from twenty thousand in 1982 to seventeen thousand in 1983. "Why are we losing heart?" asked the secretarial report. "Many people say they do not use Grassroots as an organizational tool any longer, but does this mean that Grassroots has no message to pass on?"[112]

Grassroots now had to compete with the UDF, a host of other organizations that had sprung up, and the proliferating industry of service organizations such as local advice offices, legal aid bureaus, and other media organizations like the Screen Training Project, where T-shirts and pamphlets were produced. The activists at *Grassroots* were moving on to work in other organizations, while few organizations were making people available for training in media skills. To some extent, *Grassroots* had fallen victim to its own success: it had assisted UDF member organizations in setting up their own newsletters, pamphlets, posters, and media workshops. By mid-1984, newsletters were being produced by fifteen civics, thirty CAYCO branches, and nineteen branches of the United Women's Organisation.[113]

Many activists began to see *Grassroots* as a burden, coming on top of a host of other commitments. "It is our task to identify why so many of our activists are reacting so negatively to the paper, to produce a winner again, and create the enthusiasm and excitement for this paper that existed before."[114] Paradoxically, another factor that inhibited participation was the ready availability of foreign funding: "We became dependent, taking funds for granted."[115]

Generally speaking, foreign funding proved a mixed blessing. Funds from abroad sustained many useful activities, but they also created a new elite of struggle entrepreneurs who were well versed in handling sponsors. Tensions were heightened when factionalism became mixed with the competition for funds. Access to funding could also fuel racial tensions. In the UDF generally, the treasurers were usually whites or Indians, as there were very few Africans in the Front with bookkeeping skills. As repression mounted, finances had to be handled with increasing secrecy, which again enhanced suspicions. Within the UDF, African areas routinely complained that they were starved of funds.[116] Compared to many other organizations, *Grassroots* was fortunate in having a loyal funding source that kept the financial lifeline going. Foreign funding ensured the survival of *Grassroots,* but the drawback may have been decreasing popular participation.

Grassroots in 1985–1988: Building Utopia

Until mid-1985, the Western Cape had been relatively quiescent. Of over a thousand people detained nationwide in 1984, only seven were held in the Western Cape.[117] After celebrating its successful election boycott campaign, the UDF fell into a vacuum. For about a year, no central issue emerged around which the UDF could further its mobilization and organization efforts. The UDF never came to grips with the one obvious issue that could have been a focal point of resistance: squatter struggles. The period of 1985–88 witnessed the violent government destruction of the squatter communities of Crossroads and some other squatter camps, with the residents forced to relocate in the vast new settlement of Khayelitsha. The women's and youth affiliates of the UDF made some attempts at organizing in squatter areas but had limited success. The UDF leadership had other priorities and little understanding of the dynamics of squatter politics. It failed to come to terms with the opportunistic squatter leadership: Crossroads leader Johnson Ngxobongwana was colluding with the police in driving out his rivals while he was officially still functioning as chair of the Western Cape Civic Association, a UDF affiliate.

In its endeavors to get a wide range of allies on board and to build a following among the African population of the Western Cape, the UDF was not discerning in choosing its partners. When in May 1986 the battle between the government and the squatter camps was finally lost after a series of raids by

Ngxobongwana's *witdoeke* vigilantes (who identified themselves with a piece of white cloth tied around the head) on satellite squatter camps, the UDF missed another opportunity by failing to reach out to the Africans who were forcibly resettled in Khayelitsha. Whereas Crossroads had been celebrated as the symbol of resistance and victory, Khayelitsha stood for defeat. The vast new township, which was to become home to more than three hundred thousand Africans was not "recognized" by the UDF. UDF secretary Trevor Manuel later defended the neglect of Khayelitsha by comparing the victims of these massive forced removals with scabs who take the place of workers on strike: after supporting the strikers, one could not go on to organize the scabs, until perhaps much later.[118] But blaming the victims for a situation in which they had no choice amounted to adding insult to injury.

A renewed wave of protest in 1985 was sparked off not by local Western Cape issues but by national political developments. The turning point in youth militancy was the death of Matthew Goniwe and three other activists from Cradock, which bore the hallmarks of a liquidation. The funeral of the Cradock Four in July 1985 coincided with the declaration of a partial State of Emergency. From then on, youth took to the streets to fight the police.[119] The wave of protest mounted rapidly, originating at the University of the Western Cape and then spreading to colored high schools. The school boycotts started in July 1985, lasted for most of the year, and in many high schools included a boycott of exams. On 20 August, following the example of the Eastern Cape, a consumer boycott was launched in the Western Cape, coordinated by the Consumer Boycott Action Committee, which included non-UDF organizations such as the Unity Movement, its aligned civic umbrella, the Federation of Cape Civic Associations (FCCA), and the Cape Action League (CAL). Meanwhile, a rent boycott spread through the African townships.

For the Cape Peninsula, the phase of overt repression began in July and August 1985, reaching a symbolic peak on 28 August, when police clamped down heavily to prevent a march to Pollsmoor Prison, which was called by UDF patrons to demand the release of Nelson Mandela. On 26 October, the State of Emergency was extended to the Western Cape and the Boland. It was lifted in May 1986 and then reimposed on 12 June. The peak of popular insurrection in the Cape Town area fell between August 1985 and June 1986, when the imposition of a nationwide State of Emergency forced many activists into hiding.

Becoming a UDF Mouthpiece

In view of the origins of *Grassroots,* it was natural that the paper made itself willingly available as an organizing tool for the UDF. The *Grassroots* staff, although then operating in the context of a nationwide protest movement, initially kept formulating their own editorial policy: they decided on the priorities and on the most effective coverage. But beginning in 1985, the UDF leadership began to exercise direct control over the paper. In this phase, *Grassroots* became caught up in an insoluble dilemma: it became too radical for much of its adult colored readership, but radicalized youth thought the paper increasingly irrelevant.

"From 1985, we were at the beck and call of the UDF. Then, when the UDF almost disintegrated under repression, it left *Grassroots* without direction. What was our role now?"[120] Fahdiel Manuel, *Grassroots* organizer from 1988 to 1991, believed that the newspaper missed its chance by not redefining its role. It drifted along with the tide of militancy, but it no longer provided any direction. During the period of heightened politicization in 1985–86, *Grassroots* missed the boat. If a more popular formula had been used, it would have been possible to reach people who were now prepared to know about politics.

Moreover, it became increasingly clear that "the people" were far from a homogeneous bloc: militant youth surged ahead, with the unemployed manning the barricades and the student leadership trying to provide some political and ideological guidance. But they left behind people like a real-life Mrs. Williams from Manenburg: ordinary people in colored areas often became infuriated when they saw police beating up their children, but it did not follow that they were turning in great numbers toward the ANC. As repression became harsher and resistance increasingly violent, many simply became scared and preferred to stay out of politics.

The coverage of events in *Grassroots,* reflecting the priorities of the UDF's largest constituency, focused on student struggles in secondary and postsecondary institutions. Grassroots came out strongly in support of the school and exam boycotts. "You know why I am not going to write?" it quoted a boycotting student, "because my friends were killed by the police and I cannot go on writing exams with a guilty conscience. I personally would feel like a traitor." Boycotting exams was presented as the moral thing to do, without examining whether these boycotts indeed contributed to the weakening of the state. No allowance was made for dissenting opinions. "All the organisations of the people agree: we cannot write under these conditions. Exams are a small sacrifice when so many of our brothers and sisters have been arrested, shot, killed on our doorsteps."[121]

Another prominent topic was the consumer boycott, which began in August 1985 and continued until January 1986. The boycott provided ample opportunity to link stories on the Western Cape to developments in other parts of South Africa and to evoke a sense of historical continuity through references to the boycott campaigns of the 1950s and 1979–80. The boycott was presented as a tactic empowering ordinary people. *Grassroots* admitted that the boycott weakened considerably after the declaration of the State of Emergency on 26 October 1985, but "a significant number of people remained loyal to the boycott call and stuck to buying black." In the Western Cape, the consumer boycott was not nearly as effective as in the more militant Eastern Cape.

Considerable attention was given to the radicalization of the Cape Muslims. Beginning with the death of Imam Abdullah Haroon in detention in 1969, the Muslim population of the Cape had become increasingly politicized. In September 1985, the funeral of Ebrahim Carelse, who was killed as a result of police action, drew an unprecedented crowd of mourners to Salt River, one of the Cape Town suburbs. Police shot at the crowd, seriously wounding one of the mourners and incensing thousands of Muslims. A small group came forward, disarmed one policeman, and beat him to death. Emotions again ran high in November 1985, when police entered the Park Road Mosque with their boots on. This incident marked a turning point in Muslim radicalism. The police desecration of the mosque drove some Muslims to join the ANC.

In this phase of popular insurrection, the generation gap widened. A youth leader recalled later how parents—especially mothers—would be quite supportive when their own children were harassed, beaten up, or detained. But while the youth in general were gripped by revolutionary fever, parents lived in fear.

> The youth agenda in 1985 was: insurrection. And the youth took over; they did not care about other considerations. We left the older people behind; we went on to make revolution. Many civics collapsed when the leadership was detained. Youth leadership went into hiding or was also detained. Organizations were not very strong, but then the revolution does not wait for organizations to materialize. It swept everything aside. Revolution has a dynamic of its own. You don't sit back and evaluate. We were making a revolution; the others would follow. We hardly slept, sometimes an hour in a school building.[122]

By this time, militant youth thought *Grassroots* largely irrelevant. They no longer dressed respectably to take the paper into people's houses and engage residents in discussions on rents or schools. They were more eager to learn how to make the most effective use of firebombs and how to neutralize the effects of tear gas. *Grassroots* had become too militant for its adult readership; in colored areas such as the working-class town of Mitchell's Plain, *Grassroots* came to be perceived as "an 'African' paper, because it was so militant and focusing on politics."[123] One youth activist commented on this change:

> In 1985–86, the UDF leadership began determining the content of the paper. We became a UDF mouthpiece, making UDF pamphlets. [UDF Western Cape secretary] Cheryl Carolus walked into our offices and told us what stories to write, when to be on the streets, and so on. From then on we followed the line of the

UDF, but we got more and more removed from the community. We assumed that everybody shared the anger of us activists. We had these angry funerals, toyi-toying through the streets. It actually scared away a lot of the community. We called people *comrade,* but if you would say that to an ordinary worker, he'd probably slap you and say that he is not a communist. . . . The colored community is conservative. They could relate to civics, but not to barricades and stone-throwing.[124]

This verdict is shared by Ryland Fisher, who during these years was the news organizer for *Grassroots.* During the peak of militancy, the staff lost sight of the community they were supposedly serving and confused activist consciousness with popular consciousness. "That heavy high-profile political stuff put many people off. It became more an activist paper than a community paper. . . . You have to keep in mind the character of the Western Cape; you have to start from people's consciousness. Activists assumed that ordinary people supported the ANC, violence, nonracialism, and all that."[125]

The ANC assumed increasing prominence in the pages of *Grassroots.* The first major front-page treatment came in March 1986, when *Grassroots* opened with the story of the funeral in Guguletu of seven young men who had been killed in a shoot-out with police. The funeral with ANC and SACP banners reportedly drew thirty to forth thousand people and was presented as a "massive show of support" for the ANC.[126] From then on, *Grassroots* continued openly to popularize the ANC and its leaders.

The Utopian Phase: People's Power

"Power to the People" ran the bold caption over the center spread in the February 1986 issue of *Grassroots,* and it was no longer talking about electricity. Civics were now portrayed as organs of people's power, not as community organizations lobbying for lower rents and a more convenient date to pay electricity fees. Beyond the street battles emerged a vision of a new society. As an example of what the promised land would look like, *Grassroots* described the co-op formed by dismissed Sarmcol workers in Natal: "The co-op is run democratically. The workers share all the profits according to what they need. And all the workers together decide how the co-op will be run." The workers explained how they worked without bosses or supervisors. This example, *Grassroots* concluded, "is showing us how our factories can be in the future—when the workers control the factories and share equally in the profits. Co-ops like this are a real way of building workers' power—and of building a new South Africa."[127]

By this time, it must have become obvious to the readers that this promised land could materialize only in a socialist order. This vision, of course, was by no means limited to *Grassroots*. Speaking at the *Grassroots* 1986 Annual General Meeting, COSATU (Congress of South African Trade Unions) secretary general Jay Naidoo spoke about building workers' power in the factories and in the communities. "The time for shouting socialist slogans is over. It is time to implement a socialist programme."[128] The struggle had advanced from protest to challenge. In the activists' strategic perspective, the next phase would be the revolutionary takeover of power. People's power had to manifest itself in all aspects of life, including the media. "Building the People's press is also building People's Power," was the message of *Grassroots* organizer Saleem Badat at the same meeting: "Rejecting the structures of the Apartheid State is no longer enough. It is now also necessary to replace the Apartheid Structures . . . with democratic bodies which are well organised and have strong support from the people. . . . The task of the People's Press is to challenge the power of the ruling class media, to minimise its influence and eventually take over state media and commercial newspapers, and use their institutions to serve the interests of the people."[129]

In the search for people's culture, break dancing and graffiti were portrayed as "a form of culture originated by the people themselves, understood by them and appreciated by them."[130] This equation of activist youth culture with "people's culture" sounds oddly out of tune, both with a colored working-class constituency and with one of the shining examples of "people's power" that *Grassroots* held up for its readers: the Soviet Union, at the time more known for its gerontocratic leadership than for innovative cultural manifestations. Here "people's sports" was hailed: "Sports in the socialist countries is not a privilege of the rich elite, but is available to everybody. . . . Many more sports facilities are built to serve the working people. Sports is used to promote trust and friendship among nations. Sporting personalities are expected to be an inspiration to the people and to play an important role in foreign policy. The Soviet sports system is radically different from that in the West and it would be a loss if people failed to learn its lessons."[131]

Cuba, Nicaragua, Mozambique, and Libya provided other beacons of hope. "The country is governed in a very unusual way with street committees, area committees, etc. up to national people's committees. People can change the delegate to any committee at any stage and the delegates get paid in the way MP's get paid because it is not a permanent job," reported Maulana Faried Essack of the Call of Islam after a visit to Libya. He had observed that all people there had houses and were united.[132] The maulana saw only one problem with Libya: its support for the PAC (Pan Africanist Congress). But the workers' paradise could also be found closer to home: in Mozambique. Under the caption "When work is no longer a burden," a Mozambican explained worker management: "Now all the workers together plan the production for the factory. . . . Now, I am proud to be a worker. My work is no longer my burden—it is my joy."[133]

A common feature of these countries held up as models of people's power is that they were ruled by authoritarian leaders who used popular mobilization to stage demonstrations of mass support. The issue of how to reconcile the imposed consensus with democratic ideals, such as freedom of opinion, is not specifically addressed in *Grassroots.* But the paper's ideas of democracy were clearly in line with other UDF publications that were dismissive of libertarian notions of democracy. Participation, not pluralism, is seen as the paramount principle of democracy. Yet, when embarking on campaigns to muster international solidarity for the embattled alternative media in South Africa, media activists invoked precisely the libertarian notions of press freedom, "the right to differ." Was it simply a matter of tailoring the message to suit a gullible overseas audience? Or, rather, did it reflect the ambiguous nature of the UDF itself, which managed to maintain a broad front by virtue of accommodating divergent tendencies without having to make choices?

Following the ideological prescriptions, people's power ought to imply workers' power. In real life, student activists and radical academics were the most zealous advocates of people's power. Because the *Grassroots* staff was recruited from this same category, they enthusiastically joined the search for Utopia. But even among students, enthusiasm for building people's power seemed limited to activists. Elections for the student representative council (SRC) at the University of the Western Cape in early 1986--when revolutionary beliefs in the immediate coming of people's power were at a peak—showed a surprisingly low turn out. Only 28 percent of the students cast their votes for this hard-won "organ of people's power," compared to 44 percent in 1984. In analyzing the disappointing poll, *Grassroots* quoted a student leader who identified two reasons: while "student awareness" was high in 1984, students in 1986 felt somewhat demoralized, still feeling the scars of 1985 when their university had been the focus of police repression. Secondly, the SRC had neglected many UWC issues while focusing more on national political issues.[134] Even at the level of university students, support apparently depended on the capacity to deliver the goods. While the vanguard was preparing to storm the Winter Palace, the troops were lagging behind, in contrast with Lenin's observation that the masses were surging forward while leadership was found wanting.

Even more than *Grassroots* itself, the magazine *New Era* became the herald of a socialist future. *New Era*'s role as part of Grassroots Publications was to provide a more theoretical journal, which focused on socialist experiences elsewhere in the world. *New Era* was launched in March 1986 to announce the "Dawn of the New Era," as the first editorial explained. Resistance in South

Africa, it stated, had entered "an exciting period in which we find new values being developed, a new person being created and collective democratic structures being built. We are clearly well on the road to a new society."[135] *New Era* surpassed *Grassroots* in its uncritical acclaims for the Soviet Union and other socialist countries. When commemorating the Bolshevik revolution, it claimed that the Soviet Union "today . . . is the leading force in a growing world community of socialist nations. . . . Socialism has reached a new phase of development, and is preparing itself for the 21st century. 70 years after it first emerged it has become an unshakeable system."[136] A rude awakening was in store: the countries of Eastern Europe, initially depicted as fulfilling the promises of the Freedom Charter, soon would be exposed as stagnant backwaters, ridden with ethnic chauvinism. But only after February 1990 did *New Era* make a first attempt at reassessment. The March 1990 issue admonished its readers that "we cannot comfort ourselves with assertions about the inherent superiority of socialism. If socialism is to revive itself in Eastern Europe, it will have to redefine itself and build genuine democracy and economic efficiency."[137] But the editors were apparently still too overcome with shock to offer any explanations for their turnabout.

Utopia did not lie exclusively beyond South Africa's borders: it was also to be found in images of people's power in the townships. The May 1986 issue of *Grassroots* reported on popular justice as an element of people's power. People's courts, claimed UDF education officer Raymond Suttner, do not punish offenders but reeducate them. Punishment would be unfair since "crime is because of apartheid," as Suttner quoted a community leader. "We cannot punish someone for stealing because apartheid has made him poor and hungry, and unconcerned about his fellow human beings." People's courts, Suttner explained, were different from the government's courts. "They are created by people's organisations, and are completely responsible to the people of the community. They cannot do anything that the people would not approve of."[138] Suttner did make a distinction between people's justice and kangaroo courts run by youth who used intimidatory methods to win support for the struggle. People's justice convinces people to support the struggle "because they can see it is right." But there were no reports in *Grassroots* about the more seedy side of popular justice. Many experiences with popular justice in the African townships and squatter camps bore little resemblance to Suttner's idyllic picture.[139] People's courts were limited to the African townships; there are no reports of popular justice in colored areas.

And yet, even at the height of intoxication about the new society about to be born, a curious ambivalence remained. What was the struggle all about: Was it a revolutionary seizure of power? Or was it, after all, simply a reformist movement, demanding a rightful place in society for everyone? On the same page of *Grassroots* where Suttner unfolded his vision of a new society based on persuasion rather than coercion, another article criticized the new government plans for the installation of regional services councils, which would have some form of African representation. This scheme, the article stated, fell short of "the people's demand for a share in government through one person one vote."[140] Here the demand was simply for a proper place in the system rather than a total overturning of the system. Similarly, while denying the legitimacy of the government, UDF activists frequently turned to the courts to challenge a particular government decree. Commenting on the court ruling that challenged certain measures under the State of Emergency, UDF Western Cape secretary Trevor Manuel said: "We are beginning to win some victories. The courts have shown that we have a right to exist."[141] People's power deriving its legitimacy from rulings by the courts of the apartheid state was one of the curious examples of the UDF's profoundly ambivalent nature.

Repression and Survival: The State of Emergency

"Frustration is probably the word that most typifies the experience of living in South Africa today," stated the secretarial report to the *Grassroots* AGM in 1986.[142] Behind the public exhilaration about the ascendancy toward people's power sounded a note of despondency about declining participation and the increasing difficulties of keeping the paper going. The staff believed that there was still much demand for the paper, but organizational involvement in producing and distributing the paper was declining. Member organizations were reminded that building the "people's press" was not just the responsibility of the already overburdened staff.

In the first half of 1985, the *Grassroots* offices were raided twice by the security police. In the second half of 1985, staff members were repeatedly detained for some weeks. In October, the building housing the newspaper office burned down. Nevertheless, during 1985 the usual eleven issues were produced, with the print order doubling from twenty thousand copies in early 1985 to a record forty thousand in December 1985. The annual report noted a tremendous increase in the popularity of the paper, which it attributed in part to the fact that the last issues were distributed free. Under the State of Emergency, *Grassroots* continued to be distributed free, for selling the paper became increasingly difficult. Financial self-sufficiency had become an even more remote ideal. As repression mounted, the sponsors stopped urging for self-sufficiency.

When the nationwide State of Emergency was declared on 12 June 1986, it became impossible to continue an aboveground operation. The *Grassroots* office was closed temporarily when staff members went into hiding. Coordination became difficult, with meetings being held in cars and involving an

occasional nightly encounter with some UDF leaders still at large. Publication was interrupted for six weeks. But once the staff had adjusted to the new
conditions, *Grassroots* was back on the streets again in August 1986. Apart
from the increasingly draconian press regulations, the survival of *Grassroots*
was at stake because of the government's threatened clampdown on foreign
funding in 1987.

Police searches, detentions, and harassment became a permanent feature of
working for *Grassroots* until 1990. With activists scattered all over, it was difficult to develop a coherent policy. The staff assumed that state brutality, rather
than bread-and-butter issues, was now people's immediate concern. But in
reporting on repression, a publication that appeared at five-week (or more)
intervals had obvious handicaps. For the daily accounts of street battles, police
brutality, detentions, and trials, the daily papers were more adequate vehicles.
On this score, *Grassroots* could not compete with the "commercial press." The
Cape Times had gained the reputation among daily newspapers of providing
the most thorough coverage of events under the State of Emergency. Gradually, the ANC and its leaders were also making their way into the mainstream
press. With his interview with ANC president Oliver Tambo, recorded during
a holiday visit to Britain, *Cape Times* editor Tony Heard cleared the way for
the rehabilitation of the ANC leadership in the mainstream media.[143]

Grassroots in 1988–1990: A Prisoner of the Activists

"We need to question what is wrong with our ability to organise on a mass
level and challenge our whole style of work. We need to channel our activists
into organisations where the masses have always been based so that they can
organise more effectively."[144] This assessment, drawn up at the end of 1988, is
indicative of the sense of loss of direction felt by the *Grassroots* staff. Organizations such as civics had all but collapsed. With the arrival of the new weekly
paper *South* on the Western Cape scene in 1987, *Grassroots* was forced to redefine its role. The result was a two-pronged policy: continuing to popularize
the ANC and reverting to the paper's original calling, covering local community issues. In view of the near collapse of community organizations,
rebuilding organizations was an obvious priority. But unlike in the early years,
Grassroots no longer managed to muster community involvement. "From
1988–1990, *Grassroots*'s staff was lost, without direction," recalled Fahdiel
Manuel, who at the time worked as the *Grassroots* organizer. "We became quite
despondent of working with organizations. We were mainly guided by the
staff assessments."[145]

In August 1987, the government introduced new emergency regulations
that allowed for a three-month closure of publications carrying "subversive

propaganda." Previously the alternative media had been hit by detentions, bannings, long-drawn-out legal proceedings, and various other forms of harassment; now their very survival was at stake. In March 1988, *New Nation* was closed down for three months, to be followed by *South* in May 1988 and by *Grassroots* and *New Era* in 1989. The common threat helped produce a united response: representatives from a broad range of media and media organizations in the Western Cape came together in May 1988 to launch the Save the Press Campaign, with the ubiquitous Johnny Issel in the strategic position of treasurer. Anticipating a banning, the *Grassroots* staff began setting up a new publication to serve as a backup. A first trial issue of a four-page newsletter, the *Shield,* was produced in June 1988.

In February 1988, the government imposed restrictions on eighteen organizations, including the UDF, and further tightened the curbs on the media. With open political activities by extra-parliamentary groupings virtually outlawed, community papers had obvious difficulties with their role of promoting organization. Moreover, there was an uncomfortable gap between the aspirations of media activists and the interests of the average reader. A readership survey conducted by the new alternative weekly paper *South* in 1988 suggested that "politics" was low on the list of reader preferences, especially in certain relocated colored areas. In the African townships, the survey established 80 percent support for the UDF with a concomitant interest in politics, while in Mitchell's Plain the UDF registered only 20 percent support.

When *Grassroots* began reexamining its role in the changing circumstances of the 1990s, it came up with similar results. A feasibility survey conducted in 1991 to explore the potential market for *Grassroots* in a new formula as a free sheet, run on advertising revenue, found that people were interested in reading a local paper, but it should feature a picture of the spring queen rather than Nelson Mandela on the front page. The spring queen was a beauty queen, elected annually as part of a spring festival of the textile workers—a prime example of what media activists would have labeled a despicable specimen of petty bourgeois gutter stories. In the Witwatersrand region, a Mandela picture on the front page ensured that the paper would be sold out in a couple of hours. Not so in the Western Cape: to celebrate Mandela's release in early 1990, the COSATU textile union SACTWU (South African Clothing and Textile Workers' Union) produced a special issue of its newsletter, running a five-page picture story on the ANC leader. It was distributed free by the union, but union activists met with little interest: forty-five thousand of the sixty thousand copies were returned to the union office.[146]

The *Grassroots* staff members were not unaware that the paper's highly political profile alienated the more conservative readership in the colored areas. Circulation remained at around thirty thousand copies, of which eight thousand copies, with pages inserted in Xhosa, went to the African townships. But because copies were distributed free, it was unclear whether they actually reached residents or kept piling up under people's beds. "We cover a-political issues in a political way," noted the 1989 assessment. "We have a township readership which is more politicised and a different culture. How do we cope with this in that we also have a coloured readership. We must consult with organisations on these changes." However, in practice, "consulting organisations" meant consulting with a limited circle of activists.[147]

The AGM in August 1990 decided to suspend the publication of *Grassroots* and to conduct a feasibility study for the paper to become a commercially run free sheet. But although staff members now believed in a professional and commercial operation, other activists were less flexible in adjusting to the new mood of the time. The once innovative way of producing a community paper now worked as a brake: clinging to the collectivist models of the past blocked new initiatives. The people's paper had become a prisoner of the activists. *Grassroots* had outlived itself, as Fahdiel Manuel frankly acknowledged in an assessment of the last years of *Grassroots:* "Basically, we were producing papers because the funders wanted to see a paper being produced."[148]

This clash between the nostalgia for the heady days of the struggle and the sober mood of the early 1990s was at the center of the *Grassroots* eleventh Annual General Meeting in October 1991, where two options were on the agenda: cease publication altogether or go commercial.[149] "Why should we change now, just because the people in Russia are changing?" asked CAHAC chair Wilfred Rhodes. "We have to be wary of the capitalists." *Privatization* and *commercialization* might have been the new buzz words in Eastern Europe and Russia, but why should these winds of change induce South Africans to sell out the heritage of the 1980s to market forces? But this AGM itself reflected the sobering reality of changing times. Gone were the days when the *Grassroots* AGM was a major social event in progressive circles. Only some thirty-five people turned up for this meeting in a bare community hall in Manenberg, a colored working-class area on the Cape Flats. After waiting one and a half hours in the vain hope that a sufficient number of people would arrive to achieve a quorum, it was decided to carry on anyway. In spite of invitations sent to the townships, no Africans attended.

Efforts to transform the "struggle paper" into a commercial free sheet never took off. In 1992 it was decided to cease publication of *Grassroots* altogether. Fading away through a series of ill-attended meetings was a rather inglorious end for an experiment that in its heyday had captured the imagination of many supporters. Nevertheless, with more than ten years of effective life, *Grassroots* had outlived all similar ventures elsewhere in South Africa. Having followed *Grassroots* through its turbulent history, we can now attempt to draw up the balance sheet.

Ten Years as an Organizing Tool: A Balance Sheet

February 1990 should have signaled the beginning of a new growth period, now that new space had been won for the alternative media, but it was the start of a period of decline. Many alternative papers failed to develop a constructively critical approach to the ANC and could not adapt to the changing conditions of the 1990s. Most did not manage to make a qualitative leap from struggle paper to the wider world where politics was not the be-all and end-all. Those papers that did, such as the *Weekly Mail,* did not suffer from a decline in reader interest. The extreme dependency on foreign funding proved a mixed blessing. Donor charity for alternative media was drying up, as donors were reorienting their efforts toward development or education. With money and causes running out, demoralization crept into the alternative newsrooms. The question of the raison d'être of *Grassroots* can now be examined with the benefit of hindsight.

Building Organizations

The relationship between community media and community organizations was not as clear-cut as the Leninist recipe had promised. In the first stage of organization building, *Grassroots* proved a useful tool, providing organizers with a "foot in the door" to engage residents in a discussion. But once organizations got on their feet, *Grassroots* was increasingly felt as a burden. As the staff noted at the many assessment and evaluation meetings, the newspaper was as strong as the organizations were. When the organizations collapsed in the second half of the decade, *Grassroots* operated in a vacuum.

Both *Grassroots* and the community organizations relied on a fairly limited circle of activists, which suffered from "activist burnout" and from a lack of talented new recruits. Moreover, many activists were students or recent graduates, most of whom would sooner or later want to settle into paid jobs and have some kind of a family life. Although student activists provided a useful input in terms of skills, enthusiasm, and their access to the resources of universities and technikons (postsecondary institutions that provide professional training), the heavy reliance on students had obvious drawbacks.

Short-term excitement did not usually result in sustained involvement. The "new South Africa" was not going to be built on people's power, as activists believed in the mid-1980s. Civics were revealed as weak structures that were not equipped to evolve into organs of local government. With hindsight, several key *Grassroots* activists shared the verdict of trade unionist David Lewis that community organizations were basically organizations of activists. As one *Grassroots* activists admitted: "Civics speaking 'on behalf of the people' were run by ten to twelve people." Issues that captured the imagination of the activists were not necessarily the most pressing priorities in the communities. Joe Marks was openly scornful of the activists' obsession with politics: "The working class might die out because of AIDS, while the activists are discussing workers' power."[150]

The participatory ideal behind the slogans of people's power was that people would take control over their own lives: "they were going to run the schools, the factories, the towns, everything."[151] But permanent participation proved an elusive ideal. *Grassroots* tried to be responsive to the changing needs of the time. After the initial emphasis on organization building, the paper played more of a campaigning role, trying to tie local issues to the national liberation struggle. But somewhere during the peak of popular mobilization in the Western Cape, between August 1985 and June 1986, the paper became increasingly irrelevant. Getting the paper onto the streets became an end in itself, an act of defiance.

For many, student activists as well as a fair number of people with a working-class background, *Grassroots* and the community organizations had nevertheless provided an important learning experience. People (although not "The People") learned to stand up for themselves, to speak up, to conduct a meeting, to take things into their own hands. Empowering something as amorphous as "a community" almost invariably means that the most ambitious and enterprising members of the community take advantage of the new possibilities and in the process strengthen their own power base.

Because it failed to adopt a more popular appeal, *Grassroots* did not manage to attract new recruits. There is a remarkable continuity in the core of people who, in one way or another, were involved in the *Grassroots* project over the decade. In this respect as well, the newspaper reflects the experience of the UDF Western Cape as a whole. When interviewed in 1991, Saleem Badat, the *Grassroots* organizer from 1983 to 1986 as well as one of its ideologues, drew up a realistic balance sheet that seems valid for both *Grassroots* and the UDF Western Cape:

> The UDF had a very wide appeal. It reached into all kinds of corners where the ANC had not had a basis. For example, the Western Cape, rural areas, a place like Cradock. Its strong point was mobilization, but it was weak in terms of organization. The UDF never built strong organizations. It was carried by activists: that explains the high rate of activist burnout in South Africa. . . . A big problem is that the political leadership in the Western Cape had not been reproduced. If you look at the people who are active now, they are mostly the same people who were leading ten years ago. There was no middle layer which could take over. It was a group of people in their mid-twenties, who are now in their mid-thirties, who are basically still the political core here.[152]

The unbanning of the ANC had a demobilizing effect, pointedly underlining the limitations of the participatory ethos. When the ANC leadership returned home, ordinary folks thought that the struggle was over and that they could now sit back while the leaders sorted out the problems. "Being involved in the struggle is not a natural thing for human beings," as *Grassroots* godfather Johnny Issel had to conclude.[153] Willie Simmers had a similar experience in Mitchell's Plain: "In colored areas, people wait for the 'new South Africa' to come along. They don't realize that they have to build it."[154]

Bridging the African-Colored Divide

How did *Grassroots,* and the UDF Western Cape as whole, fare in the attempt at bridging the divide between Africans and coloreds by forging a common identity, either as "the oppressed" or as "workers"?

A common perception among activists was that bridging the African-colored divide amounted to bringing coloreds into the ANC fold. On this score, the 1994 election results present a clear failure. A large majority of colored voters in the Western Cape voted for the National Party. But divisions continued not only outside the Charterist fold but also within the ANC Western Cape.

Working for *Grassroots* brought colored activists into the African townships for the first time. Folding the newspaper provided a meeting point for African and colored youth. The Cape Youth Congress and, after the fusion, the United Women's Congress effectively managed to set up racially integrated organizations. But overall, the UDF Western Cape had been dominated by coloreds. When the ANC was set up in the Western Cape, Africans seized it as "their" organization. The first ANC executive elected at the regional Western Cape Conference in 1990 was strongly dominated by Africans. The role of whites in the ANC proved less contentious than the old African-colored divide. At the next regional conference, in September 1991, ANC chair Nelson Mandela made a personal intervention to redress the balance. He berated local ANC members for having voted an executive into office that was heavily dominated by Africans and thus not representative of the demographic composition of the Western Cape. Mandela's intervention was difficult to tolerate for many seasoned local activists, both colored and African, for whom this line of argument smacked of the old arguments of apartheid ideologues. Whether or not Mandela's campaigning for colored candidates was the decisive factor, the newly elected executive counted a fair number of prominent coloreds, including the new chair, Allan Boesak.

The UDF, with *Grassroots* as one of its tools, did indeed manage to establish an ANC presence among colored people in the Western Cape, but the extent of that presence was limited. Moreover, class lines to a large extent continued to coincide with race. No amount of populist rhetoric could obscure the fact that many colored working-class families in Mitchell's Plain were hiring domestics from Khayalitsha. On the other hand, when African nationalist tendencies in the ANC began to overshadow the discourse of nonracialism, coloreds felt left in the cold, fearing that they would be left behind when the ANC would deliver jobs, housing, and education to "their people." In the 1994 election campaign, the National Party indeed claimed the coloreds as "our people." The NP was also aided by the deep sense of religion among many colored people, who were antagonistic to the ANC because of its links with the SACP.

Some ANC leaders came to regret the dismantling of UDF structures in the Western Cape. The demise of the UDF marked the revival of "colouredism," the rejection of nonracial ideology in favor of colored identity. In the Western Cape, the ANC suffered a defeat worse than anticipated: in the provincial elections of 1994, the National Party won 53 percent of the vote compared to a mere 33 percent for the ANC. Over 90 percent of the Africans, but only 27 percent of coloreds, voted for the ANC.

At the time of my interviews in 1991, the consensus view on both sides of the African-colored divide seemed to be that progress had been made in the UDF years, but that there was still a long way to go. Africans still perceived the position of coloreds as ambivalent, sitting on the fence and hedging their bets. "Some are petty bourgeois; they aspire to be like white people. Coloreds now are more progressive that they used to be, thanks to the UDF and COSATU. Now when there is a stay-away, coloreds also stay way. . . . I think the ANC is now accepted among coloreds, but you never know because they don't sign up as members."[155]

Joe Marks agreed with this assessment: "In every colored man, woman, and child, there is the white person trying to break out. That is the legacy of slavery. People have been freed of the chains on their wrists, but not yet of the chain in their head." Marks acknowledged that considerable progress had been made during the 1980s: "If we started out at zero in 1980, then we have now perhaps moved 40 percent. . . . The UDF was to unite our people across the color line . . . and the UDF has done a good job. Colored people now almost accept blacks as human beings—as long as they stay in Gugulethu. They don't want black people as their neighbors." He believed that there was still a long way to go for nonracialism to be transformed into a living reality rather than a theoretical concept. Meanwhile, "there is only one way for the ANC to draw a sizable colored vote, and that is by making clear that it is not a black organization."[156]

Grassroots, along with other media, certainly contributed to popularizing the ANC in the colored areas. Although the ANC had been unmentionable at the beginning of the 1980s, ANC symbols and slogans had become common-place toward the end of the decade. But *Grassroots* was not effective as an organizing tool across the racial divide, and probably it could not have been. A large part of the African population, notably those in the squatter camps, was illiterate and thus beyond the reach of newspapers. Africans in the town-ships were generally poorly educated: educational standards lagged behind those in the colored schools. Although the township edition of *Grassroots* with Xhosa translations was an attempt to solve the language problem, it does not appear to have been widely read. Nor could it contribute much to building bridges with colored areas. To be effective as an organizing tool, a paper needs to address a more or less homogeneous constituency. Forging a "community of the oppressed" proved an unrealistic ambition for a community paper. The success of the UDF media policy as a whole rested precisely on the opposite principle: targeting audiences meant addressing the intended audience on its own terms, rather than subsuming them into an undifferentiated public.

Grassroots was far too militant and ideologically outspoken to appeal to an essentially conservative, church-going colored public. Like the youth move-ment in the Northern Transvaal, the newspaper was not only fighting the apartheid state or the capitalists. It was as much a platform for young colored intellectuals who contested the authority of the conservative forces within the colored community, such as the churches and the educational establishment. Although it advocated community empowerment and worker leadership, the paper, in fact, represented the newfound identity of students and graduates who asserted their place among the forces of change. *Grassroots* played a key role in forging a community of young educated activists, which subsequently became the backbone of the UDF Western Cape. Its gender composition was more balanced than either the youth movement in the Northern Transvaal or the civic in Kagiso. In this environment of students and graduates, women encountered far fewer obstacles to participation. In *Grassroots,* men outnum-bered women, but women did have access to all influential positions.

Especially in its early years, the attempts by the *Grassroots* staff to give "a voice to the voiceless" proved important. After the bannings of the Black Con-sciousness papers, *Grassroots* was the first dissident voice to make itself heard. Later arrivals at the alternative scene were better, more professional papers, but *Grassroots* played a pioneering role. However, by choosing to remain an orthodox struggle paper on the fringe, it preserved its ideological purity but missed the opportunity to develop a more popular appeal. The ideologues kept a firm grip on the paper, thus preventing activists with a more practical mind and more journalistic skills to implement the stated objective of *Grass-roots,* which was "to start from where the people are." Whether it is false con-

sciousness or human nature, after a long working day many ordinary folks preferred to be distracted by the capitalist seductions of the TV series *Dallas* rather
than be educated on the workers' paradise in Mozambique.

Rehana Rossouw, a *Grassroots* activist who moved on to work for the weekly
newspaper *South,* concluded that the pioneering role of *Grassroots* as an alternative paper made an important contribution to press freedom, although not
to the concept of independent media. "The legacy of *Grassroots* as a mouthpiece is that now many organizations think they can tell us [i.e., *South*] what
to write."[157] While some *Grassroots* activists wallowed in past glories, Rossouw
was one of those who—without disowning the past—had made a clear choice
in favor of independent journalism. In the post-February 1990 period, former
"struggle journalists" found themselves caught in a "tricky balancing act
between being loyal and disciplined members and truthful journalists." Rossouw
made up her mind: South Africa needed truthful journalists.[158]

Other former *Grassroots* workers, however, continued to regard the concept
of independent media as a fraud. Those who claimed to be independent must
have ulterior motives, believed *Grassroots* former township organizer Hilda
Ndude. When discussing *South*'s editorial policy of presenting various sides of
the story, she became quite agitated: "Many of our progressive people don't
want to read it. What line are they toeing? . . . We want to know which interests *South* is serving. They write questionable stories and make ANC members
very angry. . . . If *South* claims it wants to be independent from the ANC, it
must be serving other interests.[159] She made it clear that those "other interests" could be none other than the interests of the National Party, as there
could be no neutral ground between the two main protagonists, the government and the ANC. Organizations such as the ANC or COSATU had become
steeped in the practice of prescribing the correct line. Adjustment to the more
open political climate of the 1990s proved difficult: they displayed an extreme
oversensitivity to any kind of criticism.

Part of the legacy of *Grassroots,* such as the utopian concepts of people's
power and the blind adoration of socialist models elsewhere, belongs to the
past, to the phase of popular mobilization. In style and contents, *Grassroots* was
so much the product of a particular youth culture that it could hardly have
made a lasting imprint on the world view of a broad section of people in the
Western Cape. But in a more pragmatic form, ideals of popular participation
have outlasted the utopian images of people's power.

Conclusion

From Micro Level to Macro Level

THE THREE PRECEEDING CASE STUDIES have provided some insight into the vast and at times bewildering diversity of local movements campaigning under the UDF banner. Among social movements, the UDF must surely be unique in the heterogeneity of affiliates under its umbrella: from the Johannesburg Scooter Drivers' Association to the Northern Natal Darts Club, from the Grail to the Pietermaritzburg Child Welfare Society and the National Medical and Dental Association. The three affiliates highlighted in this book represent the mainstream of UDF organizations: a youth movement, a civic, a community paper. Yet even within this mainstream, the three stories reveal a striking diversity. We are now left with the task of linking these micro narratives again to the macro story. What is the common strand between the witch burnings in Sekhukhuneland, the rent and bus boycotts in Kagiso, and the utopian project of people's power as constructed by the *Grassroots* activists? And how do they fit into the overall story of the anti-apartheid struggle inside South Africa? What is the relevance of the theoretical perspectives that have been discussed in the first part of this book, as seen from the vantage point of local studies? Which themes are missing in an historiography that is largely based on the macro story? One neglected element is the importance of religion and other belief systems as sources of legitimacy and motivation. Another aspect that has received scant attention is the relationship between local struggles and the wider anti-apartheid struggle: local agendas do not necessarily coincide with national objectives.

Secular and Spiritual Sources of Legitimacy

While religion has emerged as a central theme in the historiography of the Zimbabwean wars of liberation, it is largely ignored in the academic literature on the liberation struggle in South Africa.[1] This subject remains confined to the domain of theologians and is hardly explored by social scientists and historians. Is this because of a conceptual gap between the macro and the micro levels? How do localized narratives fit into the overall story?[2]

The master narrative features mainstream anti-apartheid resistance as a modernizing force. But some of the micro narratives do not fit neatly in this overall story of the liberation struggle. The challenge inherent in this two-track approach is to understand local struggles in their own terms, without losing sight of the dialectical interaction between macro and micro levels. The burning of witches may at first sight seem very "traditional," but it was transformed into a thoroughly modern phenomenon by the use of urban innovations such as car tires and by the generational reversal of roles. Sekhukhune youth justified their actions in struggle idiom, presenting the purge as their answer to the ANC call to make South Africa ungovernable. The absence of the spiritual dimension in the historiography of South African resistance may in part be due to a failure to understand local struggles in their own terms. There is a relative abundance of local case studies of South African resistance history. But these have mostly been undertaken as a function of the overall struggle, often seeking to draw "lessons of struggle" that can be applied at other times and places rather than as studies in their own right.

But this oversight may also be due to a conceptual gap between academic discourse and the mental map of the actors. In the academic universe, both of a liberal and of a Marxist variety, the analytical framework was thoroughly secular. But seen in the context of world history, this secular perspective is a minority view characteristic for elites in twentieth-century Western societies. In African societies, there is traditionally no dualistic world view that distinguishes between "secular" and "sacred" spheres. The forces of evil were not confined to one of these spheres. They manifested themselves in the shape of apartheid, capitalism, sin, witches, and general disharmony. All aspects of life are spheres of divine activity, explains the South African theologian Gabriel Setiloane. Salvation is when peace, order, and happiness are maintained in the community. He argues that the recorder of the history of African resistance in South Africa, being Western, has missed an important point, namely "that the African struggle all the way from Nxele (Makana) through Nongqawuse, the formation of the ANC, which follows very closely on the rise of Ethiopianism in the churches, Bullhoek, etc., is essentially a religious inspired struggle."[3]

The argument that this dimension has been lost in the historiography because of the Western antecedents of the recorders of history is not wholly convincing. The historians of the Zimbabwe liberation struggle were by and large white and Western. The religious dimension is not absent at the level of the macro narrative. The nationalist and socialist discourse used by both the ANC and the UDF at the macro level was often strongly flavored by moral or spiritual arguments. At a conference in 1983 it was proposed that the UDF declaration must be adapted into a prayer in order for it to have an appeal to the church.[4] The UDF has clearly benefited from its close relationship with churches and religious leaders. Churches and clerics rendered moral legitimacy to anti-apartheid resistance and provided the UDF with publicity, resources, protection, and advice. In the competition for legitimacy, this was an important asset for the UDF vis-à-vis the South African government. The state was vulnerable to this type of attack, as it also based itself on religious foundations. But the importance of ecclesiastical patronage went beyond the utilitarian benefits of rendering the UDF respectable (and thereby eligible for funding) at home and abroad.

Supporting the UDF was presented as the "right and moral thing to do."[5] This does not mean that morality was merely invoked as a tactical maneuver. For some strategists, the moral appeal may have been merely utilitarian, but for many others the moral tones had a persuasive resonance. The UDF's preferred tactics provided ample opportunity for the expression of moral and spiritual appeals. Boycotts and nonparticipation had a significant symbolic meaning: these campaigns were aimed at identifying and isolating the forces of evil. By manifesting their purity, their nonassociation with evil, boycotters forged moral bonds. They took part in the battle between good and evil. Sharing a sense of belonging, not only to a political community but to a moral community as well, they knew both God and history were on their side. This, as Allan Boesak observed later, proved an important distinction between the UDF years and the early 1990s. He noted a widespread nostalgia for the UDF years. "That was a period of mass involvement, a period when people took a clear stand. That had a moral appeal. Now it is difficult to get used to compromises. . . . Many people in the Western Cape now say that 'the morality of politics has gone.' The 1980s, that was 'clean politics,' morally upright, no compromises, with a clear goal."[6]

Clerics continued their attempts at restoring a moral community by driving out the forces of evil. At a news briefing in November 1994, religious leaders stated that an envisaged truth commission could not alone deal with the anger and fear permeating society. "It needs the touch of God," they said. Anglican Archbishop Desmond Tutu said a "smoking out of demons" was planned. "They will be services of exorcism. People will be splashed with water."[7] While engaging in spiritual cleansing, the churches would also call on communities to clear the streets of litter.

Religion therefore is part and parcel of the ideological baggage of the liberation movement at a national level, although its historians tend to underestimate or ignore its importance. But it is at the local level where the pervasive presence of religious beliefs is most visible, both as a resource in the struggle for legitimacy and as a source of inspiration. At grassroots level, the UDF followers expressed their world view often simultaneously in both a socialist and religious idiom, as with the Young Christian Workers in Kagiso or the Sekhukhune youth. Socialism and Christianity were not seen as contradictory but as mutually reinforcing beliefs, as in Ntlokoa's diary and Chikane's autobiography. When, after several failed attempts, the bus boycott in Kagiso finally took off, the civic leaders interpreted their success as a divine vindication: "God is on our side." The very same youth who opened the village meeting in Apel with "Viva proletarian internationalism" had played a prominent part in the witch-hunts. Christianity was not a source of inspiration for the Sekhukhune youth, as it was for the Kagiso leaders. Instead, the youth drew both on local belief systems and on orthodox Marxism to underpin their campaigns.

In this respect, there is a parallel with the Zimbabwe war, where antisorcery campaigns also upset the generational balance. Unlike the examples from Zimbabwe, the alleged witches in Sekhukhuneland were not labeled sellouts: they were not suspected of passing information to the authorities. They were simply blamed for witchcraft.[8] But in essence, this amounted to the same crime: like sellouts, witches were subverting the struggle from within.

Through the spirit mediums, the ancestors gave their blessing to the liberation struggle in Zimbabwe. Thus a revolutionary struggle could be accommodated in peasant society. Although the war thoroughly upset the pattern of social relations, this experience could be digested in terms of local value systems. The guerrillas fought for the return of the ancestral lands.

Why was this road not open to the comrades in Sekhukhuneland? Why could the BaPedi tradition of resistance against colonization and Bantustans not be tapped to legitimate a new cycle of revolt? Why could the dingaka in Sekhukhuneland not be persuaded to give their blessing and their medicine to the comrades? It seems that, for the elders in Sekhukhuneland, the memories of the 1950s for the most part functioned as a deterrent rather than an inspiration. Although ANC traditions were kept alive in a few households, for most of the elder people involvement with the ANC spelled trouble: bannings, harassment, exclusion from job opportunities, unwanted attention from chiefs and police. With the youth, historical consciousness was apparently not a source of inspiration. Moreover, youth and spiritual authorities did not occupy the same positions as in Lan's famous Dande County in Zimbabwe. Sekhukhune youth wielded sjamboks, not guns: their means of coercion were less persuasive than those of Zimbabwe African National Union (ZANU) fighters. On the other hand, spirit mediums in Zimbabwe had preserved a considerable degree of autonomy, while the dingaka in Sekhukhuneland were compromised by their dependence on the chief.

Tradition as a source of legitimacy was not absent: what was lacking was human agency to mobilize this resource. The youth revolt erupted largely spontaneously, lacking strategy and leadership and unable to link up with the elders. Generational consciousness became a much stronger motivation than any sense of continuity with past resistance. In the first phase of youth mobilization, youth had turned to the dingaka with a request for medicines to make them invulnerable and the demand to identify the culprits of witchcraft. But in turning to the dingaka, the youth bypassed the elders and the chiefs. The chiefs were so intrinsically part and parcel of the repressive status quo that it was inconceivable to win them over to the side of liberation. In the village hierarchy, the dingaka belonged to the chief's entourage. They depended on the chiefs, at whose request they performed certain rituals and from whom they needed to obtain certain permits. Therefore, the spiritual resources of the dingaka were closed off to the youth. It was only when they had established that the dingaka could not or would not deliver that they turned to another powerful medicine: Leninism. Maurice Cornforth's much-thumbed trilogy held the promise of a new potent spiritual force that could guarantee invincibility (if not invulnerability): "The Marxian doctrine is omnipotent because it is true." Armed with this doctrine, one would be able to understand nature and society—and would also be empowered to change them.

Marxism-Leninism was put to use as a secular religion. It held out the same promise of ultimate victory as Christian religions. Cornforth promised an omnipotent doctrine, but so did the Methodist Hymn Book.

> When I am all renewed,
> When I in Christ am formed again,
> And witness, from all sin set free,
> *All things are possible to me.*[9]

Muti, Marx, and Methodism all held out the promise of omnipotent medicine in the search for social harmony. African religious leaders of various denominations have emphasized that it is highly artificial to draw sharp distinctions between traditional African religion and Christianity. The Association of African Spiritual Churches in Johannesburg has lamented the labeling of African religions as pagan superstitions. "All of this makes even less sense to us when we observe that the culture and customs we read about in the Bible is far closer to our culture and customs than to Western culture of the White Churches."[10]

This search for social harmony has been described in the Kagiso story as the quest for a moral community. In the vision of Frank Chikane and the Young Christian Workers, this would be the classless society compatible with the ideals of the Kingdom of God. Countering divorce, mediating in domestic conflict, combating crime, and fighting the forces of evil were all elements in the building of this moral community. Like Gabriel Setiloane, Chikane underlines that the dualistic world view, in which the spiritual world is separated from the social world, does not fit with the African world view. Not only were the people of Kagiso involved in a battle against an oppressive state; they were, in Chikane's words, taking part in the "struggles between the forces of right-eousness (light) and unrighteousness (darkness)."[11] The anticrime campaign, the cleanups, the social isolation of the police and the town councillors, all fit in with the endeavor to cleanse the township of evil forces. In Kagiso as in Sekhukhune, evil forces and spiritual power were agents with which to be reckoned. But in Kagiso, youth were not nearly as isolated as in Sekhukhune. Although the civic leadership worried about excesses on the part of the com-tsotsis, and the youth displayed impatience with the caution of the adults, much common ground remained. In Kagiso, religion was a shared resource across the generational divide.

At first glance, religion was virtually absent from the ideological armory of the *Grassroots* activists. But the egalitarian moral and political order, as envis-aged by the Kagiso activists, resembles the participatory socialist utopia upheld by the *Grassroots* staff. In the context of the Western Cape, appropriating Christianity in the name of the struggle was a problematic option. Christian-ity belonged to the colored elite of *dominees* and other petty bourgeois mem-bers of the establishment. Those who did bring a religious legitimation to the struggle, such as Allan Boesak, came to be seen as ideological rivals by the young Marxists who dominated both *Grassroots* and the UDF Regional Exec-utive. In order to construct a counter hegemony, other ideological sources needed to be tapped. Islam, in its militant third-world version, held out some promise but never became a prominent theme in *Grassroots* columns because it was not suited for broadening out beyond the Islamic constituency. As in Sekhukhuneland, Marxism was used both as an analytical tool and as a secu-lar religion. Like the youth movement in the Northern Transvaal, *Grassroots* activists isolated themselves by drawing on an ideology that was alien to the world view of the wider community.

Can the neglect of the religious dimension in the historiography be blamed on the Western bias of the recorders of history, as Setiloane believes? Are exotic local belief systems perhaps more intriguing for Western researchers than the seemingly well trodden paths of Christianity?

Religious beliefs transcend the black-white divide between the makers of history. What about the recorders of history? Terence Ranger and David Lan have recorded the vital importance of religion in the Zimbabwe wars. But there is another school of writing on African revolution that vehemently brands religious beliefs as impediments to liberation. These authors are not white and Western, but black and angry. In his writings on anticolonial resist-ance in Algeria, Franz Fanon spearheaded the onslaught on "superstitious beliefs": "And the youth of a colonised country, growing up in an atmosphere of shot and fire, may well make a mock of, and does not hesitate to pour scorn upon zombies of his ancestors, the horses with two heads, the dead who rise again, and the djinns who rush into your body while you yawn. The native discovers reality and transforms it into the pattern of his customs, into the practice of violence and into his plan for freedom."[12]

Fanon's belief in moral regeneration through revolution, and in the necessity of revolutionary violence to liberate individuals and nations under colonial rule, became the gospel for a school of writing on African revolution. But these Fanonesque notions of the liberating qualities of revolutionary violence are not prominent in the idiom of the mainstream resistance movement in South Africa. They are, however, not totally absent. Addressing the 1985 ANC conference in Zambia, Oliver Tambo characterized the gathering as a "council-of-war that planned the seizure of power by these masses, the penultimate conviction that gave the order for us to take our country through the terrible but cleansing fires of revolutionary war to a condition of peace, democracy and the fulfillment of our people who have already suffered far too much and far too long."[13] But overall, these notions of the cleansing qualities of revolutionary war are more characteristic of the idiom of the PAC.

Ranger takes issue with Fanon and other authors and actors who have maintained that religion is bound to prevent a guerrilla war from becoming a people's war, or that it contradicts the modernizing mentality judged necessary for the construction of a new society. Ranger argues the opposite: without religious symbols and mediums, the guerrilla war might have had more difficulty in becoming a true people's war.[14]

The conceptual gap between the recorders and the makers of the South African liberation struggle cannot be explained by the skin color of the authors. Being white does not make one automatically insensitive to religious or spiritual dimensions; being black is no guarantee for receptivity. Why then is the religious and moral dimension virtually lacking in the historiography? One possible explanation is the instrumentality of much of the academic writing. Many authors aspired to go beyond a mere recording of history. Not only were the actors becoming authors, as in the case of the alternative media, but in much of the historiography, the authors became actors. They were motivated by the desire to prove certain points of ideology or strategy. For many, religion belonged to the realm of false consciousness. The prevailing race-class paradigm left no space for other dimensions of the human experience.

National Struggles and Local Agendas

The subject of "struggles within a revolution" is a common theme in much of the literature on revolution. The "struggles within the struggle" can unfold along lines of class or ideology, with various factions vying for dominance—as, for example, with the nationalists, communists, and other left-wing groupings in the ANC and the UDF. The Janus-faced nature of national liberation struggles has also been a theme of several studies on Mau-Mau and FRELIMO (Frente de Libertaçao de Moçambique), where it is argued that an internal civil war along class lines was being waged behind the broader nationalist movement. Competition for dominance can unfold along ethnic lines, as with ZANU and ZAPU (Zimbabwe African People's Union). Generational battles come out clearly in much of the literature on the Zimbabwe war and also in a revealing article by Colin Leys and John Saul on the Namibian liberation movement SWAPO (South West Africa People's Organisation).[15]

The perspective from the micro level offers perhaps a better insight into the subthemes behind the general theme of liberation struggles against colonialism or apartheid. The struggles of the 1980s in South Africa do not fit in the categories of classic guerrilla wars as in Zimbabwe or Mozambique. The South African struggle was characterized by widespread popular mobilization interspersed with low-intensity guerrilla warfare. African liberation movements generally identified the peasantry as having the most revolutionary potential. But the ANC had shifted its focus from the countryside to the cities with its strategic reappraisal in 1978–79. The main battlefield was in urban South Africa—hence my choice for two urban case studies and one rural case study. Even in the case of Sekhukhuneland, one can speak of rural struggles, but hardly of peasant struggles. Behind the overall theme of the anti-apartheid struggle, other battles were being waged. As in the case of Zimbabwe, these struggles were fought along the lines of class, ethnicity, gender, and generation.

In Sekhukhuneland, there is an element of class antagonism in the mutual hostility between youth and business owners. The main targets of attacks and extortion—the owners of bottle stores, beer halls, garages, and taxis—depended on the Bantustan government for licenses and patronage. In Kagiso, the picture was more complex. On the one hand, businessmen depended on the discredited town council for their licenses. On the other hand, business owners had reason to resent the restrictions imposed on them by the apartheid state. In the phase of the consumer boycott, local business gained a direct stake in close cooperation with the civic, for the boycott of white-owned shops resulted in an immediate increase in purchases within the township. In the townships, the relationship between UDF activists and business owners was characteristically opportunistic. Other divisions along the lines of class are more diffuse. Core activists were not exactly well-off, but neither did they belong to the poorest section of the community. In terms of their educational background, they ranked above average. For the marginalized in Kagiso township, the activities of the civic carried little attraction. Backyard tenants were more vulnerable than council tenants and possessed little scope for collective action. In spite of occasional contacts, hostel dwellers remained outsiders,

"Beyond Our Wildest Dreams"

without their own representation on the civic. Lumpen youth set their own agenda, devising their own interpretation of the struggle that legitimated the hijacking of cars and the plundering of stores and delivery vehicles.

In the Western Cape, the staff of *Grassroots* battled with class lines that largely coincided with the racial divide. The African township organizers on the staff were less educated, felt isolated, and were inclined to develop their own agenda. Most of the core staff had enjoyed at least some years of post-secondary education, which resulted in a gap between the staff and their pre-dominantly working-class constituency. The newspaper's agenda ostensibly coincided with the UDF program. But in sidelining the clergy and in advo-cating their own version of utopia in which socialism and egalitarian partici-patory populism were happily married, the *Grassroots* activists also moved beyond the UDF's primary goals. Moreover, socialism was used as a legit-imizing ideology for a particular subculture of youth activism, which became quite remote from the concerns of ordinary people. UDF activists in the West-ern Cape failed to link up with the most marginalized part of Western Cape society: the ever growing numbers of squatters.

Race or ethnicity does not emerge as a powerful force in shaping internal conflict in these case studies, except in the case of the Western Cape, where the racial divide between coloreds and Africans remained an overriding concern both during and after the UDF episode. Local agendas ostensibly coincided with the national agenda of building broad multiracial fronts. But the efforts were only partially successful. In Kagiso, which has a multiethnic population, no ethnic cleavages emerged in the course of my research. In Sekhukhuneland, with its fairly homogeneous ethnic composition, rivalry between villages developed along clan lines.

Did the struggle provide new space for women's empowerment? The picture emerging from the case studies is ambivalent. Girls were not totally absent from youth organization in Sekhukhuneland, but this movement was strongly dominated by male youth. Data are fragmentary and somewhat impression-istic, but the prevailing impression is one of competition over women, not of women's empowerment. One remarkable feature of the set of grievances expressed by high school students was that boys often complained about sexual harassment suffered by the girls. This could indicate a manifestation of student solidarity, but more often than not the boys were in fact voicing resentment against their teachers, who were snatching the girls away from them. Boys believed girls to be unreliable because they would allegedly be easily seduced by teachers, policemen, and soldiers, either under threat or with the promise of sweets or perfumes. In this competition with teachers and policemen, high school students had little to offer in terms of material inducements. Their weapon was coercion, as graphically illustrated in the "building soldiers" campaign. As in Zimbabwe, girls were forcibly removed from parental control; but unlike in Zimbabwe, there was no code against sexual intercourse. On the contrary, it was understood that one requirement of the struggle was to produce babies, an item that definitely did not figure on the national agenda of the anti-apartheid struggle.

Competition over female youth and control over women's fertility is a sub-theme that was by no means confined to Sekhukhuneland only. It was reported that in 1986 young girls in Durban were told that African girls had to become pregnant. "Every woman—married or not, at school or not—must be pregnant by February . . . to replace the black people killed in the struggle last year." An informant said that comrades had threatened to search handbags for contraceptives.[16] In their discussion on the role of women in the struggle, several authors state that social norms and household chores militated against girls' involvement, but that motherhood could be a mobilizing role. Both in actively supporting their children and in mediating functions, mothers experienced a politicization of their traditional role.[17]

This general observation makes sense in the context of Kagiso and the Western Cape, but not in Sekhukhuneland. The struggle was not an empowering experience for BaPedi mothers: they feared their children. Girls might have felt attracted to the youth movement, which provided an escape from parental control, but they played a subordinate role. Nevertheless, through the linkup with the wider world, notions of women's liberation trickled down to Sekhukhuneland. Kagiso offered the fairly unusual spectacle of a powerful woman at the center of civic affairs. But since Sister Bernard Ncube was a nun, she belonged to a different category of women, located outside the arena of male competition. Otherwise, women did not play leading roles, although KRO encouraged the involvement of women as mothers. Girls did participate in youth organization, but to a lesser extent than boys. Women did have access to the Kagiso Disciplinary Committee to present their complaints about unruly children or irresponsible husbands. As with people's courts elsewhere, the DC opposed separation and encouraged reconciliation. As discussed in the chapter on Kagiso, the envisaged new moral order was egalitarian in terms of race and class, but not in terms of gender. The courts upheld the established patriarchal norms in gender relations. Control over women emerges as a more powerful theme than women's empowerment in the struggle years.

By contrast, women played an active part in *Grassroots,* both on the staff and in the network of volunteers. The nature of the project facilitated women's involvement. The paper, particularly in its early years, dealt with bread-and-butter issues of immediate relevance to women. Involvement in *Grassroots* was not a directly confrontational activity. The intellectual environment of the Cape Peninsula, with its two universities, provided more space for women's involvement in a variety of roles. Women's issues, however, were not particularly prominent in *Grassroots* or the Western Cape UDF at large. Women who protested against rising bread prices were welcome, but women who protested against rape, domestic violence, or sexual harassment on the campus were far more contentious in UDF circles. This type of protest, after all, could be labeled "divisive," for it was not directed at the common enemy but at oppressive practices within the "people's camp."

Generation is clearly the most salient subtheme to emerge from all three case studies. In Sekhukhuneland and Kagiso as well as in the Western Cape, intergenerational battles were being waged behind the overall anti-apartheid struggle. In Sekhukhuneland, the UDF constituency was limited to youth. In Kagiso the picture is more complex, as the civic managed to involve a broad section of the community. But youth had taken the initiative for the formation of KRO; youth were the enforcers of boycotts and the anticrime campaign. They were both the main actors and the main victims, in terms of casualties. *Grassroots* proved an effective vehicle for youth to mount their revolt against the colored establishment and to articulate their own hegemonic project. In all three cases, local adaptations of Marxism-Leninism provided a legitimizing ideology for youth revolt.

It should be noted, however, that *youth* is a problematic category.[18] The youth in the three case studies differed in age, educational background, gender mix, and class. The leading actors in Sekhukhuneland were male high school students. Coercive recruitment strategies meant that most of the village youth joined willingly or unwillingly. Generational frictions were most pronounced in the case of Sekhukhuneland, where the youth movement escalated into a revolt against all authority: chiefs, dingaka, teachers, and parents. The comrades in SEYO definitely felt themselves part of the wider liberation struggle, but not only were they fighting for the liberation of Mandela—they were also fighting boredom. Once the ANC leaders returned from prison and exile to take over the lead, new worries were expressed: Would the old men understand that the youth of Apel were in urgent need of a disco?

In Kagiso, the leading actors were older than the Sekhukhune youth. They belonged to the Soweto generation: at the start of the UDF episode they were in their mid-twenties. They had left high school—with or without a diploma—but maintained an interest in further education through formal or informal channels. They were mostly unemployed or held activist-type jobs in the YCW or the trade unions. The young men who stood at the origins of KRO had learned the lessons of the Soweto revolt. Youth on their own could not bring the system down. Therefore youth had to link up with the broader community: in particular, with workers; in general, with parents. This lesson had not yet been learned by the youth in the Northern Transvaal Bantustans, where the Soweto revolt was not part of the collective memory. The street troops who manned the barricades in Kagiso in the months of confrontation were younger and more inexperienced. For lack of data, it is difficult to make a breakdown of the youth on the street: both high school students and lumpen youth would seem to be included. If the generational divide was one major source of differentiation within the community, other subthemes emerge behind the monolithic category of youth, as has been illustrated by the story of the comtsotsis of the United Front in Kagiso. As in 1976 in Soweto, the dividing line between those youth who went to school and those who did not could assume considerable importance. Similarly, the urban-rural divide cut across the category of youth. A major element in the attraction of the Sekhukhune Youth Organisation was its rural roots: while COSAS was "a thing from town," SEYO was "our own organisation."

Grassroots was largely the domain of students or former students with post-secondary education, who had first cut their teeth in the school boycotts and the community campaigns of 1980. Its volunteer network had, of course, a wider scope; it relied largely on high school students or recent graduates.

Impoverishment is often cited as an incentive for youth to engage in resistance.[19] Indeed, many of the youth leadership came from poor families, but they did not necessarily experience growing poverty. Some experienced improvements in living standards. More important than the level of poverty was a sense of grievance and a determination to be better off than their parents. Contributing to the sense of relative deprivation was a growing acquaintance with the wider world through, for example, the mass media. Not all actors had little prospect of employment. George Moiloa made a conscious decision to quit his job in order to become secretary of KRO. Ryland Fisher gave up a well-paying job when he joined *Grassroots*. The struggle attracted numerous people who could have found more profitable and less troublesome employment elsewhere. The street soldiers obviously had fewer options. But having nothing to lose is not necessarily conducive to political radicalization. Those who had a lot to lose—successful students—took high risks. Those who had least to lose—migrants and squatters—were clinging more determinedly to the little they had. The lumpen proletariat could be a recruiting ground for street soldiers, but it could be equally fertile territory for the recruitment of vigilantes or police informers.

Youth was the main constituency of the UDF, and in most of the UDF campaigns, youth played a prominent role. But in doing so, young activists also furthered their own agendas apart from the wider anti-apartheid struggle. They wanted to break out of strongly hierarchical systems; they went for excitement and at times also more material rewards; they demanded access to girlfriends; they rebelled against parents and teachers. The ANC had put ungovernability on the national agenda; youth could adapt this directive to carve out more space for themselves in local conditions.

When furthering their own agendas, youth movements could become a divisive element in the wider struggle. The phenomenon of youth sitting in judgment over elders in the people's courts was considered particularly obnoxious. The vigilante phenomenon can to some extent be explained as a backlash against the rule of the youth. Vigilantes sometimes had a class base, as town councillors and shopkeepers organized punitive expeditions to take revenge on their tormentors. But frequently vigilantes consisted of parents who were determined to teach the children a lesson. There were numerous cases of parents forcing their children with sticks or sjamboks into the schoolyard.[20]

In the intractable civil war in Natal, which in convenient shorthand is labeled the strife between UDF (or later ANC) and Inkatha, the front lines were demarcated not only by political allegiances but also by generation, class, and the urban-rural divide. Broadly, the "comrades" tended to be young, better educated, and more town-oriented, while the Inkatha fighters were older, less educated, and more rural. These elements come out clearly in an account of the battles in the Durban township of KwaMashu, as told by a former comrade. KwaMashu was a township with UDF-affiliated youth organizations. Their main enemies were the Inkatha impis, who invaded the township from nearby shack settlements. When the youth organizations tried to enforce stay-aways and consumer boycotts, these Inkatha men, firmly steeped in Zulu traditions, made it clear that they would "never let children tell them what to do" and that they would take no nonsense on Inkatha's home turf. In August 1985, Inkatha fighters moved in to "restore order" and to wipe out the youth organizations. At the other side of the front line, township residents were required to contribute at least one male member of the family for "military service" and money for the purchase of weaponry and muti.[21] Intergenerational friction was a vital element in the hostel war, which broke out in 1990 throughout the Transvaal townships.

War situations cause disruptions that are not necessarily detrimental to weaker groups. Women have often gained more space to expand their activities beyond the household sphere. During the war years, women kept the factories going in Britain, France, and the United States. The liberation wars in Mozambique and Eritrea also provided new opportunities for women, although the gains were not always consolidated after independence. Young men, being the main body of combatants, occupied positions of power and authority that would not normally be held by them. Similarly, in South Africa local power relations shifted significantly during the years of struggle. To what extent were these changes consolidated after 1990? Here, it seems that women fared better than youth. The new South African constitution treats women as equal citizens, rather than as legal minors. Since the 1994 elections, women are more numerous in government and parliament than ever before. But youth, as a SEYO activist remarked, has been "demobilized."

The ANC leadership advised the youth that it was time to go back to school and to work, to "fight, produce, and learn," while the "old men" would sort out the new order. But in many instances, schools were in chaos, money for school fees and textbooks was lacking, and jobs were not available. Under the circumstances, some youth continued fighting, although their battles were no longer sanctioned by the liberation movement.

Structural Conditions and Human Agency

Why do revolutions happen? Because structural conditions induce revolutions? Or because people make revolutions happen?

Structural conditions in the three case studies are to some extent similar. The economic crisis, high unemployment figures, the education crisis, and a crisis of legitimacy with regard to local and national government were common features in Sekhukhuneland, Kagiso, and the Western Cape. An additional factor in the Northern Transvaal is the phenomenon of widespread migrant labor. Absent is the housing crisis, which features prominently in Kagiso and the Western Cape. The inhabitants of Sekhukhuneland own their houses. Mobilization around the issue of rents and service charges, which proved such an effective focus in Kagiso and the Western Cape, was not on the agenda in Sekhukhuneland. This meant that the option of linking school and housing struggles—an effective way of forging alliances across the generational divide—was not available in Sekhukhuneland. In the townships, not only did youth perceive housing struggles as a suitable topic to mobilize parents, but they also had a direct stake in the matter. Raising rents affected the capacity of the parents to pay school fees. Conversely, the school crisis forced parents to pay attention to their children's grievances. Parents' involvement became institutionalized with the formation of the National Education Crisis Committee. In Sekhukhuneland, the school crisis served only to further alienate youth and parents. In the absence of most of the breadwinners, the female heads of household were not in a position to enter into a dialogue with the students, who demanded among other requests the formation of teacher-parent-student committees. Chiefs, who headed the school committees, were not inclined to welcome women's participation; women themselves were too shy to take the initiative. Parents and teachers generally felt that unruly youth ought to be disciplined rather than accommodated. Issues of common concern around which broad alliances could be built were virtually lacking. One potential mobilizing issue with broad appeal was the grievances against the chieftaincy. Occasionally, youth and migrant workers managed to combine forces against corrupt and exploitative chiefs, but these alliances were mostly short-lived and not a widespread phenomenon.

Structural analysis, with its focus on material conditions, provides a necessary but not sufficient explanation. In Kagiso, for example, living standards and the township environment did not change significantly between 1984 and 1986. The transition from quiescence to revolt was not caused by a sudden deterioration in material conditions but by human intervention, both from inside and outside Kagiso. The process of popular mobilization took off in a general atmosphere of rising militancy throughout the country and of escalating state repression. In December 1985, KRO managed for the first time to pull off a successful boycott campaign. But a crucial element in township rebellion was the direct experience of repression, harassment, and brutal force.

In other parts of the Northern Transvaal, similar conditions prevailed as in Apel, the village that was one of the centers of youth rebellion. Yet, certain parts remained quiet, while other remote rural areas became the scene of youth insurrection. Human agency is seen at work in the strategic planning of the students at Turfloop, who organized to set up youth movements in their home villages. The core activists of SEYO from Apel went around to establish branches in other villages with the intention of stirring up rebellion. "Tafelkop exploded within a week after our visit," recalled the chair of SEYO's Apel branch with obvious satisfaction.

Grassroots is a clear example of the explicit use of "human agency" to utilize grievances about material deprivation as a tactic for popular mobilization. Activists did not believe that material deprivation in itself would induce resistance: people needed to be "conscientised" by a newspaper. An organizing tool was required to infuse bread-and-butter struggles with a new meaning. At the same time, *Grassroots* illustrates the limitations of popular action based on undifferentiated concepts of *community*. In order to be effective as an organizing tool, a paper needs to be geared to the conditions and the cultural identity of a specific target audience. But this was not feasible in the political climate of the 1980s: to produce a paper for a colored constituency would have been deemed politically incorrect.

Human agency was crucial in focusing the direction of social change. Here, the UDF played a vital role: it may not have controlled most of the developments, but it gave political and ideological meaning to a great variety of struggles. Localized protests and bread-and-butter struggles became linked to an overall attack on the apartheid state. The Front also played an integrative role.

Highly regionalized and particularist organizations were molded into a truly national movement: thus the UDF made a significant contribution to forging a sense of national South African identity. However, its neglect of rural areas resulted in a continued sense of marginalization in the Bantustans.

To what extent were UDF organizations able to provide tangible benefits at the grassroots level? SEYO's capacity to deliver the goods was limited. It provided its own constituency with a sense of power and excitement, but this was a fleeting experience. It was hardly equipped to address the most urgent concerns in village communities: water shortages, unemployment, inadequate health care, inferior education. Youth did interfere in one pressing community issue: the fear of witchcraft. Their handling of this matter, however, served to heighten tensions rather than to promote social harmony. But for the activists themselves, the link with the UDF was meaningful in that it gave access to money (although in modest amounts), ideas, transportation, literature, propaganda material, lawyers, and hiding places.

KRO was less inclined to sloganeering and was better equipped to deal with basic issues. It could build on accumulated organizational experience and draw on a support network that provided legal assistance and limited financial support. At times, the civic proved effective in halting or delaying rent increases. Its anticrime campaign restored a sense of order and security to the township. In the months of escalating repression, KRO leadership provided residents with guidance and legal aid. Its legitimacy with residents rested to a considerable extent on this capacity to deliver the goods, although its possibilities should not be overstated. Its role in establishing a degree of social order was not without costs: it involved a considerable amount of coercion, especially in the initial phase. But in KRO's case, it seems that the benefits outweighed the costs, in the eyes of ordinary township residents.

Grassroots proved effective as an organizing tool in its early years, but it outlived its usefulness. The paper helped in the battles for more washing lines and a more convenient date for the payment of electricity bills. It was an effective tool in helping to form community organizations, but it was less useful in sustaining them over the years. Its double agenda may have hindered its effectiveness: for the media activists, addressing community issues was not an end in itself. It was a means in the battle for national liberation and socialist transformation. After a while, activists became bored with community issues and eagerly seized the opportunity to highlight national politics and ideological models. The paper proved inadequate in the period of street battles and semi-underground activities. It was not a suitable instrument to achieve one of its main objectives: bridging the divide between Africans and coloreds. Toward the end of the decade, *Grassroots* had ceased to "deliver": it faded away.

Inclusion and Exclusion: Redrawing the Boundaries

South Africa in the early 1990s was a land of paradox. As the boundaries of the apartheid state were being wiped out, other borders were redefined or underscored. As race and ethnicity were abandoned as official organizing principles of the political system, ethnicity seemed to become a more potent force in black political life than before. The apartheid state had been built on a process of ethnic mobilization by Afrikaners. Now the mainstream of Afrikaners seemed ready to move toward an inclusive concept of nationhood. While the Africans prepared to enter the corridors of power, ethnic competition within the black opposition became more pronounced.

Now that apartheid was defeated, Indians and more strongly coloreds reasserted their interests and identities. They sensed a new vulnerability as a minority group in the new South Africa, trapped between the entrenched privilege of whites and the new opportunities that would accrue mainly to Africans. But the starkest manifestation of ethnic mobilization was organized by Gatsha Buthelezi, whose appeal to Zulu traditionalism held the negotiation process to ransom until the eve of the 1994 elections. In a series of last-minute efforts, all the main players on the national field, from Inkatha to Constand Viljoen's Afrikaner Freedom Front, were ultimately incorporated in the political process.

At one point, the ANC efforts to accommodate a wide range of interests within its own camp threatened to leave an important category of South Africans in the cold. Chiefs, organized in CONTRALESA, insisted on the preservation of their powers and privileges. In terms of African customary law, women in rural areas were considered legal minors. Chiefs, fearing a reduction of their traditional jurisdiction, mounted opposition to the proposed Bill of Rights, which was based on the principle that all citizens are equal before the law. This attempt to exclude African rural women—a sizable group of South African citizens—from the equality that was now bestowed on all people in the new South Africa caused much indignation in women's organizations. Spokespersons for rural women threatened an election boycott. In the end, however, the new constitution and the Bill of Rights were inclusive of all South African citizens. Officially, the only outsiders in the new South Africa were illegal aliens. The process of incorporation seemed completed.

But at the micro level, different scenarios were being enacted, which at times deviated significantly from the peace process at macro level. In the local context, the violence had assumed its own dynamic. Some categories of South Africans who had not been included in the UDF concept of "the people" fitted seamlessly into the new South Africa: business and liberal whites were among its most ardent supporters. It is on the local level that the marginalized and the outsiders in the new South Africa become most clearly visible: farm-workers, migrants, rural communities, squatters, immigrants, and sections of the youth, now dubbed "the lost generation."

In mid-1990, clashes between hostel dwellers and residents spread to townships all over the Reef. In August 1990, the death toll exceeded five hundred in a period of ten days. The East Rand became an intractable maze of feuds involving township residents, Zulu migrants, taxi associations, and squatters. The Vaal townships became a no-go area where youth gangs ruled supreme. Tensions rose as township residents began to implement sharp increases in rents for backyard shacks. Land invasions by backyard tenants were a response to housing shortages and to rising tensions with their landlords. Gigantic new squatter camps sprang up around the main cities, caused in part by the con-tinuing exodus from the Bantustans. But many squatters were not recent arrivals on the urban scene; they emerged from backyards, had fled the hos-tels, or decided to live on their own rather than remain cramped with their rel-atives in the tiny matchbox houses. Processes of inclusion and exclusion at the local level did not necessarily follow the logic of national negotiations. At the negotiating table, the former adversaries demonstrated a surprising agility in the new game of consensus politics. But these years of hope were simultane-ously an episode of despair, as violence reached unprecedented levels and became more and more intractable. Political violence has been blamed on the "third force" (a sinister network of military men, police, and right-wingers bent on sabotaging the peace process) or on a complex of "third forces." There is convincing evidence that some of the violence was inspired and organized by elements in the defense force and the police. But the fact remains that countless recruits were available to fight the manifold battles. They apparently sensed themselves excluded from the promises of the new South Africa.

What Was It All About? The Race-Class Paradigm Revisited

The different sets of agendas, the battles fought within "the community" along other than class lines, the great variety of inspirations and aspirations demon-strate that the race-class paradigm is too narrow to capture the diversity of human experience. People were involved not only in their capacity as "blacks" or "oppressed" but also as youth and parents, as men and women, as mod-ernizers and traditionalists, as urban dwellers and rural folks, as upholders of Christianity, Islam, or other religious beliefs and ideologies. In short, people have multiple identities. Which identity prevails at any particular moment is situationally determined.

One new identity born in the struggles of the 1980s was a new broad South African identity, which was carefully fostered by Nelson Mandela in the tran-

Table 2
1994 election results in Sekhukhuneland, Krugersdorp, and the Western Cape

Sekhukhuneland
    projected numbers of voters   203,345
    number of voters national elections   149,786
    number of voters provincial elections   142,268

        provincial results

PAC	UPF	ANC	NP	DP	IFP
1,638	585	137,477	828	67	65

        national results

1,481		145,558	715	126	52

Krugersdorp
    projected number of voters   146,686
    number of voters national elections   130,916
    number of voters provincial elections   131,411

        provincial results

PAC	ANC	NP	DP	IFP
2,875	82,168	25,988	2,923	3,518

        national results

2,554	81,232	31,541	1,945	3,213

Western Cape
    projected number of voters   2,405,919
    number of voters national elections   2,151,843
    number of voters provincial elections   2,148,456

        provincial results

PAC	ANC	NP	DP	IFP
22,676	705,576	1,138,242	141,970	7,445

        national results

21,353	714,271	1,195,633	88,804	2,566

PAC: Pan Africanist Congress
ANC: African National Congress
NP: National Party
DP: Democratic Party
IFP: Inkatha Freedom Party
UPF: United People's Front (a bantustan-based political party in Lebowa which only
    contested the elections in the Northern Transvaal)

Source: Figures based on the national and provincial results released by the Election Administration Directorate, Independent Electoral Commission, on 26 May 1994. The projected number of voters is given in a list added by the Department of Home Affairs.

Note: As there was no voters' registration, the projected numbers of voters are rather rough estimates. Voters were free to vote in any polling station, provided they were in possession of one of the authorized identity documents.

sitional period up to, and beyond, the 1994 elections for the first representative parliament in South African history (table 2). This South African identity was consummated in those impressive, unending queues in which voters waited long hours, sometimes even days, in front of the polling stations. It was a therapeutic exercise: for the first time, black and white, rich and poor, participated as equals in a common ritual.

The elections were an organizational nightmare, a compromise of political horse-trading, and a straightforward miracle. It has become a truism to describe this extraordinary sequence of events, from the election days to Nelson Mandela's inauguration on the star-studded lawns of Union Buildings in Pretoria, as a miracle. The spate of indiscriminate bombings, the overheated political climate, and the widespread anxieties among both black and white South Africans on the eve of the elections gave way to a moment of trust and confidence. The euphoric mood is well captured in the headlines about these historic events: "Savouring a victory for all South Africans"; "SA becomes a beacon of hope as President Mandela takes oath of office; We're on top of the world";[22] "President Mandela sworn in for the whole of South Africa and the world; 'Let freedom reign.'"[23]

But the term *miracle* was not only used as a metaphor. For numerous voters, the elections were truly a miracle, a supernatural phenomenon, a spiritual experience. For once, the *Volksblad* in Bloemfontein captured the general mood as its reporter went out to gather comments on this extraordinary event. As befitting in the covering of a miracle, he turned, not to the politicians, but to the religious leaders of various denominations. "What should have been a political event has turned into a spiritual experience. . . . Black, white, brown, and Indian South Africans are transformed—they have found each other." Archbishop Tutu indeed believed that there could be no logical explanation for these events: it could not have happened without divine intervention.[24]

The new sense of being South African, of course, did not supplant manifestations of identity along such lines as race, class, ethnicity, generation, gender, religion, language. This new identity was added to the range of identities on which South Africans can draw. In paving the road for the unfolding of this miracle, in averting the specter of a race war, and in molding a broad sense of nationhood, the United Democratic Front—for all its faults—made a major contribution.

Note on Methodology and Sources

T HE RESEARCH FOR THIS BOOK began in 1989, when I was employed by the African Studies Centre in Leiden, the Netherlands, to write a doctoral thesis on the contemporary history of South Africa. I opted for the United Democratic Front as the subject of my research because this fascinating movement held out the promise of a multifaceted approach to the study of South African society. When studying the UDF as a national movement, one is exposed to the intricacies of "high politics." When exploring the social makeup and motivations of the UDF's multifarious affiliates, one is introduced to the complexities of politics at a grassroots level. I hoped that combining the perspectives of history from below with the broad outlines of mainstream history would contribute to my understanding of linkages between micro-level and macro-level resistance politics.

Since I had previously worked as a journalist, it seemed natural to me that this research should result not only in a thesis but also in book aimed at a more general readership. I have therefore attempted to pursue three goals: to document and analyze some aspects of South Africa's liberation struggle in the 1980s, to write an accessible book, and to meet the requirements for a doctoral thesis at the University of Leiden. Reconciling these goals was not as self-evident as it had seemed to me at the outset.

The first part of this book, notably chapter 2, summarizes various theoretical concepts and the concomitant interpretations of the South African liberation struggle. This is a much abridged and streamlined version of the first part of the original thesis.

The main body of this book is part 2—chapters 3, 4, and 5—which look in detail at three examples of local and locally inspired resistance. When I set out to explore these case studies, my mental map was largely shaped by the paradigms discussed in part 1. The plan was to situate the case studies on this mental map, pursuing the same themes when descending from the macro level to the micro level. But the theoretical explorations undertaken in preparation for the fieldwork yielded analytical concepts that at times seemed quite remote from the living experiences of the actors at grassroots level.

The race-class paradigm, which is central to most of the academic literature, and the related issue of alliance politics informed my queries as I went out to explore the social base of the UDF in Sekhukhuneland, Kagiso, and the Cape Peninsula. But once I had left the campus, this learned luggage did not take me very far. Somehow, the real people whom I met did not seem to fit in the categories that made such impressive intellectual models. This was rather disturbing, so at times I became annoyed with my informants. However forthcoming most people were, the issues remained elusive. What was even more disturbing was that, at first glance, everything seemed to fit perfectly well. Asked about their relationship with the workers' struggle, youth activists produced the politically correct answers. After all, they had digested much of the same literature, or popularized versions of it. And yet, the answers patiently offered to my impatient queries somehow did not seem to explain much when I tried to make sense of the world around me. Why was it that these people refused to fit into these learned paradigms? Didn't they know their place in history?

My frustration with my informants subsided when I finally persuaded myself to stop asking and to start listening. I abandoned my semistructured interviews and usually invited people to tell their particular story as they saw fit. The case studies are largely of a narrative nature. I do not pretend that they make significant contributions to theory, but I do hope that they contribute something to our understanding of social movement processes at the micro level. What drove the youth leadership in Sekhukhuneland, the civic activists in Kagiso, and the media workers in the Cape Peninsula? What was their vision of a future society, and how did they think they would get there? How did they become involved in the first place? How did they legitimate the power that they had assumed in opposition to the established patterns of authority?

This is not to say that race and class are irrelevant concepts at either the macro or micro level. But it does underline the observation made in the introduction: people are not one- or two-dimensional actors, intelligible only in terms of race or class, or at best in terms of race and class. Other dimensions emerged in the course of my research: alliance politics could also be discussed in terms of generation or gender, or in terms of the urban-rural divide. Next to nationalism and socialism, religion and local belief systems emerged as ideological components that motivate and legitimize people's actions. "The people" may be a one-dimensional entity, but real people have multiple identities. This confrontation with the living world of real people was initially unsettling, but later it felt as a relief. Real people proved much more interesting than the one-dimensional actors in the theoretical models.

Fieldwork

Fieldwork for this study was conducted in two stages. After an orientation visit to South Africa in January–February 1990, I spent six months in Johannesburg and the Northern Transvaal from mid-June to mid-December 1990. A second phase of two months of fieldwork in September–November 1991 was conducted in and around Cape Town and again in Johannesburg with visits to Kagiso and another brief stay in Sekhukhuneland. Some information was collected during earlier visits in 1984 and 1987, while I was working as a journalist, and again at the time of the 1994 elections, when I returned to South Africa for about one month.

A mine of information on the UDF is contained in the documentation of political trials, ranging from trials against the national leadership (notably the Pietermaritzburg Treason Trial and the Delmas Treason Trial) to a series of court cases involving local activists. A collection of records of political trials is kept in the Historical and Literary Papers Section of the University of the Witwatersrand. I have made extensive use of the Delmas Treason Trial collection, which contains documents up to mid-1985. Furthermore, I have consulted collections with UDF material in the University of South Africa (UNISA) in Pretoria, the South African Institute of Race Relations in Johannesburg (SAIRR), the African Studies Centre of the University of Cape Town, the Mayibuye Centre of the University of the Western Cape (UWC), the Centre for Adult and Continuing Education (CACE) at UWC, and the South African History Archives (SAHA) in Johannesburg. SAHA, which concentrates on collecting documents and memorabilia of liberation movements, social movements, and trade unions in the 1980s, was a particularly valuable store of information. My archival research was concluded in 1991; I have not consulted the material that continued to arrive in the SAHA office after 1991. This new material includes, for example, the documentation kept by regional UDF offices. The SAHA collection is now stored with the Historical and Literary Papers at the University of the Witwatersrand. In addition, the UDF Head Office in Johannesburg has been very helpful in providing information. Many documents in offices and private houses, of course, were confiscated during police raids in the 1980s.

This documentation has been supplemented with a series of interviews with key figures in the UDF national leadership. The case studies depend in varying degrees on a combination of published material, unpublished sources, and interviews.

I have been particularly fortunate in the timing of this research. When the research proposal was drawn up, the UDF was a restricted organization. Prominent activists were either in detention or in hiding, or they had gone into exile. My first visa request was turned down in August 1989. This proved a blessing in disguise. My renewed request was finally granted in December 1989. Arriving in South Africa in January 1990, I had the good fortune to witness the unbanning of the ANC, the UDF, and other movements and the release of Nelson Mandela. Detainees emerged from prison, refugees returned home, restrictions were lifted, documentation resurfaced in leaps and bounds. On my first visit to the SAHA office in Johannesburg, I found two almost empty rooms. As the year progressed, the rooms filled up with a steady flow of boxes with documents emerging from hiding places in garages and attics. In this new open climate, informants could afford to be more forthcoming than would have been possible under the repressive conditions of the 1980s.

Sekhukhuneland

Sekhukhuneland was selected because it promised to be an interesting case of rural rebellion. Most of the UDF documents deal with urban areas. Rural activists were generally not prolific writers. Minutes of meetings were rarely kept. The massive outpouring of media was characteristic of the UDF in the major towns but was largely absent in rural areas where facilities were lacking, service organizations unheard of, and repression much harsher. Newspapers rarely paid much attention to developments in rural areas. The story of the youth movement in Sekhukhuneland is therefore largely compiled on the basis of interviews. Reconstructing a chronological history proved more difficult in this case than in the two other cases. Many informants were not able to provide dates with their stories: events were told in relation to some salient incident in people's personal experiences—for example, "before my detention" or "after my house was burnt down." Interviews were conducted with members of the Northern Transvaal Regional Executive in Pietersburg, Seshego, and the University of the North in Mankweng, with youth activists in several villages in Sekhukhuneland but mostly in the twin villages of Apel-GaNkoane, and with former youth activists from Sekhukhuneland who were living in Johannesburg. I also consulted some teachers and ANC veterans in Sekhukhuneland, but most of the interviews were with youth activists—that is, young men in the age group of twenty to about thirty-five years. Most interviews were conducted in English, but occasionally some informants assisted as interpreters. I was largely unsuccessful in my attempts to interview girls and young women, who were much more reluctant and less fluent in English. As a result, chapter 3, "From Confusion to Lusaka," is not so much a narrative of events as an attempt to capture an example of rural revolt as it was experienced by young activists. During my visits to Sekhukhuneland I had the good fortune to enjoy the hospitality of Mrs. Gertrude Nchabeleng, widow of the murdered UDF president. Her sons and daughters were most helpful in my endeavors. I am particularly indebted to Maurice Nchabeleng, who was a patient and resourceful companion, both in the Northern Transvaal and in Johannesburg.

Kagiso

In the search for UDF affiliates that can be regarded as fairly typical of mainstream UDF organizations, a civic association seemed an obvious choice. The decision to take a closer look at the civic association in Kagiso, the township adjoining Krugersdorp, was largely inspired by the availability of source material and the accessibility of the township. A first glance at the Krugersdorp Residents Organisation (KRO) was obtained from an Oral History Project undertaken by five students of Khanya College in Johannesburg. One of these students, George Moilea, served as secretary on the KRO executive from 1981 until 1983. He has been very helpful in providing me with background information on KRO and Kagiso. Next I found that there was a substantial amount of documentation on KRO in the archives of the Historical Papers section of the University of the Witwatersrand. In early 1986, KRO had initiated legal proceedings against the minister of law and order to obtain an interdict ordering the police to stop their harassment of Kagiso residents. Both parties in this trial produced a sizable amount of evidence, ranging from affidavits and press cuttings to minutes of meetings, notebooks, and the transcripts of phone conversations by KRO leaders that had been tapped by the police. These trial documents provided much of the source material for this case study.

A first attempt to supplement this source material with interviews with past and present civic leaders in Kagiso had to be abandoned because of the outbreak of the "township war" in August 1990. Over forty Kagiso residents died in a series of attacks by Inkatha fighters who had taken over one of the migrant hostels as an operating base. In November 1990, when calm had returned, I was able to interview several civic activists in Kagiso. Because of the security situation it was not feasible to actually live in Kagiso for some weeks, as had been my initial plan. Interviews were conducted in Kagiso and Johannesburg. During my second period of fieldwork in 1991, I planned to continue this series of interviews. Meanwhile I found that I was not alone in my interest in the history of the Krugersdorp Residents Organisation. Jeremy Seekings (now at Cape Town University) had already written a conference paper on Kagiso that was largely based on the same source material. His doctoral thesis on the transition from quiescence to confrontation in the PWV (Pretoria-Witwatersrand-Vereeniging) townships also contains much information on KRO and Kagiso. He generously shared ideas and information. The chapter on Kagiso owes much to these two publications.

A second series of interviews with KRO leaders was subsequently conducted in November 1991 in Kagiso and Johannesburg, although new outbreaks of political violence meant that appointments were frequently canceled or postponed. The portrait of KRO is inevitably incomplete. Not all the main actors were available for interviews. With one exception—an interview with members of a rivaling civic—I have made no attempt to conduct interviews with residents who had not been KRO activists. One of the notable blank spots is the experience of hostel dwellers in the mid-1980s. In the period of my research, the two hostels in Kagiso had been taken over by Inkatha. Most of the original inmates had left the hostels, and in the limited time available I was not able to trace them.

There is a large gap for the period between May 1986 and 1989. During this time the KRO leadership was in detention or banned from entering Kagiso. However, the general impression is that due to heavy repression there was not much civic activity during these years.

Grassroots

One peculiar characteristic of the UDF was the creative use of a great variety of media. In the history of African liberation struggles, such a massive out-pouring of publications is surely unparalleled and deserving of closer scrutiny.

The community newspaper *Grassroots* in the Cape Peninsula was not just the first of its kind; it was also the best documented alternative paper of the 1980s. The *Grassroots* staff produced abundant documentation for its overseas sponsors, kept minutes of meetings, produced annual reports, and engaged in an almost incessant process of evaluation. *Grassroots*'s own documentation was rather scattered, as the newspaper survived a fire, police raids, and a removal. But its main and most loyal financial backer, the church-based NGO ICCO (Organisation for Development Cooperation) in the Netherlands, neatly kept both the files and a nearly complete set of the newspapers from 1980 to 1990. Both ICCO and *Grassroots* have been most helpful in providing access to this documentation. I have indicated in the notes whether the documents cited were consulted at ICCO or at the *Grassroots* office in Athlone, which has since closed.

To supplement this documentation, I have interviewed media activists who worked for *Grassroots* and some civic and youth activists who used the paper as an "organizing tool" in their communities.

In all three case studies, most of the interviews were conducted with local activists—more were with the local leadership than with the rank-and-file followers. The experiences of the average "man and woman in the street" remained outside the scope of my research. In some cases, informants asked to remain anonymous. In a few instances, I have myself refrained from naming informants since the information provided by them might still be deemed sensitive. In both cases, the notes simply refer to "interviews." When referring to documents, the notes also indicate the depository. If no depository is mentioned, the documents are in the possession of the author.

Notes

Introduction

1. *Zuid-Afrika reisgids 1985* (South Africa travel guide 1985), 25.
2. *This Is South Africa*, 30.
3. Azhar Cachalia, interview, 25 Jan. 1992.
4. Oppenheimer, quoted in Saul and Gelb, *Crisis in South Africa*, 81.
5. Hyslop, "School Student Movements," 189–91.
6. The Koornhof Bills were the Black Local Authorities Act, the Orderly Movement and Settlement of Black Persons Bill, and the Black Community Development Bill. The Orderly Movement Bill was withdrawn in 1984.
7. Popo Molefe, court testimony, Delmas trial, vol. 248, 13200.
8. Anonymous speech at the National General Council of UDF, 1985, SAHA, Johannesburg.
9. Quoted in Frederikse, *Unbreakable Thread*, 160.
10. Meeting at the Sekhukhune College of Education in Apel, Sept. 1990. I was present at the meeting.
11. Johnstone, "Most Painful to Our Hearts," 8.
12. Cf. Posel, "Rethinking the 'Race-Class Debate'"; Lipton, "Debate about South Africa."
13. Boesak, *Black and Reformed*, 116.
14. *Eastern Province Herald*, 30 June 1984.
15. *Rand Daily Mail*, 8 Sept. 1984.
16. Chidester, *Shots in the Streets*, 90.
17. *Republic of South Africa Constitution Act*, no. 110, 1983, 3.
18. Preamble of Constitution, 2.
19. Chikane, *No Life of My Own*, 38.
20. Manual of the South African Police College for Advanced Training, 54, quoted in Rauch, "Policing Discourses," 6.
21. SADF publication, quoted in Chidester, *Shots in the Streets*, 93.
22. Mayson, "Christianity and Revolution," 15.
23. Letter to the South African minister of justice, quoted in Boesak, *Walking on Thorns*, 62.
24. Summary of the Kairos document in *South Africa in the 1980s*, 70.
25. *Sunday Times Extra* (Johannesburg), 26 Aug. 1984.
26. *Race Relations Survey, 1986*, 325.
27. Sitas, "Making of the 'Comrades' Movement," 637.

28. Langa, "Quiet Thunder," 27.

29. Kasrils, *"Armed and Dangerous,"* 129.

30. Boesak, speech at SACC National Conference, June 1984, in Boesak and Villa-Vicencio, *When Prayer Makes News,* 111.

31. Minutes of meeting in Alexandra, 5 Feb. 1986, *State v. Mayekiso,* quoted in Carter, "Community and Conflict," 133.

1. The UDF and South Africa in the 1980s

1. The Congress Alliance was an alliance formed in the 1950s by the ANC (which at that time had an exclusively African membership), the Indian Congresses, the (white) Congress of Democrats, the Coloured People's Congress, and the trade union federation SACTU (South African Congress of Trade Unions). Organizations and individuals adhering to the Freedom Charter are commonly referred to as *Charterist,* meaning that they subscribe to the principle of multiracialism or nonracialism, as opposed to the Africanist and Black Consciousness organizations, which as a general rule exclude whites.

2. *Survey of Race Relations, 1983,* 41.

3. O. R. Tambo, "We Must Organise Ourselves," 2–10.

4. Allan Boesak, interview, 31 Dec. 1993.

5. Boesak, *Black and Reformed,* 116. The President's Council, an advisory body to the government, had drawn up the constitutional proposals. Colored opposition to these proposals was coordinated by the Anti–President's Council Committee (anti-PC), the colored equivalent of the anti-SAIC.

6. UDF Declaration.

7. A. Tambo, *Preparing for Power,* 146.

8. Exh. V1, Delmas trial.

9. Exh. C130, Delmas trial.

10. Seekings, "Quiescence," 190.

11. "Democratic Opposition: The Progressive Movement in South Africa." Edited text of a speech delivered by Auret van Heerden to both the NUSAS Congress in Durban and a joint sitting of the AZASO General Students Council and COSAS National Council in Durban, Nov.–Dec. 1982, exh. C127, Delmas trial.

12. Anti-SAIC Congress, exh. V21, Delmas trial.

13. Memorandum to executive members from secretariat, 4 Aug. 1983, exh. C45, Delmas trial.

14. Ibid.

15. The Indian Congresses had nonracial constitutions. The TIC demonstrated its Charterist credentials with the election of African trade unionist Samson Ndou and Soweto civic leader Nthatho Motlana to the executive. The reconstitution of the Indian Congresses had the blessing of the ANC.

16. Barrell, "United Democratic Front," 11–12.

17. Foster, "The Workers Struggle—Where Does Fosatu Stand?" address to the Second FOSATU Congress, 10–11 April 1982, 12.

18. Ibid., 18.

19. Figures from a report by the National Manpower Commission, quoted in *Southscan* 6, no. 14 (12 April 1991).

20. Report of the National Conference of the United Democratic Front held 17–18 Dec. 1983 in the Feather Market Hall in Port Elizabeth, exh. AL49, Delmas trial.

21. NEC meeting held 21–22 Jan. 1984 in Pretoria, exh. F, Delmas trial.

22. On the organizational structure of the UDF, see Lodge and Nasson, *All, Here, and Now*, 52–55, 62; Popo Molefe, interview, 30 Nov. 1990.

23. Minutes of joint national secretariat and treasury, 28 April 1984, exh. C89, Delmas trial.

24. Documentation on Million Signature Campaign in Historical Papers, University of the Witwatersrand (A 1789, box 7) and in the Archives of UNISA, Pretoria.

25. Seekings, "Quiescence," 231.

26. Diar, *Sharpeville Six*, xxvi.

27. Ibid., 4. The case of the "Sharpeville Six," who months after the event were charged with the murder of Kuzwayo Jacob Dlamini, acquired international notoriety as the six were charged under the "common purpose" doctrine declaring that individual members of a crowd could be held responsible for the behavior of the mob. After a protracted trial, the six were sentenced to death but were later reprieved.

28. Seekings, "Quiescence," 70.

29. With the new classification in provinces, the PWV area was in 1995 renamed Gauteng Province.

30. Input on organisational aspects of UDF, exh. C5, Delmas trial.

31. "The Community Organisation," paper discussed at the UDF West Rand Area Committee Workshop, 22 Dec. 1984, exh. U-11–d Delmas trial; exh. C111.18, KRO trial.

32. Charge sheet, 274, Delmas trial.

33. Lodge, "People's War or Negotiation?" 52.

34. Seekings, "Quiescence," 247.

35. UDF secretarial report, 5–7 April 1985, SAHA.

36. Lodge and Nasson, *All, Here, and Now*, 53.

37. It later transpired that the clashes in the Eastern Cape had been provoked by Military Intelligence.

38. The inquest in the Goniwe case revealed that the head of the Eastern Cape command of the South African Defence Force (SADF) General Joffel van de Westhuizen (who later was head of Military Intelligence), had given orders for the "permanent removal" of Matthew Goniwe from society. SADF officers gave conflicting evidence in court as to whether this was to be understood as an order to murder or to detain Goniwe (*Weekly Mail and Guardian*, 11–17 Feb. 1994).

39. *Race Relations Survey, 1985*, 512.

40. *Race Relations Survey, 1986*, xxiv.

41. *Political Conflict*, 184.

42. Mufson, *Fighting Years*, 102–3.

43. Aitchison, "Civil War in Natal," 457–73; Paddy Kearney, interview, 6 Dec. 1990.

44. Bell, "Different Drum," 51–52.

45. UDF secretarial report of Feb. 1986, SAHA.

46. Schärf and Ngcokoto, "Images of Punishment," 341.

47. Lodge and Nasson, *All, Here, and Now,* 187.

48. UDF Report of the National Working Committee Conference held 24–25 May 1986, SAHA.

49. Lodge and Nasson, *All, Here, and Now,* 88.

50. Cook, *War against Children.* In 1987 an International Conference on Children, Repression, and the Law in Apartheid South Africa was held in Harare to alert international public opinion.

51. Sampson, *Black and Gold,* 256.

52. The UDF delegation included Murphy Morobe, Cheryl Carolus, Arnold Stofile, Mohammed Valli Moosa, and Raymond Suttner.

53. Literature on vigilantes is scarce. One contemporary document is Haysom, *Mabangalala.* On vigilantes and squatter politics in the Western Cape, see Cole, *Crossroads;* Du Toit and Gagiano, "Strongmen on the Cape Flats."

54. Mufson, *Fighting Years,* 275–77; Baynham, "Political Violence," 114.

55. *Natal Mercury,* 10 Oct. 1986; Azhar Cachalia, interview, 24–25 Jan. 1992.

56. Du Toit, "Changing Patterns"; *Political Conflict,* 116.

57. Simon Ntombela and Ephraim Nkwe, members of the SAYCO National Executive, interview, 27 April 1987.

58. "A perspective on negotiations," delivered by Murphy Morobe, acting publicity secretary of the UDF to the Transvaal Indian Congress Consultative Conference, 30 July 1989, SAHA.

59. Sparks, *Tomorrow Is Another Country.*

60. See, for example, "The future of the UDF," a memorandum by Titus Mafolo, 11 Sept. 1990, SAHA.

61. Paper on National Civic Movement, delivered at the UDF National General Council, 1–3 March 1991.

62. Allan Boesak, interview, 31 Dec. 1993.

2. *Making Sense of Events*

1. Mayekiso, *Township Politics;* Mayekiso, "Legacy of Ungovernability."

2. For a survey of the main contributions to these debates, see Van Kessel, *Aspects of the Apartheid State.*

3. The most comprehensive accounts of the UDF episode thus far are *Fighting Years* by the American journalist Steven Mufson, and *All, Here, and Now* by Tom Lodge and Bill Nasson. Martin Murray's *South Africa: Time of Agony, Time of Destiny* was published in 1987 and therefore treats only the first half of the decade. An interesting collection of articles dealing with various aspects of popular struggles is William Cobbet and Robin Cohen, *Popular Struggles in South Africa.* Anthony Marx's *Lessons of Struggle* focuses on opposition ideology, encapsulated in different central conceptions of race, nation, and class and implying different strategies. Jeremy Seekings has published numerous articles on the UDF, exploring the specific characteristics of the Front in different regions as well as highlighting aspects of the UDF's political culture.

4. These figures are quoted by Murray, *South Africa,* 354–55, but estimates of unemployment vary considerably. Seekings ("Quiescence," 50) quotes a survey by the Bureau of Market Research in which total unemployment figures for the PWV region hover around 50 percent.

5. Seekings, "Origins of Political Mobilisation," 60.

6. Bundy, "Street Sociology," 311.

7. Van der Walt report, 15.

8. Hyslop, "School Student Movements," 185.

9. Ibid., 192.

10. Saul and Gelb, *Crisis in South Africa,* 57. Their Gramsci-inspired analysis was influential among left-wing intellectuals in the 1980s.

11. Strategy and Tactics of the African National Congress, 6.

12. Barrell, "Turn to the Masses."

13. Riordan, "Great Black Shark," 14.

14. The history of Operation Vula, a secret infiltration operation to set up an underground structure inside South Africa staffed by part of the senior ANC leadership from exile, covers the period 1986 to 1990, when it was exposed by the South African police. The story is told in detail in the book *Operatie Vula* by Conny Braam, chair of the Dutch Anti-Apartheid Movement, who assisted Operation Vula by providing disguises, couriers, and safe houses in Southern Africa.

15. Marx, *Lessons of Struggle,* 139.

16. The Kagiso Trust was set up to channel funds from overseas. There is no relationship between the Kagiso Trust and the township Kagiso, which is the subject of one of the case studies. *Kagiso* is the Tswana word for "peace."

17. Azhar Cachalia, interview, 24 Jan. 1992.

18. Murphy Morobe, interview, 28 Nov. 1991.

19. Trevor Manuel, interview, 14 Feb. 1990.

20. Jonathan de Vries, interview, 12 Nov. 1991.

21. Mohammed Valli Moosa, interview, 19 Dec. 1990.

22. Quoted in Pinnock, "Popularise, Organise, Educate and Mobilise," 149.

23. Rossouw, "Some Thoughts on Redefining the Role."

24. Jacobs, "Advocacy Journalism," 43–44.

25. *Citizen,* 21 Sept. 1984.

26. Secretarial Report to UDF Conference 1991, SAHA.

27. Lodge and Nasson, *All, Here, and Now,* 55.

28. Swilling, "United Democratic Front," 97.

29. Saul and Gelb, *Crisis in South Africa.*

30. Lipton, *Capitalism and Apartheid,* 357.

31. Marx, *Lessons of Struggle.*

32. "Errors of Populism," *Isizwe* 1, no. 2 (1986), 17.

33. Ibid., 21.

34. Thornton and Ramphele, "Quest for Community," 29–31.

35. UDF memorandum: A challenge to foreign governments, foreign business, and organised South African business, 2 August 1985, SAHA.

36. Literature on the political views of migrants and squatters is scarce. Some pio-

neering studies are Sitas, "Moral Formations"; Cole, *Crossroads;* Segal, "Human Face of Violence"; Safire, "Politics and Protest"; Du Toit and Gagiano, "Strongmen on the Cape Flats"; Ramphele, *A Bed Called Home.*

37. Mohammed Valli Moosa, "The Present Conjuncture," speech for UDF workshop, 6 April 1990.

38. The treasurers on the UDF National Executive Committee in 1983–85 were Cassim Salojee and Mewa Ramgobin. From 1985 on, it was Azhar Cachalia.

39. M. J. Naidoo, interview, 5 Dec. 1990.

40. *Natal Post,* 1 May 1988, letter to the editor.

41. Yunus Mohammed, interview, 6 Dec. 1990. He was allegedly a core member of the cabal.

42. See Wentzel, *Liberal Slideway.*

43. Some of the arguments are summed up in Lambert and Webster, "Re-emergence of Political Unionism," 20–41; Friedman, *Building Tomorrow Today.*

44. Joe Foster, "The Workers' Struggle—Where Does FOSATU Stand," speech delivered in 1982.

45. COSAS message sent to the launch meeting of the Soweto Youth Congress, Dobsonville, 31 July 1983. Police transcript of video, exh. V23, Delmas trial.

46. Seekings, *Heroes or Villains,* 9.

47. Ibid., 27.

48. Brewer, *After Soweto,* 73; Carter, "'We Are the Progressives,'" 214.

49. Trevor Osterwyk and Logan Wort, interview, 9 Oct. 1991.

50. Seekings, *Heroes or Villains,* 62–64.

51. Ibid., 82–83.

52. Delmas trial, vol. 248, 13200.

53. Majola, "Beginnings of People's Power," 59–62.

54. Seekings, "'Trailing behind the Masses,'" 17.

55. Swilling, "UDF and Township Revolt," 90–113. For a critical reaction, see Friedman, "Idealised Picture of Township Organisation."

56. Meli, "South Africa," 76.

57. The phrase is from a speech by UDF acting publicity secretary Murphy Morobe to the COSATU congress in 1987, *New Era,* Sept. 1987, 6.

58. "Democracy and Government: Towards a People's Struggle." The paper was presumably written by acting publicity secretary Murphy Morobe and presented by Andrew Boraine on behalf of the UDF on 8–9 May 1987 at a conference organized by the Institute for a Democratic South Africa (IDASA), SAHA.

59. For a survey of the literature, see Beckman, "Whose Democracy?"; Buijtenhuijs and Rijnierse, *Democratization in Sub-Saharan Africa.*

3. *"From Confusion to Lusaka"*

1. The state in cross-examination of defense witness Laurine Platzky, court record, vol. 352, Delmas trial.

2. *Grassroots,* Sept. 1986.

3. UDF press package on the death of Peter Nchabeleng and the crisis in the North-ern Transvaal, 16 April 1986, SAHA.

4. *State of the Nation,* SASPU, Feb.–March 1985.

5. UDF secretarial report, April 1985, SAHA.

6. Delius, "Sebatakgomo and the Zoutpansberg Balemi Association"; Delius, "Sebatakgomo: Migrant Organization"; Delius, *Lion amongst the Cattle.*

7. Strategy and Tactics of the African National Congress, 8.

8. Kasrils, *"Armed and Dangerous,"* 287–88.

9. Delius, "Sebatakgomo: Migrant Organization"; Delius, "Migrants, Comrades and Rural Revolt"; Delius, *Lion amongst the Cattle.*

10. *State of the Nation,* SASPU, Feb.–March 1985.

11. UDF report of the National Working Committee conference, 24–25 May 1986, SAHA.

12. UDF rural report, 1987, SAHA.

13. Keenan, "Counter-Revolution as Reform," 143.

14. Delius, "Migrants, Comrades and Rural Revolt."

15. Civic activists in Lebowakgomo, interview, Aug. 1990.

16. Mönnig, *Pedi,* 290–91.

17. Rocky Williams, "Welfare and Wham: The Lebowa Experience," *Mayibuye,* Nov. 1992, 18–19.

18. Bothma, "Political Structure of the Pedi," 179; Delius, *Lion amongst the Cattle,* 141.

19. Mbeki, *South Africa,* 47.

20. Mzala, *Gatsha Buthelezi,* 224.

21. Initially, the acronym *COTRALESA* was used, but this was later changed to *CONTRALESA.*

22. *Race Relations Survey, 1987–1988,* 922.

23. *Contralesa Newsletter,* no. 1, n.d. [1990].

24. *Weekly Mail,* 25 Sept.–1 Oct. 1987; *Financial Mail,* 15 Dec. 1989.

25. Samson Ndou, interview, 21 Sept. 1990.

26. Murphy Morobe, interview, 28 Nov. 1991.

27. Zuma, "Role of the Chiefs."

28. UDF rural report.

29. The region *Northern Transvaal* was not an administrative unit in the period under study, and therefore its geographical boundaries are arbitrary. Since 1991, the Central Statistical Services used a classification of South Africa into nine development regions: region G is the Northern Transvaal. The socioeconomic data in this chapter generally refer to region G. With some modifications, this became the new province Northern Transvaal after the 1994 elections, and in 1995 it was renamed *Northern Province.* However, in the UDF regional structure, the Northern Transvaal was under-stood as a larger territory, which also included much of the Eastern Transvaal.

30. Development Bank of Southern Africa, 1992 calendar; *Financial Mail,* 18 Oct. 1991.

31. Van der Wal, *Socio-economic Indicators,* 28.

32. These unemployment figures include an unspecified number of people in the subsistence and informal sector; Development Bank, *Lebowa,* 37, 28.

33. Van der Wal, *Socio-economic Indicators,* 14–32.

34. Ibid., 23.

35. Keenan, "Counter-Revolution as Reform"; Lodge, *Black Politics,* 261–63.

36. *Star,* 29 July 1993; *Weekly Mail and Guardian,* 1–7 Oct. 1993.

37. The de facto population includes all persons physically present at the reference date, thus excluding the bulk of the migrant workers. Development Bank, *Statistical Abstracts,* 127.

38. Mönnig, *Pedi,* 4.

39. Delius, *Lion amongst the Cattle,* 142; Development Bank, *Lebowa,* 63.

40. *Star,* 5 Feb. 1986.

41. Development Bank, *Lebowa,* 59.

42. Mönnig, *Pedi,* 9; Development Bank, *Statistical Abstracts,* 145.

43. Development Bank, *Statistical Abstracts,* 145.

44. Development Bank, *Lebowa,* 61–62; *Race Relations Survey, 1987–1988,* 165; *Race Relations Survey, 1989–1990,* 514.

45. Memorandum on the changing political complexion of the Northern Transvaal region, n.d., exh. ABA26, Delmas trial.

46. Northern Transvaal Programme of Action, n.d. [probably April 1984], exh C132, Delmas trial.

47. UDF press package on the Death of Peter Nchabeleng.

48. Kasrils, *"Armed and Dangerous,"* 97.

49. Delius, *Lion amongst the Cattle,* 178–79.

50. Elleck Nchabeleng, interview, 19 Nov. 1991; also Ellis and Sechaba, *Comrades against Apartheid,* 171.

51. Joyce Mabudafasi, interview, 13 Jan. 1990, 2 Sept. 1990.

52. Gastrow, *Who Is Who,* 3:213–17; Louis Mnguni, interview, 30 Aug. 1990.

53. *Weekly Mail,* 30 May–1 June 1991.

54. *Weekly Mail,* 24–29 April 1992.

55. Quoted in Murray, *South Africa,* 291.

56. Friedman, *Building Tomorrow Today,* 476.

57. *Sunday Tribune,* 28 Aug. 1988.

58. Thabo Makunyane, interview, 29 Aug. 1990.

59. Louis Mnguni, interview, 30 Aug. 1990.

60. Interview with four members of the South African National Students' Congress (SANSCO—the successor organization to AZASO) and the Student Representative Council (SRC), Turfloop, 31 Aug. 1990; *Race Relations Survey, 1985,* 405.

61. Dewet Monakedi, interview, 6 Feb. 1990.

62. I was present at the meeting.

63. *Sowetan,* 21 July 1987.

64. Delius, *Lion amongst the Cattle,* 159–60.

65. Philip Mnisi, interview, 29 Nov. 1991.

66. *SASPU National* 6, no. 2 (June-July 1985); Application for funding for Mankweng Civic Association, Delmas trial.

67. Members of the Seshego Civic Association, interview, 19 Aug. 1990.

68. *State of the Nation,* SASPU, Oct.–Nov. 1985.

69. Lodge and Nasson, *All, Here, and Now,* 120; *Star,* 10 April 1986; *Race Relations Survey, 1986,* 661.

70. *Star,* 25, 27 Feb. 1986, 12 March 1986; *Sowetan,* 12 March 1986.

71. Tony Harding, "Resistance and Development in Rural Areas," unpublished paper, 1990.

72. *City Press,* 29 Sept. 1985.

73. *Sowetan,* 11 Dec. 1986, 14 Jan. 1987, 2 June 1988; *New Nation,* 19–25 March 1987; *City Press,* 12 April 1987.

74. *Star,* 10 April 1986.

75. *State of the Nation,* SASPU, Oct.–Nov. 1985; *SASPU National* 6, no. 2 (June/July 1985); *SASPU National* 7, no. 3 (June 1986).

76. *Rapport,* 11 May 1986.

77. *Star,* 14 May 1986.

78. *Rapport,* 11 May 1986. [*Ons eet doringdraad vir brekfis and is regser as die AWB.*]

79. *Rapport,* 11 May 1986; *Star,* 14 May 1986; *Race Relations Survey, 1986,* 664.

80. SEYO activists, interview, 15 July 1990.

81. *Sunday Times,* 11 May 1986.

82. SEYO activists, interview, 10 July 1990.

83. Statement by the South African Council of Churches on events in the Northern Transvaal and in particular on the death in detention of Peter Nchabeleng, n.d. [1986] SAHA; interview with Maurice Nchabeleng, Johannesburg, 29 Nov. 1990.

84. Luthuli Nchabeleng, interview, Nov. 1991. He had returned to South Africa in August 1991.

85. Elleck Nchabeleng, interview, 19 Nov. 1991.

86. Ibid.

87. Nelson Diale, interview, 21 Sept. 1990.

88. Philip Mnisi, interview, 29 Nov. 1991.

89. Ibid.

90. SEYO Constitution.

91. There is some confusion as to the proper name of these villages. Sometimes Apel is used as the postal address for two villages: GaNkoane and GaNchabeleng. But people from GaNchabeleng generally refer to their village as *Apel,* while people from GaNkoane refer to their village as *GaNkoane.* I have followed local usage and use the term *Apel-GaNkoane* when referring to both villages. GaNchabeleng is also the name of another village, some six miles from Apel-GaNkoane.

92. SEYO activists, interview, 10 July 1990.

93. Richard Sekonya, interview, 25 Sept. 1990.

94. Moss Mabotha, interview, 10 July 1990.

95. Richard Sekonya, interview, 25 Sept. 1990.

96. *Grassroots,* May 1987.

97. Silas Mawele Mabotha, interview, 29 July 1990.

98. SEYO activist, interview, Aug. 1990.

99. UDF press package on the death of Peter Nchabeleng.

100. Delius, *Lion amongst the Cattle,* 29; Mönnig, *Pedi,* 109–11, 314.

101. Ritchken, "Burning the Herbs," 22.

102. SEYO activist, interview, 30 July 1990; *New Nation,* 26 July 1990.

103. *Race Relations Survey, 1986,* 702.

104. Dewet Monakedi, interview, 28 Aug. 1990.

105. Maurice Nchabeleng, interview, 30 July 1990; also interviews with students at the University of Venda, Oct. 1990.

106. There were, however, other organizations of migrant workers outside the UDF. The Hostel Dwellers' Association (HDA) of the Western Cape had its origins in the ministry to migrant workers by the Anglican Church. The HDA, formed in 1983 and formally launched in 1985, was affiliated with COSATU rather than with the UDF. See Ramphele, *Bed Called Home,* 89–99.

107. *New Nation,* 13 Aug. 1986.

108. Draft Constitution of the Northern Transvaal People's Congress, n.d., SAHA. I found only a copy of the draft constitution; it seems that there was no definite constitution.

109. "Notpeco: Bridging the gap from town to village," *SASPU National* 7, no. 4 (Nov.–Dec. 1986).

110. Draft Constitution of NOTPECO.

111. Jepson Nkadimeng, interview, 2 Sept. 1990.

112. Thabo Makunyane, interview, Feb. 1990.

113. Wilfried Monama, interview, 2 Nov. 1991.

114. "Notpeco," *SASPU National* 7, no. 4 (Nov.–Dec. 1986).

115. Ibid.

116. See, for example, "UDF Speaks," *SASPU National* 7, no. 4 (Nov.–Dec. 1986).

117. Wilfried Monama, interview, 2 Nov. 1991.

118. Jepson Nkadimeng, interview, 2 Sept. 1990.

119. O'Brien T. Malindi and Maghwendzha Mphaphuli, UDF Far Northern Transvaal, interview, Sibasa, Venda, 3 Oct. 1990.

120. The actual chair was a migrant worker from Venda, who seems to have been completely overshadowed by NOTPECO's acting chair.

121. Delius, "Sebatakgomo: Migrant Organization," 614.

122. Nelson Diale, interview, 21 Sept. 1990.

123. Dewet Monakedi, interview, 28 Aug. 1990.

124. SEYO activists, interview, 15 July 1990.

125. Dewet Monakedi, interview, 6 Feb. 1990.

126. Ritchken, "Introduction to Section Four," 394.

127. Philip Mnisi, interview, 29 Nov. 1991.

128. Morwamoche Makotanyane, interview, 24 Sept. 1990. Makotanyane owned several stores in Mohlaletse, the head village of Sekhukhuneland. In 1989 he was elected to the Lebowa Parliament. He became deputy minister of education in March 1990.

129. M. W. Makgaleng, interview, Aug. 1990.

130. M. W. Makgaleng, interview, Aug. 1990; Morwamoche Makotanyane, interview, 24 Sept. 1990; Maurice Nchabeleng, interview, 30 July 1990.

131. M. W. Makgaleng, interview, Aug. 1990.

132. James Nchabeleng, interview, Aug. 1990.

133. Richard Sekonya, interview, 25 Sept. 1990.

134. Ibid.

135. Maurice Nchabeleng, interview, 30 July 1990.

136. *New Nation,* 26 March 1986.

137. *Sunday Times,* 11 May 1986.

138. *Race Relations Survey, 1986,* 663.

139. SEYO activists, interview, 10 July 1990.

140. Nelson Ramodike was the chief minister of the Lebowa Bantustan.

141. Chris Hani was chief of staff of Umkhonto we Sizwe (MC).

142. "The Spear of the Nation" in SeSotho.

143. SEYO activists, interview, 15 July 1990.

144. Richard Sekonya, interview, 25 Sept. 1990.

145. M. W. Makgaleng, interview, Aug. 1990.

146. *Sunday Times,* 20 April 1986.

147. SEYO activist, interview, 29 Nov. 1991. Unfortunately, I did not succeed in hearing the story from the point of view of the girls.

148. SEYO activist, interview, Aug. 1990.

149. Sauwe Idah Mamaganyane and Damaris Maditsi, interview, Aug. 1990.

150. Maurice Nchabeleng, interview, 30 July 1990.

151. Female high school students in Apel, interviews, Aug. 1990.

152. Joyce Mabudafasi, interview, 17 Jan. 1990.

153. Ritchken, "Experiences of Secondary Schooling."

154. Female high school students, interviews, Aug. 1990.

155. Mr. Kgopa, interview, Aug, 1990.

156. Philip Mnisi, interview, 21 Nov. 1991.

157. Female students in Apel and Mankopane, interviews, Aug. 1990.

158. Silas Mawele Mabotha, interview, 29 July 1990; Moss Mabotha, interview, Oct. 1990.

159. Female students in Apel, interviews, Aug. 1990.

160. *New Nation,* 5 Nov. 1987; *SASPU National* 6, no. 2 (March 1985).

161. Clarification was provided when discussing a draft version with Petrus and Maurice Nchabeleng, Johannesburg, 26 March 1993. For an exposé on the confusion between tribes, clans, and lineages in Southern Africa, see Kuper, *Wives for Cattle,* notably chapter 4, "States, clans, Lineages and Ruling Lines."

162. Richard Sekonya, interview, 25 Sept. 1990.

163. SEYO activists, interview, 30 July 1990.

164. Mönnig, *Pedi,* 303.

165. The Pedi *ngaka* combines various roles such as diviner, priest, medicine man, magician, and "witch doctor." The plural form is *dingaka.* In other Bantu languages this functionary is known as *nyanga, nganga,* or similar cognates.

166. Discussion with SEYO activists, Apel, Nov. 1991.

167. *Race Relations Survey, 1984,* 540.

168. Ibid. p. 539. The chieftainess died before the trial took place.

169. *Star,* 16 April 1986.

170. *Sunday Times,* 20 April 1986.

171. *Star,* 17 April 1986.

172. *Business Day,* 17 April 1986.

173. SEYO activists, interview, 10 July 1990.

174. *Business Day,* 17 April 1986; Gertrude Nchabeleng, interview, July 1990.

175. *Star,* 25 June 1987; *Race Relations Survey, 1988,* 566.

176. *Business Day,* 17 April 1986.

177. Anderson, "Keeping the Myth Alive," 38. Anderson's thesis is based on the trial records.

178. Ibid., 48. Anderson does not mention the name of Maurice Nchabeleng but instead refers to him as X.

179. Chief Phasha was quoted in *Sowetan,* 18 April 1986. He has since died, so it was not possible to get a clarification of his views. This account is based on contemporary newspaper reports and on interviews with Maurice Nchabeleng in July and Aug. 1990 and Nov. 1991 in Apel; Silas Mawele Mabotha in July 1990 in Apel; Petrus Nchabeleng, Moss Mabotha, Freddy Maphutha, Victor Monakedi, and Republic Monakedi in July 1990 in Johannesburg; Dewet Monakedi in Feb. 1990 in Pietersburg; Philip Mnisi in Nov. 1991 in Johannesburg; and a series of other, more informal discussions. In a later discussion with Petrus and Maurice Nchabeleng in March 1993, they provided some further clarifications.

180. For further details on this belief, see Hammond-Tooke, *Boundaries and Belief,* 100–103. In his research among the Kgaga, a Sotho-speaking people near Tzaneen, Hammond-Tooke found a widespread belief that killing for medicine is rife. It is believed that every shop, on its establishment, is medicated with human flesh by the burial of some body part. Another example was Venda, which in the late 1980s was shocked by a wave of ritual murders in which bodies of victims were mutilated in order to be used as medicine. These "muti murders" led local youth movements to organize manhunts in order to find the culprits and to protect the community against further harm. The alleged culprits were burned as witches.

181. Mönnig, *Pedi,* 80–97; on the ambiguity in the perceptions of the role of the ngaka, see also Schoffeleers, "Folk Christology in Africa."

182. Sekhukhune youth were by no means alone in the belief that the dingaka were able to deliver this medicine. During the bitter railway strike in 1987, union members called in a sangoma from Swaziland to administer medicine that would make them immune to police bullets. In Natal, the use of protective muti is a common practice on both sides of the battlefront. *Inyangas* in Natal have also been killed on suspicion of having used their powers to favor the other side. These examples are mentioned in the *Weekly Mail,* 23–29 March 1990.

183. Moss Mabotha, interview, 10 July 1990.

184. Wilfried Monama, interview, 2 Nov. 1991.

185. Ritchken, "Burning the Herbs"; Ritchken, "Comrades, Witches and the State"; Keenan, "Reform and Resistance"; I. Niehaus, "Witchhunting and Political Legitimacy."

186. Ritchken, "Burning the Herbs," 18.

187. Schutte, "Understanding Ritual Killings," 16; *State of the Nation,* SASPU, Feb.–March 1985.

188. Geschiere and Van de Wetering, "Marginaal," 150–54; Chidester, *Shots in the Streets,* 51.

189. Sipho Jacobs, "Burn the Witches!" *Drum,* April 1994; *Weekly Mail and Guardian,* 10–16 June 1994; *Guardian,* 22 Sept. 1994.

190. Evans, "On brûle bien les sorcières"; Evans, "'Scapegoat Intended.'" Some data on witch burnings and muti murders in Venda, Lebowa, and KwaZulu are provided in a paper by Minnaar and Payze, "Witch-Burnings and Muti Use."

191. *Citizen,* 30 Jan. 1986.

192. Silas Mawele Mabotha, interview, 29 July 1990.

193. Maurice Nchabeleng, interview, 30 July 1990.

194. SEYO activists from Mphaaneng, interview, Aug. 1990.

195. Mutwa, *Let Not My Country Die.*

196. Lelyveld, *Move Your Shadow,* 249–56.

197. Clarifications provided in March 1993.

198. These volumes were first published in 1952 and 1953. There are numerous subsequent reprints and several revised editions. I have used the 1987 reprints. These volumes belonged to the classics of the South African Communist Party.

199. Cornforth, *Materialism and the Dialectial Method,* 15.

200. Ibid., 10.

201. Ibid., 12.

202. Lenin, *The Three Sources and Three Component Parts of Marxism,* quoted in Cornforth, *Materialism and the Dialectical Method,* 14.

203. Cornforth, *Materialism and the Dialectical Method,* 28.

204. Ibid., 51.

205. Ibid.

206. "Notpeco," *SASPU National* 7, no. 4 (Nov.–Dec. 1986).

207. Ritchken, "Introduction to Section Four," 391.

208. *Grassroots,* May 1987.

209. *Race Relations Survey, 1986,* 39.

210. Thabo Makunyane, interview, Feb. 1990.

211. O'Brien T. Malindi and Maghwendzha Mphaphuli, interview, 3 Oct. 1990.

212. Louis Mnguni, interview, 30 Aug. 1990; Joyce Mabudafasi, interview, 13 Jan. 1990.

213. SAPA report, 5 March 1990, quoted in *Facts and Reports* 20 (23 March 1990).

214. UDF Northern Transvaal to UDF Head Office. Affiliates per 18 Jan. 1991, SAHA. The South African National Students Congress (SANSCO) was the successor organization to AZASO.

215. Financial statement, UDF Northern Transvaal, 1 July 1990–30 September 1990, SAHA.

215. Samson Ndou, interview, 21 Aug. 1990.

217. Samson Ndou, interview, 24 Oct. 1990.

218. *Lebowa Mirror,* 24 Aug. 1990.

219. Lawrence Phokanoka, an ANC and SACP veteran who served a sixteen-year sentence for MK activities, interview, Aug. 1990.

220. John Phahla was sentenced to thirty years in one of the 1978 terrorism trials. On his release in 1990, he was appointed ANC convenor for the Northern Transvaal.

221. Statement of the conference of the Union of Traditional Healers held at GaPhaahla, 12 Jan. 1991, SAHA.

222. John Phala, interview, 4 Nov. 1991.

223. For this warning, see *Weekly Mail*, 15–21 Feb. 1991.

224. Based on interviews conducted in November 1991. It seemed then that CON-TRADOSA had already collapsed. Interviews with Geelbooi Mmanonyane Mokgwadi, vice-chair of the Union of Traditional Healers, Schoonoord, 2 Nov. 1991; second interview on 4 Nov. 1991 in the presence of two more union members; with Moses Letokoa, Tsatana Matlala branch of the Congress of Traditional Doctors, 3 Nov. 1991; two dingaka in Mohlaletse who were summoned by the paramount chief. Most of these conversations were conducted through an interpreter. Interview with John Phala, GaPhaahla, Nov. 1991. Documents of the Union of Traditional Healers and minutes of the 12 Jan. 1991 meeting in Lobethal, SAHA, unsorted boxes. The Union of Traditional Healers purported to be a national organization, but all members of the Working Committee were from Sekhukhuneland. There was also a South African Traditional Healers Council (SATHC), which claimed to have three hundred thousand members. SATHC general secretary was Peter Erasmus, a former captain in the Rhodesian Army, who was reportedly planted in SATHC by South African military intelligence. According to a series of articles in the *Weekly Mail*, SATHC was founded in 1986 with a 300,000 Rand loan from the SADF. *Weekly Mail*, 21–27 Feb. 1992; 15–23 April 1992.

225. I was present at the launch of GaNkoane Civic Association.

4. *"Yah, God Is on Our Side"*

1. In the course of its history, KRO changed its name several times. It was formed in 1981 as the Kagiso Residents Organisation. After a merger with a community organization in the neighboring township of Munsieville, KRO was rebaptized Krugersdorp Residents Organisation, named after the white town of Krugersdorp for which both Kagiso and Munsieville served as African satellite townships. In 1990, after some years of inactivity, KRO was relaunched as the Kagiso Civic Association (KCA).

2. Estimates of the numbers of inhabitants vary considerably. According to a Kagiso council spokesperson, 73,060 people were resident in Kagiso and Munsieville in 1987. But the minister of constitutional development and planning stated in the same year in Parliament that there were 101,140 people in Kagiso and Munsieville. See Mashabela, *Townships of the PWV*, 89. The 1985 census put Kagiso's population at 42,930, while the *South African Township Annual* gives an estimate for 1987 of between 76,000 and 80,000 inhabitants. See *South African Township Annual, 1988*, 9, and *1989*, 72.

3. Figures for 1987 were taken from Mashabela, *Townships of the PWV*, 89. But again, different figures are provided by the *South African Township Annual, 1989*, which lists the statistics for 1989 as an average of 6 occupants per formal housing unit and 4.13

occupants per shack, which—given the 5,800 shacks—brings the total number of shack dwellers to nearly 24,000.

4. *South African Township Annual, 1990,* 76.

5. Mashabela, *Townships of the PWV,* 90.

6. Seekings, "Quiescence," 53.

7. Diar, *Sharpeville Six,* xxii.

8. Mashabela, *Townships of the PWV,* 88.

9. *Kagiso News* 1, no. 1 (Jan.–Feb. 1984).

10. Isaac (Ike) Genu, interview, 29 Oct. 1990.

11. "KRO Oral History." This is a paper written in 1989 by four students (including George Moiloa) of Khanya College in Johannesburg.

12. Bafana Seripe, interview, 21 Nov. 1991.

13. Uhuru Moiloa, quoted in "KRO Oral History."

14. Bafana Seripe, quoted in "KRO Oral History."

15. Bafana Seripe, interview, 21 Nov. 1991.

16. "KRO Oral History."

17. Uhuru Moiloa, quoted in "KRO Oral History."

18. KRO Constitution, exh. 5, KRO trial.

19. "KRO Oral History."

20. KRO trial, court record vol. 6.

21. "KRO Oral History."

22. Sister Bernard declined to be interviewed.

23. *The State v. Mary Bernard.* Documents for this 1983 trial are included in the documentation for the KRO trial.

24. Chikane, *No Life of My Own,* 31–33.

25. Ibid., 34–38.

26. Ike Genu, interview, 29 Oct. 1990.

27. The Kairos document is briefly discussed in the introduction to this book.

28. Chikane, *No Life of My Own,* 103–4.

29. Ibid., 5–6.

30. For example, Trevor Manuel, secretary of the UDF Western Cape, who held several portfolios in Mandela's first cabinet; Sam Ntuli, president of CAST (Civic Associations of the Southern Transvaal, who was assassinated in Oct. 1991; Shepherd Mati from COSAS.

31. This section on the YCW is largely based on YCW publications and on an interview with the following members of the YCW National Executive in Johannesburg, 11 Nov. 1991: President Pogiso Molapo, National Organizer Busang Moiloa (from Kagiso), Treasurer Jacob Modimoeng (from Oukasie near Brits), and Secretary Duma Caluzar (from the Eastern Cape). When I approached them in 1991 with a request for some background on their organization, the members of the YCW National Executive were most forthcoming, although they also expressed surprise that my other interviewees had mentioned their YCW background to me. They stated that, until recently, this was "almost unmentionable," certainly "not something that people would advertise to outsiders." This interview is subsequently referred to as the YCW interview.

32. The Young Christian Workers organization is known in Belgium and the Netherlands as the *Katholieke Arbeidersjeugd.*

33. Ntlokoa made this statement while in detention in 1978. Exh. 137, KRO trial.

34. YCW Declaration of Principles, 9 (capitalization in the original). The Marxist analysis of society was further elaborated in the International Manifesto of the Working Youth, published in 1985.

35. Ntlokoa's statement to the police in 1978, exh. 137, KRO trial.

36. From a letter by Lawrence Ntlokoa, 2 Aug. 1980, exh. 111.3, KRO trial.

37. Exh. 111.2, KRO trial.

38. "Die YCW se selfstandigheid (autonomy) in verhouding met ander groepe en organisasies" [The YCW's autonomy in relation to other groups and organizations], YCW, 1984.

39. YCW interview.

40. Ibid.

41. Ibid.

42. Tizza Moiloa, interview, 19 Nov. 1990.

43. George Moiloa became a full-time organizer for the YCW in 1983 after his resignation as KRO secretary. Interview, 13 July 1990.

44. Lawrence Ntlokoa, interview, 16 Nov. 1991; KRO trial documents.

45. Mpho Malela and Zandisile Musi, interview, 20 Nov. 1991.

46. Seekings, "Organisation and Repression," 4.

47. George Moiloa, interview, 13 July 1990.

48. Ike Genu, interview, 29 Oct. 1990.

49. Joe Makgothlo, interview, 19 Nov. 1990.

50. Serge Mokonyane, interview, 14 Nov. 1991.

51. George Moiloa, interview, 13 July 1990.

52. Ike Genu, interview, 29 Oct. 1990.

53. Letter from KRO to WRAB, 21 July 1981, exh. C2.1, KRO trial.

54. Newspaper clippings from the *Sowetan* and *Star* in KRO trial exhibits, n.d. [but probably July 1981].

55. *Sowetan,* 28 July 1981; *Star,* 30 July 1981.

56. Ike Genu, interview, 29 Oct. 1990.

57. "KRO Oral History."

58. Exh. 128, KRO trial.

59. *Star,* 30 July 1981.

60. George Moiloa, interview, 9 Feb. 1990.

61. Letter from the Ministry of Cooperation and Development to attorney Sello Monyatsi, 3 June 1983, exh. C2.1, KRO trial.

62. Ike Genu, interview, 29 Oct. 1990.

63. *The State v. Mosotho Izak Genu,* 4 July 1983. The court record is part of the evidence in the KRO trial. [*Mandela wat op Robbeneiland is. Klaarblyklik 'n gevangene.*]

64. Affidavits in the case against Izak Genu, notably a statement by Dina Nojikile, 9 March 1983, exh. 37, KRO trial.

65. George Moiloa, interview, 9 Feb. 1990.

66. "KRO Oral History."

67. Seekings, "Organisation and Repression," 4.

68. George Moiloa, interview, 13 July 1990.

69. Lawrence Ntlokoa, interview, 11 Nov. 1990.

70. Lawrence Ntlokoa, interviews, 11 Nov. 1990, 16 Nov. 1991; Joe Makgothlo, interview, 19 Nov. 1990.

71. Exh. 45, KRO trial. The literal quotation from "What Is to Be Done" reads: "Without a revolutionary theory there can be no revolutionary movement."

72. Exh. 40, KRO trial.

73. *Star,* 17 April 1985.

74. KRO press statement, exh. 47, KRO trial.

75. Minutes of KRO meeting, 31 March 1985, exh. 41, KRO trial.

76. *Sowetan,* 19 April 1985.

77. *Rand Daily Mail,* 11 Feb. 1985.

78. KRO minutes, 3 March 1985, exh. 39, KRO trial.

79. *Sowetan,* 16 Jan. 1985; *City Press,* 25 Jan. 1985; *Rand Daily Mail,* 7 March 1985.

80. *Rand Daily Mail,* 28 Jan. 1985.

81. *Rand Daily Mail,* 1 March 1985.

82. Minutes of KRO meeting, 20 March 1985, exh. 40, KRO trial.

83. Exh. 54, KRO trial.

84. KRO minutes, 3 March 1985, exh. 39, KRO trial.

85. Bafana Seripe, quoted in "KRO Oral History."

86. Nomvula Mkhize, interview, 14 Nov. 1991. Since she had married Serge Mokonyane, she was now known as Nomvula Mokonyane.

87. Ibid.

88. Federation of South African Women Transvaal Workshop, exh. U5–c, Delmas trial.

89. Ibid.

90. Exh. 38, KRO trial. The document is not dated and mentions no author; possibly it was authored by Sister Bernard.

91. Lipman, *We Make Freedom,* 130.

92. Tennessee Maleke, interview, 10 Nov. 1991.

93. Seekings, "Gender Ideology," 82.

94. Zandisile Musi, interview, 20 Nov. 1991.

95. KRO minutes, 25 May 1985, exh. 42, KRO trial.

96. Serge Mokonyane, interview, 14 Nov. 1991.

97. Exh. 42, KRO trial.

98. KRO trial, court record, vol. 5.

99. Zandisele Musi, interview, 20 Nov. 1991.

100. KRO minutes, 5 June and 12 June 1985, exh. C43, KRO trial.

101. KRO trial, court record, vol. 9.

102. Police unrest reports, exh. 57, KRO trial.

103. Serge Mokonyane, interview, 14 Nov. 1991.

104. *Star,* 17 Sept. 1985.

105. Seekings, "Organisation and Repression," 2.

106. Seekings, "Quiescence," 22.

107. Makgothlo in consultations with lawyers, vol. 3, KRO trial.

108. Evidence by Ntlokoa, court record, vol. 5, KRO trial.

109. Makgothlo in consultations with lawyers, vol. 3, KRO trial.

110. Ntlokoa in consultations with lawyers, vol. 3, KRO trial.

111. Chikane, *No Life of My Own,* 101–2.

112. Lawrence Ntlokoa, interview, 16 Nov. 1991.

113. Tizza Moiloa, interview, 19 Nov. 1990.

114. George Moiloa, interview, 13 July 1990.

115. Robert Mangope and Zweni Nyathi, interview, 28 Nov. 1991. Mangope was regional organizer of AZANYU until his arrest in June 1986. He was then sentenced to nine years for PAC activities, but on appeal the term was reduced to three years. After his release in 1989, he became a PAC official for the West Rand. He was co-opted to the KCO executive. KCO secretary Nyathi had Africanist sympathies but was not a card-carrying PAC member.

116. Ibid.

117. *Star,* 29 Nov. 1985.

118. Leaflet, "Asinamali: Black December" by the Consumer Boycott Committee, exh. C132, KRO trial; *Sunday Star,* 15 Dec. 1985.

119. *Star,* 13 Dec. 1985.

120. Makgothlo in consultations with lawyers, vol. 3, KRO trial; Seekings, "Organisation and Repression," 12.

121. Makgothlo in consultation with lawyers, KRO trial.

122. Affidavit by Makgothlo, KRO trial.

123. *Star,* 13 Dec. 1985.

124. *Star,* 11 Dec. 1985.

125. *Star,* 20 Dec. 1985.

126. *Business Day,* 18 Dec. 1985.

127. Police recordings of phone conversations, exh. 142, KRO trial. The files of the KRO trial include transcriptions of recordings of phone conversations tapped by the police, who had apparently bugged the phones of all leading activists. These files cover the period from 24 Dec. 1985 to 24 April 1986. They are subsequently referred to as "police recordings."

128. *SASPU National* 7, no. 1 (Jan. 1986).

129. Robert Mangope and Zweni Nyathi, interview, 28 Nov. 1991.

130. *Sowetan,* 13 Dec. and 20 Dec. 1985.

131. Makgothlo in consultations with lawyers, KRO trial.

132. KRO trial, affidavit by Louisa Williams.

133. Tizza Moiloa, interview, 19 Nov. 1990.

134. Evidence by Ntlokoa, court record, vol. 5, KRO trial.

135. *Star,* 3 Jan. and 7 Jan. 1986.

136. Makgothlo in consultations with lawyers, KRO trial.

137. *Star,* 7 Jan. 1986; police recordings: Ntlokoa speaking to reporter, 6 Jan. 1986, exh. 142, KRO trial.

138. Police recordings: Makgothlo phoning Ntlokoa, 6 Jan. 1986, KRO trial.

139. *Race Relations Survey, 1986,* 203.

140. Ibid.; *Sowetan,* 6 March 1986.

141. *Star,* 5 Feb. 1986.

142. *Star,* 6 Feb. 1986.

143. Police unrest reports, exh. 57, KRO trial.

144. *Race Relations Survey, 1986,* 204.

145. Serge Mokonyane, interview, 14 Nov. 1991.

146. Police recordings: *Star* phoning Ntlokoa, 24 Feb. 1986, exh. 142, KRO trial.

147. Makgothlo in consultations with lawyers, KRO trial.

148. *Star,* 26 March 1986; *Sowetan,* 2 April 1986.

149. *Star,* 7 April 1986.

150. *Star,* 10 April 1986.

151. Serge Mokonyane, interview, 14 Nov. 1991.

152. [Original in Afrikaans: *Kaffir, jy het niks om te sê nie* and *Fok of, meid.*] Ntlokoa in consultations with lawyers, vol. 3, KRO trial; also affidavits in KRO trial; *Sowetan,* 28 Jan. 1986.

153. Tennessee Maleke, interview, 10 Nov. 1991.

154. *Star,* 3 Feb. 1986; police recordings, *Star* phoning Ntlokoa, 30 Jan. 1986, exh. 142, KRO trial.

155. Mpho Malele and Zandisile Musi, interview, 20 Nov. 1991.

156. Police recordings, exh. 142, KRO trial.

157. *SASPU National* 7, no. 1 (Jan. 1986).

158. Ibid.

159. Police recordings: *Star* phoning Ntlokoa, 9 Jan. 1986, exh. 142, KRO trial.

160. *Sowetan,* 14 Jan. 1986.

161. Police recordings: various phone conversations with Ntlokoa and Sister Bernard, exh. 142, KRO trial.

162. Police recordings: phone conversation with Sister Bernard, 21 March 1986, exh. 142, KRO trial.

163. Police recordings: supermarket owner phoning Sister Bernard, 25 March and 11 April 1986, exh. 142, KRO trial.

164. Lawrence Ntlokoa, interview, 16 Nov. 1991.

165. Mpho Malele and Zandisile Musi, interview, 10 Nov. 1991.

166. Police recordings: phone conversation between Sister Bernard and Ntlokoa, 19 March 1986, exh. 142, KRO trial.

167. Police recordings: phone conversation between Makgothlo and Ntlokoa, 27 April 1986, exh. 142, KRO trial.

168. Sister Bernard in consultations with lawyers, vol. 2, KRO trial.

169. Counsel for the minister of law and order, court record, vol. 8, KRO trial; interview with Ike Genu, 29 Oct. 1990.

170. Makgothlo in consultations with lawyers, vol. 2, KRO trial.

171. Evidence by Ntlokoa, court record, vol. 5, KRO trial.

172. *Sunday Star,* 9 March 1986; also Seekings, "Organisation and Repression," n. 50.

173. *Sunday Star,* 9 Feb. 1986.; *Star,* 14 Feb. 1986.

174. Police recordings: *Star* phoning Ntlokoa, 24 Feb. 1986, exh. 142, KRO trial.

175. Ike Genu, interview, 29 Oct. 1990.

176. Affidavit by Lawrence Nanne, KRO trial.

177. Affidavit by Makgothlo, KRO trial.

178. *City Press,* 2 Feb. 1986.

179. *Race Relations Survey, 1986,* 545.

180. *Vaderland,* 31 Jan. 1986.

181. *Star,* 24 Feb. 1986.

182. *Krugersdorp News-Nuus,* 17 Jan. 1986.

183. *Vaderland,* 25 Feb. 1986 [*Sowaar as die Here*]; *Beeld,* 25 Feb. 1986.

184. *Sunday Star,* 9 March 1986.

185. Medical reports, exh. 2.3, KRO trial.

186. *Sunday Star,* 9 March 1986; *Race Relations Survey, 1986,* 545.

187. *Sowetan,* 10 April 1986.

188. *Beeld,* 21 March 1986; *Star,* 22 and 23 March 1986.

189. Seekings, "Organisation and Repression," 18.

190. *Star,* 18 Feb. 1986; *Beeld,* 18 Feb. 1986.

191. *Race Relations Survey, 1986,* 864.

192. Ibid., 514.

193. Evidence by Ntlokoa, court record, vol. 5, KRO trial.

194. Seekings, "Organisation and Repression," 19.

195. Ntlokoa in consultations with lawyers, vol. 2, KRO trial.

196. Joe Makgothlo, interview, 19 Nov. 1990.

197. Serge Mokonyane, interview, 14 Nov. 1991.

198. *Sowetan,* 20 March 1986.

199. Joe Makgothlo, interview, 19 Nov. 1990.

200. Jerry Kgofela, interview, 10 Nov. 1991. He served on the DC.

201. Police recordings: various phone conversations, March–April 1986, KRO trial.

202. Robert Mangope and Zweni Nyathi, interview, 28 Nov. 1991; Jerry Kgofela, interview, 10 Nov. 1991.

203. Police recordings: phone conversations with Sister Bernard, 27 March 1986, exh. 142, KRO trial.

204. Interview.

205. Interview.

206. Interview.

207. Exh. 45. KRO trial.

208. Photo exh., KRO trial.

209. Makgothlo in consultations with lawyers, KRO trial.

210. Exh. 76 and exh. 106, KRO trial.

211. *Rapport,* 2 March 1986. [*Die kinders ruim rommel op, hou die strate skoon. Die betreklik netjiese parkies heet Biko Park, Nelson Mandela Park en "the Fallen Heroes." Die verklaarde doel van al hul bedrywighede is om daarmee te probeer sê dat hulle doeltreffender as die stadsrade is.*]

212. Ibid.

213. Affidavits by residents, KRO trial.

214. Makgothlo in consultations with lawyers, vol. 3, KRO trial.

215. *Sunday Star,* April 1986.

216. Carter makes a similar observation in an article on Alexandra. See Carter, "Community and Conflict."

217. Chikane, *No Life of My Own,* 103–4.

218. *SASPU National* 7, no. 1 (1986).

219. YCW activist, interview.

220. Ibid.

221. Lawrence Ntlokoa, interview, 11 Nov. 1990.

222. Mpho Malela and Zandisile Musi, interview, 20 Nov. 1991.

223. Serge Mokonyane, interview, 14 Nov. 1991.

224. Baskin, *Striking Back,* 353.

225. NACTU (National Confederation of Trade Unions) had been formed as a result of the merging of Africanist and BC unions.

226. There is disagreement about the origins of KCO. Although KCO activists maintain that their civic organization was constituted in 1984, the members of KRO insist that KCO was not formed until 1989.

227. Tizza Moiloa, interview, 19 Nov. 1990; Serge Mokonyane, interview, 14 Nov. 1991.

228. Robert Mangope and Zweni Nyathi, interview, 28 Nov. 1991.

229. Letter from Kagiso residents to Kagiso Town Council, 2 Dec. 1989; minutes of KICC meeting, n.d.

230. Ike Genu, interview, 29 Oct. 1990.

231. Tizza Moiloa, interview, 19 Nov. 1990.

232. Draft constitution of the Krugersdorp Civic Association, n.d. [1990]; Lawrence Ntlokoa, interview, 16 Nov. 1991; Ike Genu, interview, 29 Oct. 1990; Tizza Moiloa, interview, 19 Nov. 1990.

233. *Daily Mail,* 7 Aug. 1990; *Weekly Mail* 24–26 Aug. 1990; *Star,* 7, 8, 22, and 23 Aug. 1990, 3 Sept. 1990; Ike Genu, interview, 29 Oct. 1990; Ntlokoa, interview, 11 Nov. 1990.

234. *Race Relations Survey, 1991–92,* 324 and 505.

235. *Weekly Mail,* 17–23 May 1991; Minnaar, "Hostels and Violent Conflict," 18.

236. *Star,* 19 and 20 Nov. 1991; *Sowetan,* 20 Nov. 1991; personal communication with Uhuru Moiloa, 20 Nov. 1991.

5. Grassroots

1. Tomaselli, "Progressive Press," 163.

2. Maree, "General Workers' Union," 128–48.

3. Cole, *Crossroads,* 40.

4. Ibid., 82.

5. Nasson, "Opposition Politics and Ideology," 93.

6. Alexander, "Non-collaboration in the Western Cape," 187.

7. Pillay, "Trade Unions and Alliance Politics"; Maree, "General Workers' Union."

8. Francis, "UDF in the Western Cape."

9. Maree, "General Workers' Union," 147.

10. See, for example, the concluding part of Nasson's chapter on the Western Cape in Lodge and Nasson, *All, Here, and Now,* 232.

11. Lenin, "Where to Begin," 20.

12. Ibid., 22.

13. Lenin, "What Is to Be Done?" 375.

14. Johnny Issel, interview, 16 Oct. 1991.

15. Ibid.

16. Youth activist, interview, Oct. 1991.

17. UDF leader, interview, Nov. 1991.

18. Leila Patel quoted in Orford, "*Grassroots* 1980–1984."

19. Badat, "Political Importance and Achievements."

20. Ibid.

21. Johnny Issel, interview, 16 Oct. 1991.

22. Saleem Badat, interview, 2 Oct. 1991.

23. Shaun Johnson, "Resistance in Print I," 194.

24. Rehana Rossouw, interview, 11 Oct. 1991.

25. *Grassroots,* June 1981.

26. *Grassroots,* Aug. 1984, Feb. 1985.

27. Jonathan de Vries, interview, 12 Nov. 1991.

28. Ibid.

29. Issel, "Setting up *Grassroots.*"

30. *Grassroots,* April 1984. [*Ons sien oral in die koerante hoedat mense probeer om hierdie man se naam sleg te maak. Ons vra aan die mense: hoe maak jy die naam sleg van iemand wat die geestelike vader van 700 miljoen Christene is?*]

31. *UDF News, Nuusblad van Suid-Wes Kaap,* n.d. [1984]. [*'n Wêreld-leier praat*]

32. Project description, Saamstaan Publikasies, 1984, ICCO. *Saamstaan* also received funding from church-based NGOs in the Netherlands.

33. *Grassroots,* Aug. 1984. [*Dit is 'n keuse wat berus op die evangelie van Jesus Christus.*]

34. *Kleurlinge kan nie saamstaan nie.*

35. *Grassroots* project description, n.d. [1983?], ICCO.

36. Rashid Seria, interview, 15 Feb. 1990.

37. Lenin, "What Is to Be Done?" 355.

38. Andrew Boraine, interview, 26 Nov. 1991.

39. Rehana Rossouw, interview, 11 Oct. 1991.

40. Wilfred Rhodes, interview, 22 Oct. 1991.

41. An editorial board was formed, which included seven people who from the beginning had been involved in the newspaper project: Dr. Jakes Gerwel, lecturer at the University of the Western Cape, who in the next decade was to become rector of UWC and a leading light in the ANC and the SACP; the Reverend Moses Moletsane, a priest in the African township of Langa; Dr. Ramsey Karelse, a psychiatrist; Essa Moosa, an attorney; James Matthews, former executive member of the UBJ, writer,

and poet; Qayoum Sayed, printer, publisher, and former UBJ member; and Rashid Seria, journalist and former UBJ member. In addition, three new people were included on the board: Dr. Allan Boesak, chaplain at UWC; Aneez Salie, journalist and chair of the Writers' Association of South Africa (WASA); and Moegsien Williams, journalist, secretary of the WASA executive, and later the first editor of *South*. This board acted as a board of trustees. Once the paper was on its feet, the board resigned to be succeeded by a central committee representing the participating organizations.

42. Essa Moosa, interview, 22 Oct. 1991.

43. ICCO *notitie*, 1987. ICCO also provided financial support to SASPU and *Ukusa*, a community paper in Durban, and later to *South*. *Saamstaan* was funded by the Vastenaktie, a solidarity organization that was run by the Catholic Church in the Netherlands and that funded third-world projects. Toward the end of the decade, the European Community set up a fairly substantial program of financial support for alternative media in South Africa, which benefited such publications as *New Nation*, *Vrye Weekblad*, *Weekly Mail*, and *South*.

44. Report on *Grassroots*' policy directives for AGM, March 1982, *Grassroots*.

45. *Grassroots* chairperson's report, 1980, ICCO.

46. *Grassroots* project description, n.d. [1983?], ICCO.

47. Ryland Fisher, interview, 2 Oct. 1991. Fisher was the *Grassroots* news and production organizer from 1984 to 1987. He then went to work for bigger alternative papers such as *New Nation* and *South* until 1990, when he joined one of South Africa's largest commercial papers, the *Sunday Times*, which planned to launch a new edition aiming at a colored readership in the Western Cape. At the same time, however, he remained involved in *Grassroots*.

48. *Grassroots* news/production officer's report, 1980, ICCO.

49. *Grassroots* secretarial report, 18 Jan. 1981, ICCO.

50. Report of the fund-raising committee investigating all aspects of *Grassroots* community newsletter, 18 Jan. 1981, ICCO.

51. *Grassroots*, March 1982.

52. Ibid.

53. Notes from conversation between ICCO representative and Rashid Seria, *Grassroots* secretary and treasurer, 25 Oct. 1982, ICCO.

54. Report of the investigation committee to *Grassroots* publications, second AGM, March 1982, *Grassroots*.

55. News-gathering committee report for AGM, March 1982, *Grassroots*.

56. *Grassroots*, May 1982.

57. Ibid.

58. *Grassroots*, June 1983.

59. *Grassroots*, Oct. 1982. [*'n onnodige rondgooi van groot woorde. . . . Dit is meer soos 'n University lecture as 'n grassroots meeting. Hoekom praat hulle nie dat 'n mens kan verstaan nie.*]

60. Organiser's report for *Grassroots* meeting, 5 Sept. 1980, *Grassroots*.

61. Lynn Matthews, interview, 10 Oct. 1991.

62. *Grassroots*, June 1983.

63. Statement by the Manenberg Civic Association, Parkwood Tenants Association and BBSK Residents Association, n.d. [1983], CACE, UWC; draft reply to the statement by BBSK, Parkwood and Manenberg on their withdrawal, n.d. [1983], CACE, UWC.

64. Ryland Fisher, interview, 2 Oct. 1991.

65. *Grassroots* project description, n.d. [1983], ICCO.

66. Leila Patel, "The Way Forward," *Grassroots* AGM, 1983, *Grassroots*.

67. Ibid.

68. *Grassroots,* Nov. 1987.

69. Essa Moosa, interview, 22 Oct. 1991.

70. Organizer's report, Feb. 1984, ICCO.

71. Chairperson's address, AGM, 27 April 1985, *Grassroots*.

72. Mampe Ramotsamai, interview, 8 Oct. 1991.

73. Ibid.

74. Ibid.

75. Trevor Osterwyk and Logan Wort, interview, 9 Oct. 1991; Trevor Osterwyk, interview, 17 Oct. 1991.

76. Report of the investigation committee to *Grassroots* publications, second AGM, March 1982, *Grassroots*.

77. Zollie Malindi, interview, 21 Oct. 1991.

78. Organizer's report, AGM, 1983, *Grassroots*.

79. Mildred Leseia, interview, 7 Oct. 1991.

80. Township report, 1984 and 1985, *Grassroots*.

81. Velishwa Mhlawuli, interview, 16 Oct. 1991.

82. Ryland Fisher, interview, 2 Oct. 1991.

83. *Grassroots,* Dec. 1980.

84. *Grassroots,* May 1982.

85. *Grassroots,* June 1985.

86. *Grassroots,* Dec. 1982.

87. Trevor Osterwyk and Logan Wort, interview, 9 Oct. 1991.

88. David Lewis, interview, 23 Oct. 1991.

89. News-gathering committee report, April 1984, *Grassroots*.

90. Secretarial report, AGM, 1983, *Grassroots*.

91. Organizer's report, 5th AGM, 1985, ICCO.

92. Trevor Osterwyk and Logan Wort, interview, 9 Oct. 1991.

93. *Grassroots,* June 1984.

94. *Grassroots,* Nov. 1984. [*Ek het by die stembus gestaan. Ek het die bybel en die stemmery by mekaar gebring—tussen daar's 'n gaping. Toe bring ek die UDF en die bybel saam—dis net kontak! Toen gaan ek verby die stembus.*]

95. *Grassroots,* Dec. 1983.

96. *Grassroots* secretarial report, Oct. 1983, ICCO.

97. CAYCO secretarial report, 20 April 1985, CACE.

98. For the UDF's handling of the Crossroads crisis, see Cole, *Crossroads*.

99. News and production report, AGM, April 1985, ICCO.

100. UDF Western Cape treasurer Andrew Boraine, quoted in Francis, "UDF in the Western Cape."

101. Jonathan de Vries, interview, 12 Nov. 1991.

102. Joe Marks, interview, 15 Oct. 1991. In the interview, Marks kept repeating the word *polatiek,* with a look of disgust, to make it clear that "politics" was considered bad taste among ordinary colored folks.

103. *Grassroots,* Nov. 1984.

104. Ryland Fisher, interview, 2 Oct. 1991.

105. Saleem Badat, interview, 2 Oct. 1991.

106. See, for example, *Learning Roots,* Feb. 1986.

107. "Which way forward?" by *Grassroots* organizer [Saleem Badat], assessment report by *Grassroots,* Sept. 1984, ICCO.

108. *Grassroots,* June 1983.

109. *Grassroots,* Feb. 1985.

110. *Grassroots,* Aug. 1984.

111. Lynn Matthews, interview, 10 Oct. 1991.

112. *Grassroots* secretarial report, 1983, ICCO.

113. WACC evaluation report, Oct. 1984, ICCO.

114. Chairperson's report, assessment meeting, Oct. 1983, ICCO.

115. Rehana Rossouw, interview, 11 Oct. 1991.

116. Andrew Boraine, interview, 26 Nov. 1991.

117. Coleman and Webster, "Repression and Detentions," 116.

118. Trevor Manuel, interview, 14 Feb. 1990.

119. Johnny Issel, interview, 16 Oct. 1991.

120. Fahdiel Manuel, interviews, 15 July 1991, 22 Oct. 1991.

121. *Grassroots,* Nov. 1985.

122. Trevor Osterwyk, interview, 17 Oct. 1991.

123. Willie Simmers, interview, 8 Oct. 1991.

124. Rehana Rossouw, interview, 11 Oct. 1991.

125. Ryland Fisher, interview, 2 Oct. 1991.

126. *Grassroots,* March 1986.

127. *Grassroots,* Feb. 1986.

128. *Grassroots,* May 1986.

129. Saleem Badat, "Building the People's Press Is Also Building People's Power," AGM, 1986, *Grassroots.*

130. *Grassroots,* March 1985.

131. *Learning Roots,* Nov. 1988.

132. *Grassroots,* Oct. 1986.

133. *Grassroots,* Dec. 1986.

134. *Grassroots,* May 1986.

135. *New Era,* March–April 1986.

136. *New Era,* Nov. 1987.

137. *New Era,* March 1990.

138. *Grassroots,* May 1986.

139. Schärf and Ngcokoto, "Images of Punishment," 341–71.

140. *Grassroots,* May 1986.

141. *Grassroots,* Aug. 1986.

142. Secretarial report, *Grassroots* AGM, 1986, ICCO.

143. *Cape Times,* 4 Nov. 1985.

144. *Grassroots* assessment, Dec. 1988, ICCO.

145. Fahdiel Manuel, interview, 22 Oct. 1991.

146. Ibid.

147. *Grassroots* assessment, 1989, ICCO.

148. Fahdiel Manuel, interview, 11 Oct. 1991.

149. I was present at the meeting.

150. Joe Marks, interview, 15 Oct. 1991.

151. Saleem Badat, interview, 2 Oct. 1991.

152. Ibid.

153. Johnny Issel, interview, 16 Oct. 1991.

154. Willie Simmers, interview, 8 Oct. 1991.

155. Zollie Malindi, interview, 21 Oct. 1991.

156. Joe Marks, interview, 15 Oct. 1991. Marks left the ANC and the SACP in 1993 and joined the Democratic Party, explaining that he was thoroughly disillusioned with the ANC's disregard for the concerns of ordinary people and the lack of internal democracy. See *Vrye Weekblad,* 2 April 1993.

157. Rehana Rossouw, interview, 11 Oct. 1991. Rossouw later moved on to the *Mail and Guardian.*

158. Rossouw, "Some Thoughts."

159. Hilda Ndude, interview, 23 Oct. 1991.

Conclusion

1. For Zimbabwe, see Ranger, *Revolt in Southern Rhodesia;* Ranger, "Death of Chaminuka"; Ranger, *Peasant Consciousness;* Lan, *Guns and Rain;* Werbner, *Tears of the Dead;* Kriger, *Zimbabwe's Guerrilla War.* A tentative discussion that does include South Africa is found in Huizer, "Folk Spirituality," which presents a review of some of the relevant literature.

2. A stimulating essay on this subject is Du Toit, "Understanding South African Political Violence."

3. Setiloane, "Salvation and the Secular," 77.

4. Exh. AL49, Delmas trial.

5. UDF Western Cape REC secretary Cheryl Carolus, quoted in Francis, "UDF in the Western Cape," 40.

6. Allan Boesak, interview, 31 Dec. 1993.

7. *Sowetan,* 17 Nov. 1994.

8. Werbner, *Tears of the Dead.* The notion that the witches in Sekhukhuneland were deemed guilty as *impimpis* (traitors) appeared only in newspaper coverage, not in my local interviews.

9. Methodist Hymn Book 548, quoted in Setiloane, "Salvation and the Secular," 76 (emphasis added).

10. African Spiritual Churches Association, *Speaking for Ourselves* (Braamfontein, South Africa: ASCA, 1985), 21, quoted in Huizer, "Folk Spirituality," 49–50.

11. Chikane, *No Life of My Own,* 103–4.

12. Fanon, *Wretched of the Earth,* 45.

13. A. Tambo, *Preparing for Power,* 151.

14. This issue is discussed in Schoffeleers, "Review Article: Peasants, Mediums and Guerillas," 147–52.

15. Leys and Saul, "Liberation without Democracy?"

16. *City Press,* 21 Jan. 1986, quoted in Cock, *Colonels and Cadres,* 37.

17. Beall, "African Women," 101; Cock, *Colonels and Cadres,* 182.

18. As illustrated by Seekings, *Heroes or Villains?* Sitas, "Making of the 'Comrades' Movement"; Naidoo, "Politics of Youth Resistance."

19. Naidoo, "Politics of Youth Resistance," 150.

20. Mohammed Valli Moosa, interview, 19 Dec. 1990.

21. Oscar Gumede, "My Life as a Comrade," *Weekly Mail,* 30 May–6 June 1991.

22. *Star,* 10 May 1994.

23. *Beeld,* 11 May 1994. [*Pres. Nelson Mandela ingehuldig voor die hele SA en die wêreld; "Laat vryheid regeer."*]

24. *Die Volksblad* is quoted in Setiloane, "Spirit of Africa," 14. [*Wat 'n politieke gebeurtenis moes gewees het, het in 'n geestelijke ervaring verander. . . . Swart, wit, bruin en Indiër Suid-Afrikaners is getransformeer—hulle het mekaar ontdek.*]

Bibliography

Depositories

African Studies Institute, University of Cape Town Centre for Adult and Continuing Education (CACE), University of the Western Cape

Daily News Library, Durban

Grassroots, Athlone

Historical and Literary Papers Library of the University of the Witwatersrand, Johannesburg. Collections consulted in this library include:

The Krugersdorp Residents Organisation and four others versus the Minister of Law and Order, referred to in the text as "KRO trial," catalogue number AK 2145

The State versus Patrick Mabuya Baleka and twenty-one others, referred to in the text as the "Delmas trial," catalogue number AK 2117

Various boxes with UDF material, catalogue number A 1789

Inkatha Institute, Durban

Inter Church Organisation for Development Cooperation (ICCO), Zeist (the Netherlands)

Mayibuye Centre, University of the Western Cape

The South African History Archives (SAHA), Johannesburg

South African Institute of Race Relations (SAIRR), Johannesburg

Star Library, Johannesburg

University of South Africa (UNISA), Pretoria

Werkgroep Kairos, Utrecht (the Netherlands)

Interviews

Saleem Badat, *Grassroots* organizer, 1983–86

Guy Berger, editor, *New Era* and later *South*

Allan Boesak, patron of the UDF; chair, ANC Western Cape, 1991–94

Andrew Boraine, NUSAS president, 1980–81; treasurer, UDF Western Cape, 1983–85; member, UDF National Executive Committee (NEC)

Azhar Cachalia, treasurer of the UDF NEC, 1985–91

Firoz Cachalia, Transvaal Indian Congress

Phiroshaw Camay, secretary general, CUSA

Cheryl Carolus, secretary, UDF Western Cape, 1983–91

Moss Chikane, secretary, UDF Regional Executive Committee (REC), Transvaal, 1983–85

Josette Cole, representative, The Ecumenical Action Movement (TEAM), UDF Western Cape

Speedo Dau, interim committee, UDF Northern Transvaal

Nelson Diale, advice office, Jane Furse, Sekhukhuneland

Sandile Dikene, Student Representative Council, University of the Western Cape

A. Docrat, veteran Indian activist, Durban

George Du Plessis, member, UDF NEC, 1983–85

Zora Ebrahim, civic activist, Cape Housing Action Committee

Federation of Cape Civic Associations (FCCA)

Ryland Fisher, news and production organizer, *Grassroots,* 1984–87

Isaac Genu, vice chair, KRO

Johnny Issel, organizer, *Grassroots,* 1980

Adli Jacobs, *New Era*

Mansoor Jaffer, news and production coordinator, *Grassroots,* 1983–88

Zubeida Jaffer, volunteer, *Grassroots,* 1980–85

Essop Jassat, chair, Transvaal Indian Congress

Joe Jele, secretary, ANC Political-Military Committee

Paddy Kearney, member, UDF REC Natal, 1983–85

Jerry Kgofela, member, Disciplinary Committee

Mr. Kgopa, principal, Mankopane High School

Mildred Leseia, United Women's Organisation

Moses Letoka, Tsatane branch, Congress of Traditional Doctors

David Lewis, secretary general, General Workers' Union

Lucas [no surname given], SEYO; teacher, Apel high school, Sekhukhuneland

Moss Mabotha, SEYO

Silas Mawele Mabotha, secretary general, SEYO, 1986

Joyce Mabudafhasi, secretary, UDF Northern Transvaal

Damaris Maditsi, high school student, Apel, Sekhukhuneland

Desmond Mahasha, trade unionist

M. W. Makgaleng, chair, Sekhukhune Parents' Crisis Committee

Joe Makgothlo, chair, KRO, 1981–89

Morwamoche Makotanyane, secretary, Sekhukhune Parents' Crisis Committee

Thabo Makunyane, vice-chair, UDF Northern Transvaal

Tennessee Maleke, treasurer, Kagiso branch, FEDTRAW

Mpho Malela, chair, KAYCO

O'Brien T. Malindi, Far Northern Transvaal Coordinating Committee of the UDF, Sibasa, Venda

Zollie Malindi, president, UDF Western Cape, 1985–91

Sauwe Idah Mamaganyane, high school student, Apel, Sekhukhuneland

Robert Mangope, AZANYU regional organizer, Pan-Africanist Congress

Fahdiel Manuel, organizer, *Grassroots,* 1988–91

Trevor Manuel, secretary, UDF Western Cape, 1983–91

Freddy Maputha, SEYO, Turfloop

Philemon Maputha, Masemola Youth Congress

Joe Marks, vice-president, UDF Western Cape, 1983–85

Lynn Matthews, secretary, *Grassroots* executive; convenor, news-gathering
    committee, 1981–85

Velishwa Mhlawuli, township organizer, *Grassroots,* 1985–90

Louis Mnguni, chair, UDF Northern Transvaal

Philip Mnisi, SEYO.

Maghwendzha Mphaphuli, Far Northern Transvaal Coordinating Committee of the
    UDF, Sibasa, Venda

Ismail Mohamed, chair, Anti-President's Council Committee

Yunus Mohammed, secretary, UDF REC Natal; member, UDF NEC; trustee,
    Kagiso Trust

George Moiloa, secretary, KRO, 1981–83

Tizza Moiloa, vice-chair, KRO, 1990–

Geelbooi Mmanonyane Mokgwadi, vice-chair, Union of Traditional Healers

Nomvula [Mkhize] Mokonyane, representative of FEDTRAW, KRO general council

Serge Mokonyane, trade union representative, KRO

Popo Molefe, general secretary, UDF, 1983–91

Dewet Monakedi, publicity secretary, SEYO

Republic Monakedi, SEYO

Victor Monakedi, SEYO

Wilfried Monama, acting chair, NOTPECO

Strini Moodley, publicity officer, AZAPO

Essa Moosa, attorney; chair, *Grassroots* executive

Mohammed Valli Moosa, acting secretary, UDF, 1985–90

Murphy Morobe, acting publicity secretary, UDF, 1985–90

Zandisile Musi, COSAS, KAYCO

M. J. Naidoo, vice president, Natal Indian Congress until 1987

Elleck Nchabeleng, Apel, Sekhukhuneland

Gertrude Nchabeleng, Apel, Sekhukhuneland

James Nchabeleng, veteran Sebatakgomo and ANC activist

Lizzy Nchabeleng, Apel, Sekhukhuneland

Luthuli Nchabeleng, Apel, Sekhukhuneland

Maurice Nchabeleng, SEYO

Petrus Nchabeleng, SEYO

Samson Ndou, vice-president, UDF Southern Transvaal, 1985–89; director of projects, CONTRALESA

Hilda Ndude, township organizer, *Grassroots,* 1983–85

Don Nkadimeng, chair, AZAPO Northern Transvaal, 1989–90, then secretary-general, AZAPO

Jepson Nkadimeng, secretary, NOTPECO

Ephraim Nkwe, SAYCO National Executive

Lawrence Ntlokoa, secretary, KRO, 1984–90

Simon Ntombela, SAYCO National Executive

Zweni Nyathi, secretary, Kagiso Civic Organisation

Trevor Osterwyk, president, CAYCO, 1983–84

N. G. Patel, Transvaal Indian Congress, participant, Anti-SAIC conference

John Phala, ANC convenor, Northern Transvaal

Lawrence Phokanoka, ANC and MK veteran

Mampe Ramotsamai, Women's Front

Wilfred Rhodes, chair, CAHAC, 1981–88; then organizer, CAHAC

Rehana Rossouw, journalist, volunteer worker, *Grassroots*

Frangelina Sekhukhune, chair, ANC branch Apel-GaNkoane, Sekhukhuneland

K. K. Sekhukhune, acting paramount chief, Mohlaletse

Richard Sekonya, SEYO

Rashid Seria, journalist, treasurer, *Grassroots* executive

Bafana Seripe, YCW national president, 1982–84; KRO, 1981–82 and 1990–

Willie Simmers, Mitchell's Plain Civic Association

Jonathan de Vries, publicity secretary, UDF Western Cape, 1983–85

Logan Wort, CAYCO

Young Christian Workers: Pogiso Molapo (president), Busang Moiloa (national organizer), Jacob Modimoeng (treasurer), Duma Caluzar (secretary)

Linda Zama, lawyer, ANC REC Southern Natal

Selected Secondary Sources

Adam, Heribert. "Racist Capitalism versus Capitalist Non-racialism in South Africa." *Ethnic and Racial Studies* 7, no. 2 (1984): 269–82.

Adam, Heribert, and Kogila Moodley. *South Africa without Apartheid: Dismantling Racial Domination.* Perspectives on Southern Africa no. 39. Berkeley: Univ. of California Press, 1986.

Aitchison, John. "The Civil War in Natal." *South African Review 5,* 457–73. Johannesburg: Ravan Press, 1989.

Alexander, Neville. "Non-collaboration in the Western Cape, 1943–1963." In *The Angry Divide,* ed. James and Simons, 180–91.

Anderson, R. L. "Keeping the Myth Alive: Justice, Witches and the Law in the 1986 Sekhukhune Killings." B.A. thesis, University of the Witwatersrand, 1990.

Badat, Saleem. "The Political Importance and Achievements of the *Grassroots* Newspaper." Paper presented at the conference entitled "A Century of the Resistance Press in South Africa," University of the Western Cape, 6–7 June 1991.

Barrell, Howard. *MK: The ANC's Armed Struggle.* London: Penguin Books, 1990.

———. "The Turn to the Masses: The African National Congress' Strategic Review of 1978–79." *Journal of Southern African Studies* 18, no. 1 (1992): 64–92.

———. "The United Democratic Front and National Forum: Their Emergence, Composition and Trends." *South African Review 2,* 6–20. Johannesburg: Ravan Press, 1984.

Baskin, Jeremy. *Striking Back: A History of COSATU.* Johannesburg: Ravan Press, 1991.

Baynham, Simon. "Political Violence and the Security Response." In *South Africa in Crisis,* ed. Blumenfeld, 107–25.

Beall, Jo, et al. "African Women in the Durban Struggle, 1985–1986: Towards a Transformation of Roles?" *South African Review 4,* 93–103. Johannesburg: Ravan Press, 1987.

Beckman, Björn. "Whose Democracy? Bourgeois versus Popular Democracy." *Review of African Political Economy,* no. 45/46 (1989): 84–97.

Bell, Paul. "A Different Drum." *Leadership* 6, no. 6 (1987): 48–54.

Berger, Guy. "The Cabinet Minister, the Communist and the Ex-Editor." Paper presented at the conference entitled "A Century of the Resistance Press in South Africa," University of the Western Cape, 6–7 June 1991.

———. "The Great Participation Debate." *Work in Progress,* no. 55 (Aug.–Sept. 1988): 24–28.

Bhana, Surendra, and Bridglal Pachai, eds. *A Documentary History of Indian South Africans.* Cape Town: David Philip, 1984.

Blumenfeld, Jesmond, ed. *South Africa in Crisis.* London: Croom Helm, 1987.

Boesak, Allan. *Black and Reformed: Apartheid, Liberation, and the Calvinist Tradition.* Maryknoll NY: Orbis Books, 1984.

———. "If This Is Treason, I Am Guilty." In *Hammering Swords into Ploughshares,* ed. Tlhagale and Mosala, 279–88.

———. *Walking on Thorns: The Call to Christian Obedience.* Geneva: World Council of Churches, 1984.

Boesak, Allan, and C. Villa-Vicencio, eds. *When Prayer Makes News.* Philadelphia: Westminster Press, 1986.

Boonzaier, Emile, and John Sharp, eds. *South African Keywords: The Uses and Abuses of Political Concepts.* Cape Town: David Philip, 1988.

Boraine, Andrew. "Building Broad Alliances: The Unity and the Contradictions." *South African Labour Bulletin* 13, no. 8 (1989): 28–39.

Bothma, C. V. "The Political Structure of the Pedi of Sekhukhuneland." *African Studies* 35, nos. 3–4 (1976): 177–205.

Bozzoli, Belinda, and Peter Delius. "Radical History and South African Society." In *History from South Africa,* ed. Brown et al., 3–25.

Braam, Conny. *Operatie Vula.* Amsterdam: Meulenhof, 1992.

Brewer, John D. *After Soweto: An Unfinished Journey.* Oxford: Clarendon Press, 1986.

Brewer, John, D., ed. *Can South Africa Survive? Five Minutes to Midnight.* Basingstoke GB: Macmillan, 1989.

Brown, Joshua, Patrick Manning, Karin Shapiro, and Jon Wiener, eds. *History from South Africa: Alternative Visions and Practices.* Philadelphia: Temple Univ. Press, 1991.

Buijtenhuijs, Rob, and Elly Rijnierse. *Democratization in Sub-Saharan Africa, 1989–1992.* Research Report no. 51. Leiden: African Studies Centre, 1993.

Bundy, Colin. "'Action, Comrades, Action!' The Politics of Youth-Student Resistance in the Western Cape, 1985." In *The Angry Divide,* ed. James and Simons, 206–17.

———. "Around Which Corner? Revolutionary Theory and Contemporary South Africa." *Transformation,* no. 8 (1989): 1–23.

———. "Street Sociology and Pavement Politics: Aspects of Youth and Student Resistance in Cape Town, 1985." *Journal of Southern African Studies* 13, no. 3 (1987): 303–30.

Cabesa, Quadro. "From Ungovernability to Revolution: Some Burning Issues of Strategy and Tactics." *African Communist,* no. 104 (first quarter, 1986): 28–40.

Campbell, Catherine. "The Township Family and Women's Struggles," *Agenda,* no. 6 (1990): 1–22.

Carter, Charles. "Community and Conflict: The Alexandra Rebellion of 1986." *Journal of Southern African Studies* 18, no. 1 (1992): 115–42.

———. "'We Are the Progressives': Alexandra Youth Congress Activists and the Freedom Charter, 1983–85." *Journal of Southern African Studies* 17, no. 2 (1991): 197–220.

Chidester, David. *Shots in the Streets: Violence and Religion in South Africa.* Boston: Beacon Press, 1991.

Chikane, Frank. *No Life of My Own.* Johannesburg: Skotaville, 1989.

Cobbett, William, and Robin Cohen, eds. *Popular Struggles in South Africa.* London: Review of African Political Economy in association with James Currey, 1988; Trenton NJ: Africa World Press, 1988.

Cock, Jacklyn. *Colonels and Cadres: War and Gender in South Africa.* Cape Town: Oxford Univ. Press, 1991.

Cole, Josette. *Crossroads: The Politics of Reform and Repression, 1976–1986.* Johannesburg: Ravan Press, 1987.

Coleman, Max, and David Webster. "Repression and Detentions in South Africa." *South African Review 3,* 111–36. Johannesburg: Ravan Press, 1986.

Collinge, Jo-Anne. "The Privately-Owned Media in South Africa: Villains or Victims in the Struggle for Democracy?" *Development Dialogue,* no. 2, (1989): 57–71.

———. "The United Democratic Front." *South African Review 3,* 248–66. Johannesburg: Ravan Press, 1986.

"'Communist Influence in South Africa': US State Department Report to Congress," *Transformation,* no. 3 (1987): 90–99.

Cook, Helena. *The War against Children: South Africa's Youngest Victims.* New York: Lawyers for Human Rights, 1986.

Cornforth, Maurice. *Dialectial Materialism: An Introduction*. Vol. 1, *Materialism and the Dialectical Method*. Vol. 2, *Historical Materialism*. Vol. 3, *The Theory of Knowledge*. London: Lawrence & Wishart, 1952–53; rev. ed., 1987.

Cullinan, Kerry. "Youth Politics: Dispelling the Myths." *Work in Progress*, no. 90 (1993): 21–22.

Davis, Stephen. *Apartheid's Rebels*. New Haven: Yale Univ. Press, 1987.

"Debating Alliance Politics." *Work in Progress*, no. 34 (1984): 12–15.

Delius, Peter. *A Lion amongst the Cattle: Reconstruction and Resistance in the Northern Transvaal*. Johannesburg: Ravan Press, 1996.

———. "Migrants, Comrades and Rural Revolt: Sekhukhuneland, 1950–1987," *Transformation*, no. 13 (1990): 2–26.

———. "Sebatakgomo: Migrant Organization, the ANC and the Sekhukhune Revolt." *Journal of Southern African Studies* 15, no. 4 (1989): 581–615.

———. "Sebatakgomo and the Zoutpansberg Balemi Association: The ANC, the Communist Party and Rural Organization, 1939–55." *Journal of African History* 34, no. 2 (1993): 293–313.

Development Bank of Southern Africa. *Lebowa: Introductory Economic and Social Memorandum*. Midrand, South Africa: Development Bank of Southern Africa, 1988.

———. *Statistical Abstracts on Self-Governing Territories in South Africa*. Midrand, South Africa: Development Bank of Southern Africa, 1987.

Diar, Prakash. *The Sharpeville Six*. Toronto: McClelland & Stewart, 1990.

Dollie, Na-iem. "The National Forum." *South African Review 3*, 267–77. Johannesburg: Ravan Press, 1986.

Du Toit, André. "The Changing Patterns and Limits of Political Violence." *South African Foundation Review* 12, no. 7 (July 1986): 2.

———. "Understanding South African Political Violence: A New Problematic?" Geneva: United Nations Research Institute for Social Development, April 1993.

Du Toit, Pierre, and Jannie Gagiano. "Strongmen on the Cape Flats." *Africa Insight* 23, no. 2 (1993): 102–11.

Ellis, Stephen, and Tsepo Sechaba. *Comrades against Apartheid: The ANC and the South African Communist Party in Exile*. London: James Currey, 1992.

Evans, Jeremy. "On brûle bien les sorcières: Les meurtres muti et leur répression." *Politique Africaine*, no. 48 (Dec. 1992): 47–57.

———. "'Scapegoat Intended': Aspects of Violence in Southern KwaZulu." In *Patterns of Violence*, ed. Minnaar, 215–26.

Fanon, Frantz. *The Wretched of the Earth*. Harmondsworth: Penguin, 1977.

Francis, Matthew. "The UDF in the Western Cape." B.A. thesis, University of the Western Cape, Bellville, 1984.

Frederikse, Julie. *The Unbreakable Thread: Non-Racialism in South Africa*. Johannesburg: Ravan Press, 1990.

Freund, Bill. "Some Unasked Questions on Politics: South African Slogans and Debates." *Transformation*, no. 1 (1986): 118–29.

Friedman, Steven. *Building Tomorrow Today; African Workers in Trade Unions, 1970–1984.* Johannesburg: Ravan Press, 1987.

——. "Idealised Picture of Township Organisation." *Die Suid-Afrikaan,* no. 26 (Aug. 1989): 28–32.

——. "The Struggle within the Struggle: South African Resistance Strategies." *Transformation,* no. 3 (1987): 58–70.

Gastrow, Shelagh. *Who Is Who in South African Politics.* Vols. 1–4. Johannesburg: Ravan Press, 1985–.

"General Workers' Union and the UDF." *Work in Progress,* no. 29 (1983): 11–18.

"General Workers' Union on the United Democratic Front." *South African Labour Bulletin* 9, no. 2 (1983): 47–62.

Gerhart, Gail. *Black Power in South Africa: The Evolution of an Ideology.* Berkeley: Univ. of California Press, 1978.

Geschiere, Peter, and Wilhelmina van de Wetering. "Marginaal: Zwarte magie in een onttoverde wereld." *Sociologische Gids* 36, nos. 3–4 (1989): 150–54.

Grundy, Kenneth. *The Militarization of South African Politics.* Oxford: Oxford Univ. Press, 1988.

Gwala, Nkosinathi. "State Control, Student Politics and the Crisis in Black Universities." In *Popular Struggles in South Africa,* ed. Cobbett and Cohen, 163–82.

Hammond-Tooke, W. D. *Boundaries and Belief: The Structure of a Sotho Worldview.* Johannesburg: Witwatersrand Univ. Press, 1981.

Haysom, Nicholas. *Mabangalala: The Rise of Right-Wing Vigilantes in South Africa.* Johannesburg: University of the Witwatersrand, Centre for Applied Legal Studies, 1986.

Hill, C. R. *Change in South Africa: Blind Alleys or New Directions?* Totowa NJ: Barnes & Noble, 1983.

Huizer, Gerrit. "Folk Spirituality and Liberation in Southern Africa." *Travaux et Documents,* no. 29–30, 1991. Centre d'Etude d'Afrique Noire, Bordeaux.

Hyslop, Jonathan. "School Student Movements and State Education Policy: 1972–87." In *Popular Struggles in South Africa,* ed. Cobbett and Cohen, 183–209.

——. "Schools, Unemployment and Youth: Origins of Student and Youth Movements, 1976–1987." *Perspectives in Education* 10, no. 2 (1988–89): 61–69.

Images of Defiance: South African Resistance Posters of the 1980s. Johannesburg: Ravan Press, 1991.

Issel, Johnny. "Setting Up Grassroots: Background, Aims and Process." Paper presented at the conference entitled "A Century of the Resistance Press in South Africa," University of the Western Cape, 6–7 June 1991.

Jacobs, Adli. "Advocacy Journalism: Has It Advanced Truth or Is It Merely the Flip Side of the Propaganda Coin?" *Rhodes University Journalism Review* 1, no. 2 (1991): 43–44.

James, Wilmot, and Mary Simons, eds. *The Angry Divide: Social and Economic History of the Western Cape.* Cape Town: David Philip, 1989.

Johnson, Shaun. "Resistance in Print I: *Grassroots* and Alternative Publishing, 1980–1984." In *The Alternative Press in South Africa*, ed. Tomaselli and Louw, 191–206.

———, ed. *South Africa: No Turning Back*. Basingstoke GB: Macmillan, 1988.

Johnstone, Frederick. "Most Painful to Our Hearts: South Africa through the Eyes of the New School." *Canadian Journal of African Studies* 16, no. 1 (1982): 5–26.

Kasrils, Ronnie. *"Armed and Dangerous": My Undercover Struggle against Apartheid*. Oxford: Heinemann, 1993.

Keenan, Jeremy. "Counter-Revolution as Reform: Struggle in the Bantustans." In *Popular Struggles in South Africa*, ed. Cobbett and Cohen, 136–54.

———. "Reform and Resistance in South Africa's Bantustans." *South African Review 4*: 115–36. Johannesburg: Ravan Press, 1987.

Kitchen, Helen, ed. *South Africa: In Transition to What?* New York: Praeger, 1988.

Kriger, Norma. "The Zimbabwean War of Liberation: Struggles within the Struggle." *Journal of Southern African Studies* 14, no. 2 (1987–88): 304–22.

———. *Zimbabwe's Guerrila War: Peasant Voices*. Cambridge: Cambridge Univ. Press, 1992.

Kuper, Adam. *Wives for Cattle: Bridewealth and Marriage in Southern Africa*. London: Routledge, 1982.

Labour Monitoring Group. "Report: The November Stay Away," *South African Labour Bulletin* 10, no. 6 (May 1985): 74–100.

Lambert, Rob, and Eddie Webster. "The Re-emergence of Political Unionism in Contemporary South Africa." In *Popular Struggles in South Africa,* ed. Cobbett and Cohen, 20–41.

Lan, David. *Guns and Rain: Guerrillas and Spirit Mediums in Zimbabwe*. London: James Currey, 1985.

Langa, Mandla. "The Quiet Thunder: Report on the Amsterdam Cultural Conference. *Sechaba* 22, no. 3 (March 1988): 26–27.

Lelyveld, Joseph. *Move Your Shadow: South Africa Black and White*. London: Michael Joseph, 1986.

Lenin, V. I. "What Is to Be Done? Burning Questions of Our Movement." *Collected Works,* vol. 5. Moscow: Progress, 1977.

———. "Where to Begin." *Collected Works,* vol. 5. Moscow: Progress, 1977.

Leys, Colin, and John S. Saul. "Liberation without Democracy? The SWAPO Crisis of 1976." *Journal of Southern African Studies* 20, no. 1 (1994): 123–47.

Lipman, Beata. *We Make Freedom: Women in South Africa*. London: Pandora Press, 1984.

Lipton, Merle. *Capitalism and Apartheid: South Africa, 1910–1986*. Aldershot: Wildwood House 1986.

———. "The Debate about South Africa: Neo-Marxists and Neo-Liberals." *African Affairs* 78, no. 310 (1979): 57–80.

Lodge, Tom. "The African National Congress after the Kabwe Conference." *South African Review 4,* 6–17. Johannesburg: Ravan Press, 1987.

———. "The African National Congress in South Africa, 1976–1983: Guerrilla War and Armed Propaganda." *Journal of Contemporary African Studies* 3, nos. 1–2 (1983–84): 153–80.

———. *Black Politics in South Africa since 1945.* Johannesburg: Ravan Press, 1983.

———. "'Mayihlome!—Let Us Go to War!' From Nkomati to Kabwe, the African National Congress, January 1984–June 1985." *South African Review 3,* 226–47. Johannesburg: Ravan Press, 1986.

———. "People's War or Negotiation? African National Congress Strategies in the 1980s." *South African Review 5,* 42–55.Johannesburg: Ravan Press 1989.

———. "The Politics of Refusal." *Leadership South Africa* 5, no. 1 (1986): 19–23.

———. "The Second Consultative Conference of the African National Congress." *South Africa International* 16, no. 2 (1985–86): 80–97.

———. "The United Democratic Front: Leadership and Ideology." In *Can South Africa Survive?* ed. Brewer, 206–30.

Lodge, Tom, and Bill Nasson. *All, Here, and Now: Black Politics in South Africa in the 1980s.* Cape Town: Ford Foundation/David Philip, 1991.

Lonsdale, John, ed. *South Africa in Question.* Cambridge: Association of Cambridge African Studies Centre, in association with James Currey and Heinemann, 1988.

Louw, P. Eric. "The Emergence of a Progressive-Alternative Press in South Africa with Specific Reference to *Grassroots.*" *Communicatio* 15, no. 2 (1989): 26–32.

———. "The Libertarian Theory of the Press: How Appropriate in the South African Context." *Communicatio* 10, no. 1 (1984): 31–37.

———. "Resistance in Print II: Developments in the Cape, 1985–1989: *Saamstaan, Grassroots,* and *South.*" In *The Alternative Press in South Africa,* ed. Tomaselli and Louw, 207–11.

Majola, Sisa. "The Beginnings of People's Power: Discussion of the Theory of the State and Revolution in South Africa." *African Communist,* no. 106 (1986): 55–66.

Manganyi, Chabani N., and André du Toit, eds. *Political Violence and the Struggle in South Africa.* Halfway House, South Africa: Southern, 1990; New York: St. Martin's Press, 1990.

Manning, Richard. *They Cannot Kill Us All: An Eyewitness Account of South Africa Today.* London: Taurus, 1988.

Maré, Gerhard, and Georgina Hamilton. *An Appetite for Power: Buthelezi's Inkatha and South Africa.* Johannesburg: Ravan Press, 1987.

Maree, Johann. "The General Workers' Union, 1973–1986." In *The Angry Divide,* ed. James and Simons, 128–48.

Marks, Shula, and Stanley Trapido, eds. *The Politics of Race, Class and Nationalism in Twentieth Century South Africa.* London: Longman, 1987.

Marx, Anthony W. *Lessons of Struggle: South African Internal Opposition, 1960–1990.* Cape Town: Oxford Univ. Press, 1992.

Mashabela, Harry. *Townships of the PWV.* Johannesburg: South African Institute of Race Relations, 1988.

Matiwana, Mizana, et al. *The Struggle for Democracy: A Study of Community Organisations in Greater Cape Town from the 1960s to 1988.* Bellville, South Africa: University of the Western Cape, Centre for Adult and Continuing Education, 1989.

Mayekiso, Mzwanele. "The Legacy of Ungovernability." *Southern African Review of Books* 5, no. 6 (Nov.–Dec. 1993): 24.

———. *Township Politics: Civic Struggles for a New South Africa.* New York: Monthly Review Press, 1996.

Mayson, Cedric. "Christianity and Revolution: A Battle Fought on Many Fronts." *Sechaba* 21, no. 10 (Oct. 1987): 12–15.

Mbeki, G. *South Africa: The Peasants' Revolt.* London: International Defence and Aid Fund, 1964; reprint, 1984.

Meli, Francis. "South Africa and the Rise of African Nationalism." In *The National Question in South Africa,* ed. Van Diepen, 66–76.

———. *South Africa Belongs to Us: A History of the ANC.* Harare: Zimbabwe Publishing House, 1988.

Minnaar, Anthony. "Hostels and Violent Conflict on the Reef." In *Communities in Isolation,* ed. Minnaar, 10–47.

———, ed. *Communities in Isolation: Perspectives on Hostels in South Africa.* Pretoria: Human Sciences Research Council, 1993.

———. *Patterns of Violence: Case Studies of Conflict in Natal.* Pretoria: Human Sciences Research Council, 1992.

Minnaar, Anthony, and Catherine Payze. "Witch-Burnings and Muti Use." Pretoria: Human Sciences Research Council, May 1994.

Mlambo, Solomon. "Popular Front or United Front." *South African Labour Bulletin* 13, no. 8, (1989): 22–37.

Mönnig, H. O. *The Pedi.* Pretoria: Van Schaik, 1988.

Mufson, Steven. *Fighting Years: Black Resistance and the Struggle for a New South Africa.* Boston: Beacon Press, 1990.

Murray, Martin. *South Africa: Time of Agony, Time of Destiny.* London: Verso, 1987.

Mutwa, Credo. *Let Not My Country Die.* Pretoria: United Publishers International, 1986.

Mzala. *Gatsha Buthelezi: Chief with a Double Agenda.* London: Zed Books, 1988.

Naidoo, Kumi. "The Politics of Youth Resistance in the 1980s: The Dilemmas of a Differentiated Durban." *Journal of Southern African Studies* 18, no. 1 (1992): 143–65.

Nasson, Bill. "Opposition Politics and Ideology in the Western Cape." *South African Review 5,* 91–105. Johannesburg: Ravan Press, 1989.

Niehaus, Carl. *Om te Veg vir Hoop.* Kaapstad: Human & Rousseau, 1993.

Niehaus, Izak. "Witchhunting and Political Legitimacy: Continuity and Change in Green Valley, Lebowa, 1930–91." *Africa* 63, no. 4 (1993): 498–530.

Nyawuza. "The National Question and Ethnicity: The Case of the United Democratic Front and the National Forum." *African Communist,* no. 98 (1984): 20–33.

Orford, John. "*Grassroots* 1980–1984: An Assessment of the Role and Significance of *Grassroots* in the Western Cape." B.A. thesis, University of Cape Town, 1990.

An Overview of Political Conflict in South Africa: Data Trends, 1984–1988. Indicator Project South Africa, Centre for Social and Development Studies, University of Natal, Durban, March 1989.

Pillay, Devan. "Trade Unions and Alliance Politics in Cape Town, 1979–1985." Ph.D. thesis, University of Essex, 1989.

Pinnock, Don. "Culture as Communication: The Rise of the Leftwing Press in South Africa." *Race and Class* 31, no. 2 (1989): 17–35.

———. "Popularise, Organise, Educate and Mobilise: Culture and Communication in the 1980s." In *The Alternative Press in South Africa,* ed. Tomaselli and Louw, 133–54.

Political Conflict in South Africa: Data Trends, 1984–1988. Indicator Project South Africa, Centre for Social and Development Studies, University of Natal, Durban, December 1988.

Posel, Deborah. "Rethinking the 'Race-Class Debate' in South African Historiography." In *Southern African Studies: Retrospect and Prospect; Proceedings of a Seminar Held in the Centre of African Studies.* Edinburgh: University of Edinburgh, 1983.

Race Relations Survey. Johannesburg: South African Institute of Race Relations, 1984–. (Prior to 1984 the title was *Survey of Race Relations.*)

Ramphele, Mamphela. *A Bed Called Home: Life in the Migrant Labour Hostels of Cape Town.* Cape Town: David Philip, 1993.

Ranger, Terence. "The Death of Chaminuka: Spirit Mediums, Nationalism and Guerrilla War in Zimbabwe," *African Affairs* 81, no. 324 (1982): 349–70.

———. *Peasant Consciousness and Guerrilla War in Zimbabwe: A Comparative Study.* London: James Currey, 1985.

———. *Revolt in Southern Rhodesia 1896–7: A Study in African Resistance.* London: Heinemann, 1967.

Rauch, Janine. "Policing Discourses and Violence in South Africa." Policing Research Project, Centre for the Study of Violence and Reconciliation, University of the Witwatersrand, Johannesburg, 1992.

Republic of South Africa Constitution Act, no. 110, 1983.

Reynolds, Andrew, ed. *South Africa Election '94: The Campaigns, Results and Future Prospects.* London: James Currey, 1994.

Riordan, Rory. "The Great Black Shark: An Interview with Chris Hani." *Monitor,* Dec. 1990, 10–19.

Ritchken, Edwin. "Burning the Herbs: Youth Politics and Witches in Lebowa." *Work in Progress,* no. 48 (July 1987): 17–22.

———. "Comrades, Witches and the State: The Case of the Brooklyn Youth Organisation." African Studies Seminar Paper, University of the Witwatersrand, Sept. 1987.

——. "Experiences of Secondary Schooling in the Mapulaneng District, Lebowa 1989." Research Report no. 4. Johannesburg: University of the Witwatersrand, Jan. 1990.

——. "Introduction to Section Four: Rural Politics." *South African Review 5*, 390–402. Johannesburg: Ravan Press, 1989.

——. "The KwaNdebele Struggle against Independence." *South African Review 5*, 426–45. Johannesburg: Ravan Press, 1989.

Rogerson, Christian, and Essy Letsoalo. "Rural Underdevelopment, Poverty and Apartheid: The Closer Settlements of Lebowa, South Africa. *Tijdschrift voor Economische en Sociale Geografie* 72, no. 981 (1981): 347–60.

Rossouw, Rehana. "Some Thoughts on Redefining the Role of Progressive Journalists. Paper presented at the conference entitled "A Century of the Resistance Press in South Africa," University of the Western Cape, 6–7 June 1991.

Safire, Hilary. "Politics and Protest in Shack Settlements of the Pretoria-Witwatersrand-Vereeniging Region, South Africa, 1980–1990." *Journal of Southern African Studies* 18, no. 3 (1992): 670–97.

Sampson, Anthony. *Black and Gold: Tycoons, Revolutionaries and Apartheid*. London: Hooder & Stoughton, 1987.

Saul, John S, and Stephen Gelb. *The Crisis in South Africa*. London: Zed Books 1986.

Schärf, Wilfried, and Baba Ngcokoto. "Images of Punishment in the People's Courts of Cape Town, 1985–87: From Prefigurative Justice to Populist Violence." In *Political Violence and the Struggle in South Africa*, ed. Manganyi and Du Toit, 341–71.

Schoffeleers, J. M. "Folk Christology in Africa: The Dialectics of the Nganga Paradigm." *Journal of Religion in Africa* 19, no. 2 (1989): 157–83.

——. "Review Article: Peasants, Mediums and Guerillas," *Journal of Southern African Studies* 14, no. 1 (1987): 147–52.

——. "Ritual Healing and Political Acquiescence: The Case of the Zionist Churches in Southern Africa." *Africa* 61, no. 1 (1991): 1–25.

Schutte, Gerhard. "Understanding Ritual Killings: Witchcraft Accusations and Social Transformation." *Indicator South Africa* 2, no. 4 (1985): 14–16.

Seekings, Jeremy. "Civic Organisations in South African Townships." *South African Review 6*, 216–38. Johannesburg: Ravan Press, 1992.

——. "From Quiescence to 'People's Power': Township Politics in Kagiso, 1985–1986." *Social Dynamics* 18, no. 1 (1992): 20–41.

——. "Gender Ideology and Township Politics in the 1980s." *Agenda*, no. 10 (1991), 77–88.

——. *Heroes or Villains? Youth Politics in the 1980s*. Johannesburg: Ravan Press, 1993.

——. "Organisation and Repression in the Transition to Confrontation: The Case of Kagiso, 1985–1986." African Studies Seminar paper, presented at the African Studies Institute, University of the Witwatersrand, Feb. 1990.

——. "The Origins of Political Mobilisation in PWV Townships, 1980–84." In *Popular Struggles in South Africa*, ed. Cobbett and Cohen, 59–76.

——. "People's Courts and Popular Politics." *South African Review 5*, 119–35. Johannesburg: Ravan Press, 1989.

——. "Quiescence and the Transition to Confrontation: South African Townships, 1978–1984." Ph.D. thesis, Oxford University, 1990.

——. *South Africa's Townships, 1980–1991: An Annotated Bibliography.* Stellenbosch, South Africa: Research Unit for the Sociology of Development, University of Stellenbosch, 1992.

——. "'Trailing behind the Masses': The United Democratic Front and Township Politics in the Pretoria-Witwatersrand-Vaal Region, 1983–1984." *Journal of Southern African Studies* 18, no. 1 (1992): 93–114.

Segal, Lauren. "The Human Face of Violence: Hostel Dwellers Speak." *Journal of Southern African Studies* 18, no. 1 (1992): 190–231.

Setiloane, Gabriel M. "Salvation and the Secular." In *Hammering Swords into Ploughshares,* ed. Thlagale and Mosala, 73–83.

——. "The Spirit of Africa." *Sash* 37, no. 1 (1994): 14–17.

Shamuyarira, N. M., ed. *Essays on the Liberation of Southern Africa.* Dar es Salaam: Tanzania Publishing House, 1975.

Sisulu, Zwelakhe. "People's Power: A Beginning, Not an End." In *South Africa: In Transition to What?,* ed. Kitchen, 155–64.

Sitas, Ari. "The Making of the 'Comrades' Movement in Natal, 1985–91." *Journal of Southern African Studies* 18, no. 3 (1992): 629–41.

——. "Moral Formations and Struggles amongst Migrant Workers on the East Rand." *Labour, Capital and Society* 18, no. 2 (1985): 372–401.

South Africa in the 1980s: State of Emergency. London: Catholic Institute of International Relations, 1987.

The South African Township Annual. Rivonia, South Africa: IR Research Surveys.

Sparks, Allister. *The Mind of South Africa.* New York: Knopf, 1990.

——. *Tomorrow Is Another Country: The Inside Story of South Africa's Road to Change.* New York: Hill & Wang, 1995.

Survey of Race Relations. Johannesburg: South African Institute of Race Relations, 1982–. (Beginning in 1984 the title was changed to *Race Relations Survey*.)

Swilling, Mark. "Die Lesse van '85–'86: 'Onregeerbaarheid' of Onderhandeling?" *Die Suid-Afrikaan,* no. 18 (Dec. 1988): 33–36.

——. "Stayaways, Urban Protest and the State." *South African Review 3,* 20–50. Johannesburg: Ravan Press, 1986.

——. "The United Democratic Front and Township Revolt." In *Popular Struggles in South Africa,* ed. Cobbett and Cohen, 90–113.

Tambo, Adelaide, comp. *Preparing for Power: Oliver Tambo Speaks.* London: Heinemann 1987.

Tambo, O. R. "We Must Organise Ourselves into a Conquering Force." Speech delivered on 8 January 1983 at the 71st anniversary of the ANC. *Sechaba* 17, no. 3 (March 1983): 2–10.

This Is South Africa. South African Communication Service, 1992.

Thornton, Robert, and Mamphela Ramphele. "The Quest for Community." In *South African Keywords,* ed. Boonzaaier and Sharp, 29–39.

Tlhagale, Buti, and Itumeleng Mosala. *Hammering Swords into Ploughshares: Essays in Honor of Archbishop Mpilo Desmond Tutu.* Grand Rapids MI: William B. Eerdmans; Trenton NJ: Africa World Press, 1987.

Tomaselli, Keyan. "The Progressive Press: Extending the Struggle, 1980–1986." In *The Alternative Press in South Africa,* ed. Tomaselli and Louw, 155–74.

Tomaselli, Keyan, and P. Eric Louw. "Impact of the 1990 Reforms on the 'Alternative Media.'" In *The Alternative Press in South Africa,* ed. Tomaselli and Louw, 222–26.

——, eds. *The Alternative Press in South Africa.* London: James Currey, 1991.

Tomaselli, Keyan, and Don Pinnock. "Underdevelopment and the Progressive Press in South Africa." *Fuse,* Nov. 1984–Jan. 1985, 19–24.

Trevor, Hugh. "The Question of an Uprising of the Whole People: The Role of the Masses in Our Liberation Struggle." *African Communist,* no. 97 (1984): 62–73.

Turok, Ben, ed. *Revolutionary Thought in the 20th Century.* London: Zed Press, 1980; reprint, 1991.

"UDF and AZAPO: Evaluation and Expectations." *Work in Progress,* no. 49 (1987): 26–33.

"United Fronts and Political Unity." *Work in Progress,* no. 29 (1983): 40–45.

Van der Wal, Alie. *Socio-economic Indicators of Development in South Africa: A Case Study of Region G and Lebowa in Particular.* Amsterdam: Vrije Universiteit, Centre for Development Cooperation Services, National Resource Management Unit, August 1994.

Van der Walt, Tjaart. "Report on the Investigation into Education for Blacks in the Vaal Triangle Following upon the Occurrences of 3 September 1984 and Thereafter." RP 88/1985. Cited as Van der Walt report.

Van Diepen, Maria, ed. *The National Question in South Africa.* London: Zed Books, 1988.

Van Kessel, Ineke. "Afrique du Sud: La Prépration des Discussions." *Année Africaine 1989:* 61–84. Bordeaux: Centre d'Etudes d'Afrique Noire, 1990.

——. "L'ANC en 1990: Une Rentrée Mouvementée," *Politique Africaine,* no. 41 (1991): 153–59.

——. *Aspects of the Apartheid State: A Bibliographical Survey.* Research Report no. 34. Leiden: African Studies Centre, 1989.

——. "'From Confusion to Lusaka': The Youth Revolt in Sekhukhuneland." *Journal of Southern African Studies* 19, no. 4 (1993): 593–614.

——. "The United Democratic Front en Afrique du Sud." *Politique Africaine,* no. 38 (1990): 126–32.

Van Rensburg, Patrick. "Democracy and the Media in Southern Africa." *Development Dialogue,* no. 2 (1989): 39–56.

Wentzel, Jill. *The Liberal Slideaway.* Johannesburg: South African Institute of Race Relations, 1995.

Werbner, Richard. *Tears of the Dead: The Social Biography of an African Family.* Edinburgh: Edinburgh Univ. Press, 1991; Harare, Zimbabwe: Baobab Books, 1992.

Wessels, Elsabé. "The Role of the Independent Alternative Grassroots Media in South Africa: A personal perspective." *Development Dialogue,* no. 2 (1989): 72–79.

Wright, H. M. *The Burden of the Present: Liberal-Radical Controversy over South African History.* Cape Town: David Philip, 1980.

Zuid-Afrika: Reisgids, 1985. South African Tourism Board, 1985.

Zuma, Thando. "The Role of the Chiefs in the Struggle for Liberation." *African Communist,* no. 121 (1990): 65–76.

Index

Abrahams, Liz, 229, 268

African National Congress. *See* ANC

Afrikaans (language), 228, 246–47, 259, 265

Afrikaner Weerstandsbeweging (AWB), 85, 101, 204–5

age regiments, 107

Alexander, Neville, 231

Alexandra, 39, 48, 200, 212–13

Alexandra Youth Congress, 68

Algeria, 293

alliance politics, 10, 48, 53, 66–69, 115, 231–32, 254, 262–65, 301

ANC: Kabwe Conference (1985), 37, 294; in Kagiso, 168–69; position on chieftaincy, 82–83, 143, 146; relationship with UDF, 17, 46, 49–50, 54–55, 141, 184, 211, 222; and SACP, 66, 233; strategy, 54, 295; unbanning of, 45, 218; in Western Cape, 231, 284; Women's League, 46, 173; Youth League, 46, 140, 147, 221. *See also* armed struggle; South African Communist Party; UDF; Umkhonto we Sizwe

Anglo-American Corporation, 3

Angola, 84

Anti–South African Indian Council Committee (anti-SAIC), 15, 33

Apel, 92, 103–6, 112, 115, 123–26, 135, 145, 147–49

Apostolic Faith Mission, 157, 159–61, 170

armed struggle, 54, 78, 79, 145, 167, 295. *See also* Umkhonto we Sizwe

Association of African Spiritual Churches, 292

Atteridgeville, 26, 109

Azaadville, 186

Azanian People's Organisation (AZAPO), 18, 21, 38, 99–100, 151, 156, 167, 169, 187, 208

Azanian Students Movement (AZASM), 38, 96

Azanian Students Organisation (AZASO), 19, 89, 93, 96, 103, 106–7, 140

Azanian Youth Organisation (AZANYU), 38, 187, 192, 208–9

Badat, Saleem, 239, 275, 283

Bantu Authorities Act, 78, 82

Bantustans, 17, 21, 42, 46, 75–76, 84–86, 109–10, 138, 141, 143, 147, 305. *See also* Ciskei; Gazankulu; KwaNdebele; KwaZulu; Lebowa; Venda

BaPedi, 102, 116, 124, 133, 138, 291

Bekkersdal, 193, 195

Beyers Naudé, C. F., 161

Bible, 7, 160, 163

Bill of Rights, 44, 304

black, definition of, 18, 21, 232

Black Consciousness (BC), 18, 20, 92, 151, 158, 169, 225, 231, 237

Black Consciousness Movement (BCM), 45, 93, 96, 186

Black Local Authorities, 30, 156

Black Local Authorities Act, 3, 37, 151, 155, 185

Black People's Convention (BPC), 18

Black Sash, 104

Boesak, Allen, 6–9, 15–16, 35, 47, 57, 71, 244–45, 284, 290

Boraine, Andrew, 247

Boshielo, Flag, 92, 102

Botha, Nico, 245

Botha, President P. W., 4, 27, 43, 94, 205

Botha, Stoffel, 57

boycotts, 230; bus, 41, 193–97, 232; consumer, 33, 41, 139, 175, 183, 188–89, 190–91, 196, 206, 271; rent, 30, 41, 271; school, 25, 30, 34, 97 197, 199, 233, 271–72; as a strategy, 54, 188–89, 199–200, 215, 221, 227, 290; tricameral elections, 25

Broederbond, 96

Buthelezi, Mangosutho (Gatsha), 21, 70, 117, 304

cabal, 63–65
Cachalia, Azhar, 2, 40
Calata, Fort, 30
Call of Islam, 228, 265, 275
Cape Action League, 231, 271
Cape Flats, 227
Cape Herald (Cape Town), 249
Cape Housing Action Committee (CAHAC), 233, 247, 252, 254–55, 259–60
Cape Malays, 228
Cape Times (Cape Town), 279
Cape Town Municipal Workers Union, 229
Cape Youth Congress (CAYCO), 68, 235, 258–59, 284
capitalism, 29, 52, 59, 66, 161, 255–56, 269
Cardijn, Cardinal Jozef, 162
Carelse, Ebrahim, 273
Carolus, Cheryl, 57, 273
Castro, Fidel, 78–79
Catholic Church, 159, 161–63, 170, 206
Chamdor Industrial Area, 152, 154, 170, 175, 217
Charter for Change, 15
Chemical Workers Union, 175
chiefs, 42, 78, 147–48, 301. *See also* Congress of Traditional Leaders of South Africa
chieftaincy, 78, 82, 302; UDF position on, 80, 83–84, 110, 116, 120
Chikane, Frank, 6, 32, 35, 156–57, 159–61, 163, 168, 214, 290, 292–93
Chikane, Moss, 32–33
Christianity, 158–163, 214, 222, 265, 290–93
Churches' Urban Planning Commission (CUPC), 237
circumcision. *See* initiation
Ciskei, 20, 267
Citizen (Johannesburg), 58
Civic Associations of the Southern Transvaal (CAST), 219
civics and civic organizations, 28–29, 46, 81, 84, 109, 142, 145, 150–52, 176; rela-
tionship with UDF, 185–86, 210, 212–13, 221–223; in the Western Cape, 233–235, 250–51, 254
civil society, 46, 222–23
colored identity, 227–29, 232, 244–46, 285
coloreds, position of, 4, 47, 284–86, 304
Coloured Labour Preference Policy, 227, 230
Coloured People's Congress, 230, 267
Colyn, Stoffel, 7
Communist Party of South Africa, 77–78. *See also* South African Communist Party
community councils, 156, 172. *See also* Black Local Authorities
comtsotsis, 41, 202, 299
Conference for a Democratic Future, 45, 140
Congress Alliance, 15, 78, 230
Congress, American, 28
Congress of South African Students (COSAS), 19–20, 27, 51, 89, 93, 96, 98, 103–4, 299; banning of, 32, 34, 183, 193; branch in Kagiso, 156, 158, 168, 179, 182
Congress of South African Trade Unions (COSATU), 22, 35–36, 45, 146, 217, 275, 287; relationship with UDF, 42–45, 66. *See also* trade unions
Congress of Traditional Doctors of South Africa (CONTRADOSA), 144
Congress of Traditional Healers, 141, 144. *See also* Union of Traditional Healers
Congress of Traditional Leaders of South Africa (CONTRALESA), 42–43, 83–84, 111, 141–42, 144, 148, 304. *See also* chiefs; chieftaincy
Conservative Party, 85, 200, 205
constitution (1983), 4, 6, 15, 233, 241, 265; interim constitution (1993), 301
consumer boycotts. *See* boycotts
Cornforth, Maurice, 136–37, 292
corporal punishment, 121, 147, 167, 184, 199, 209
Council of Unions of South Africa (CUSA), 22, 27, 154, 169
Cradock, 30, 271

Crossroads squatter camp, 39, 41, 230, 266, 270
Cuba, 71, 209

Dan Pienaarville, 204–5
defiance campaigns, 44, 140
De Klerk, President F. W., 43, 140, 142, 148
Delius, Peter, 79, 107
Delmas treason trial, 27, 32–33, 75
Detainees Support Committee (DESCOM), 95
De Vries, Jonathan, 56–57, 243–44, 267
Diale, Nelson, 92, 103, 143
dialectical materialism, 8, 136, 233
Disorderly Bills Action Committee (DBAC), 233
District Six, 227, 237
Dlamini, Bongani, 207
Dlamini, Mayor Kuzwayo Jacob, 26
Driekop, 116
"dual power," 34, 69–70
Durban, 36
Dutch Reformed Church, 7, 228
Dutch Reformed Mission Church, 228

Eastern Cape, 21, 30–33, 188, 200
elections (1994), 285, 301, 307
Electricity Petition Campaign, 240–41, 252
Essack, Maulana Faried, 275
ethnicity, 111–12, 124, 219–220, 229, 243, 296, 304. *See also* nonracialism
European Community, 28
Evaton, 26

Fanon, Franz, 293–94
farm workers, 61, 77, 85, 101, 305
Fathers' Congress, 207
Federation of Cape Civic Associations (FCCA), 271
Federation of South African Trade Unions (FOSATU), 18, 22, 27
Federation of South African Women (FEDSAW), 180–81, 257
Federation of Transvaal Women (FED-TRAW), 159, 179–80
feminism, 180–81, 257

Fisher, Ryland, 249, 256, 274
Food and Beverage Workers Union (FBWU), 154, 169
Food and Canning Workers Union (FCWU), 229, 234, 262–63
forced removals, 77, 85
Foster, Joe, 22
Freedom Charter, 15, 103, 225, 231, 233, 243, 268, 277; UDF and, 4, 5, 16, 19, 239
FRELIMO, 42, 295

GaMasemola, 103
Gandhi, Mahatma, 23
GaNkoane, 105, 115, 124–27, 130, 145–47, 148
GaPhaahla, 143
Gazankulu, 124, 140, 142
Gelb, Stephen, 59
General and Allied Workers Union (GAWU), 22, 154, 169–70
General Workers Union (GWU), 229, 234, 263–64
generational conflict, 36, 108, 112, 132, 148–49, 184, 222, 289, 293, 298
Genu, Isaac (Ike), 157, 169, 173–75, 196, 203, 218–19
German Democratic Republic, 8, 71
Gerwel, Jakes, 231
Goldstone, Judge R. J., 206
Goniwe, Matthew, 30, 33, 271
Gqabi, Joe, 92
Gramsci, Antonio, 23, 247
Grassroots: and African-colored divide, 241–43, 257–61, 284–86; and ANC, 248, 255, 268, 287; funding, 248–49; ideology, 247, 255–57, 274–78, 286; language debate, 246, 260, 286; Leninist inspiration, 236, 238–39, 246; as model for community papers, 225–26; notions of democracy, 240–41, 250–55; relationship with trade unions, 234, 261–64; and UDF, 265–67, 269–70, 271–72
Greyhound bus company, 172, 175, 178, 193–96, 202, 215
Groblersdal, 99, 128
Group Areas Act, 227–28, 242

Guguletu, 228, 274, 285
Gumede, Archie, 16, 36

Hani, Chris, 145
Harare Declaration, 44–45
Heard, Tony, 279
Hendrickse, Allen, 241
Hinduism, 7
homelands. *See* Bantustans
hostel dwellers, 62, 264, 300, 305; in
    Kagiso, 153–54, 171–72, 195–97,
    219–220. *See also* migrant workers
House of Delegates, 25
House of Representatives, 25
hunger strike, 43, 93, 140

ICCO (Interchurch Organization for
    Development Cooperation), 248–49
idealism, 8
impimpis, 9, 127, 132
Indian Congresses, 18, 21, 23, 63–65, 230.
    See also Natal Indian Congress; Trans-
    vaal Indian Congress
Indians, 4, 15, 18, 30, 63–65, 270
influx control, 3, 80, 87, 109, 227
initiation, 107, 120, 130
Inkatha, 17, 21, 36, 45, 70, 85, 146, 154,
    192, 219–20, 300
Institute of Contextual Theology,
    159–60
Interdenominational Youth Christian
    Club (IYCC), 158, 160, 163
Internal Security Act, 31, 206
Isizwe, 60
Iskra, 236–38
Islam, 7, 228, 265, 273, 293
Issel, Johnny, 237–38, 250, 258, 280, 284

Jacobs, Adli, 58
Jane Furse, 104–5
Johannesburg, 15, 39, 90–91, 139, 141,
    146, 161, 186

Kagiso, 158, 171, 178; profile of, 152–56;
    Kagiso African Chamber of Com-
    merce (KAFCOC), 190–91; Kagiso
    Civic Association (KCA), 218–21;
    Kagiso Civic Organisation (KCO),

187, 191, 208–9, 217; Kagiso Interim
    Co-ordinating Committee (KICC),
    217–18; Kagiso Taxi Association, 178,
    194, 218, 221
Kagiso Trust, 55
Kagiso Youth Congress (KAYCO), 183,
    193, 201, 203
Kairos document, 7, 160
Kasrils, Ronnie, 8, 78
Khayelitsha, 270–71
Khumalo, Lucky, 99
Kinikini, Tamsanqa, 35
Koornhof Bills, 4, 16, 23, 233
KRO. *See* Krugersdorp Residents
    Organisation
Krugersdorp, 152, 200, 204, 218;
    Krugersdorp Action Group, 204;
    town council, 204
Krugersdorp Residents Organisation
    (KRO), 152, 174–76, 297–98, 303;
    affiliation to UDF, 175; constitution,
    157; Consumer Boycott Committee
    (KCBC), 190, 191, 193, 200, 215
Kwadi, Amanda, 179, 181
KwaNdebele, 39, 42, 75, 83, 86, 126, 142
KwaNobuhle, 30, 35
KwaZulu, 36

Labour Party, 230
Langa, 30, 228
language, debate on, 246–47. *See also*
    Afrikaans; Xhosa
Lebowa, 75, 85–89, 114, 124, 141–42,
    148–49; Lebowa Development Cor-
    poration, 81; Lebowa Police, 92, 99,
    100, 114, 127–28, 139; schools, 88–89,
    121–22; UDF in, 79, 99–100
Lebowakgomo, 100
Legwate, Maki, 198, 203
Lekganyane, Bishop Barnabas, 94, 100
Lekoa Council, 26, 155
Lekota, Patrick ("Terror"), 24, 32–33, 56
Lenin, 23, 176, 224, 262; on the use of
    media, 236–39, 246
Lewis, David, 263, 282
liberation theology, 7, 160–62. *See also*
    Kairos document
Libya, 275

Lobethal, 104, 143–44
Lusaka, 94, 248, 258
Lutheran Church, 104, 169

Mabasa, Goodman, 183
Mabotha, Moss, 132
Mabotha, Silas, 129–30, 135
Mabudafhasi, Joyce, 93, 95, 96
Maditsi, Solomon, 125
Mafokoane, Shadrack, 99
Magnet Heights (Sekhukhuneland), 113
Maharaj, Mac, 248
Mahlangu, Prince Klaas Makhosana, 83
Mahlatsi, Esau, 155
Mahwelereng, 99
Makeleng, Alf, 94
Makgaleng, M. W., 114–15, 145
makgothla, 207
Makgothlo, Joe, 157, 169, 192, 194–95,
    202, 212, 219
Makotanyane, Morwamoche, 113–15
Makunyane, Thabo, 92–93, 95, 139
Maleke, Tennessee, 198
Malindi, Zollie, 260
Mamaro, Steve, 144
Mamelodi, 134
Mandela, Nelson, 45, 94, 135, 145, 148,
    159, 173, 271, 280, 284, 305
Mandela, Winnie, 186, 213
Mangope, Robert, 187–88
"Manifesto of the Azanian People," 21
Mankweng, 91, 93, 95, 98–99
Mankweng Youth Congress (MAYCO),
    95, 98
Manuel, Fahdiel, 272, 279, 281
Manuel, Trevor, 57, 233, 278
Mao Tse-tung, 23
Mapulaneng, 107, 133
Marks, Joe, 267, 283, 285
Marogo, Chief, 116
Marx, Anthony, 59
Marxism-Leninism, 53, 71, 136–38, 161,
    226, 236–39, 243–44, 298
Masha, Chief, 125, 142
Mashigo, Steven Rooi, 190
Mass Democratic Movement (MDM),
    43, 55, 84, 217
Matshogo, Stephen, 204–5

Matthews, Lynn, 266
Metal Workers Union (MAWU), 95, 154
Mayekiso, Mzwanele, 48
Mayibuye, 173
Mbeki, Govan, 82
Mbeki, Thabo, 8
Mbuli, Mzwakhe, 118
media, 31, 56–58, 224–25
Meli, Francis, 70
Mhlawuli, Velishwa, 261
migrant workers, 59, 61–63, 77–81,
    86–87, 108–13, 138, 171, 196, 219–20,
    234, 264, 299, 305
Million Signature Campaign, 25
Mitchell's Plain, 17, 233, 240–41, 252,
    273, 280
MK. *See* Umkhonto we Sizwe
Mkhize, Nomvula. *See* Mokonyane,
    Nomvula
Mkhonto, Michael, 30
Mmesi, Modiri, 196
Mnguni, Louis, 92–93, 95–96, 146
Mnisi, Philip, 104
Moeketsi, Mayor Edward, 177–78, 185,
    191, 207
Mohamed, Ismail, 32
Mohlakeng, 186, 193, 198, 218
Mohlaletse, 125
Moiloa, Busang, 168
Moiloa, George, 157, 168, 170, 172–75
Moiloa, Tizza, 168, 186, 219
Mokaba, Peter, 83, 93–95, 116, 146
Mokonyane, Nomvula, 168, 179
Mokonyane, Serge, 168–69, 197, 207
Molefe, Popo, 19, 24, 32–33, 58, 69
Monakedi, Dewet, 108, 112
Monama, Wilfred, 109–13
Mönnig, H. O., 107
Mono, Joseph, 211
Montoedi, Morgan, 208
Moosa, Essa, 248
Moria, 94, 100
Morobe, Murphy, 15, 45, 56, 77
Motatema, 99
Motlana, Nthatho, 71, 186
Motsoaledi, Aaron, 104
Motsoaledi, Elias, 102
Moutse, 83, 109

Mozambique, 84, 139, 269, 275–76
Mpetha, Oscar, 16, 229, 268
Mphaaneng, 106
Munsieville, 153, 179, 204–5, 220–21;
    Munsieville Development Committee,
    175; Munsieville Youth Congress, 193
muti, 8, 292
Mutwa, Credo, 136

Naidoo, Jay, 63, 275
Namibia, 139
Natal, 36, 41, 64–65, 300
Natal Indian Congress (NIC), 18, 36, 64.
    See also Indian Congresses
National Confederation of Trade Unions
    (NACTU), 217
National Education Crisis Committee
    (NECC), 34, 114, 197
National Educational Union of South
    Africa (NEUSA), 121
National Forum, 21
nationalism: African, 4, 5, 11, 18, 228;
    Afrikaner, 4, 5, 304
National Party, 6, 41, 45, 85, 87, 205, 228,
    284
National Union of Metalworkers of
    South Africa (NUMSA), 217
National Union of South African Stu-
    dents (NUSAS), 19, 21, 259
Native Affairs Department, 82
Nchabeleng, Elleck, 92, 94, 103, 105
Nchabeleng, Gertrude, 128
Nchabeleng, Luthuli, 103
Nchabeleng, Maurice, 103, 105, 129–30,
    145, 149
Nchabeleng, Peter, 92, 102–5, 113, 124,
    128, 139
Nchabeleng, Petrus ("Mpho"), 105, 124
Nchabeleng, Chief Richard, 129, 148
Ncube, Sister Mary Bernard, 159, 169,
    172–73, 179, 191, 198–99, 200–202,
    208, 213, 297
Ndou, Samson, 82, 142
Ndude, Hilda, 261, 287
"necklace," 9, 35, 127, 133, 213
Nederduits Gereformeerde Kerk
    (NGK). *See* Dutch Reformed Church
Nederduits Gereformeerde Sendingkerk.
    See Dutch Reformed Mission Church

Netherlands, 248
New Era, 58, 276–77, 280
New Nation, 109, 280
New Unity Movement (NUM), 68, 151,
    231, 263, 271
ngaka, 126, 132, 143, 292. *See also* sangoma
Ngxobongwana, Johnson, 230, 270–71
Nicaragua, 71, 166, 275
Nkadimeng, Don, 100
Nkadimeng, Jepson, 111
Nkadimeng, John, 92, 102
Nkondo, Curtis, 19, 186
nonracialism, 60, 63, 231–32, 235, 243,
    285. *See also* ethnicity
Northern Transvaal, 43, 75, 85–95,
    141–42; Northern Transvaal Civics
    Association, 141; Northern Transvaal
    Coordinating Committee of the
    UDF, 89, 91–95; Northern Transvaal
    Council of Churches, 91, 104, 140;
    Northern Transvaal People's Con-
    gress (NOTPECO), 81, 91, 108–13,
    138
Ntlokoa, Lawrence, 158, 162–63, 166,
    175–76, 186, 193–94, 198, 200, 202,
    216, 219, 221, 290
Ntsimane, Ben, 219
Nyanga, 228
Nzima, Lettie, 157, 160, 173, 179
Nzo, Alfred, 84

Operation Vula, 55, 65
Oppenheimer, Harry, 3
Organisation of African Unity, 44
Oudtshoorn, 245

Pan Africanist Congress (PAC), 5, 18, 45,
    106, 151, 275, 294; in Kagiso, 156, 187,
    208–9, 220
parliament. *See* tricameral parliament
participation debate, 23–24, 230–31, 290
Patel, Leila, 238, 254, 256
Pathudi, Cedric, 127
people's courts, 9, 37, 116, 118, 206–10, 277
people's power, 9, 37, 55, 69–70, 75, 83,
    137, 200, 240, 274–78
people's war, 37
Phala, John, 143–44
Phalaborwa, 101

Phasha, Chief, 115, 130–31, 146
Pietermaritzburg, 36
Pietermaritzburg Treason Trial, 32, 160
Pietersburg, 91, 93, 98, 139, 143
Pollsmoor Prison, 271
populism, 60, 241, 296
Port Elizabeth Black Civic Organisation (PEBCO), 33, 151
Potgietersrus, 99
Pretoria-Witwatersrand-Vereeniging (PWV), 27, 212

race-class debate, 5, 48, 52, 305
racial capitalism, 21, 52
Radio Freedom, 162, 169, 173
Reagan administration, 27
Ramodike, Nelson, 141–42, 148
Ramushu, Sydney, 118, 149
Rapport (Johannesburg), 162, 211
referendum, 23–24
Release Mandela Campaign, 20
religion, 6–11, 158, 214, 244–45, 289–94
RENAMO, 84, 139
rent boycott, 30, 41, 271. *See also* boycotts
Rhodes, Wilfred, 247, 281
Riekert Commission on Manpower, 3
Robben Island, 77, 92, 103, 128, 140, 145, 173, 175
Roman Catholic Church. *See* Catholic Church
Rossouw, Rehana, 247, 287
Russian revolution, 277

Saamstaan (Oudtshoorn), 244–45
SAAWU. *See* South African Allied Workers Union
SACP. *See* South African Communist Party
SACTU. *See* South African Congress of Trade Unions
SADF. *See* South African Defence Force
Salojee, Cassim, 32
sangoma, 8. See also *ngaka*
SAP. *See* South African Police
Sathekga, Emma, 26
Saul, John, 59
Save the Press Campaign, 280
SAYCO. *See* South African Youth Congress

school boycotts. *See under* boycotts
Schoonoord, 128, 149
Sebatakgomo, 78–79, 91–92, 102, 108–10, 112
Sebokeng, 26
Sechaba, 7, 159
Seekings, Jeremy, 68–69, 182
Sekhukhune Youth Organisation (SEYO), 98, 102, 104–7, 122, 129, 140, 147, 299, 302
Sekhukhune, K. K. (acting paramount chief), 142, 146
Sekhukhune, Morwamoche (acting paramount chief), 82
Sekhukhuneland, 75, 82, 99; Sekhukhune Chamber of Commerce, 88, 113; Sekhukhune College of Education, 125; Sekhukhune Parents' Crisis Committee (SPCC), 113–15. *See also* Sebatakgomo; Sekhukhune Youth Organisation
Sekonya, Richard ("Taylor"), 105
Seripe, Bafana, 156, 167
Seshego, 91, 93, 98–99
Setiloane, Gabriel, 289, 292–93
Sexwale, Mosima ("Tokyo"), 92
Sharpeville, 26
Simmers, Willie, 284
Sisulu, Albertina, 16, 32, 179
Sisulu, Walter, 43, 140, 145
Slovo, Joe, 145
socialism. *See* Marxism-Leninism
Sonto, Roseberry, 259–60
sorcery. *See* witchcraft
South (Cape Town), 279, 287
South African Allied Workers Union (SAAWU), 22, 89, 94, 96, 229, 234
South African Clothing and Textile Workers' Union (SACTWU), 280
South African Communist Party (SACP), 30, 32, 45, 65, 66, 145, 169, 231, 233, 267, 285. *See also* Communist Party of South Africa
South African Congress of Trade Unions (SACTU), 92, 229, 263, 268
South African Council of Churches (SACC), 7, 18, 55, 110, 161, 171, 206
South African Defence Force (SADF), 7, 82, 97, 100, 104, 138–39, 195, 206, 305

South African Police (SAP), 6–7, 128,
170, 196, 189–99, 203–6, 305
South African Students Organisation
(SASO), 93
South African Youth Congress
(SAYCO), 42, 83, 93, 106, 139, 140
Soviet Union, 275, 277
Soweto, 77, 92, 98, 136, 145, 174, 186, 189;
Soweto Civic Association (SCA), 71,
151, 160, 169, 186; Soweto Parents Crisis Committee, 34, 197; uprising
(1976), 20, 78, 98, 109, 160, 298
spirit mediums, 291
squatters, 62, 230, 234, 266, 270, 299
Star (Johannesburg), 191
State of Emergency: first, 31–32, 33, 37,
184, 189, 201, 271; second, 38–43, 97,
100, 136, 139, 196, 199, 206, 216, 278
stay-away, 26, 27, 54, 62, 67, 101, 175, 220
Steelpoort, 95, 101
strikes, 40, 54, 148, 229; "Fatti's and
Moni's," 232, 237; "red meat," 232
Strydkraal, 125
student representative council (SRC),
34, 97–98, 122, 167, 184, 199, 217, 276
student-worker alliance, 27, 67, 237, 268.
See also alliance politics
Sunday Star (Johannesburg), 204
Sunday Times (Johannesburg), 102, 119
Suttner, Raymond, 277
Swanieville, 220
SWAPO (South West Africa People's
Organisation), 295

Tafelkop, 105–6, 302
Tambo, Oliver, 15, 35, 39, 159, 201, 268,
279, 294
Tembisa, 109, 144
Terreblanche, Eugène, 204
Tompi Seleki, 105–6
Township News (Cape Town), 260
trade unions, 19, 22; and community
organizations, 36, 232–34, 261–64;
and Freedom Charter, 16; in Kagiso,
154, 217; and migrant labor, 61; and
nationalist movements, 66, 263; in
Northern Transvaal, 94; reform of
legislation, 3; and UDF, 22, 36, 263;

in Western Cape, 229–30, 232–34.
See also alliance politics; Congress of
South African Trade Unions; Federa-
tion of South African Trade Unions;
General and Allied Workers Union;
General Workers Union; National
Confederation of Trade Unions;
strikes; South African Allied Workers
Union; South African Congress of
Trade Unions
Transport and Allied Workers Union, 195
Transvaal, 33, 63, 89, 152, 154, 219
Transvaal Consumer Boycott Commit-
tee (TCBC), 189
Transvaal Indian Congress (TIC), 15
Transvaal United African Teachers Asso-
ciation (TUATA), 121
tribalism, 124, 148
tricameral parliament, 4, 23, 226, 231, 265
Trotskyites, 231. *See also* New Unity
Movement
Tshwete, Steve, 5, 47
tsotsis, 201, 207, 222
Turfloop. *See* University of the North
Tutu, Desmond, 6, 35, 290
two-stage strategy, 66
Tyacke, Eric, 162

UDF (United Democratic Front): and
ANC, 27, 39, 46, 49–50, 54–55, 141,
211, 222; and AZAPO, 30, 38; class
composition, 58; declaration, 16–17,
60; funds, 40, 55; ideology, 69–71;
and Inkatha, 21, 30; launch, 17;
National General Conference (1983),
23; National General Council, 24, 30,
60; National Executive Committee
(NEC), 24; National Working Committee, 24; in Northern Transvaal,
91–93, 95, 116, 139–42; origins of,
15–17; patrons, 17; Programme of
Action, 4; Regional Executive Committees, 24, 30; restriction of, 43;
rural policy, 77–85; West Rand Area
Committee, 186; Western Cape, 24,
57, 233, 235, 243–44, 260, 270; working principles, 17, 60
Uitenhage, 30, 33

Umkhonto we Sizwe (MK), 8, 23, 38, 55, 78, 92–95. *See also* armed struggle
unemployment, 50; in Lebowa, 86
"ungovernability," 35, 106, 108, 118, 135, 300
Union of Black Journalists, 248
Union of Traditional Healers, 143–44. *See also* Congress of Traditional Healers
UNITA, 84
United Democratic Front. *See* UDF
United Front, 16, 22
United Front (Kagiso), 201–2, 299
United Nations, 44
United Women's Congress, 235, 284
United Women's Organisation (UWO), 257–58, 264
Unity Movement. *See* New Unity Movement
University of the North, 91–92, 94–98, 107, 136, 140
University of the Western Cape, 231, 237, 247, 276
University of Venda, 96
University of Zululand, 21
Urban Training Project, 162

Vaal Civic Association (VCA), 26
Vaal Triangle, 26, 51, 175, 305; uprising, 58
Valli Moosa, Mohammed, 24, 56–57
van Heerden, Auret, 20
van Warmelo, P., 96
Venda, 47, 109, 140, 142
Vietnam, 54
vigilantes, 39, 63, 85, 139, 203–5, 300; "witdoeke," 271
Viljoen, Minister Gerrit, 179
Vlakfontein, 109

Vlok, Adriaan, 194
Volksblad (Bloemfontein), 307

Wessels, Leon, 205, 212
Western Cape, 21, 31, 33, 47, 68, 161; profile of, 227–35; Western Cape Civic Association (WCCA), 235, 259–60, 270; Western Cape Council of Churches, 237; Western Cape Inter Church Youth, 17; Western Cape Traders Association, 61; Western Cape Youth League, 231
Winning Hearts and Minds (WHAM), 39–40
witchcraft, 8, 123–36, 143–44, 289–92, 303
Witwatersrand, 31, 33, 219, 280
women, 11, 179–82, 192, 214, 257–58, 286, 296–98, 300–301; in rural areas, 80–81, 108, 120; in youth organizations, 68–69, 122–23, 168
Women's Front, 257–58

Xhosa (language), 227, 247, 260–61, 280, 286

Young Christian Workers (YCW), 156, 158, 161–68, 170, 174, 209, 215, 290, 292

Zihlangu, Dorothy, 268
Zimbabwe, 92, 288–95; Zimbabwe African National Union (ZANU), 291, 295; Zimbabwe African People's Union (ZAPU), 295
"Zimzims," 5
Zion Christian Church (ZCC), 39, 94, 100, 106, 208
Zoutpansberg Balemi Association, 78
Zulu migrants, 219, 305